KING ALFRED'S COLLEGE
WINCHESTER

To be returned on or before the day marked below :—

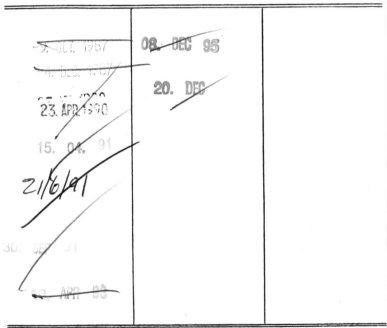

-5. OCT. 1987   08. DEC 95

4. DEC. 1987   20. DEC

23. APR 1990

15. 04. 91

21/6/97

30. SEP 91

APR

PLEASE ENTER ON ISSUE SLIP:

Somerset 1625-1640

A County's Government
During the "Personal Rule"

Somerset 1625-1640

A County's Government
During the "Personal Rule"

by Thomas Garden Barnes

Oxford University Press
London

Distributed in Great Britain by Oxford University Press, London

Publication of this book has been aided by a grant from the Ford Foundation

Made and printed in Great Britain by
William Clowes and Sons, Limited, London and Beccles

À JEANNE-MARIE

Preface

The reign of Charles I has exercised more historians for a greater number of years than almost any other short span of time in England's history. The result has been a spate of published works, commenced by the fact-finding compilation of Rushworth, mightily advanced by the narration of Gardiner, and latterly continued with the analyses of historians of similar stature. The debates of parliament have been published, papers of government transcribed or indexed, and biographies of those who played both major and minor roles have appeared in increasing numbers. Learned scholars have minutely dissected events of momentous import and traced social, economic, legal, and intellectual development during this short period of history. They have even employed the new medium of the broadcast word to cultivate their ideas in the minds of many long removed from the intellectually vivifying experience of more formal instruction. All this has not been without good reason. For the prime subject of the scholars' endeavors died by his people's hand, and out of the turmoil revolving around his death grew England's present constitution. As well, some Englishmen for conscience's sake founded a new civilization in the wilderness beyond the seas—an event which has never ceased to attract the heirs of that new civilization, who have in good measure added to the literature on the old.

This scholarly ferment has tended to bypass the institutions of local government and the persons into whose hands those institutions were committed. The omission has not been for any want of evidence, since it is from these years that most counties have preserved the written vestiges of their administration. Nor can the omission be put down wholly to ignorance of the importance of those institutions; if local government has not been duly appreciated, many have intimated that it should be more fully investigated. Rather, it appears that the omission is due to the greater appeal to the historians' sensibilities of those organs of government in which was focused the struggle culminating in rebellion, regicide, and a vastly altered constitution.

Local government at any point in England's growth is worthy of consideration. It was, and is, the essence of government; governance refined and brought to bear in almost daily contact on the humblest individuals. It permeates more niches of society than any of the greater organs which call it into being. In the reign of Charles I, especially in the first sixteen years of his reign, local government has an even greater claim to attention. For in these years, the established institutions of local government were required to implement those acts of state which proved the catalyst of civil strife. The men who led the revolt—and those who led the counterattack—were largely the men who had administered royal policy in their counties during those sixteen years.

A worthwhile study of local government demands an intimacy between the student and his subject which is not possible if his attention is diffused over the whole realm, or sunk so deeply into the structure of one county's government that he loses sight of the institution as a totality. This consideration limits such a study to one county and to that level of government within its bounds which exercised control over all subordinate administrative units. At that level in seventeenth-century England were found the justices of the peace, the lord and deputy lieutenants, and the sheriff. These officers comprised a "triarchy" whose authority to govern was peerless within the county, derived as it was directly from the king and the law of the land.

The members of the "triarchy" may conveniently be termed the local governors—a term by which they will be identified throughout this work. Drawn from the large yet well-defined class predominant in wealth and prestige, they served as the resident unpaid instruments for the administration of the county. In their collective hands was gathered virtually the whole power of the Crown within the county which they were to apply as occasion required, under the direction of the ministers of the Crown. Government in its main aspects—judicial, executive, military—was their immediate responsibility, and they were accountable not to those below, but to their master above, and to the law. Only the

King and the law limited their authority, and to the mass of their neighbors who were the governed, those limitations seemed hardly significant.

During the eleven years of Charles' "personal rule," more than in many decades preceding or many decades that would follow, the local governors stood in exceedingly close relationship to their master. If they had always been accountable to the central authority from whence they derived their power, during these years that authority seemed more intent than ever that they should exercise their power towards clearly ordained ends. Under strict surveillance, the local governors were repeatedly called upon to expend more time and effort in the King's service than had been required of their predecessors in office. The pattern of their labor was one of increasing demand and increasing control from above. In themselves, such demands and their accompanying control bore heavily enough. What gave particular sting to them was that the programs comprised in the demands were sure to evoke unusual resistance on the part of the governed. This ever-mounting resistance made far more wearisome and difficult the labor of the local governors which, by its novelty and by the programs that elicited it, bore with unprecedented weight upon them.

This study is intended to reveal the magnitude of the demands, the means by which they were enforced upon the local governors, and the extent of the county's resistance to them. As well, the activities of the local governors must be presented against the backdrop of a struggle among themselves for political supremacy in the shire which promoted the disruption of county government and the royal programs dependent upon it. The investigator must, in the absence of a previous study of the county's administration, dwell at some length on the institutions called upon to effect the programs. He has denied himself the satisfaction of treating the years of turmoil that followed these sixteen years, and therefore he will refrain from propounding one more theory to explain the events of the succeeding turbulent decade. None the less, he feels himself competent to describe the reaction of Somerset's local governors to the unprecedented demands made on them. And if their reaction

1*

proved to be common to their counterparts elsewhere in the realm, he is willing to suggest that it had grave consequences in the era following the "personal rule," in the decade dominated by conflict and civil strife.

This study and its author have benefited from the assistance of many who have graciously given of their time and energy that this book might be less imperfect than would otherwise be the case. To acknowledge their contributions is to testify to the corporate nature of scholarship and the intellectual companionship that eases the solitude of search while it does not relieve the searcher of his sole responsibility for the finished work. This study has been some ten years in preparation; it is with grateful appreciation that I remember the aid and encouragement that has been given me at every stage along the way.

The undergraduate course on Stuart history given by Professor W. K. Jordan at Harvard provided the initial impetus that turned me to research in early Stuart local government. Though burdened with administrative tasks, teaching, and his own splendid research, Professor Jordan gave me immediate attention and direction and has continued to be interested in my research. A longish honors essay at Harvard was the foundation for this study. In its preparation Professor Jacob Price of the University of Michigan, then a tutor at Harvard, provided the guidance that enabled me to cope with my first sortie into archives. In its first form, this book was an Oxford doctoral thesis directed by Professor R. B. Wernham. No expression of gratitude is adequate recompense for the help he gave me, neither can I assess the debt I owe him for the many insights which molded my thinking and consequently this study. I hope it is worthy of his effort.

To many in Somerset I render thanks, not only for considerable scholarly assistance, but also for a warm hospitableness that made Somerset a second homeland. Lord and Lady Hylton, the late Mr. Geoffrey Luttrell and Mrs. Luttrell, Mr. and Mrs. George Wyndham, and Mr. and Mrs. Hugh Foster provided both in good measure. Mr. and Mrs. C. W. H. Rawlins have a large claim on my gratitude, and I owe much to the studies of Mrs. Rawlins (formerly Miss S. W. Bates-Harbin) in

Somerset's history. Mr. A. W. Vivian-Neal has had an influence on my development as an historian hardly less important than that provided by more formal instruction. His profound knowledge of Somerset's history, his intuitive comprehension of past reality, and his gently proferred criticism of and comments on my work have been freely given me from my first days in Somerset. To him and Mrs. Vivian-Neal I am grateful, too, for many happy hours at Poundisford.

Mr. T. J. Hunt of Taunton, who took time from his own research to act as a foil for my ideas (some of which, I fear, were unworthy of his consideration) has been a good friend and a valued critic. The same qualities in Mr. Ivor P. Collis, county archivist of Somerset, are to be reckoned in as part of the great contribution he has made to this work. He handed me that invaluable tool (and showed me how to use it properly) which is so inadequately termed the "archive approach" to research. Without his assistance at every step of the research process, this study would show some ugly birthmarks. His able staff—Mr. Donald Mirams, Mr. Derek Shorrocks, Mrs. Frank Elkins, Mrs. Paul Besley, and Miss Ethel White—will forgive me if I make mere passing reference to an obligation for help, encouragement, and kindness so considerable that the friendship of a lifetime will not discharge it.

The two examiners of this in thesis form brought to it their own vast knowledge of the period and the institutions here treated and the criticism that enabled me to right much which was amiss: Dr. W. G. Hoskins of Oxford and Mr. H. C. Johnson, principal assistant keeper of the Public Records. During the five years since that thorough (somewhat discomfiting) appraisal, the latter has given yet more aid to me. And I must thank his colleagues at the Public Record Office, especially Mr. E. K. Timings, Dr. N. J. Williams, Mr. A. W. Mabbs, Dr. R. A. Brown (now at King's College, London), and Dr. R. F. Hunnisett, for countless favors and many assists. All students of English history will join me in appreciation of the services afforded by Miss Winifred D. Coates, the national registrar of archives, and her friendly staff in guiding the student to invaluable muniments in private hands. My thanks are due also to the staff of the British Museum, printed books and manuscripts departments, for their aid; to the staff of the Bodleian Library, especially

Dr. W. O. Hassall and Dr. D. M. Barratt; to Mr. A. Ringrose and his always helpful assistants at the library of Lincoln's Inn.

I am grateful to the President and Fellows of Corpus Christi College, Oxford, particularly Mr. W. F. R. Hardie and Mr. Michael Brock, for their encouragement and their generosity in providing financial assistance on three pressing occasions, and for an environment still touched by the spirit of Richard Hooker. Mr. R. C. Latham's seminar at the Institute of Historical Research, London, provided intellectual stimulation of the most valuable kind; the opportunity to undergo the rigors of criticism at the hands of one's co-aspirants under serene tutelage is gratefully acknowledged. That unique institution, the seminar of Sir John Neale and Professor Joel Hurstfield at the Institute, provided me last year with the chance to rethink—sometimes out loud—the arguments put forth here, on the eve of the book's going to press. I thank all there for suffering me in many flights of fancy.

A special debt of gratitude is owed Professor Wallace Notestein of Yale. I was never afforded the opportunity of studying under him in a formal way. But during the past seven years, following a chance meeting in the Somerset Record Office, he has provided much information and encouragement; with the legion of his own disciples, I must acknowledge him *magister*. To a number of my contemporaries I am greatly obligated, and I rejoice in the expectation of becoming more so in the years to come: Dr. William J. Jones, Dr. George Abernathy, Dr. G. E. Aylmer, Dr. A. Hassell Smith, Dr. Joyce Mousley, Miss Nancy Briggs, and Miss Carol Czapski. Here, too, I render thanks to Professor Cyrus H. Karraker of Bucknell University, whose pioneer work on the seventeenth-century sheriff answered many questions, for graciously setting aside his scholarly and humanitarian pursuits in order to read and to criticize what I had to say about the sheriff.

I credit two beloved colleagues at Lycoming College, Professors Loring B. Priest and Roger E. Cogswell, with the friendship that sustained me in my first teaching job and encouraged me to conclude this work. James Jeffers, a senior student at Lycoming, expertly executed the maps. Miss Nancy Leonard uncomplainingly grappled with an abominable draft in typing the greater part of the manuscript, much of it in her own time. For such service as these have given, I render heartfelt thanks.

I thank the Public Record Office, the Somerset Record Office, the British Museum, and other custodians and owners of manuscripts for permission to quote briefly from manuscripts in their care.

To the Harvard University Press I register my gratitude for undertaking the publication of this study. Miss Ann Orlov, the editor, deserves special mention, her careful attendance to the details of publication and her unfailing courtesy to a procrastinating author being much appreciated.

Finally, I humbly record the obligation in which I am bound to my dear friends Sydney and Margaret Templeman: to them both for their affectionate encouragement and hospitality over many years, to Sydney for bringing the keenness of the English equity lawyer's mind to bear on the work at every stage. In my wife and my mother, I possessed two careful typists, to cast no higher my debt to them. In the first draft of this study, my mother and my father proved sharp critics, and what lucidity it possesses is traceable to them. My father, who was my first and finest teacher, did not live to see this book in which he is so deeply concerned. It is a memorial to his devotion, the book he never wrote, the product of his inspiration above all other.

Thomas Garden Barnes

Berkeley, California
All Saints' Day 1960

Contents

Maps

For outlines and political divisions, these three maps are based on John Speed's map of Somerset in Theatre of the Empire of Great Britaine *(1611). However, Ordnance Survey maps and other cartographic materials were used for physical features, roads, towns, and the seats of justices of the peace.*

Somerset 1625-1640

A County's Government
During the " Personal Rule "

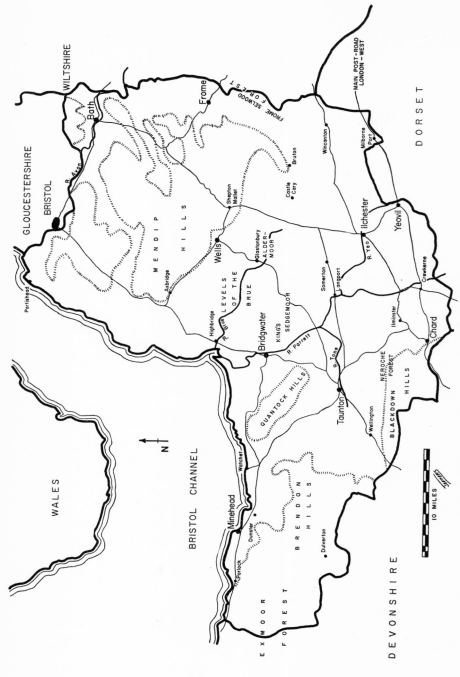

FIG. 1.—*The main physical features, towns, and roads of Somerset in 1630.*

Chapter I ❧ *The County*

In area Somerset is the seventh largest county of England. Arched round the Bristol Channel, it is bordered by Gloucestershire to the north, Wiltshire to the east, Dorset to the south and east, and Devon to the south and west.

Diversity is the keynote of Somerset's terrain. Windswept Dunkery, 1706 feet up on Exmoor, contrasts with the damp lowness of fenland Sedgemoor; the lush meadows of the Vale of Taunton Deane with the abrupt Cheddar Gorge and the marred plateau of the Mendips. This diversity of terrain has had a marked effect on the determination of the population of the county. In a mainly agricultural community with poor communications—and such was Somerset in the seventeenth century—it vitally affected the relationship of the county's administrators with the central government.

The Mendip Hills stretch from very near Weston-super-Mare eastwards until they become lost in the rolling country around Frome. About fifteen miles wide at its greatest breadth, the Mendip plateau rises sharply north of the Levels of the Brue and skirts Axbridge, Wells, and Shepton Mallet. On the north, it drops off gradually into the hilly region around the River Avon that continues into Gloucestershire. In the seventeenth century the roads over Mendip were so poor—churned up by miners' plough carts—and the climb so steep, that these hills provided an effective barrier to any but the most necessary intercourse between the central part of the county and the narrow though populous northern strip of Somerset comprising the area south of the Avon as far as Bath and the terrain north of that city. This northern strip partook much more of Gloucestershire than of Somerset for the Avon proved less of an effective natural boundary than the Mendips. To the southeast, from Frome to Yeovil, Somerset merges imperceptibly into Wiltshire and Dorset. Similarly, Exmoor to the west is common to Somerset and

Devon—the natural boundary would be along the Brendons, Exmoor's foothills, from Watchet on the sea to Wellington. Only to the south does Somerset's political boundary follow nature's division. The Blackdown Hills, stretching southeasterly from Wellington to Chard, rise suddenly from the Vale of Taunton Deane and largely isolate Somerset's central region from Devon. Within these bounds, the long central portion of the county, extending from the Brendons in the west through the Vale across Sedgemoor and into the rolling country around Bruton in the east, is territory peculiar to Somerset.

This central portion has been traditionally the center of the county's life. The most populous area,[1] it contained most of the county's incorporated towns, her finest churches, and it possessed an almost exclusive monopoly of Somerset's great houses. Naturally, marshy Sedgemoor and the Levels of the Brue must be excluded from this statement. Here, the villages were few and far between, oases in a watery desert peopled by a race of amphibious folk.[2] It was the rest of this central area which the contemporary observer, Thomas Gerard, epitomized as "inhabited by wealthy and substantiall men though none the best bredd."[3] It contained the great fair and market towns which comprised the commercial heart of the county.

The land of the Brendons and Exmoor was sparsely populated and given over primarily to sheep grazing. Only in the southwest corner, Dulverton, and the northwest coastal area around Minehead, were there any appreciable settlements and much commercial activity. The Mendips, save that they were peopled by lead and coal miners, were much like Exmoor demographically. Civilization was on the fringe of the Mendips, never on the hills themselves. No great manor houses, such as were to be found north and especially south of this forbidding plateau, were built on the Mendips. Their intrinsic unattractiveness was heightened by opencast mining operations. But to the north around Bristol and Bath, the country was well populated, housed many, and had villages in good number. Already the villages to the immediate south of Bristol had begun to take on the appearance if not the function of suburbs to a great center of urban activity.

[1] Dr. E. G. R. Taylor reckoned Somerset to have been the third or fourth most densely populated county in England, on the basis of the number of able-bodied men enumerated in 1588 militia statistics, *An Historical Geography of England before 1800* (1951), p. 360.

[2] While this is at variance with Dr. Thirsk's picture of the not dissimilar Lincolnshire Fens, *Fenland Farming in the Sixteenth Century* (1953), the Somerset sessions records tend to support the contemporary view, though it was exaggerated, of Sedgemoor.

[3] Thomas Gerard, *The Particular Description of the County of Somerset, 1630* (1900), p. 125.

Somerset's prosperity was very real. To contemporaries, particularly the Privy Council, it was a populous and rich county. It is worth noting that only Devon, Yorkshire, and London were assessed more for ship money, 1635–1637.[4] To William Camden, his eye on the countryside, it was a plentiful country.[5] Mainly agricultural, it was also one of the foremost cloth-producing counties in the kingdom. Its lead mines were at their peak. Its harbors sustained a phenomenal coastwise traffic for their size, especially with Ireland. In bountiful harvest years it was a granary for surrounding counties.

But Somerset's occasional distress was no less real than its evident prosperity. Bad harvests caused terrible corn scarcity in 1622–1623 and 1629–1631. Coupled with depression in the cloth industry which resulted from stoppages of trade, these scarcities fell most heavily on the many clothworkers who had no means of support other than their trade.[6] The action that the government took to cope with this distress will be discussed fully in another chapter. It was a remedy that was not sufficient to erase from the minds of the mass of people the memory of starvation and unemployment. Somerset was a prosperous community, but some people were more prosperous than others. There could be nothing idyllic about life under an economy so unpredictable.

By the seventeenth century, Somerset's agriculture was mixed; a workable balance had been struck between pasturage and crops. The type of terrain determined to a large extent the type of agriculture. It is interesting, though, to find the stony, shallow-soiled hills north of the Mendips planted with corn. Although the yield here was not so high as elsewhere, the quality appears to have been good. Perhaps there was some truth, too, in the locals' argument that the stones kept the soil from being blown away. The Mendips were agriculturally fit for nothing save sheep grazing. The wooded area around Frome, adjacent to Wiltshire, was given over largely to grazing. The ill effects of the corn scarcity was felt here most acutely because all food had to be transported into the district. It was in the central portion that both cattle grazing and corn growing were most successfully carried on. Gerard's description of Martock fits the whole area: "A place seated in the fattest place of

---

[4] W. R. Ward, *The English Land Tax in the Eighteenth Century* (1953), p. 9. Dr. Ward holds that the ship-money assessment was a good criterion of a county's wealth in the 1630s.

[5] William Camden, *Britannia* (1722), I, 67.

[6] E. Lipson, *The Economic History of England* (1931), II, 66, 68. Prof. Lipson's contention that the clothworker was almost wholly divorced from the soil is supported by the picture of misery around Frome, 1629–1631.

the Earth of this Countie, especially for errable."[7] The land around Somerton was noted for cattle grazing, and that already decayed town's one source of prosperity was a great and continuous cattle fair, lasting from April to June. Taunton and its surrounding soil was a garden of orchards. Apple trees could be seen there where the gasworks now obtrude. Even Sedgemoor, damp though it was, furnished useful cattle ground in summer. The Vale of Taunton Deane with its rich soil produced rich corn. Exmoor's not inconsiderable service to agriculture was as a sheep and cattle run. It was not so populous as to require extensive crop production, and thus its people did not suffer in 1629–1631 as did the landless cloth cottagers around Frome. An accurate measure of Somerset's agricultural productivity—in times of good harvest—was the contribution the county made toward feeding Bristol and the central portion's export of butter and the famous cheddar cheese to Wiltshire, Dorset, and Devon, and of corn to Devon.[8] When for reasons of Somerset's own survival this trade had to be stringently curtailed in 1629–1631, the old customers suffered.

Enclosure was not a burning issue in Somerset at this time. In the western half of the county enclosure of open fields (where open fields had existed at all) had been largely accomplished by the end of the sixteenth century.[9] In the eastern part it was in process during this period, though without manifestations of strong opposition or much upheaval. Neither the 1607 agrarian riots nor the Western Rising of 1628–1631 in Wiltshire, Gloucestershire, and Dorset affected Somerset.[10] The King's own efforts, however, in disafforesting and enclosing Neroche and Frome Selwood forests and in enclosing and improving Sedgemoor met with considerable obstruction. The sole instance extant of antienclosure vandalism was the destruction of a duck decoy pond in Kennmoor belonging to Lord Poulett. The two husbandmen charged with the offence alleged in justification that it was "for the good of the country"; such high motives are suspect inasmuch as one of them had been charged previously with a dastardly

---

[7] Gerard, p. 123. This description of the county owes much to *An Historical Geography of England before 1800*, chs. ix–xi.

[8] Licenses of laders, badgers, etc., granted at Somerset quarter sessions give some indication of the extent of the legally tolerated trade—the illicit trade must have been even greater.

[9] W. E. Tate, *Somerset Enclosure Acts and Awards* (1948), p. 22, and *An Historical Geography of England before 1800*, pp. 345–346.

[10] Tate, p. 21. See D. G. C. Allan, "The Rising in the West, 1628–1631," *Econ Hist Rev*, series 2 (1952), V, 76–83 for a full discussion of this trouble.

assault on two poor milkmaids![11] Were there more Star Chamber proceedings extant for the period, it might well appear that Somerset produced other incidents, though probably nowhere near the scale of those which made the Midlands notorious during this period and impelled the Attorney-General to lay information against as many as two hundred at one time.

Two commissions were issued in 1635 for Somerset as well as other counties directed to local gentlemen and the Surveyor-General authorizing them to enquire of depopulating enclosures.[12] We do not know what came of this, but the situation in Somerset probably did not warrant intense investigation or action. Since much of Somerset's enclosure was of waste, enclosure was unlikely to cause extensive depopulation. It was corn scarcity and depression that beggared people living on the margin of poverty. Enclosure did not in itself improve farming methods, and so could not remedy scarcity. By the same token, enclosure can hardly be blamed for the economic ills that afflicted the community.

Somerset's chief commercial industry was the production of wool cloth. The industry did not present a very prosperous appearance in this period for it had suffered at the hands of Alderman Cockayne and the continental war limited its traditional markets. Four powerful interests concerned themselves with the industry, and seldom did they agree or cooperate. The Merchant Adventurers who controlled the export market were at loggerheads with the Staplers who had lost control of export but were still the principal wool dealers. Both were united in their dislike of middlemen who had grown up locally, such as the market spinners. The local clothiers, dependent on the Merchant Adventurers for export and largely dependent on the Staplers for their wool, were impatient of both. The Privy Council, intent upon keeping order in the industry, tended to side with the Merchant Adventurers. The industry was the "almost continual concern of the government" in this period.[13] The Council was often misguided, and its actions were wholly insufficient to avoid seasonal unemployment of the cloth artificers and recurrent depressions like those of 1622 and 1629–1630. Evasion of cloth-making regulations was common practice among West Country clothiers, and an investigator sent down by the Council in the early 1630s was ducked

[11] SRO, Sess Rolls, 72, nos. 25–26, 51–52, Mich. QS 1635.
[12] See p. 160.
[13] G. D. Ramsay, "*The Report of the Royal Commission on the Clothing Industry, 1640*," EHR (1942), LVII, 482.

in the Avon.[14] As the 1630s saw little improvement in the situation, a commission was appointed in 1638 to investigate the whole broadcloth industry of the West, though it reported too late for its far-reaching proposals to be implemented.[15] It was the spinners and the weavers who felt the full force of endemic depression. However, for the Somerset clothiers who controlled the industry locally it was still a lucrative vocation. The Civil War appears to have afforded some of these men the opportunity of attaining social and political recognition commensurate with their wealth.

The industry was centered principally in two areas. On the eastern end of the Mendips, around Bath and Frome and as far as Shepton Mallet, it was the furthermost extension of the Cotswold cloth industry. The cloth manufacture centered to the south on Taunton, Bridgwater, Wellington, and Chard was the beginning of the Devon broadcloth industry. There were isolated cloth manufacturing centers, such as the linsey-woolsey manufactures of Milborne Port on the Dorset border and, most notably, the Dunster yarn spinners in the northwest. "Bridgwaters" and "Tauntons" were household words in seventeenth-century England.

Mendip was the location of the other great commercial enterprise of the county; its lead mines reached their productive peak in this period.[16] Usually a small entrepreneur, the Mendip miner staked his claim and worked it either by open-cast or shallow shafting. In times of scarcity he felt the pinch of want, and the late years of his life might be as a pauper on the poor rates. Speculators such as Bristol merchants, neighboring gentlemen, and even publicans, were often ready to advance capital in return for shares. "Adventurers," similar to Sir Bevis Bulmer in Elizabeth's time, occasionally tried large-scale operations with government encouragement. These met with little success.[17] The small miners—"groviers"—were jealous of their trade even if it was not particularly rewarding. They were a sturdy, independent, and often riotous people. It was the lords of the manors on Mendip who found lead mining most profitable. In addition to appreciable royalties, they had the profits

[14] *Ibid.,* p. 484; PRO, S.P.16/180, no. 74, remonstrance of the Merchant Adventurers to PC [1630?] and S.P.16/454, no. 29, petition of West Country clothiers, 20 May 1640.

[15] Ramsay, pp. 482–493. The commission, composed of clothiers, recommended central control of the industry, strict sealing of cloths, and summary punishment of offenders against the regulations.

[16] J. W. Gough, *The Mines of Mendip* (1930), p. 157.

[17] *VCH Som* (1911), II, 374–375; Gough, pp. 126–128.

of the courts which administered the peculiar law and custom of Mendip that controlled the industry. Doubtlessly, those who marketed the lead ingots made good money, for besides the government's purchase of lead, there was a considerable export black-market to Spain. English veterans of the Low Countries knew the effectiveness of Mendip lead when cast into round shot by the Spaniards.

Coal mining on Mendip was also a rising enterprise. What soil the lead groviers did not tear up, the coal miners did. Dr. Nef estimates the yield of Mendip (including some Dorset mines) in 1551–1560 at 10,000 tons per year; in 1681–1690 at 100,000 tons.[18] The coal miner like the grovier was usually a small prospector. He sank his pits in the same way. He was as subject to depression and ruin as the grovier. But he did not come within the jurisdiction of a peculiar code and court as did the grovier, and therefore was freer and often more irresponsible in his work. Likewise, through royalties, the lords of the manors profited most. This coal was for a limited market, mainly domestic in character.[19] Camden noted that Mendip's coal was "made use of by smiths as most proper to soften iron".[20] Small-coal was utilized in lime kilns thus serving another minor industry fairly widespread in the county.

In the Bristol Channel west of the Parrett's mouth, fishing was a common occupation. Inshore school fish were captured in weirs, usually owned by the manor lords. The Luttrells, besides their yarn market at Dunster, worked extensive weirs in the Minehead region. Porlock was already by 1624 a herring port of some note. Building stone, the glory of Somerset, came from two places. The honey-colored stone of the county's Perpendicular church towers came from Ham Hill. The freestone, evident in Wells and Glastonbury, was quarried at Doulting near Shepton Mallet. Even alabaster was cut in small quantities at Blue Anchor— another Luttrell enterprise.

It is difficult to estimate the extent to which Somerset men of wealth engaged in speculative enterprise. That the county was alive to this mode of making money is amply proven by the readiness with which the mayor of Bridgwater allowed the Virginia Company to hold a lottery in 1620 to distribute stock.[21] Investments made by the great gentlemen of

[18] John U. Nef, *The Rise of the British Coal Industry* (1932), I, 19–20. Of the 10,000 tons in 1551–1560, Somerset accounted for 4000 and Kingswood Chase, Dorset, 6000.

[19] J. A. Bulley, "To Mendip for Coal," *SANHS Proc* (1952), XCVII, 61–62.

[20] Camden, I, 87.

[21] *SANHS Proc* (1943), LXXXIX, 79 ff.

the county were not uncommon. Sir Thomas Wrothe, JP, was a large shareholder of the Virginia Company and on the Council for New England.[22] Sir Thomas Wyndham of Kentsford, JP, invested heavily in the Earl of Dorset's fens-draining project—and lost.[23]

The numerous fairs of Somerset, most of them established in the later Middle Ages and still flourishing in this period, give an indication of commercial activity in the county. They do not tell us much about the county's internal trade since few records exist previous to the next century of the staple commodities of particular fairs.[24] But the fairs' positions do confirm the impression that the central portion of the county was the center of agricultural activity and generally the most prosperous area. In this region some fairs, such as Bridgwater and Wells, attracted traders from far beyond the county's borders. Others, like Taunton, Glastonbury, and Chard, were at least county-wide in influence. These were big marts where nearly everything could be bought and sold. Combined with the smaller, more specialized cattle and wool fairs they formed a network of commercial centers engaged in fairly continuous activity. Even recurring depression could not destroy their vitality. Too, from the fairs' geographical positions, it is possible to determine with some certainty the main routes of communication in the county. "All roads lead to a fair" aptly fits Somerset, and the emphasis on roads is very well founded. Water transport was not extensive in the county, for with the exception of the Avon, Somerset's rivers were small sluggish streams. There was an extensive carriage trade on the Avon, through Bristol to Bath and thence into Wiltshire, and Gerard noted a small traffic in barges up the River Parrett as far as Langport.[25] Most of the Parrett's traffic stopped at Bridgwater, the county's premier port, which sustained a heavy legal traffic with Ireland and not a little illicit trade with the continent.[26] Some goods were carried in lighters up the Tone to Taunton. John Mallett, JP, undertook in the 1630s a too-ambitious project to make navigable the Tone as far as two miles west of Taunton.[27]

[22] *DNB*, XXI, 1080.

[23] H. A. Wyndham, *A Family History* (1939), I, 173.

[24] N. F. Hulbert, "A Survey of Somerset Fairs," *SANHS Proc* (1936), LXXXII, 158.

[25] Gerard, pp. 131–132.

[26] PRO, E.159, records of proceedings for cancelling and levying recognizances by merchants, entered into to land goods only in Ireland, provide material on Bridgwater's trading activity.

[27] PRO, Index 4212, commission of 6 March 1637/8 to John Coventrye *et al.* to compound with mill owners on the Tone touching improvement of navigation to be made by John Mallett.

Somerset's life moved mostly by its roads. While the main routes linked the principal commercial and political centers, the condition of the roads was such as to impede traffic rather than accelerate it—cross country might have been faster. Quarter-sessions records constantly remind one of the ruinous state of the dirt roads, rutted and mired by the passage of plough carts, colliers' wagons, and pack horses. Inundation made the roads across Sedgemoor impassable in winter and spring. It was for the next century of turnpike trusts and canal companies to provide really effective communications. Government suffered because of these poor arteries. London was a three-day ride for the fastest messenger of the Chamber, and it was a stout nag that could carry a magistrate from his house near Bath to Taunton quarter sessions in two days and a night.

Though what urban life there was had long centered primarily in the towns in the central portion of Somerset, Bath in the northeast was the premier city of the county. As early as 1447 this city had been granted autonomy from the county's magistrates. Camden found it a "flourishing place, both for the woollen manufacture and the great resort of strangers."[28] Though it had not yet attained the eminence it was to achieve in the coming century, Bath was the county's great jewel. Nevertheless, the boroughs and towns in the central portion were those in the mainstream of county life. Taunton, enriched through trade and cloth, had usurped from the enfeebled town of Somerton the status of county-town. With Wells, Bridgwater, and Ilchester, Taunton shared quarter sessions; the autumn assizes were, with few exceptions, held there. Even though its lord was the powerful Bishop of Winchester, its burgesses were an independent and prosperous lot. Taunton largely escaped control by a county family because the nearby Portmans exerted only a persuasive influence there. The same cannot be said of the decayed town of Ilchester, whose steward was Sir Robert Phelips. Ilchester's only distinction was the county gaol, one of the county sessions, and the shire court. It was a very minor borough. Still, Sir Robert Phelips secured its "restoration" as a parliamentary borough in 1621, probably to ensure himself a seat if, as in 1614, he failed to carry a county election.[29] Minehead, prosperous as an *entrepôt* of Irish trade, was firmly under the Luttrells' control. When the burgesses fell afoul of George Luttrell, he secured the revocation of their charter in 1603 and barely failed in his attempt to have the

[28] *British Borough Charters, 1307–1660* (1943), p. 101; Camden, p. 90.
[29] E. de Villiers, "Parliamentary Boroughs Restored by the House of Commons, 1621–1641," *EHR* (1952), LXVII, 187–188.

borough disenfranchised.[30] During Charles' reign, the town did as its
lord desired. Milborne Port, geographically in Dorset, was "restored" to
a parliamentary franchise in 1628, much to the advantage of various
Dorset families. Wells, the cathedral city, avoided control by any great
family, though it was particularly receptive to pressure exerted by the
dean and chapter on the one hand and by the bishop on the other.
Bridgwater was rich and sturdily independent, but by 1640 its recorder,
Sir Thomas Wrothe, JP, whose seat was at North Petherton nearby,
appears to have obtained mastery of the borough's stormy politics. It
returned him to the Long Parliament where he distinguished himself
as a Parliamentarian. Most of the lesser towns, such as Wiveliscombe,
Crewkerne, and Frome, came within the orbit of a neighbouring large
family. Unenfranchised and with no more borough rights than a market
or a fair, they had no independent existence. By and large, however, all
the towns were prosperous in this area. Gerard noted new buildings at
Yeovil and also at Chard; in the latter case he attributed it to the importance of the place as an assize town.[31] During this period two towns received full borough liberties, including a recorder and virtual freedom
from the jurisdiction of the county magistrates: Taunton in 1627 and
Chard in 1641.[32] Without overemphasizing the dependence of most of the
towns on a county family, it is safe to say that the political ferment of
the period was focused in the country and only reflected in the towns.
Therefore, a picture of county politics is valid even if the towns are
largely ignored.

The relationship of Somerset to the great metropolis on its northern
border, always close, was perhaps closer in the seventeenth century than
ever before. Bristol, a separate county since the fourteenth century, a
tremendous commercial and industrial center, the port of colonial plan-
tation, relied largely on Somerset as well as Wiltshire and Gloucestershire
for its daily bread. It was a center of "conspicuous consumption" that
drew off all the surplus corn from the strip of Somerset north of Mendip,
from Gloucester, and western Wiltshire. The badgers' licences in the
Somerset quarter sessions order books indicate that despite the poor roads
over Mendip the central part of the county also carried on a good trade
in corn, butter, and cheese with Bristol. In times of plenty this was

[30] H. C. Maxwell-Lyte, *A History of Dunster* (1909), pt. 1, p. 174.
[31] Gerard, pp. 171–173, 72–73.
[32] PRO, C.66/2376, no. 2, for Taunton's charter, and C.66/2895, no. 10, for Chard's
charter.

profitable for the county's farmers. In times of scarcity it was tragic for the landless poor and unemployed of Somerset. Without anticipating a later chapter, mention must be made here of the almost universal reproach Somerset justices heaped on Bristol corn-carriers for draining the county of corn in 1630–1631. Yet it was not normally a one-way trade. Bristol shared with Bath preeminence as the market of northern Somerset. Socially, Bristol continued to give much to the county. The number of Somerset's gentle families that had sprung from Bristol merchants surpassed those descended from Londoners. In the realm of intangibles, Bristol set a tone that all urban life in Somerset appears to have aped, and which even county families, perhaps not oblivious of their forbears, found acceptable despite their exalted station in rural society.

For a county of its wealth, size, and beauty it seems strange that Somerset had but two noble families seated there, and both of them brand-new creations. Sir James Ley of Beckington, successively Lord Chief Justice of Ireland, of England, and Lord Treasurer, was advanced to a barony in 1624 and created Earl of Marlborough in 1626. An extremely successful lawyer of gentle birth, turned politician, he was succeeded upon his death in 1629 by his son Henry. John Poulett of Hinton St. George, the son and grandson of two Elizabethan courtiers and royal servants, was created Baron Poulett of Hinton St. George in 1627 for services rendered the King and Buckingham, and rather more than ordinary obsequiousness. Except for these two newly risen stars, the county would have had no resident peers. The older Ley was absorbed in affairs of state, and neither spent much time at Beckington, the younger Ley preferring his Wiltshire seat. Poulett, on the other hand, remained at home and played the courtier by post, though not always with the greatest success.

What the county lacked in nobility it more than made up for in gentry. At the top of the social hierarchy were about twenty-five families. The head of each was generally, though not invariably, a knight. Most of them had origins in the county, but it is safe to say that their preeminence depended upon monastic lands purchased usually with the profits of royal service under Elizabeth and James I. These families had recently built and were then living in the mansions that are such a feature of the county. It was to this group that the King and Council looked for leadership in local government, that the county looked to for its representatives at Westminster, and from which both sides sought leadership during the Civil War. Preeminent in land, wealth, and, above all, social standing, they dominated the rural bench and furnished almost all of the deputy lieutenants. These were the county's magnates. Below them were the seventy-five or so heads of families of undoubted gentility from which were drawn the majority of the justices of the peace—though not all men of the magisterial class were magistrates. Their origin was not unlike that of the magnates, but more of them owed their wealth to mercantilist forbears than to wealth gained through royal service. The line between these men and the magnates, like all social lines in this period, was more apparent than real. It is a mistake to think of them as inferior in status to the magnates, for no magnate would have considered them as less than equals on the bench. Nevertheless, they did not wield the power and influence in the county and at Westminster that the greatest men did, and this was the feature that most clearly distinguished them from the magnates. When in this period and during the Civil War they were active in politics they leant upon the magnates for leadership. John Symes, Esq., a merchant's son, opposed the free-gift in the county, but he did so in the wake of that dreadnought, Sir Robert Phelips, heir of a late Master of the Rolls.

Below the magisterial class were the many families who can be called "lesser gentry." Many of these had substantial estates and were respected as lords of manors. Those at the top were usually on the way to becoming members of the group above—those at the bottom faded imperceptibly into the numerous yeomen in the country or burgesses in the town. This group included some few men with the title of "Esquire." A man with "gent." after his name was certainly of this group unless he was the heir of an "Esquire." Of particular interest is the fact that during this period very few of the top families in this strata appear to have attained the level above. It would take a large increment of wealth to enable the lesser gentleman to become of such status as to be placed on the commission of the peace. For reasons that are best left to another study and to social historians, this increment was not forthcoming in Somerset in the 1620s–1630s.

Below the "lesser gentry" anonymity reigns, save where for a brief moment the little men gain a place in the records because they witness —or commit—a crime, petition a court, or come within the orbit of the poor law. They cannot be ignored because they were the mass of the governed.

There are numerous indications that Somerset's yeomanry were many in number, fairly prosperous, and decidedly ambitious. Especially is this true of those in the central portion of the county. When a yeoman appeared as the accused before quarter sessions it was invariably for an assault on a servant or some village husbandman, or for a theft done in vengeance rather than for gain, occasionally with a *bona fide* claim of right. A yeoman's examination before a justice portrays an arrogant, selfish, but slightly frightened man. During the corn scarcity they were the bulk of those informed against for engrossing and forestalling corn. These were the "wealthy and substantiall men though none the best bredd ... [who] have money in their purses to make them gentlemen when they are fitt for the degree."[33] Apparently, there was little chance in this period for these men to advance to that "degree." They paid a large proportion of the taxes and filled the onerous hundredal and parochial offices. They were politically conscious and a study of Civil War Somerset might show them to have become politically important as well.

So little can be discovered about the vast majority of the "lower orders" —husbandmen, laborers, artisans, and vagrants—that they are best treated geographically rather than socially. Mendip was almost exclusively populated by miners. These were violent, hard-drinking men. Alehouses, which were literally dens of thieves, covered the hills and could not be suppressed.[34] Sporadic outbursts of violence resulting in bloodshed were commonplace, giving Mendip the dubious distinction of representing the single greatest problem of law enforcement in Somerset. Because virtually no justices lived there, the hills did not come under the constant surveillance of the magistrates; a surveillance which elsewhere contributed greatly to keeping the peace. Much the same was true of Sedgemoor. The amphibious folk who lived in that watery wilderness existed by fishing, netting ducks, subsistence farming, and not a few by thieving. Exmoor and the Blackdowns, less populous, were also less disorderly, and the nearby justices working with the subordinate officers exerted an effective control. If this picture seems to do less than justice to the vast mass of Somerset's folk by concentrating on the more disorderly among the husbandmen and laboring people, it has still provided an impression

[33] Gerard, p. 125.
[34] SRO, Sess Rolls, 2, no. 81, Eas. QS 1607. This order of quarter sessions suppressing *all* alehouses on Mendip was ineffective. The order recited that the alehouses were "remote from the eye and view of ... officers."

justifiably held by their superiors. It should not be forgotten that in seventeenth-century England innocent merriment might in a moment become riot bordering on rebellion. A local squire needed precious little imagination in order to see in a drunken husbandman staggering homewards a potential threat to the King's peace.

In religion, Somerset presented a well-ordered countenance. The diocese of Bath and Wells, coterminous with the county, possessed churches as beautiful as any in the realm. Most men worshipped in these churches either through choice or from fear of penal statutes. Even those who did not were little bothered, provided they kept quiet.

Roman Catholic recusancy was not really a threat to good government in this county. Just under two hundred recusants were presented at quarter sessions in this period, according to hundred presentments in the sessions rolls. Three-fifths of the presented recusants came from five hundreds in the central portion.[35] In most cases, the recusants were concentrated in one or two gentle families in the hundred. A recusant gentleman's house might contain his family, distant relatives, Roman Catholic friends and servants. The whole household would refuse to attend church, be presented for nonattendance and recusancy, and be fined by quarter sessions. There is no evidence to link these people with sedition, Jesuits, or clandestine Masses. They were accorded such respect as befitted their social status in the community. The Council's licence to travel outside the county was readily given to some of them. When on Council order of November 1625 they were disarmed after thorough searching, the handful of corselets, the ancient battle-axe and odd pistol or two collected by the deputy lieutenants did not go far toward equipping the trained bands.[36] Even during periods of marked severity towards recusants in general, such as the autumn of 1625 and the spring of 1630, they were little troubled. Attorney-General Heath's letter of 9 December 1625 to the clerk of the peace ordering a return of recusants' names and more stringent enforcement of the penal law was carefully entered in the sessions rolls and then apparently forgotten.[37] Seminarians and sedition were another matter, however. Sir Thomas Wrothe, as recorder of

[35] SRO, Sess Rolls, *passim*. The recusant rolls—PRO, E.377—confirm this estimate. The five hundreds were: Abdick and Bulstone, Milverton, Stone and Catsash, Whitley, Williton and Freemanors.

[36] PRO, S.P.16/10, no. 48, DLs of Somerset to PC, 28 Nov. 1625. The DLs in a later report said that the recusants' arms would not equip ten men, PRO, S.P.16/32, no. 76, 29 July 1626.

[37] Enrolled in SRO, Sess Rolls, 58 pt. ii, no. 63, Epiph. QS 1626/7.

Bridgwater, zealously examined a young Irish priest arrested there in 1639. John Hodges of Kilton, gent., regularly presented as a recusant by the Wilton and Freemanors hundred jury, pronounced some indiscreet words concerning an "alteration" in religion. He was examined closely by the two next justices, spent three weeks in London in the custody of a messenger, and was finally bound over by the Lord Chief Justice to Somerset quarter sessions where he suffered no ill. Chief Justice Bramston did not take a serious view of the case, and found Hodges a quiet and harmless man.[38] Professor Jordan's opinion that through "the country as a whole the recusants were rarely molested" during the 1630s, is certainly supported by Somerset's experience.[39] The county was sufficiently far from London, its fears and rumors, and the recusants so few and so quiet that little ill feeling was manifested toward them. After all, and four aged Roman Catholic spinsters of Whitestaunton were hardly a threat to the safety of the realm.

When the Civil War came, Somerset proved to be predominantly puritan in religious sympathy. It would be a mistake, though, to look in the Somerset of the 1630s for the clear divergence that appeared in 1642, and an even graver error to consider puritan inclinations in an individual as evidence of political disloyalty to the King. To the magnate, the lesser gentleman, and the yeoman in the 1630s, what we call puritanism was the established faith practised in the established Church. It was unfortunate for these people that William Pierce, Bishop of Bath and Wells from 1632 until deprived by Parliament in 1641, was so staunch a follower of Laud. Bishop Pierce came to a diocese of laymen who were quietly enjoying their "lecturers" and receiving their infrequent communions from a deal table in the nave. When he left it—for the Tower— the diocese was not so quiet but even more determined to follow its old practice. Laudianism in Somerset, as elsewhere, lacked roots among the parochial clergy and the people. It probably did manage through oppressive measures in the diocesan court to raise the level of uniformity and decency a very slight degree. But it left an immense residue of resentment that under the disorder of war destroyed all religious uniformity and ultimately the established Church.

There is the barest hint of puritan conventicles in this period, and those

---

[38] PRO, S.P.16/420, no. 50, examination by Wrothe of Cornelius O'Connor, 4 May 1639, 326, no. 5, Bramston, CJ, to PC, 11 June 1636.

[39] W. K. Jordan, *The Development of Religious Toleration in England* (1936), II, 184.

2 +

only in the five years before 1640. Sir Thomas Wrothe was rather indiscreetly involved in one.[40] Far too much has been made of the churchales dispute which erupted in Somerset in 1633 as an indication of the county's deep commitment to militant puritanism; that commotion grew from the feud of county factions merged with a private quarrel between Laud and Chief Justice Richardson rather than from a puritanical loathing for these boisterous and occasionally unruly parish fetes.[41] The repercussions of the churchales affair certainly did promote religious discord and might indeed have been largely responsible for the appearance of conventicles in the county a year or so later, the expulsion of clergy who would not read the King's Book of Sports providing the conventicles with militant leadership. If the justices had any particular religious sympathies, they were overwhelmingly against the Laudian practice rather than for the Geneva practice. This was as true of John Lord Poulett, the Court's best friend in the county, as it was of Hugh Pyne, JP, who was removed from the commission in 1626 for seditious opposition to the government. The magistrates saw no threat in puritanism and thus they deemed unnecessary any repressive action. Even the clerical justices, including Bishop Pierce, do not seem to have urged attention to be paid to puritanism, though admittedly this might have stemmed from characteristic Laudian jealousy for ecclesiastical independence from the secular arm. Since most puritans were attenders at church, they did not run afoul of the secular law.

The puritans did run afoul of Bishop Pierce. He attempted to compel "lecturers" to conform by making them read the prayers before preaching and wear surplice and hood instead of a cloak. In 1634 he gave effect to the royal injunction that the communion table should be railed in at the east end of the church. About one hundred and fifty parishes appear to have complied without audible protest. One parish most vehemently did protest. The Beckington churchwardens' refusal to move their table was the county's most serious puritan reaction to Bishop Pierce's Laudianism. The churchwardens' appeal to the court of Arches failed through royal intervention, and they were excommunicated and gaoled by assizes. The whole parish supported them, even with force, for there

---

[40] In 1635, Wrothe wrote a mildly seditious letter to a Dr. Stoughton in London, who appears to have preached to puritan groups in the West, PRO, S.P.16/297, no. 39. Wrothe was appointed a county justice in 1636 by virtue of being recorder of Bridgwater.

[41] T. G. Barnes, "County Politics and a Puritan Cause Célèbre: Somerset Churchales 1633," *Trans RHS* (1959), 5th series, IX, 103–122.

was a riot in Beckington Church in 1637. Convicted at assizes, the rioters were required to make a particularly humiliating public submission to the bishop or suffer the full penalty of the law. As late as March 1639–1640, one intransigent rioter had still not submitted.[42] Bishop Pierce had awakened in one parish a spirit of naked resistance which spread throughout the diocese when civil strife weakened the sanctions that caused the timorous to conform.

To claim for any one of the kingdom's two-score counties that it was "typical" of the nation as a whole would be not only presumptuous, it would be impossible. That claim is not made here for Somerset. Yet, Somerset in its economic, social, and religious aspects avoided the extremes that can be found in some other counties. Economically, it was relatively prosperous in agriculture while also possessing a full measure of the industry of the age. Socially, it was stable, untroubled by the monolithic influence of a few great noble families. Governed by a broadly based, solid gentry, not too new risen, it was blessed also with a numerically strong, well-to-do yeomanry. Religiously, it was neither a stronghold of Roman Catholicism nor a haven for the *avante garde* in puritanism— extremes not uncommon in the north and east of England, respectively. It was a big county, an important county, and a county receptive to new influences from every quarter. This is not the basis for a claim for Somerset's "typicality." It is justification for a study of the local government of that county in the crucial years, 1625 to 1640.

[42] *VCH Som,* II, 44; the churchwardens' reasons are in PRO, S.P.16/375, no. 84; *Som Asz Ords,* no. 161. Dr. Addleshaw cites the Beckington affair as the "classical instance" of the impact of visitation injunctions on parochial life, *The Architectural Setting of Anglican Worship* (1948), p. 128.

Chapter II   *The Local Governors*

In the sixteen years that preceded the convention of the Long Parliament, one hundred and eight lords and gentlemen (all of them resident in Somerset save the lords lieutenants and a few justices who lived in adjacent counties) served the King and the county in the three main offices of Somerset's government. At least something can be found out about each in addition to the mere fact that he appeared on the commissions of the peace or lieutenancy, or served as sheriff. Each is interesting as an individual and, though portraits of some emerge more clearly than of others, all must be viewed within the society from which they sprang and over which they ruled. A picture of their background, their status, and their education, will help to explain the peculiar place they held in their society and the reason they held it. On this subject, the dean of present-day historians of the era has sounded a note of warning, and we must heed it: "With all that has been said about the country gentleman, there remains something elusive about the best of them."[1] Though the depiction here presented might be misleading if drawn too vigorously, it can perhaps give a measure of life to men three centuries dead.

There could be no doubt as to the gentility of these men. Every one possessed a coat of arms, either given or confirmed by the College of Arms on visitation of a herald. With these arms, they decorated their houses, sealed their letters and graced the parish church; when they died they were laid to rest under them.

Pride in arms was no indication of the antiquity of the gentle family. Some of the families were of long tenure in the county. Stawells had lived at Cothelstone, Frauncises at Combe Flory, Rodneys at Rodney Stoke, Gorges at Wraxall, Spekes at Whitelackington, and Luttrells in Dunster Castle and had served as justices, sheriffs, knights of the shire,

[1] Wallace Notestein, *The English People on the Eve of Colonization, 1603–1630* (1954), p. 60.

18

and commissioners long before the seventeenth century. However, the majority of the families who furnished the local governors of Charles' era would have found it difficult to find a wealthy and well-established ancestor in the county before 1539. For most of the families the sure establishment of their gentility rested on the lands of the monasteries, purchased by men who had come to the county via the Court, Westminster Hall, or counting house.

Indeed, no family of magisterial rank in Charles' reign appears to have established itself during the preceding century solely by careful husbandry and estate management.[2] A large influx of outside wealth had been required for a minor gentle family before the Dissolution, to purchase the monastic lands that raised it and sustained it in such status that seventy-five years later it was yet able to produce a local governor. The Baber family, which furnished three justices in this period, is a case in point. As late as 1559 the family was of "inconsiderable importance." But Serjeant Baber acquired former monastic lands at Chew Magna from the sequestered estates of the Duke of Somerset. Serjeant Baber's grandfather had died in 1527—a husbandman.[3] This is an exceptional success story. More modest ascent (though from a more advantageous starting point) attended the Berkeleys. Sir Maurice Berkeley, who died in 1581, was a gentleman of the privy chamber and a "staunch adherent" of Thomas Cromwell. He received the lands of Bruton Priory as well as some of Glastonbury's estates.[4] To his heirs he left the two manors of Bruton and Yarlington, seats of two of the greatest magnates of our period. Monastic lands also made the Hoptons. Sir Ralph Hopton of Witham, who died in 1572, was probably in Cromwell's service. He was marshal of the Household to both Henry VIII and Edward VI. Witham Friary was granted to him in 1544 as well as lands of Glastonbury, and his famous namesake of the seventeenth century resided at Witham. The Malletts' fortunes in part rested on the wealth of Baldwin Mallett, Solicitor-General to Henry VIII.[5] Sir Edward Rogers, esquire of the body to Henry VIII, a chief gentleman of the privy chamber to Edward VI, a prisoner under Mary, and finally a privy councillor to Elizabeth,

[2] This tends to confirm the same point made by Prof. H. R. Trevor-Roper in *The Gentry, 1540–1640* (1953), p. 13.

[3] F. A. Wood, *Collections for a Parochial History of Chew Magna* (1903), p. 140.

[4] S. W. Bates-Harbin, *Members of Parliament for the County of Somerset, 1258–1832* (1939), pp. 118–119.

[5] John Collinson, *The History and Antiquities of the County of Somerset* (1791), I, 92–93.

secured the Cannington Priory lands that sustained two justices in this period. Of the estates of the ninety-three Royalist baronets, which were considered by the Parliamentary Committee for Compounding in the 1640s, that of Sir William Portman, fifth baronet, was the greatest. The wealth of the Portmans of Orchard Portman derived from a Marian Lord Chief Justice, and the dynasty had weathered the death of three heirs in the space of nine years.[6] Service to the Tudors was the way to fortune for the Spekes of Whitelackington, and for the Wyndhams of Orchard Wyndham, too. Of more recent wealth was Sir Thomas Wrothe, whose father was a very successful Kent lawyer; the father's fortune enabled his son to buy Petherton Park from an insolvent cousin in 1614 and in so doing to establish himself as one of the richer gentlemen in the county.[7] Sir James Ley of Beckington rose faster and further than many of his fellows. A gentleman of modest background, he died as first Earl of Marlborough. Custos rotulorum of Somerset in both James' and Charles' reigns, his climb had been the steady trek from a Welsh judgeship through the chief justiceship of Ireland, attorney of the court of Wards, Lord Chief Justice of England, and Lord Treasurer (1624–1628). He was fabulously wealthy. Yet even Ley's wealth could not match that of the two scions of the county's two premier families. That chief justice of "unwearied diligence,"[8] Sir John Popham, amassed one of the greatest fortunes in an age of great fortunes, and his son, a county magistrate in Charles' reign, intended that it should not be diminished. Like Popham, Sir Edward Phelips, Attorney-General, Speaker of the Commons, and Master of the Rolls, found the law remunerative. He built one of the kingdom's greatest houses in an age of great houses, a rival to the châteaux of the Loire. Sir Robert Phelips, his son and heir who will figure prominently in this study, left his son a somewhat diminished estate, though Montacute remained the social center of the county for over two hundred years.

Emphasis on wealth made in service of the Crown and in the practice of the law should not obscure the number of magisterial families that descended from prosperous merchants. John Symes, a long-lived and

---

[6] See E. L. Klotz and G. Davies, "The Wealth of Royalist Peers and Baronets during the Puritan Revolution," *EHR* (1943), LVIII, 219; *Burke's Peerage, Baronetage and Knightage* (1949), p. 1618; *SANHS Proc* (1943), LXXXIX, 50. Henry, 2nd Bart., *o. s. p.* 1623; John, 3rd Bart., *o. s. p.* 1624; Hugh, 4th Bart., *o. s. p.* 1632; William, the fourth of the brothers, succeeded Hugh. The family was hard hit twice for wardship for John and Hugh.

[7] Collinson, III, 69; *DNB*, XXI, 1080–1081.

[8] Camden, I, 73.

hard-working magistrate (of somewhat radical politics), was the son of
a Chard merchant who had acquired Poundisford Lodge through wise
marriage, and had secured a comfortable fortune by hard work. Any
question as to John's gentility was dispelled by the fact that he married
a Horner of Mells—a soundly county family that had picked up extensive
lands when Glastonbury fell.[9] The indefatigable justice seated at Nailsea
Court, Richard Cole, was the son of a Bristol merchant who had married
a co-heiress. Richard himself married a Hopton, thereby taking a good
step upwards. Most of the Somerset families that came from merchant
forbears were descended from Bristol rather than London men. In every
case the pattern of rise closely resembled that of Symes and Cole. First
came the money, then the house and land, and finally a suitable marriage.
With good reason, gentlemen were careful in the choice of their
daughters-in-law and in the disposition of their own daughters. Orchard
Wyndham came to John Wyndham, a Norfolk courtier of Henry VIII,
through marriage with an heiress of the Sydenhams. The most notable
example of statesmanlike marriage alliances is afforded by those arranged
by Chief Justice Popham. He married his four daughters into four of the
most prominent county families—the Malletts, Rogers, Horners, and
Warres of Hestercombe. His heir, Sir Francis, married a Luttrell.

Wealth came through royal service, law, and trade; but one enterprise
yielded more advantages than another. With only a single exception,
none of the twenty-five families of magnate status sprang from and
ascended by a fortune made in trade. The magnate's station of preeminence in county society, county politics, and county government was
founded upon lavish expenditure in the county and influence at Westminster. Trade might well supply the money to allow the former, but
it alone could never furnish the latter.

Royal service brought the magnate into the shadow of the throne and
provided him with tremendous prestige in the county. For this purpose
the law can rightly be termed royal service, because as well as the fortune
possible, the successful lawyer usually advanced to the position of a
royal servant—a King's serjeant, a master of Requests, an official in
Chancery or a law court, perhaps ultimately a judge. It was the path of
royal service that John Lord Poulett's father and grandfather had followed, that the Berkeleys, the Rogers, the Haringtons, and the

[9] *Abstracts of Somersetshire Wills* (1887), I, 53; *SANHS Proc* (1950), XCV, 10; S. W. Bates-
Harbin, p. 130. John Symes retained his townhouse at Chard.

Wyndhams had followed; the path of royal service and law that the
Pophams, Phelipses, Malletts, Portmans, Leys, and Coventryes had followed. It was the path upon which the Caroline magnates intended their
sons should tread. Sir Robert Phelips had held the reversion of the office of
the clerk of the Petty Bag. John Lord Poulett was warden-keeper of
Neroche Forest, and he pushed his sons at Court for office.[10] Sir Francis
Popham married his daughter to the son of a Secretary of State and labored
to have his heir sworn a gentleman of the King's privy chamber. Sir
Thomas Wyndham succeeded where Popham failed, his heir, Edmund,
was a gentleman of the privy chamber. Royal service was a source of wealth,
and Prof. Trevor-Roper in *The Gentry, 1540–1640*, has rightly given
proper emphasis to this. It was much more. Even when, as in the case
of Poulett's keepership of Neroche, it became a financial encumbrance it
still provided the holder with ready ears in the Court and the Council
chamber.

Of necessity a magnate had his friends at Westminster. Poulett
carefully courted Edward Nicholas, secretary to Buckingham and later
clerk of the Council. He tardily provided Lord Conway with the much
sought after cheddar cheeses, when they were available! He thanked
Secretary Lord Dorchester for affording him esteem among his neighbors
and friends "by manifestinge the interest I have in you."[11] Sir Francis
Popham used his son-in-law's father, Lord Conway, to advance his son
and even to intervene in his favor in a suit in Arches.[12] Sir John Stawell
had the feodary's father secure a most searching appraisal—personal
and economic—of a Somerset gentleman's widow in whom Lord Dorchester was matrimonially interested![13] Sir Ralph Hopton had served in
Bohemia and the Low Countries, and was well known and well liked
at Court. John Harington of Kelston, son of that star of Elizabeth's
Court, Sir John Harington, was not a courtier to his father's measure,
but he was Lord Treasurer Marlborough's son-in-law. Even Sir Robert
Phelips, though suspect by the government, assiduously and successfully

[10] Poulett was keeper of Neroche from about 1619 until 1636, jointly with his son and heir
apparent, John, from 1625. His two sons were to attend the Earl of Danby on his embassy
to France, PRO, S.P.16/141, no. 62, Poulett to Sec. Dorchester, 28 April 1629.

[11] PRO, S.P.16/153, no. 54, Poulett to Sec. Dorchester, 14 Dec. 1629.

[12] PRO, S.P.16/158, no. 30, Thomas Grove to Endymion Porter, 9 Jan. 1629/30;
S.P.16/267, no. 83, Lord Cottington to Sir John Lambe, 13 May 1634.

[13] PRO, S.P.16/158, no. 31, Sir John Stawell to Sec. Dorchester, 10 Jan. 1629/30. The
lady was the widow of Sir Francis Hele; Poulett first called Dorchester's attention to her
in October 1629. Dorchester, however, married Viscountess Bayning in June 1630.

cultivated Edward Nicholas.[14] He was his father's son, and despite his apparent radicalism Phelips' voice could not be ignored by those in Whitehall. Through royal service the fathers of these magnates—and some of the magnates themselves—had attained wealth in the county and influence at the seat of government. Even though their sons, the present magnates, appeared less involved in the duties of Crown office, they carefully tended their contacts. Influence at Westminster was one of the two pillars upon which rested their status as magnates in the county.

The other pillar was placed firmly in Somerset. It was power in the county. These magnates dominated rural society. They directed and controlled through the instrument of county government all aspects of the county's life. Their power was based directly on the King's commission, though ultimately upon their own wealth and the respect that all classes accorded them. As landed wealth was the basis of their gentility so it was the foundation of the deference which society yielded them. If a magnate lost large portions of his estate, quite aside from the consequent loss of reputation, he would be forced to retrench his finances and limit the lavish expenditure that marked him a great man. If he lost enough, he might well drop out of the magisterial class altogether, a fate that befell Edward Popham of Huntworth, a deputy lieutenant and justice who was outlawed for debt in 1626.[15] The wealth of the magnate had to be an ostentatious wealth in an ostentatious age. His great house had to dominate its neighbors; his parks had to contain the largest herd of deer; his retinue had to be the largest when he moved into the assize or sessions town. In his dress, the accoutrements of his person, even in the harness of his horse, the magnate perforce displayed a richness to dazzle with its splendor, regardless of the cost to him.[16] The architecturally overpowering and heraldically perfect tomb of the magnate's father was as much a help to the magnate in his search for recognition as it was often a monument to his (or the deceased's) bad taste. It proclaimed that the lord of the manor was a very great man indeed. That was his reputation among the lesser folk.

[14] Sir Robert made good use of his son, who resided in London: Sir Robert to Edward Phelips, early 1637, "Listen now and then at the Council Chamber after Ilchester, Hodges, and me." SRO, Phelips MSS, vol. C, f. 42.

[15] He was again outlaw in 1640, PRO, P.C.2/51, p. 299. His father had left him a moderate estate in lands valued ("clear yearly value") by the feodary at £56, PRO, Wards 5/36, feodary's certificate, 1602. Five other justices were at one time or another outlaw.

[16] Sir Henry Portman, Bart., owed £347 9s to London tradesmen when he died, almost £110 of it to a silkman, PRO, Wards 10/24, note of Portman's debts, 12 May 1623.

Among those of his own station his reputation depended rather less on outward show and more on his hospitality and conviviality. The ideal were men like Lord Poulett, Sir John Stawell, and Sir Robert Phelips, whose mansions were always open, and who enjoyed, almost to the point of inanity, the sociable and hospitable pleasures of the hunt. Magnates who kept the miserable establishments for which the gossip Aubrey criticized Sir Francis Popham or were as notoriously antisocial as Sir Hugh Smyth of Long Ashton courted unpopularity among their fellows.[17] While such unpopularity would not immediately affect their status as magnates, over a period of years it corroded the good opinion of their fellows from which they derived much of their influence. Gerard's description of Sir John Wyndham, that "he hath made . . . [Orchard Wyndham] ye cheife place of his abode, in which hee strives rather to please his affection then to suite himself according to his rank,"[18] is revealing. Sir John, though an active justice of good lineage, did not wield the influence either in Court or country that might have been expected of one of his station.

The magnate's power, then, was based in both Court and country. At Court his influence secured for him and his children office, a ready ear, and a reputation in the country that he was a man who counted. In the country his influence secured him a seat in Parliament, afforded him a place of leadership in all county affairs, and gave him a reputation at Westminster as a power in the county that could not be ignored. Newly risen men with no firm roots in the county, like Sir Edward Powell, Bart., a master of Requests, Robert Henley, chief clerk of enrollments in the King's Bench, and Sir John Gyll, an esquire to the Queen, might have been well placed to exert influence at Westminster, but they did not have the good opinion of their countrymen and the power at home that entitled them to the rank of magnates.

To a lesser extent, the same was true of the magnates who had not kept up their contacts at Court. The Luttrells had largely cut themselves off from Court; they had produced no royal servants in Tudor times, received no sudden influx of outside wealth, neither had they opened new channels of influence. They can just barely be termed magnates, for the power they wielded in the county was the power of a great name though little influence at Court. The Horners and the Spekes were in

---

[17] Sir John Popham "left a vast estate to his son, Sir Francis . . . he lived like a hog," John Aubrey, *Brief Lives* (1950), p. 246. Sir Hugh Smyth's wife wrote a relative that her husband was desirous of total privacy, R. Gorges, *The Story of a Family* (1944), p. 114.

[18] Gerard, p. 27.

similar circumstances. Through choice, circumstances, or carelessness, these families had grown away from Court. Yet all these men retained their status as magnates because they retained a large measure of influence in the county; given inclination and an opportunity they could reassert their power and regain abundant influence in Court as well. Strangely enough, the opportunity presented itself in the form of civil war. In that conflict, though Sir Thomas Horner and George Speke were on opposite sides, there was no questioning their power both in the county and in their respective "courts."

Wills, inquisitions post mortem, feodaries' surveys, conveyances, and returns of the commissioners for subsidies, privy seal loans (1625–1626), and distraint of knighthood (1631) afford sufficient evidence to allow some tentative comparisons of wealth to be made among the local governors. Such comparisons can only approximate reality, for the evidence is in places incomplete, in others contradictory. The sheer quantity of the evidence and the myriad pitfalls it contains have precluded systematic use of it for this study. Somerset's gentlemen, in common with their brethren elsewhere, await a searching investigation of their economic positions.

The magnates were preeminent in wealth as in everything else. Sir William Portman, Bart., John Lord Poulett, Sir Francis Popham, the Earl of Marlborough, and Sir Robert Phelips were the richest men in Somerset. Recent fortunes made through royal service or the law accounted for their prosperity. At the same time, others of magnate status, though not reinforced by such recent fortunes, were rich. The Luttrells, while largely isolated from the great sources of wealth for the preceding hundred years, were major land owners, and the commercial activity of Dunster and Minehead brought them a steady and considerable income. Sir Edward Rodney of Rodney Stoke appeared prosperous, his vice-admiralty of Somerset and Bristol supplementing his estates' income. The feodary's estimates of the annual values of the magnates' real estates placed them in excess of £100, while the estates of the non-magnate magisterial gentry were more usually clustered around the £50 mark. A wide gap in terms of real wealth in the county separated John May and his small estate on Mendip valued at £41 *per annum* from Edward Rogers with his extensive holdings in central Somerset valued at £140 and George Luttrell with his widespread holdings in the northwest of the county valued at £302.[19] For some of the magnates, there is too little evidence to draw any conclusions. However, they presented highly prosperous countenances and yet avoided bankruptcy.

Perhaps the evident wealth of Sir John Wyndham can be ascribed to his striving to "please his affection then to suite himself according to his ranke," for, though wealth was greatest among the magnates, so too was indebtedness and bankruptcy. Mention has been made of Edward Popham's outlawry. The same fate befell Sir Nicholas Halswell, John Mallett, and Sir Robert Gorges, all magnates. Sir Baldwin Wake of Clevedon, Bart., died deeply indebted, his son requiring letters of protection and his wife selling her jointure to satisfy his creditors. Sir Thomas Phillips of Barrington Court, Bart., sold his lands with his superbly beautiful mansion to the upstart William Strode, and still went to the grave in debt.[20] Even Sir Robert Phelips, though he succeeded to one of the largest inheritances in the county, was constantly concerned with creditors. Before death, he made over in trust to his heir a manor and appurtenances to discharge his obligations.[21] Phelips must have incurred tremendous expense in his political activities. He lived sumptuously even by the standards of the day. His letters in the 1630s to Edward, his son and heir apparent, reflect a shaky financial state. On receiving news of the birth of his grandson, he wrote Edward, "I pray lett my example make you carefull and be not as I have been, expensive to the prejudice of your famelye."[22] Edward succeeded to a great house and a fair estate, but the dowry of his wife, auditor of the Exchequer Sir Robert Pye's daughter, was a considerable help in recouping the family fortunes. Edward's two sisters, who went without marriage portions, paid the price for Sir Robert's indebtedness. The most extravagant magnate of all was probably Lord Poulett. It is ironic

---

[19] PRO, Wards 5/36–37, feodaries' surveys and certificates, which must be used with caution. The figures cited are from three surveys by the same feodary, 1628–1630. I include lordships, franchises, advowsons, rectories, etc., as well as lands and tenements, in the term "real estate."

[20] Gerard, p. 122. His will specified that his interest in 1200 acres of Neroche forest should be sold to pay his debts, *Abstracts of Somersetshire Wills,* I, 77. His patrimony had not been very large in the first place.

[21] *Somerset Enrolled Deeds, 1536–1655* (1936), p. 272. As early as 1617, Phelips had sold a large manor and appurtenances, part of his inheritance, for £4000. In 1631, he made over to his heir Edward and Anne Pye in jointure the better parts of his estate including Montacute House, retaining right of use for his and his wife's lives, PRO, C.142/571/157. Sir Robert's real estate at death was valued at only £99 *p.a.,* including Montacute, PRO, Wards 5/36, feodary's survey, 1640.

[22] SRO, Phelips MSS, vol. C, f. 54, Sir Robert to Edward Phelips [c. 23 Nov.] 1636.

and peculiarly fitting that he should complain in a letter to Lord Dorchester that people lived at such a height that the loss of a coach horse was able to break a man.[23] Poulett found the politician's and the courtier's expenses heavy indeed.

For the local governor who had an outside income assured by his own toil, economic difficulties were seldom encountered. The first Earl of Marlborough was, however, the only magnate actively engaged in a profession. Sir Thomas Wrothe (who cannot be considered a magnate) kept up a lucrative practice at the bar. He was wealthy enough to take an active part in politics. Others of less than magnate status who followed the law did well. Hugh Pyne was prosperous, and though anathema at Whitehall, his income does not appear to have suffered. Robert Henley of Leigh held the highly remunerative office of chief clerk of enrollments in the King's Bench. He did rather well; a series of commissions were issued to investigate alleged extortions by him and his associate in the office.[24] Both Sir Edward Powell, Bart., a master of Requests, and Serjeant Thomas Mallett were wealthy, the latter gathering much fruit from the inexhaustible tree of Stuart patronage, capped by a judgeship in 1641. Sir John Gyll, an esquire to the Queen, did not wax rich on his £100 *per annum* stipend,[25] but he appears to have prospered by taking advantage of the opportunities household office opened up.

Those who were merely country gentlemen and who attempted to supplement the income of their lands by investment outside the county found many opportunities in that speculative era. But the risks were great; allusion has already been made to Sir Thomas Wyndham's losses in the Earl of Dorset's schemes. Despite the risks, such investment was attractive to men tied to their land and its diminishing real value. If however, the country gentleman readily accepted the limitations of his economic position and suited his mode of living accordingly, he could live comfortably and according to his status. This was not difficult for the

[23] PRO, S.P.16/150, no. 39, 7 Oct. 1629.

[24] PRO, Index 4212, commission tested 26 Oct. 1637 to discover unlawful exactions by Robert Henley and Samuel Wightwicke; and see Index 4212, pp. 288, 318, 356 for renewal commissions of the same nature. The office had brought Sir John Roper £3500 *p.a.*, Trevor-Roper, p. 11. Henley was also under attack for extortion in his former office of one of the six clerks in Chancery, PRO, E.165/51 f. D4v. In 1646, Henley compounded for his support of the Royalist cause by a fine of £9000, PRO, Index 4213, p. 48. Dr. G. E. Aylmer's forthcoming book, *The King's Servants: The Civil Service of Charles I, 1625–1642*, will contain detailed information as to Henley's activities in office.

[25] PRO E.403/3041, pp. 299–300.

justices of mere magisterial rank. It proved well-nigh impossible for most of the magnates.

The land imposed social as well as economic limitations. It ensured that county society would be very much county society. The difficulties of travel conditioned the gentlemen to living at home and to taking an active part in affairs that could be conveniently seen to in seldom more than a day's ride. The almost annual proclamations directed to local governors in London to repair to their country seats were applicable to only three or four of Somerset's magnates who, for reasons of pressing business or the necessity of attending Court, occasionally went to Town. With the exception of the lords lieutenants, the Earls of Marlborough, Sir Edward Powell, Bart., Serjeant Mallett, Robert Henley, and perhaps Sir Thomas Wrothe, none of Somerset's local governors kept a London house. Poulett, newly-created baron, ill with an attack of gout, returned home by his coach because he could not "abide the incommodities" of his "hired lodging" in London.[26] Later, he often stayed with Lord Dorchester. Sir Robert Phelips appears to have made the house of Sir Robert Pye (his son's father-in-law) his London quarters. Poulett and Phelips were the two greatest magnates. Nevertheless, save during parliament and Poulett's brief tour with the fleet, neither man spent more than about one month in twelve away from his seat. The proportion was even less for lesser gentlemen. The limitation imposed by land and the necessity of its constant oversight, the difficulties of travel, and the fact that county society provided its own diversions guaranteed the continued existence of county government by the magisterial class. Despite the need the King and Council felt for proclamations against and even a Star Chamber prosecution[27] for absenteeism in London, England was never in danger of the fate that befell French local government in the seventeenth century.

---

[26] PRO, S.P.16/72, no. 35, Poulett to Sec. Conway [July 1627].

[27] William Palmer, Esq., of Fairfield, Somerset (not a justice) paid a fine of £200 imposed in Star Chamber in Mich. 1632 for residing in Sussex instead of in Somerset, Lincoln's Inn, MS "Starrchamber" in press C.4, f. 17. In the returns by local officials in November 1632 of the names of gentlemen resident in London and its environs *contra* the proclamation of 20 June 1632 for gentlemen to return to their country seats, no Somerset local governors were given as resident in the City of London, and only Sir John Stawell in Chancery Lane ("gone" was noted against his name in a different hand), Robert Henley and family in the liberties of Westminster, and possibly John Symes and family in St. Martin's-in-the-Fields were returned as resident in the environs, Bodl, Bankes MSS, bundle 62, nos. 32 and 34. Taken as a whole, the returns indicate that only a small proportion of the nation's landed aristocracy had town houses—a great many resided in lodgings of one sort or another.

The limitations of county life had a marked effect on that paramount social institution, marriage. A large pedigree shows thirty-five local governors in this period linked by marriage alliances contracted sometime within the present and preceding two or three generations. The effect of this intermarriage on local government cannot be overstressed. The resulting social cohesiveness, the deep, impelling feeling of being related by some tie greater than mere common interest to almost all the other men of importance in the county, was a powerful force working for cooperation. An intruder, regardless of the unsuitability of his lineage, might find acceptance in the society of the bench provided he was married into it. Otherwise, he was an outsider and even the King's commission (if it were granted him) could not make him anything else. Robert Henley of Leigh and James Rosse of Shepton Beauchamp, JPs, are proof enough of this. They were not "county," and even some vulgar drunkards in a Wells inn where the justices stayed knew it and reminded them of it once.[28]

Despite its limitations, country life provided ample diversion. Assizes and quarter sessions were important social events and the social side of these meetings undoubtedly provided attractions. Entertainment in the great houses, especially at the festive seasons, alleviated the boredom of confinement. The hunt, restricted to an all-too-short season, was the foremost diversion. If the conversation there had ever been recorded, discussion of business, both private and public, might appear to have eclipsed all other talk. The magnitude of his party both in dogs and servants was an integral part of the great man's reputation. The hunt had a hold on the sensibilities of these men that is barely comprehensible to us today. When in the early 1630s Lord Poulett was restricted in the exercise of his keepership of Neroche by royal fiat, he felt even more keenly than the King's displeasure the loss of his deer-hunting privileges in the forest. His letters were full of preparations for the hunt.[29] Sir John Mallett, a justice in James' reign, sent his apologies for being unable to attend quarter sessions due to private business—which proved to be arrangements for a hunt.[30] Even Sir Robert Phelips of serious mien and great

[28] SRO, QSOB, 1627/8–1638, Epiph. QS 1633/4, memo after no. 23, Thomas Meryfeild said that "he did not care for Henley neither for Rosse." Sessions left it to Henley to inform the Attorney-General of the matter, SRO, Sess Rolls, 71 pt. ii, no. 38, Epiph. QS 1633/4.

[29] PRO, S.P.16/530, no. 58, Poulett to Sec. Dorchester, 20 May 1629; SRO, Sanford MSS box 51, John Poulett to Richard Wykes [c. 1614].

[30] SRO, Sanford MSS, box 51, no. 114, Sir John Mallett to Richard Wykes, 13 Sept. [1614?].

application was passionately fond of hunting. The countryman's translation of the Phelips motto, *Pro aris et focis*, yet current around Montacute, was apt: "For hares and foxes."

Litigation provided a welcome excuse for breaking out of the confines of county life, since an action usually required both the plaintiff and the defendant to journey to London. The interminability of pleading allowed ample time for gossip. This form of social outlet was not restricted to magnates. For many of the local governors of minor status, the occasional trips to Westminster as a party to a suit appear to have been the few instances when they left the county. At one time or another most of them were involved in litigation. To mention the social advantages of legal actions is by no means to obscure the earnestness with which they were fought. Men like Sir Edward Powell (as a master of Requests he resided in London anyway) pursued legal actions for what they could get out of them. Powell and Sir Francis Popham were two outstanding litigants. Popham, always acquisitive, always ready to go to law, moved suits in a most vexatious manner. Nonetheless, for more temperate gentlemen litigation provided a welcome and often the sole means of obtaining an intimate and lengthy contact with the outside world.

Yet, thirty-two of the local governors had at one time or another a contact with the outside world that had more effect on local government and the county's politics than any other contact possible. Thirty-two had sat as members of Parliament up to and including the Short Parliament. Twenty-two of them had served more than once; seven had sat in five or more Parliaments.[31] One, Sir Robert Phelips, was a parliamentarian of the first rank. Naturally, the county seats went to magnates, and such was the competition for seats that men of magnate status scrambled for the seats of the county's seven enfranchised boroughs and even sought borough seats elsewhere. However, one-third of the thirty-two magistrate-members were not of magnate status.

The political effects of the large number of the local governors who had parliamentary experience will be treated in later chapters. We are interested here in the effect on local government which was just as considerable if not so important. For men active in local government and largely isolated from others who fulfilled the same function in other

---

[31] Sir Charles Berkeley, Edward Kyrton, Sir Henry Ley (afterwards second Earl of Marlborough), Sir Robert Phelips, Sir Francis Popham, Sir Edward Rodney, and Sir Thomas Thynne sat in more than five Parliaments from 1597.

counties, attendance at a Parliament allowed the exchange of ideas as well as gossip. The diffusion of universally useful information to persons engaged in local government now provided by the Home Office and other ministries had no counterpart in the seventeenth century, and Council letters, despite their concern for minuteness, could not serve the same purpose. This accounts for some amazing variations throughout the realm in quarter-sessions procedure and even in the application of law.[32] The discussion that took place around a Parliament enabled men to return to the county with a knowledge of local governmental affairs in other areas. Though the influence is hard to detect, the increasing uniformity in administration by the local governors throughout the kingdom, which is a feature of the early seventeenth century, might have owed as much to the table-talk occurring during parliamentary sessions as to pressure from the Council expressed in letters and through the judges at assizes.

The most prolonged contact with the outside world that the majority of the local governors had enjoyed was the year or two most of them had spent at a university, an Inn of Court, or both. The Elizabethan age witnessed tremendous advances in the broadening of education of the gentry both at school and at the university and Inn of Court. Unfortunately, little evidence exists to determine the extent to which the local governors were subjected in their younger days to a formal schooling. Fortunately, the figures for the numbers who left the county for a brief exposure to higher education are readily available. At least eighty of the one hundred and eight resident local governors attended either a university or an Inn of Court. Of these, thirty-six attended both; twenty-six attended only a university, and eighteen attended an Inn. Of the sixty-two who matriculated at a university, twenty took a degree—of which, ten were clergymen, leaving only ten laymen who pursued study to its conclusion. Likewise, of the total of fifty-four who attended an Inn of Court, only fifteen were called to the bar.

Since the average age of matriculation was sixteen and most of the future local governors limited their sojourn at Oxford or Cambridge to a year or two, the academic benefit of their brief exposure to higher education must have been minute. Like George Luttrell, who had a room in the master's lodging at Caius during his sixteenth year, the young gentleman might receive some salutary training in good manners

[32] For example, in Lancashire the father of a bastard was usually whipped (as well as the mother), though in Somerset, seldom, *Lancashire Quarter Sessions Records, 1590–1606* (1917).

but very little understanding of philosophy. The same was true of those who spent a year at an Inn of Court. Contemporary accounts, with a kernel of truth lurking in an abundance of exaggeration, speak of the rowdy life spent by the young gentleman at those honorable societies. Still, any knowledge of the law they might have received there would later serve them in good stead. Oxford may claim credit for having awakened in Thomas Lyte the interest in antiquities that caused him to value above all else his library. John Harington of Kelston, requesting aid from his friend Selden in learning Arabic at the age of sixty-three, had doubtless received something from his few years at Trinity, Oxford.[33]

The significance of these high figures of attendance at the universities and the Inns of Court of men who were later called upon to govern the county is not that they indicate any particular academic benefit accruing to the future local governors. Rather, these men had undergone a broadening experience largely denied their predecessors in office and most of their contemporaries not in office. This afforded them a distinct advantage in that it enabled them to undertake more successfully those duties of county government which most of them entered upon at a very early age and pursued without cease until they died. Moreover, it exposed them to the radical ideas of the age which, while they might be outgrown, still left their mark on the future local governors' thinking.

Eight of the men who served the King in the county in this period are of supreme interest. They can be selected from the rest for closer examination because sufficient material exists to gain a clear impression of their personalities. They impressed their character upon many aspects of local government, every action of the local governors. As they furnished the leadership in county government, so too they led in the political life of the county. Out of a personal dispute between two of them grew two factions which in the 1630s divided the county and its governors. Another one of them was called upon to heal the cleavage. Two were above the fray and to their selfless diligence was due in large part the preservation of order and the effectual continuance of county government.

Philip Herbert, fourth Earl of Pembroke and Earl of Montgomery,

[33] BM, Eger. MS 2711, f. 94, John Harington "To the incomparable his highly honoured friend John Selden Esqr.," 11 Oct. 1652 (draft). It was noted of a Jacobean justice, Sir Francis Hastings, that his "studdie of bookes and other implements thereof . . . was praised att tenn poundes because he was a scholler," PRO, St.Ch.8/1/40, answer sworn to 17 April 1611.

was lord lieutenant from 1630 to 1640.[34] Nineteen at James' accession, Herbert was that King's first favorite and rose from glory unto glory until Carr eclipsed him. In 1630 he succeeded to his elder brother's earldom of Pembroke, and took his place as lord lieutenant of Somerset. Like his brother, he exerted considerable influence in parliamentary elections. He was a bitter enemy of that grandee, the Duke of Buckingham, and his hatred for Strafford expressed itself in the vote he gave for the bill of attainder in 1641. Soon afterwards the Lord Chamberlain's staff was taken from him, and he joined irrevocably with the Parliamentary party. His biographer has stressed his vile temper, but perhaps Clarendon gives a better clue to his personality in stressing Herbert's self-effacement at the time of Carr's ascendency.[35] Though quick of temper, and at odds with many of his peers, he had the capacity to play smoothly the arbiter among his subordinates. Pembroke the arbiter never ceased to be Pembroke the superior. His handling of the last great dispute between Sir Robert Phelips and Lord Poulett is indicative of a man who would work quietly and patiently to restore order, but would crush with impunity a subordinate who disobeyed him. No matter how great a disservice he later did Charles, while he held that sovereign's commission in Somerset he served him well.

John Coventrye of Barton Grange, second son of the Lord Keeper, was custos rotulorum from 1636 to 1641.[36] Obviously intruded into this office by his father, Coventrye had lived in the county only since his marriage to Elizabeth Colles a few years before. That he was at all tolerated by his colleagues of the bench was due solely to his father's position and the fact that he had married properly. Possessed of the politician's mentality and ambitions, he found little outlet for them in Somerset of the 1630s. Leadership in the political arena had long before been firmly centered on Sir Robert Phelips and Lord Poulett. Coventrye's character, vacillating and often petty, was not such as to recommend him to likely followers, and he had to rest content with the role of Phelips' ally. Nevertheless, he possessed abundant influence at Court which was both his strength and, because of the suspicion and jealousy it doubtless

[34] Principal sources for this sketch: *DNB*, IX, 659–663; GEC, X, 415–418; V. A. Rowe, "The Influence of the Earls of Pembroke on Parliamentary Elections, 1625–1641," *EHR* (1935), L, 242–256; SRO, Phelips MSS, vol. A, *passim*.
[35] *DNB*, IX, 659; Earl of Clarendon, *The History of the Rebellion* (1712), I, 59.
[36] Principal sources: Collinson, III, 285; SRO, Phelips MSS, vol. B, *passim*; SRO, QS OB, 1627/8–1638; SRO, Sess Rolls; Clarendon, vol. I.

raised among his fellows, his weakness. Like many men of more inferior status, the Civil War afforded John Coventrye his first opportunity to exert independent political power in the county. As a Royalist, he did— and managed to disrupt the whole Royalist camp.

Hugh Pyne of Curry Mallet served as deputy custos rotulorum (chairman of quarter sessions) until removed in 1626 from the commission of the peace for his patent animosity towards the King and Buckingham.[37] Pyne is of more interest as a type than as an individual. Socially, he was the "judicious lawyer" who did well enough to buy a modest manor that had once belonged to a peer, but not well enough to consider exchanging Lincoln's Inn for Serjeants' Inn. Politically, he was the not-so-judicious lawyer of the genus that William Prynne would make notorious. Pyne carried with him from Parliament into the county a vociferous and irresponsible espousal of the "country's rights," and a consuming hatred for Buckingham. When in 1626 he used his chair at Ilchester quarter sessions to pervert the solemn charge to the grand jury into a scathing attack on royal policy and later uttered words touching the King's own person, Pyne's loose talk brought him within the shadow of the gallows. Only a strict interpretation by the judges of the Statute of Treason prevented him from being tried and surely hanged.[38] Yet Pyne said nothing at the quarter sessions at Ilchester in 1626 that was not said by others in Parliament in 1640. It was the intervening fourteen years and the changed place that made all the difference. Of insufficient status in the county to lead, he was not even suffered to follow. Sir Robert Phelips carefully avoided the loose-tongued lawyer whom Poulett uncharitably but truthfully likened to a "madde dogge." Ironically, Pyne's daughter, a female counterpart of her father,[39] became the beloved nurse of Charles, Prince of Wales.

By far the most attractive personality of all the county's gentlemen was Pyne's successor as deputy custos. John Harington of Kelston, son of the famed Elizabethan courtier of the same name, eschewed the Court and lived the quiet life of a country gentleman.[40] Possessed of a profound intellect and catholic interests, Harington was of the same stuff as

[37] Principal sources: Taunton Castle, Brown MSS, vol. 7; S.P.16; Gerard, pp. 62–63.
[38] George Croke, *Reports* (Charles I), pt. 3 (1683), p. 117.
[39] "Nihil muliebre praeter corpus gerens," Clarendon, II, 641.
[40] Principal sources: BM, Eger. MS 2711; F. J. Poynton, *Memoranda Relating to the Parish of Kelston*, pt. 3 (1885), pp. 32–34; Anthony Wood, *The Life and Times of Anthony Wood* (1892), II, 352–353; SRO, Sess Rolls, 1626–1638. Ian Grimble's excellent recent study, *The Harington Family* (n.d.), somewhat slights John in favor of his more eminent kin.

Selden, Cotton, and Wotton. Algebra, geometry, Arabic, Welsh, medicine, the law, and theology comprised his existence. Harington was the political neutral in an age which knew no neutrality; the man of tender conscience in an age which understood neither tenderness nor conscience. A puritan, he was not a Parliamentarian. A magnate, he was not a politician. His fellows of the bench respected him because his intellect, his honesty, and his selflessness raised him above them and their bickering. In his charges to quarter sessions, Harington exhorted his fellow justices to look for God, follow His word, and serve Him, and though they did not fully comprehend, they listened. When the disputes of the two factions led by Poulett and Phelips divided most of the local governors, Harington kept peace and carried on the routine administration of magistracy. Until the Civil War he served with total fidelity a King and his ministers with whom he could not agree and whom he did not trust. When war came, he reluctantly took up arms against that King. When war was over, he labored to the end of his life in 1654 to rebuild the damage that war had wrought. Neither God, the King, nor his countrymen could find fault in John Harington.

In Sir Ralph Hopton, Knight of the Bath, of Evercreech Park, the county's lieutenancy found its counterpart to Harington.[41] A professional soldier, Hopton exemplified chivalry—a quality all too rare in so many of his contemporaries. Veteran of both the Palatinate and the Low Countries, he foresaw with an expert's eye the failure of the Cadiz expedition. Declining to serve therein, he chose rather to retire to his seat, where he took up the duties of the country justice and deputy lieutenant. For Hopton, politics held no attractions and though he sat in Parliament both before and after the "personal rule," it was with the same obvious reluctance with which he had retired to Witham. Once retired he turned all his energies and his tremendous ability into Somerset's lieutenancy. When lieutenancy became the arena of struggle for political supremacy in the county, he refused to either faction his adherence and the influence it would have provided. While his colleagues fought and lied, Hopton quietly carried on the training of the militia for the civil struggle which he must have foreseen. Though he advocated Strafford's attainder in Parliament, when the issue became clearly one

<hr/>

[41] Principal sources: *DNB*, IX, 1241–1243; GEC, VI, 576–577; Ralph Hopton, *Hopton's Narrative of the Civil War, 1642–1644* (1902); C. R. Hoare, *Monastic Remains of the Religious Houses at Witham, etc.* (1824); Taunton Castle, Brown MSS, vol. 9, pp. 118 ff.; PRO, S.P.16; D. Lloyd, *State Worthies* (1670), pp. 1008–1014; Clarendon, vols. I and II.

of rebellion against lawful authority, he was the King's foremost champion in the west. In war as in peace he was above politics and his honesty in opposing the treaty of Breda cost him the new King's favor. Respected, even loved, by his enemies, Hopton had served faithfully and with self-abnegation a cause and two kings to which he was morally and spiritually far superior.

Sir John Stawell, Knight of the Bath, of Cothelstone stood in marked contrast to Hopton.[42] Stawell's only personal distinction was a dilettante's passion for medicine, the rules of which he followed to the extent of never eating breakfast. This might account for the choleric unevenness of his temper and the impatient rashness and wrath he so often exhibited. Of mediocre attainments as a politician and as a soldier, Stawell played at being both. In the political struggle in the county he served Lord Poulett as a totally subservient lieutenant. The influence that Stawell possessed was the influence of the man he served. The cause he espoused was the cause Poulett espoused. He professed the "King's interest," but he could hardly have fathomed it. At least he was constant, and when the time came, courageous. The Civil War called forth from Stawell these qualities, and to his credit he showed them. His later career is pathetically inscribed on his monument in Cothelstone church:

> Post perditam rem familiarem aedium ruinam, carceres aliasque calamitates exoptatissimo regis Caroli Secundi reditu laetans Diem obiit....

Only in his suffering did Stawell approach the nobility of Sir Ralph Hopton.

Around two major antagonists revolved the politics of pre-Civil War Somerset. In temperament widely different, John Lord Poulett and Sir Robert Phelips were at variance in all matters, public and private. They indelibly impressed their personal hostility upon the fabric of the county's political life and in so doing altered the whole garment. Both were descended from Elizabethan officers of state, both were wealthy men, both were magnates. Here all similarity ended—save that each was consumed with overwhelming desire to exercise absolute supremacy within the county, and each was ready to use almost any means to attain that end.

[42] Principal sources: *DNB*, XVIII, 1007–1008; G. D. Stawell, *A Quantock Family* (1910); Gerard, p. 54; Taunton Castle, Brown MSS, vol. 19, p. 731, vol. 15, p. 555; Collinson, III, 249 ff.; Clarendon, vols. I and II; SRO, Phelips MSS, vol. A, *passim*; PRO, S.P.16.

John Poulett, Baron Poulett of Hinton St. George, secured his peerage in 1627.[43] It was a costly honor. For nearly a year Poulett had been the host at Hinton St. George of the Duc de Soubise, the exiled Huguenot leader. He had regularly reported to Secretary Conway the attitude and intentions of his restless guest. There was truth in Hugh Pyne's words that the King had "committed Monsieur de Soubize to Mr. Poulettes custodie, because hee knewe him to bee a good gaoler."[44] The bellicose *emigré* was a distinct diplomatic embarrassment to Charles and his rustication at Hinton removed the embarrassment from Court. This hectic year, however, gave Poulett his first important contact with Secretary Conway and brought him to the notice of Buckingham, whom henceforth he obsequiously cultivated. His reward was the barony and influence at Court such as he had never before possessed. In 1627, the new Lord Poulett had attained the position from which he would for the next decade do battle with his old rival for supremacy in the county.

That success so seldom attended Lord Poulett can be laid to the man's two inherent weaknesses in the face of Sir Robert Phelips' many strong qualities. Poulett was lazy, and he was not exceptionally intelligent. Not uncomely, his obsequiousness and courtly manners doubtless made a satisfactory first impression. However, he failed invariably to follow up his initial advantage with hard work. In his keepership of Neroche forest, in his activities in county government, in his many disputes with Phelips, Poulett never ran the course of his own volition, but required considerable pressure from others to finish. His letters to Dorchester and Conway promised much and delivered little; Conway waited a long time for his cheddar cheese. Procrastination while not fatal to the courtier, cost the politician pitted against an opponent capable of the greatest sustained effort, skirmish after skirmish. Perhaps aware of his inability to work steadily to an end, Poulett allowed himself to take rash action, to his own disadvantage. Poulett was not well; he suffered continually from gout which was the price paid for overindulgent living. Undoubtedly gout took its toll on his nervous system. It caused him in 1635 to relinquish the command of the King's ship, the *Constant*

---

[43] Principal sources: *DNB*, XVI, 229–230; GEC, X, 615–616; SRO, Phelips MSS, vol. A, *passim*, Sanford MSS, box 51; Poulett MSS; PRO, S.P.16, especially correspondence of Poulett with Buckingham, Dorchester, Conway, and Nicholas; Clarendon, vols. I and II. Poulett's father, Sir Anthony, Governor of Jersey, was the second son of Sir Amyas Poulett, Elizabethan privy councillor and gaoler of Mary Stuart.

[44] PRO, S.P.16/40, no. 58, affidavits against Hugh Pyne [Nov. ?] 1626.

Reformation, after having served with the fleet only three and one-half months. This retirement closed off one of Poulett's most valuable contacts with Court on the eve of his final and greatest battle with Sir Robert Phelips.

Nor was Poulett's intellect on a par with his opponent's. Poulett's mind worked in devious ways, and though he grasped detail, he could not construct in broad outline the telling argument that characterized Phelips' logic. At times he was clever enough, and his political maneuvering showed occasional finesse. Of average intelligence, had Poulett been capable of a fraction of his opponent's application, his more favorable initial position might well have given him final victory.

Sir Robert Phelips of Montacute possessed in like measure those qualities of mind that made his father one of the foremost politicians and lawyers of his age.[45] Phelips was capable of intense application and sustained activity. He was the indefatigable "little dark man" of tremendous energy. His nervous, slanted, near-illegible scrawl, covering reams of paper was characteristic of the lawyer who could use a pen like a sword and with like facility. He marshalled facts in impressive array, all neatly arranged to do the most damage to his opponent's argument. Eliot, who knew him so well in Parliament, said that his oratory was ready and spirited though somewhat marred by redundancy and exuberance. The same was true of his writings. Exuberance arose from his energy, redundancy from the conviction that he was right and his striving to convey that conviction to his audience. Phelips' greatest weapon was his seemingly prodigious memory. In reality, it was no memory but merely the careful recording of all he thought and said, all that others wrote which concerned him. When occasion demanded that he recall before the King and Council any events many years past, Phelips was always ready. In warfare carried on by word written and spoken, Phelips was at a distinct advantage. Not brilliant, yet very shrewd, he set himself a task, minutely mapped it out, and worked slavishly and without faltering until he had attained his end.

When the struggle between Poulett and Phelips began in earnest in 1627 the contestants were hardly on equal footing. Poulett with his newly won barony and the influence it had brought him at Westminster

[45] Principal sources: *DNB,* XV, 1030–1031; SRO, Phelips MSS; PRO, S.P.14 and 16; E. Farnham, "The Somerset Election of 1614," *EHR* (1931), XLVI, 579–599; *Commons Debates, 1621* (1935); *The Commons Debates for 1629* (1921); S. R. Gardiner, *History of England, 1603–1642* (1883), vols. IV and V.

had a distinct advantage over Phelips, at the same moment handicapped by his removal from the commission of the peace and from lieutenancy and his disgrace at Court. Ten years later, it was Phelips who had triumphed. Many battles had been fought and Phelips had won all. Regardless of the preponderance that court favor, title, and an attractive cause could give, victory did not go to the indolent man of desultory intellect battling in the realm of words with the man of energy and shrewdness.

These one hundred and eight men governed the county in this period by virtue of the King's commission. His Majesty's commission could have been given to few others in the shire. By reason of their background and the landed wealth it afforded them they alone possessed the social distinction which made them the natural rulers of their society. In a country yet provincial their horizons were broader than those of any they were called upon to govern. Some among them possessed both the influence at the seat of government and the power to control their lesser countrymen that raised them to preeminence in county government. It exalted them as well to dominance in the political arena which the county became during the eleven years of "personal rule."

Chapter III   *Magistracy*

Without an understanding of the routine functions of the justices, the lord and deputy lieutenants, and the sheriff to serve as a point of departure and a basis of comparison, the extraordinary labor required of them by Charles and his ministers will fail to make the impression on us that it made on the thinking of the local governors. For that reason, this and the following two chapters on lieutenancy and shrievalty are intended to provide the point of departure. Quite aside from the necessity of such a detailed investigation of county administration in its day-to-day workings to the study as a whole, the factual information provided might possess interest and usefulness to the reader. However, the emphasis in these three chapters will be on the weight of those offices upon the local governors: the nature of the duties involved, the effort expended in their fulfillment, and the relative efficiency or inefficiency of the administrative machines on the eve of the royal programs that must have made the old routine seem light and easy in comparison with the new.

Edward III could scarcely have foreseen the place that his conservators of the peace would occupy in Tudor-Stuart government. From the humble and circumscribed policemen of 1 Edward III, c. 16, they had become the principal executors of royal justice and administrators of royal policy in the counties. Justices of the peace were in a sense as much a creation of the Tudor monarchy as was the lord lieutenant. The Tudors inherited an institution little more powerful or useful than it had been under the last Plantagenets and with their peculiar genius transformed it into the foundation of royal power in the shires. They did this by multiplying the responsibilities of these local gentlemen, and so multiplied the burden of their work. It was no accident that Lambarde's "not loads, but stacks of statutes" bearing upon the justices, first appeared in the 1602 edition of

Eirenarcha—striking testimony to the effect of a century of Tudor rule on the institution of county magistracy.

This chapter is intended to portray that institution as it existed in 1630. In the next year, the full weight of Tudor legislation was placed by the hands of a Stuart monarch and his advisers upon the backs of the justices of the peace.

One hundred Somerset men chose to serve the King as justices of the peace in the sixteen years before the Long Parliament. They held office

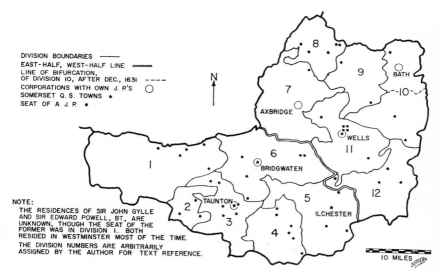

DIVISION BOUNDARIES ——
EAST-HALF, WEST-HALF LINE ══
LINE OF BIFURCATION,
OF DIVISION 10, AFTER DEC., 1631 ━━━━
CORPORATIONS WITH OWN J. P'S ○
SOMERSET Q. S. TOWNS ★
SEAT OF A J. P. ●

NOTE:
THE RESIDENCES OF SIR JOHN GYLLE AND SIR EDWARD POWELL, BT., ARE UNKNOWN, THOUGH THE SEAT OF THE FORMER WAS IN DIVISION 1. BOTH RESIDED IN WESTMINSTER MOST OF THE TIME.
THE DIVISION NUMBERS ARE ARBITRARILY ASSIGNED BY THE AUTHOR FOR TEXT REFERENCE.

10 MILES

FIG. 2.—*The seats of the Justices of the Peace in July 1631.*

by authority of the King's commission issued out of Chancery under the great seal. No commission for Somerset contained more than fifty-seven or less than thirty-seven names of locally resident justices. On each commission was included the Lord Keeper and other privy councillors as well as the two judges of assize. The commission named the justices, appointed one of them custos rotulorum and a number of them to be of the quorum. It summarized their duties and stated the authority by which they were to execute their office. In all, fifty-two such commissions for this county were issued as letters patent between May 1625 and December

1640, at rather irregular intervals.[1] Since the withdrawal or addition of a justice voided the entire commission, a new one was issued on such occasions. It appears to have been Chancery practice to issue commissions of the peace for all the counties which required adjustment at about the same time. Once issued, the commission was transmitted to the clerk of the peace, and the new justices took the oaths of office, allegiance, and supremacy at the next assizes. They were then empowered to execute the office of justice of the peace until the King willed that they be removed from the commission.

The officer responsible for appointing the justices was the Lord Keeper. It is difficult to determine to what extent the King, the Council, or individual councillors directed the Lord Keeper in his appointments. Buckingham took spasmodic interest in the appointment of justices and the Secretaries' of State voices carried weight. The large-scale changes made in the commissions of a number of counties preceding the free gift of 1626 were obviously Council actions. It is hard to say how far the lord lieutenant and the judges of assize, who had ostensibly the closest contact with local affairs, influenced the Lord Keeper. In a 1601 parliamentary debate concerning corrupt justices, a member had said that the Lord Keeper appointed justices on a commendatory certificate from the judges of assize. The member alleged that too often the certificate was procured from the judges, ignorant of local affairs, by a note signed by some justices of the peace.[2]

What is not in doubt is that the initial nomination of a new justice came from some magnate in the county itself. John Poulett, with the growth of his influence at Westminster indicated by his direct contact with the omnipotent Buckingham and his advancement to the peerage in 1627, became increasingly the avenue to a justiceship in the county. By direct intercession with Buckingham and Secretary Conway, Poulett

[1] Thirty-three of these letters patent are preserved in the SRO. See T. G. Barnes and A. Hassell Smith, "Justices of the Peace from 1558 to 1688—a Revised List of Sources," *Bulletin of the Institute of Historical Research* (1959), XXXII, 221–242 for a detailed discussion of the validity of various sources for determining the names of justices at any given time and the procedure for appointment of justices. At least 11 Somerset justices were at one time or another also in commissions of the peace for other counties: two each for Wilts., Dorset, Devon, Hants, and the liberty of Westminster, and one for Gloucestershire.

[2] *The Lancashire Lieutenancy under the Tudors and Stuarts*, pt. 1 (1859), p. xlvi. The MP's rather cryptic remark, that the Lord Keeper on receipt of the judges' certificate put the new justices into the commission at the next assizes, meant that the newly appointed justices took the oaths at the next assizes. James Whitelocke was placed in the Oxfordshire commission on a note from the judge of assize, James Whitelocke, *Liber Famelicus* (1858), p. 60.

secured the appointment of his uncle, George Poulett, and Sir Francis Rogers in 1627.[3] As early as 1623 his influence had been sufficient to secure William Walrond's appointment. Nor did Sir Robert Phelips fail to exercise power in the nomination of justices. He appears to have secured the appointment of John Harbyn in 1623/4 and, in his own words, "got in" Thomas Lyte later.[4] Like Poulett, his influence extended throughout the shire. A magnate, especially if he was about to retire, usually pressed successfully for the appointment of his heir in his place.

It is significant that the initial impetus for appointment came from the county. On the one hand, it indicates that despite the weight of its duties the office was eagerly sought. To men of magnate status the office allowed the maximum of power both parochially and county-wide and a continuing contact with the central government. Conversely, loss of office for the greatest magnate meant a drastic reduction of local power and the rupture of his relations with the central government that was a mark of his rank. Sir Robert Phelips is an excellent illustration of this. When out of the commission from 1626 to 1629, he lost a large measure of control over Ilchester despite his stewardship of the borough, control that he was never able to regain entirely. He also patently ceased to wield the influence at Westminster that was a mainstay of his power in the county. By the same token, Phelips' reappointment in 1629 also illustrates the fact that a man of his status in county society could not long be kept from office save on very strong grounds. These same considerations operated to a lesser extent with all other magnates; it was unlikely that the lord of Dunster or the owner of Orchard Portman would fail to be named in the commission if he so desired. In the case of lesser gentlemen, appointment to the office was sought not only for the power it brought but for the prestige it conferred. Unlike the magnates, they had no prescriptive claim to the office. Since magistracy functioned largely through the efforts of these numerous lesser men, it was essential to county government that the office of justice should remain attractive, an object to be obtained at any cost.

On the other hand, the impetus from below is significant because it meant the central government was limited in its choice of justices not only

[3] PRO, S.P.16/53, no. 88, John Poulett to Edward Nicholas, 12 Feb. 1626/7; SRO, Commissions of the peace, 1625–1638/9, commission of 22 Nov. 1627.

[4] SRO, Phelips MSS, vol. A, ff. 87–88, 93. The parliamentary counterpart to such local impetus for the appointment of justices is evident throughout Sir John Neale's *The Elizabethan House of Commons* (1949).

by the number of men willing to serve, but by the influence that certain great men in the county exerted upon the government. The appointment of magnates was little affected by the swing of the political pendulum. However, unless the gentleman of mere magisterial rank desirous of obtaining office was promoted by a magnate who was then most in favor with the government, it was unlikely that he would be appointed. As the political battle between Lord Poulett and Sir Robert Phelips surged, carrying first one and then the other to momentary ascendancy, so the appointment of justices depended on the favor of the ascendant magnate. The result was a growing factionalism intruded onto the rural bench which was not calculated to increase efficiency. Nor did the King necessarily obtain the services of the best possible men. Save in the appointment of a few clergymen, barristers and some others, the government took little direct interest in the nomination of justices. It relied upon the promotion of new men by the magnate in the county who professed most convincingly, at the moment, the "King's interest." Poulett's appeal to Buckingham (through his secretary), when asking for the inclusion of two new justices undoubtedly fell on sympathetic ears: "but yet since in the good choise of governers for ye provinces depends much ye successe of his majestys affairs, tis not a matter unworthy my lords [Buckingham's] care, and more in thease tymes then heretofore."[5] When Phelips was ascendant, he could and did make the same claim, and the government was then as wont to listen to him as it had been to his opponent.

This marked tendency on the part of the county's political leaders to promote their adherents for magisterial office was somewhat controlled by the basis of appointment. With the exception of those magnates who could not very well have been omitted, new justices were appointed only when needed, and the need was interpreted as being at least two active justices in each division. Even before the Book of Orders of 1630/1 gave final definition to divisions (out of sessions administrative areas) the government intended that justices should be evenly distributed over the county. The Book of Orders established finally the need for two active justices in each of the twelve divisions of two or more hundreds (see map on p. 41). Thus, John Harington of Kelston was appointed in December 1625 because John May of Hinton Chartehouse had dropped

[5] PRO, S.P.16/53, no. 88, Poulett to Edward Nicholas (Buckingham's secretary), 12 Feb. 1626/7.

from the commission the preceding spring, leaving the large division (no. 10) surrounding Bath without two justices. A decade later, the growing inactivity of the aged William Frauncis in division no. 3 made imperative the appointment of the Rev. Edward Kellett, rector of West Bagborough. The appointment of lesser gentlemen with respect to divisions was so invariable that it proves beyond doubt that this was the basis of appointment applied by the government. Poulett, in pressing for his uncle and the son of an aged magnate to be appointed justices, emphasized to Secretary Conway that these two men were needed at once to serve in a division vacated by the outlawry of two justices, the retirement of two others, and the impending retirement of a fifth.[6] The acceptance by the political leaders in the county of the division as the basis of appointment coupled with the government's intention to allow only necessary and active justices in the commission forestalled any attempt at large-scale packing of the bench with adherents of either faction in the county. Neither faction, however, passed up an opportunity to promote a friend when there was the slightest excuse for the appointment of a new justice.

Another restriction on the county politicians' nominations of new justices in this period was the government's own choice of ten clergymen to serve as justices. The bishop of Bath and Wells had long been appointed a justice and in the commission of July 1622 like honor was accorded the dean of Wells. Henceforth, with the exception of Laud who even as bishop of Bath and Wells (1626–1628) was too involved at Westminster to take much part in county and diocesan affairs, the bishop and dean appeared in every commission. As early at 1617/8, two canons of Wells were appointed, and in 1623 the first parochial cleric appeared in the commission. It is interesting that all the clergymen-justices were doctors of divinity and held exceptionally good livings. Their participation in magistracy was not an instance of Laudian sacerdotalism, as one local scholar has suggested,[7] since it commenced long before Laud attained his supremacy in either church or state. There were never more than five and usually only four clergymen on the commission at one time, and this was as true under Archbishop Laud as it had been under Archbishop Abbot. The episcopal and chapter clergy can be termed magnates by any

[6] PRO, S.P.16/526, no. 5, Poulett to Sec. Conway, 29 Jan. 1626/7.
[7] E. H. Bates in the introduction to *Quarter Sessions Records for the County of Somerset, Charles I* (1908), p. xix.

definition, and had a good claim to office. The parochial clergy were in
every case appointed with an eye to their usefulness in the divisions.
Doubtless the government appointed these clergymen-justices because
they were above faction and had unique intellectual gifts needed in rural
magistracy. Regular attenders at quarter sessions, they were among the
most active justices out of sessions.

The government's desire to have real legal talent represented on the
bench also imposed one final limitation to political promotion of new
magistrates. Fifteen barristers were named in the commissions over the
period, and some of them no doubt were included by the Lord Keeper's
own choice. Sir Edward Powell, Bart., a master of Requests, Thomas
Mallett, serjeant-at-law, and Robert Henley, chief clerk of enrollments
in the King's Bench, were appointed with some intention of reinforcing
the rural bench with men learned in the law. The quorum had lost its
original significance,[8] and with the growing complexity of the criminal
law quarter sessions needed expert direction. It was in quarter sessions
that these capable professionals made their contribution; only Robert
Henley was active out of sessions. Excepting the recorders of boroughs,
the few other barristers appointed fit into the pattern of appointment
with respect to divisions. All these men, most of them practising though
some were retired, furnished an important leavening of expert knowledge.
The inclusion of some of the recorders of Somerset boroughs in the
county commission leaves the impression that their appointment was to
help ease possible jurisdictional disputes and increase cooperation between
borough and county benches.[9] The recorders, without exception resident
in the county, were fairly active both in and out of sessions. Though
most appear not to have had an exceptionally large private practice, they
were well-versed in the criminal law, which gave them particular usefulness.

[8] Originally, some justices learned in the law were named to the "quorum," at least one
of whom had to be present at a sessions for that sessions' acts to be valid, William Lambard,
Eirenarcha (1619), p. 48. By this period over three-fourths of Somerset's justices were of the
quorum, most of whom obviously had no special knowledge of the law. However, one of
the quorum was still required at every sessions and out-of-sessions meeting; the growth of
the latter accounts for the increased numbers of the quorum, though the prestige of being
"of the quorum" doubtless contributed to the inflation.

[9] George Browne, recorder of Taunton, county JP 1618–1625 and 1629–1630; Thomas
Southworth of Wells, 1613 (at least)–1625; John Baber of Wells, 1626–1631; Sir Thomas
Wrothe of Bridgwater, 1636 *et seq.* John May, county JP 1613 (at least)–1628, was recorder
of Axbridge in 1599 and perhaps later. The recorder of Bath was apparently never in the
county commission.

The Somerset justices were limited in the exercise of their power to the county, which did not include for most magisterial purposes the cities and boroughs of Bath and Wells and the boroughs of Axbridge, Bridgwater, and (after 1627) Taunton. The relations existing between Somerset's justices and those of neighboring counties and these five boroughs were, with the exception of one borough, perfectly satisfactory. Since the malefactor was no respecter of jurisdictions and the law was, cooperation was in the interest of all those sworn to preserve the King's peace. The apprehension of felons, settlement of paupers, and the coercion of reputed fathers to ensure the performance of bastardy orders were successfully handled by the jurisdictions involved usually without friction. Intercounty pauper settlement and the repair of bridges lying in two counties which proved too difficult for solution via polite letters were left to assizes for a plenary order. Although Somerset's justices never attempted to exercise jurisdiction in another county, they were not always careful in dealing with the five boroughs. None of these boroughs' charters contained an explicit *non se intromittant* clause, though each borough possessed a recorder and other justices thus being entitled to their own quarter sessions. However in this period the magistrates of these boroughs occasionally committed for trial at the county sessions criminals who had perpetrated a crime in and were taken within the borough. Axbridge's charter of 1623 explicitly denied the borough justices cognizance of felonies.[10] In the case of Taunton, all the criminals sent to county sessions were thieves who had stolen goods valued over 12d—capital felons. The same appears true of the few persons sent for trial from Bridgwater. This indicates that in some cases borough sessions preferred to leave, or by law were required to leave the trial of those accused of capital felony not sent to assizes to the county bench. With respect to borough quarter-sessions' administrative (as against criminal-judicial) powers, even less can be ascertained. But the one extant case in which the Somerset justices fell afoul of borough magistrates evidently turned upon the question of the borough's immunity to the county sessions' administrative orders.

The dispute involved Wells. Two of its recorders had been county justices successively from 1614 to 1631 but the outstanding dispute

---

[10] *British Borough Charters, 1307–1660*, pp. 100–101. Bath's quarter sessions had the same powers as a county quarter sessions. At one time in this period, seven of its fourteen justices were also Somerset JPs and county magnates.

between the county and Wells justices occurred almost eight years after John Baber, the recorder, had dropped from the county commission. Baber complained at the Lent assizes 1638/9 that the county justices had pretended jurisdiction in the borough. Chief Justice Finch ordered Baber and the Somerset justices to meet at the county's next sessions, agree on the issues to be submitted, and attend him in chambers that term.[11] The outcome is unknown. As early as 1627 the borough officers had refused leave to a county justice to take recognizance of some malefactors within the borough, but the catalyst of the dispute that reached assizes was probably an order made at the county sessions in January 1638/9. The Somerset bench had peremptorily ordered readmission to the town of an artisan (likely to become a charge on the borough) whom the mayor and recorder had expelled a few days before at the borough quarter sessions.[12] Such jealous assertion of their privileges by the burgesses did not extend to criminal cases, for more felony suspects were remanded by Wells magistrates to the county sessions for trial than from all the other boroughs combined. Much depended on the temperament of the mayor and recorder; evidently Baber was not a man to be trifled with. The motive of the Somerset justices in invading another jurisdiction might well have been the laudable one of seeing justice done. In no sense did they stand to profit by it, and if the borough was upheld, their unlawful act might have resulted in very stiff damages.

There could be no jurisdictional disputes with the courts-leet and hundred courts. At law and in fact the relationship of the justices with these historic courts was that of master and servant, of a master compelled to do much of his servant's work as well as his own. The leets and hundred courts were largely impotent, and to judge by numerous complaints against them at quarter sessions prone to corruption. The power of quarter sessions was frequently required to compel a man presented by a leet to undertake a constableship or tithingmanship, a consideration which prompted the Cavalier Parliament (by 14 Charles II, c. 12) to transfer to the justices the leet's jurisdiction in appointment. Where reference to a leet appears in the sessions records, it is generally

---

[11] *Som Asz Ords*, no. 146. Baber claimed a clause of *non se intromittant* in the Wells charter, though no such clause appears there, *Wells City Charters* (1931), pp. 15–16. Without that clause in its charter, Wells had no valid legal ground to complain of the county bench's intrusion.

[12] SRO, Sess Rolls, 60, no. 44, Mich. QS 1627, Ralph Barlow, JP, to Christopher Browne, 15 Sept. 1627; 78, no. 32, Epiph. QS 1638/9.

in a matter of this sort. Presentment of bridges and roads in disrepair, usually made by hundred juries at quarter sessions, were seldom presented at the hundred courts, and in any case executive action lay with quarter sessions. Petitions against unlawful distraint upon leet process, complaints of leets having over-rated a tithing at the instigation of other tithings, and other petty appeals meant more work out of sessions for those justices delegated to investigate the matter. Because the leets and hundred courts were often far from impartial, they were a vehicle by which the unscrupulous escaped justice. A man indicted at quarter sessions for receiving a pauper pleaded (groundlessly) that it was a matter determinable only in the hundred court.[13] The emasculated state of the Taunton leet, its duties and powers gathered mostly into the justice's hands, was not untypical of these old courts.[14] Save for the adjustment of very petty disputes and the appointment of inferior officers—the latter with constant supervision by the justices—they served little useful purpose in local government. From the point of view of magistrates already amply employed they were certainly more trouble than they were worth. That there was no demand from the bench for their activities to be further restricted can be ascribed, perhaps not very charitably, to the number of justices who enjoyed the profits of the old courts.

The relations of the justices with the ecclesiastical jurisdictions—archdiaconal, diocesan, and High Commission—were limited. On occasion the county bench and the local ecclesiastical authorities did impinge on one another. Suffice it to say here, the justices stepped warily in those cases before them touching the ecclesiastical authority; such usually involved concurrent actions in the local ecclesiastical courts or the numerous illegalities perpetrated by the officers of those courts. Quarter sessions was wont to refer the matter to clergy-justices (especially the bishop and the archdeacons) on the bench. Very occasionally and only in minor matters did the central ecclesiastical authority utilize the justices as its agents in the shire. Its network of ecclesiastical officials made use of the justices unnecessary, no matter what other considerations moved the Establishment to keep its affairs in its own hands. At the county level, on the whole the two jurisdictions kept their respective distances.

[13] SRO, Sess Rolls, 73 pt. i, nos. 25–26, mids. QS 1635.
[14] R. G. Hedworth Whitty, *The Court of Taunton in the Sixteenth and Seventeenth Centuries* (1934), p. 124, the seignorial court of the bishop of Winchester—virtually a hundred court so wide was its jurisdiction.

Within the confines of their jurisdiction the county justices had sufficient power to discharge the judicial and administrative duties committed to them by their commission, the common law, statutes, and royal
and conciliar direction. The line between their judicial and administrative
functions remained blurred until the day two and one half centuries
later when the justices reverted to an almost purely judicial capacity.
For convenience, however, this study will treat the functions as separate.

Justices of the peace had been created originally to deal with crime,
and that is virtually their sole function today. In the sixteenth and seventeenth centuries the justices, despite the increasing burden of their
administrative duties, were not allowed to slacken in their traditional
warfare against the criminal. In fact, the long process of the justices'
usurpation of the criminal law functions of the sheriff reached its culmination in these centuries. By the hand of Parliament and upon the
example of the Council in Star Chamber, the criminal law was expanding. Much of the weight of that expansion fell on the justices of the
peace.

The early years of the 1630s were especially busy ones, for they were
years marked by famine and depression and consequent lawlessness.
The calendars of prisoners at sessions (in the quarter-sessions order
books and the sessions rolls) reflect the hardship of the poor and the
unemployed around 1630. There was a marked increase in the number
of sessions trials in these years. The examinations before justices out of
sessions indicate that larceny of food mostly comprised the increase; the
normally more common thefts of sheep and clothes yielding pride of place
to theft of food. The rise in larcenies of food was accompanied by an
increase in assaults and other forms of disorderliness. If the criminal
records of assizes were yet extant the picture would be complete. It is
complete enough to show that at the same time the justices were undertaking added administrative duties, their sessions agendas were crowded
with trials, and much more of their time between sessions was spent
in the examination of criminals.

In one direction, however, the justices in quarter sessions were losing
some of their power. The act, 34 Edward III, c. 1, had authorized them
to hear and determine virtually all felonies and their commission still
gave them power *ad omnia et singula felonias ... audiendum et
terminandum.* In practice, however, quarter sessions was far advanced
on the road that ended in the next century with the loss of its power to

inflict the death penalty. The first inroads had been made by two
Marian statutes which, while ordaining the examination of felons by the
justices, required them to certify the examinations and informations to
assizes.[15] Though this did not remove the justices' authority to hear and
determine indictments for felony brought before them, through judicial
interpretation trial of the more serious felonies was increasingly assumed
by assizes. The reformed commission of the peace, first issued in 1590 and
followed subsequently, by expressly exhorting the justices to leave *casus
difficultatis* to the judges spurred on this development. Lambarde, with
an uncharacteristic lack of precision, informed his justices that "they are
not now adaies much occupied" with the trial of felonies, while in the
same paragraph he reassured them that their power was "no whit
restrained to proceed before the comming of" the judges.[16] Dalton, his
successor as a handbook author, was more explicit and told the justices
to try only "pettie Larcenies and small felonies" and other felonies
definitely assigned them by statutes.[17] The practice of the Somerset justices
fell between these two complementary authorities. A case of rape—
casus difficultatis in the extreme—was sent to quarter sessions for
trial, though the outcome is unknown because of a gap in the indictment
rolls and silence in the calendar of prisoners.[18] It was only an *ignoramus*
returned on a bill of indictment by a quarter-sessions grand jury that
prevented the justices from trying the case of a woman charged with
strangling and then secreting the body of her illegitimate child—a
statutory variety of murder with involved rules of evidence.[19] Allowing
for the greatest latitude in interpretation of Dalton's admonition to the
justices to try only small felonies, these cases should have gone to assizes.
The fact that such cases are extremely rare in the sessions rolls implies
that assizes had assumed in practice the trial of virtually all felonies save
larceny.

Quarter sessions treatment of cases of grand larceny provides further
evidence of the progressive shrinkage of that court's power to try felonies.
Grand larceny was capital felony; petty larceny (theft of goods valued at

[15] 1 & 2 Philip and Mary, c. 13; 2 & 3 Philip and Mary, c. 10 extended examination to all
cases of felony.
[16] Lambarde, p. 553.
[17] Michael Dalton, *The Countrey Justice* (1655), p. 58.
[18] SRO, Sess Rolls, 68, no. 89; 67 pt. i, no. 62; 69 pt. ii, nos. 33, 73, Mich. QS 1632 to
Eas. QS 1633.
[19] SRO, Indictment rolls, 63, Epiph. QS 1630/1; Sess Rolls, 64 pt. ii, nos. 264–265. See
Dalton, *Countrey Justice*, p. 352, and 21 James I, c. 27 for the statute.

12d or less) was not. To judge from the examinations of criminals, many
of the larcenies sent to quarter sessions for trial were grand larcenies. Yet
it is significant that in this period only eight persons were hanged by
quarter sessions for grand larceny. Such mercifulness was accomplished
by the legal abuse of "clergy," the occasional refusal of grand juries to
return *billa vera* on a bill of indictment for grand larceny that they
considered should be petty larceny, and the persistent undervaluation of
stolen property by trial juries which reduced the theft to petty larceny.
There was a limit, though, to the extent to which a jury could conscientiously undervalue goods, and the most lenient jury would have stuck at
valuing a gold ring at 10d. In fact, a quarter sessions' trial jury was never
asked to use the truth so hardly for the simple reason that the larcenies
tried there seldom involved goods whose real value much exceeded 12d.
This is the surest evidence that the court had relinquished to assizes
the trial of greater larcenies. Nonetheless the court had not relinquished
the power to inflict the lawful penalty for grand larceny if it and the
jury thought that necessary. About the cases of seven of the eight who
hanged there remains ample evidence; in each there were exceptional
circumstances that aggravated the crime.[20] Six of the cases were heard
at Michaelmas sessions, 1625, and the size of the calendar and such
unusual severity indicate that both justices and jurors might have felt
that hitherto the law had not been enforced rigorously enough. These
eight found the justices' punishment no less stringent than that of the
judges.

There can be little doubt that there was some line, though not perhaps
hard and fast, between the larcenies the justices might try and those
they were to leave to the judges. This line was based on the value of
the stolen property. A knowledgeable justice wrote to the clerk of the
peace that though he had bound two suspects to assizes for theft, they
had "made suite" to be tried at sessions "but because I belive it wilbe
above the vallew, I doe think it will nott be tryed at the sessyons."[21] As
there are no examinations of these two suspects in the sessions rolls it
can be inferred that their trial was at assizes. The goods stolen, though
not valued in Hopton's letter, were three pairs of stockings taken in
Frome market. This was a theft typical of many whose perpetrators
were tried at quarter sessions. It is impossible to say at what value the

20 SRO, Sess Rolls, 53 pt. i, nos. 47–48, 81–83, 114–115; 77 pt. i, nos. 66–67.
21 SRO, Sess Rolls, 73 pt. ii, no. 24, 13 Jan. 1634/5.

line was drawn, since many who had stolen goods of greater value than three pairs of stockings were tried at quarter sessions. Still, the fact that most larcenies tried at quarter sessions involved goods of small value and that rape, robbery, and homicide cases very rarely appear in the sessions rolls is sufficient proof that sessions was indeed restricted to trying "small felonies."

It is hardly credible that the expansion of the *casus difficultatis* clause of the commission was more than an excuse to restrict the justices' powers in felonies. It can be argued that the muddled (and expanding) law of larceny bred many more knotty problems of both substantive and adjective law than the better defined crimes of rape, arson, and robbery. Neither King nor Parliament exhibited particular concern for the rights and safety of the prisoner at the bar. There is a more satisfactory explanation. As the local magistrates did not possess in like measure as the awesome judges the dignity and power in their persons and places sufficient to coerce a grand jury into returning a true bill and a trial jury a conviction that meant the noose, so felons were not brought to justice as King, Council, and judges required. Anyone aware of the relative lawlessness of the age is even more aware of the unending exertion of the Council to suppress it. The King and Council did not scruple to reduce the justices' powers in felonies for the better preservation of the King's peace.

If the government and the judges saw fit to curtail the justices' powers over felony, the vacuum was amply filled with misdemeanors. These non-capital, indictable trespasses were principally the product of the Tudors' zeal to make the long outmoded criminal code an efficient instrument to preserve order in a modern state. Since misdemeanors were largely statutory creations, the authority to hear and determine them was usually clearly assigned in the originating act, to the justices of the peace as well as the judges. Even if authority to hear and determine was not assigned in the originating statute, the commission of the peace provided the justices with full power in all misdemeanors. The first two Stuarts' only notable additions to the multitude of misdemeanors were statutes against drunkenness and alehouse nuisances—the full weight of which could hardly have rested upon any other authority than the justices, alone possessed of the requisite local knowledge to enforce the law adequately. It requires only a quick glance at the calendar of any quarter sessions to see how these statutory creations and extensions of the previous two centuries had come to dominate the judicial functions of Stuart justices. Misdemeanors ranging from such high offences as riot and abuse of legal procedure to petty assaults and drunkenness outnumber the older felonies, three to one. Master Dalton did not exaggerate when he wrote that "the numbers of which Statutes [establishing misdemeanors] are exceedingly increased of late years, to the overburthening of all the Justices. . . ."[22]

Misdemeanors brought to criminal procedure two innovations, which, quite aside from the profusion of these new crimes, meant a considerable increase in the work of quarter sessions. The first of these was the form of trial known as the traverse. Like the older felonies, misdemeanors were indictable offences; that is, the action was brought on the Crown's behalf by the presentation of a bill to the grand jury which if returned *vera* brought the offender to trial. In fact most of the serious misdemeanors appear to have been brought to trial by indictment. The mode of trial followed in misdemeanor cases, however begun (though never felony), was usually the traverse. In traverse, the offender came in of his own volition and pleaded his exception to the charge, in marked contrast to the felon who was either brought in for arraignment by an officer or by compulsion of a bail bond. The pleading of the traverse resembled pleadings in a civil suit, with pleas and counterpleas, all taking considerable time. Once the traverse was ended and the pleas settled, it appears that the offender was then bound to a subsequent sessions for the actual hearing and determining. This is the significant difference in procedure between felony and misdemeanor. The felon was indicted, arraigned, tried, and sentenced all in one sessions; the offender in misdemeanor took up a large measure of the court's time in two sessions. The actual trial of both types of crime was the same, and the demurrer, justification, and other time-consuming weapons of the defendant were sacred to both actions. So general was the use of the traverse at Somerset quarter sessions that an attorney for a complainant in a wounding case then before the court wrote the clerk of the peace that he would not bring in his witnesses until the following sessions, since he understood the "course . . . upon those processes" would mean the trial would be then.[23]

The second innovation in criminal procedure wrought by misde-

---

[22] Dalton, *Countrey Justice*, p. 21.

[23] SRO, Sess Rolls, 73 pt. i, no. 90, Walter Liffe to Christopher Browne, 1635. Lambarde, pp. 538–554, gives a sound if brief comparison of the two forms of trial, traverse and arraignment.

meanors was the common informer. Though the more heinous misdemeanors such as riot were brought on indictment and many offences against administrative statutes (highways in disrepair, ditches unscoured, etc.) by presentment, the vast majority of the minor misdemeanors were brought on information which had the same effect as indictment in bringing the offender to trial. An information could be laid by the injured party, or on behalf of the King, or on behalf of the King and the informer. The common informer built his livelihood upon the last, dividing the fine with the King. It could be a very steady livelihood since the numbers were legion of those who sold ale or transported corn without licence, pursued a trade without previous apprenticeship, built a cottage with less than four acres of land attached, and committed like petty offences. It was not unusual for any one of the six most successful informers to present twenty to forty informations a sessions, with fully three-quarters of them successfully prosecuted or compounded for. Though many of these men were illiterate (their informations signed by mark), they had money to retain a part-time scribe, attorneys, and even counsel. While the informers were not employees of the court, Elizabeth's statutes of informers had given the judges and justices power to fine and enjoin an informer never to inform again upon conviction for violation of the statutes or for malicious prosecutions.[24] Somerset's justices did treat with marked severity two informers who had brought malicious prosecutions, one of them spending over a year in gaol for want of bail.[25] The government's only contribution in this period to the regulation of these prosecutors was a proclamation of 1635 enjoining common informers to certify their composition to a royal patentee so that the Crown might not be cheated of its half of the composition fee.[26] Composition by the defendant with the informer (after the traverse) became more common in the 1630s. This was probably a result of the increasing number of informations brought against corn engrossers and unlawful laders and badgers. It was in the interests of the justices to allow such composition, for the offender was punished, the Crown received its money, and the court was saved the hearing of another case.

[24] 18 Elizabeth I, c. 5 and 27 Elizabeth I, c. 10. Mr. Copnall overstates the position of the common informers in saying they were employed by the court, *Nottinghamshire County Records* (1915), pp. 20–21.

[25] SRO, QSOB, 1627/8–1638, Eas. QS 1631, calendar, and Epiph. QS 1631/2, no. 15. Assizes gaoled another informer, who practiced at both quarter sessions and assizes, for malicious prosecution, *Som Asz Ords*, no. 109.

[26] *Foedera* (1732), XIX, 682, proclamation of 6 Sept. 1635.

3*

However, the number of compositions between informers and defendants never came near to equalling the total number of informations sworn out and tried at sessions. The informers justified their existence as an instrument for the enforcement of the law, but the main burden fell on a court which even without common informers had more than enough business to fill its three or four-day sittings.

In the battle against lawlessness that perhaps had impelled the government to restrict the justices' powers in felonies and which had called forth the multitude of new misdemeanors, the justices were the main weapon of society against the criminal. As well as hearing and determining the lesser felonies and misdemeanors in their quarter sessions, they still performed a police function out of sessions that had been their *raison d'être* from the first. This might be literally detective work, such as justice Edward Lancaster's instructions to a constable to set a trap to catch a thief.[27] Usually it was the more prosaic examination of the captured criminal in which the justice fulfilled much the same function as the *juge d'instruction* does in France today. Professor Holdsworth stresses the inquisitorial aspect of the examinations and points out how this had the desired effect of drafting a ready case against the accused before he was brought before the grand jury.[28] He also sees in this the influence of Star Chamber procedure on the common law.

Without attempting to depict every quarter sessions as a county *Camera Stellata*, there seems to have been some parallel in county magistracy to the development of new weapons against the criminal taking place in Star Chamber, though the former authority was much more closely restricted by existing law in its innovations. One innovation, seemingly without statutory basis or explicit conciliar sanction, was the justices' examination of offenders in misdemeanor as well as in felony. Neither the Marian statutes, Lambarde, nor Dalton gave any direction that in cases of misdemeanor the offender's examination should be taken.[29] Yet, among the sessions rolls appear many such examinations certified to quarter sessions, which formed the basis of an indictment for misdemeanor. It was a wholly natural development, and it extended the useful

[27] SRO, Sess Rolls, 53 pt. ii, nos. 111–113, Eas. QS 1625.
[28] W. S. Holdsworth; *A History of English Law* (1945), V, 191. For a fuller discussion of the examination and the advantages it secured to the accused, see my note in *SDNQ* (1955), XXVII, 39–42.
[29] 2 & 3 Philip and Mary, c. 10; Lambarde, pp. 212–213; Dalton, *Countrey Justice,* pp. 56–57, 369–374.

inquisitorial procedure to the many lesser offences which were increasingly the concern of the justices.

The readiness to find a remedy to any wrong that could conceivably lead to a breach of the peace which was characteristic of Star Chamber is discernible in the increasing use made of surety for good behavior by the justices. Surety for good behavior was firmly rooted in statute and developed by judicial authority. Akin to the surety for the peace, it was a more supple weapon since the breaking of the bond for good behavior did not require a breach of the peace but merely actions or words "which shall tend to the breach of the peace."[30] By the time Lambarde and Dalton wrote, it could be sworn out on application to a justice against drunkards, defamers, incontinent couples, persons of "evil fame" —in short, against those who, though they had committed no indictable offence, might bring about a breach of the peace. Although the bond was intended to prevent a breach of the peace it was in practice used by the justices as punishment for acts not themselves indictable at law. An illustration of this is its use against defamers by words. Defamatory words as a criminal offence fell solely within the jurisdiction of the ecclesiastical courts and Star Chamber. However, should a person defame another by words, he could be brought before a justice on application by the injured party and required to find bond with two sureties (usually in £20 each) to be of good behavior. Failing such bond he was committed to gaol until released by quarter sessions. Since in many cases sureties were not forthcoming, such use of the bond for good behavior had a definite penal effect.[31] This convenient weapon was readily employed, and almost superseded the older and more rigid peace process.

However, while stressing the readiness of the justices to use with maximum effectiveness every instrument the law allowed them, it must be remembered that they dared not wander far from the path of established law. Star Chamber punished attempted felonies as attempts; quarter sessions could only charge a man who had attempted rape with common assault.[32] In another case, a man was convicted of assault (albeit

[30] Dalton, *Countrey Justice*, pp. 212–218. The statutory basis was 34 Edward III, c. 1.

[31] The use of a bond to enable the bench to commit summarily was given judicial sanction by Crew, CJKB. He held that quarter sessions or assizes could control alehousekeepers who brewed *contra* statute by indicting offenders, thus ensuring that they would be bound over to quarter sessions or assizes "wher they are to be committed yf ther be cause." Bodl, Bankes MSS, bundle 15, no. 5, certificate of Crew, 12 Oct. 1626.

[32] SRO, QSOB 1627/8–1638, mids. QS 1632, kalendar, and Eas. QS 1633, kalendar. See J. F. Stephen, *A History of the Criminal Law of England* (1883), II, 223–224.

assault with all possible aggravating circumstances included in the indictment) who might well have been convicted of the capital crime of buggery
a year later after the ruling of the judges in Castlehaven's Case.[33] There
were many sharp-eared attorneys about the court most willing to inform
a person indicted on tenuous legal grounds as to his rights and justices
were not wholly immune from prosecution in Star Chamber by parties
who, no matter how groundlessly, felt they had been injured.[34] The
removal of a case to Westminster by writ of *certiorari* was a constant
and unappealing possibility for the justices and one which made them
cautious in stretching the law merely to catch another criminal. With
the maximum use of the tools the law allowed them and with their
small though effective refinements of those tools in practice, the justices
were able to preserve the King's peace and to a remarkable extent provide
a remedy for a wrong.

Lambard's plaintive "Then, how many Justices, (thinke you) may now
suffice (without breaking their backs) to beare so many, not loads, but
stacks of statutes, that have since ... [Henry VII's] time bene laid upon
them"[35] referred chiefly to the acts of Tudor Parliaments that transformed
the justices from judges into the principal county administrators. Even
at the beginning of Elizabeth's reign, the justices were still basically
judicial officers. By the time of the Queen's death there could be no
mistaking the fact that they had become administrators as well. It was
as administrators that the justices made their greatest contribution to
local government in the seventeenth century, and it was as administrators
that they suffered the greatest burden of governance. Unfortunately, the
burden reposed only slightly on the traditional body of the justices in
quarter sessions. It fell with increasing weight upon the individual
justice or group of two or more justices out of sessions—upon the justices
at the level where they were least able to bear the weight conveniently.

The two final statutes on the Tudor "stack" were heaviest of all.

[33] SRO, Sess Rolls, 62, nos. 5–6, and Indictment rolls, 65, Mich. QS 1630. In Castlehaven's Case tried in Lords eight months later, the judges held that buggery could be committed even "sans penetration, car le use del corps despend le seede in tiel cases fait ceo
Buggery," Dalton, *Countrey Justice*, p. 341. See *A Complete Collection of State-Tryals* (1719),
I, 270 for the case.

[34] John Baber, as recorder of Wells, and other borough magistrates were acquitted in
Star Chamber in 1628 of conspiracy to indict a woman as an accessory to a murder, the
charge being dismissed with a fine *pro falso clamore* upon the prosecutor and damages to
the defendants, on the basis that in examining suspects the magistrates were merely doing
their duty, HLS, L. MS 1128, no. 58.

[35] Lambarde, p. 34.

The two poor laws of Elizabeth's last years were so great in magnitude and so far-reaching in importance that Chapter VII is devoted to them. It will suffice to say here that as these acts established poor relief on a parochial basis, so they required the supervision of the program at a parochial level. This supervision was specifically assigned to two justices of the peace to whom the parish officers were to look for guidance and authority in the execution of their offices, and upon whom the government relied for the oversight of the parish officers. This relationship of the justices to both their servants and their master was the foundation of poor relief—a foundation centering on two justices out of sessions, not on a bench of justices.

Two important aspects of the justices' concern with poverty must be mentioned here as they will not be treated in the later chapter, being not wholly relevant to the 1630/1 Book of Orders. The routine of settlement of the poor and the granting of extraordinary relief were little affected by the Book of Orders.

For a pauper to receive aid from a parish he had to be settled in that parish. The law as to what constituted settlement was exceedingly vague until 1633, when the so-called "resolutions of the judges of assize" gave it some degree of definition.[36] Not unexpectedly, every parish attempted to disown a pauper, but a man born and reared in one parish was undoubtedly settled there. Disputes between parishes over a pauper or one likely to become a pauper arose when the individual moved to another parish, either to work or merely to live. Save for a few disputes between parishes in two different counties which went to assizes, these disputes were invariably brought to quarter sessions, usually by the parish that had the pauper and wished to be rid of him. A settlement hearing was a lengthy process, and with both sides normally being represented by counsel, a forensic affair too. But until the mid-1630s quarter sessions seldom underwent this tedious experience. Of the fifty-five settlement disputes brought before the Somerset bench prior to 1634, the hearing of three-fourths of them was delegated to two or more justices out of sessions. The case of John Parker's child was not untypical. Glastonbury complained to the midsummer sessions 1631 that Parker's orphaned child had been living in Shapwick where its father had been lawfully settled, but that the Shapwick overseers brought the child to Glastonbury (its birthplace) and left it on the church doorstep. The matter was referred

[36] See p. 188.

to Sir Edward Rodney and Rev. Paul Godwyn, JPs, who met, heard innumerable witnesses, and in a lengthy report certified that the child ought to be settled at Shapwick. At the Easter sessions 1632, Shapwick appealed against this finding and it was again referred to the same two justices, who again met, reexamined, and returned the same certificate. Midsummer sessions 1632 merely confirmed the certificate as an order.[37] One year and two lengthy hearings before two very busy justices had been required to settle one baby!

Fire, flood, and plague were common scourges of the age and the Elizabethan poor laws and 1 James I, c. 31 made provision for the extension of relief to sufferers. A hospital fund was established for each half of the county with a yearly income through rates of about £100 each. This "county stock" was to pay for the maintenance of poor prisoners, the building and upkeep of the houses of correction, and for special aid to needy persons. It was constantly on the verge of insolvency since expenditure was heavy and the funds were regularly raided to make disbursements for which the stock was not intended, such as to pay the salary of the muster master of the militia. In all, there were twenty-three grants from the county stock for extraordinary relief; once, the insolvency of the fund prevented the disbursement. When disaster was widespread or the number of poor in one parish great, the hospital fund was unable to supply the requisite cash so that special rates on neighboring parishes or on the whole county had to be made. Provision for such special rates was included in 1 James I, c. 31, which dealt specifically with plague. In 1625 Bridgwater was hard hit by the Death; the Michaelmas quarter sessions were adjourned from that town to Taunton for fear of it. The full responsibility for raising the special rate, overseeing the exclusion of strangers from the stricken town, and supervising the nauseating tasks that followed the disease's visitation reposed wholly on two nearby justices. The arrears on the special rate—to be expected—were ordered collected under supervision of three other justices. The labor of all was in vain, for the plague spread to Taunton, and the justices near that town assumed the same job. The looting that follows such disaster provided added tasks of law enforcement for the few justices already well occupied.[38]

[37] SRO, QSOB, 1627/8–1638, mids. QS 1631, no. 5; Eas. QS 1632, no. 9; mids. QS 1632, no. 7; Sess Rolls, 67 pt. ii, nos. 79, 81.

[38] SRO, QSOB, 1620/1–1627, mids. QS 1625, no. 16; Epiph. QS 1625/6, no. 2; Sess Rolls, 57 pt. ii, nos. 65–67, Eas. QS 1626.

Illegitimate children, one of the most prevalent social evils of the age, provided the justices out of sessions with a truly enormous task. 18 Elizabeth I, c. 3 established the procedure by which such unfortunate children could be kept off the parish poor rates and their parents punished. This quasi-judicial proceeding was committed to the care of the two "neighboring" justices to the child's birthplace. Before the child's birth, the woman was examined as to the child's paternity and the putative father then bound to quarter sessions. After the birth of the child, the mother and usually the father were convented before the two justices. Following exhaustive investigation, including testimony of the midwife as to any statement regarding paternity the girl had made during labor, the putative father was bound to provide a certain sum for the child's maintenance until it could be apprenticed. Either or both parents were to be sentenced to corporal punishment, though in Somerset the father was not corporally punished if convicted only on the mother's testimony.[39] The mother was to undergo the barbarous chastisement of being "whipped until her back be bloody," or was sent to the house of correction. Practice often tempered this severity, many mothers escaping the lash and very few being sent to the house of correction for a first offence as the law required. The order of the two justices was certified to quarter sessions, there confirmed and enrolled in the order book. There were exactly two hundred and fifty such orders certified to quarter sessions from 1625 to 1638; an average of over four per sessions.

The duties on the justices out of sessions imposed by bastardy up to the certification of the order were onerous and time-consuming enough. Moreover, with characteristic Tudor thoroughness the act allowed an appeal to be entered at the quarter sessions to which the order was certified. Appeal was generally brought by the putative father, who disclaimed paternity. Since quarter sessions could merely confirm or disallow the order, but could not name a new putative father,[40] the court often referred the whole matter back to the ordering justices or, occasionally, to two or more disinterested justices for rehearing and reordering. Appeals were many, and the involved questions of fact and even law raised by

[39] This in marked contrast to both Lancashire and Nottinghamshire where both were whipped, *Lancashire Quarter Sessions Records* (1917), p. xxiii, and *Nottinghamshire County Records*, pp. 122 *et seq.* An assize order in 1637/8 required the Somerset justices to "take speciall care" that the father was corporally punished, *Som Asz Ords*, no. 124.

[40] Opinion in chambers of Davenport, CB, and Denham, B, entered in SRO, QSOB, 1627/8–1638, Epiph. QS 1634/5. This was the practice of Somerset quarter sessions before this decision.

them were appalling. Bastardy, both at first instance and on appeal, enjoyed the distinction of providing more out-of-sessions work of a more difficult nature than any other single matter of routine that came within the justices' purview.

The crude bridges and roads which made so difficult the easy intercourse necessary to efficient government also cost the justices a great deal of time in efforts—usually futile—to keep them in repair. The bridges, slowly disintegrating or regularly washed out by floods, and the roads, almost wholly impassable in winter and spring, were largely beyond the help of seventeenth-century Englishmen. It required a better knowledge of bridge construction and a McAdam before any noticeable improvements were made. What could be done within the technical limitations the Tudor monarch left to the justices of the peace out of sessions.

The machinery for the repair of bridges as enjoined in 22 Henry VIII, c. 5 was at least more realistic than that for road repair. After an initial inquiry by quarter sessions or four justices as to who ought to bear the cost of the bridge's repair, two surveyors were appointed charged with undertaking the repairs. On order of the justices, the surveyors could obtain men, equipment, and materials with the funds supplied them by those responsible for the bridge's upkeep. Most large bridges appear to have been "county bridges," and thus the funds for their repair were raised by hundred rates throughout the county, the broadest tax base the age's thinking would allow. The surveyors and the collectors of the rate in each hundred (the hundred constables) were responsible to the justices. This was a workable system. By 1625 the surveyors in Somerset had become virtually professional construction engineers who repaired bridge after bridge, being allowed probably a bit more than the statutory "reasonable costs."[41] But the sheer weight of technical difficulties combined with apparent reluctance on the surveyors' parts to expend more time and money than was necessary to present a comely veneer to the justices' inspection, defeated the law and the genuine concern of the justices to enforce it. For example, in 1625 Stanmore bridge was repaired at considerable cost. A decade later it was again in a ruinous state.[42]

[41] Thomas Anthonye repaired bridges throughout the county and petitioned quarter sessions for his fees, SRO, Sess Rolls, 56 pt. i, no. 2, Mich. QS 1626.

[42] SRO, QSOB, 1620/1–1627, mids. QS 1625, no. 2; Sess Rolls, 71 pt. i, no. 69, Mich. QS 1634.

Road repair was accomplished under a Marian statute which erected a system of parochial endeavor resembling the later Elizabethan poor laws.[43] Two parish surveyors, appointed annually, were for six days in the year to direct the repair of highways in the parish. Men and equipment were obtained in the form of a cart and two men from every person who held a "plow-land" or more in the parish, and the services of every able-bodied householder. Quarter sessions or two justices were to take account of the surveyors, and in case of failure to repair, make presentment at sessions or fine the parish outright. *Corvée* labor under the direction of two householders was an impossible substitute for genuine workmen and engineers, despite the simplicity of the roads. Stanmore Bridge had its equivalent in many of the county's roads which, with monotonous regularity, were virtually unserviceable.

The statute for road repair should have rested less heavily on the justices than that concerning bridges because it established machinery which was intended to require a minimum of magisterial oversight. In reality, however, roads provided recurrent difficulties to vex the justices. A parish might be amerced for nonrepair of a highway, but that seldom resulted in the road's immediate amendment. The recurrent breakdown of the parochial machinery for repair resulted in justices out of sessions being required by sessions to take "speedy order" for the repair of a road. This often meant personal direction of the repairers by a justice as William Every, JP, provided in Bathealton.[44] If, as frequently happened, some refused to send a cart, claiming they did not have a plow-land, the justices had to hold a hearing to settle the vexed question of what constituted a plow-land. In this they received little help from quarter sessions. A general order of Epiphany sessions 1627/8 defining a plow-land as thirty acres appears to have been cancelled (for unknown reasons) before it was issued.[45] A common complaint to quarter sessions was that persons who held lands though they did not reside in the parish, refused to send a cart. Every such case was referred to some justices out of sessions to examine all parties and take order for repair. The referee justices received small consolation from a Privy Council directive which informed them of what they knew already—namely, that such landowners were liable for

[43] 2 & 3 Philip and Mary, c. 8. The most helpful printed account of roads at this time is in S. and B. Webb, *English Local Government: The Story of the King's Highway* (1913).
[44] SRO, QSOB, 1627/8–1638, Mich. QS 1637, no. 5.
[45] SRO, QSOB, 1627/8–1638, Epiph. QS 1627/8, no. 5.

road repair.[46] The Council's direction that small landowners should be grouped to furnish a single cart merely complicated matters further. In bridge repair, the same difficulties attended the justices out of sessions. The repair of a county bridge to be paid for by hundred rates was generally a source of interminable rating disputes, always referred to justices out of sessions for settlement. In fact the whole procedure of enquiry, supervision of the two surveyors, and inspection of the finished bridge, had long since devolved on the four justices out of sessions. The case of one bridge, which took two years and six sessions orders to repair, furnishes all the complications that could afflict the justices. Lyng causeway fell into disrepair, and on petition of Lyng parish the bench at Epiphany sessions 1631/2 assigned three justices to take "speedy course" for its repair or certify the next sessions their "opinions therein." After a hearing, at which four elaborate documents containing the testimony of at least twenty-eight persons were considered, liability for repair was settled on Lyng. The "richer sort" of the parish refused to obey the surveyors' directions for repair, and allegedly spoke disparagingly of the justices' order. The causeway was not repaired. After another reference to the same three justices, and the personal supervision of yet another justice, the causeway was finally made passable.[47] Lyng causeway was something of an exception, but only in so far as it produced most of the complications which singly can be found in every one of the twenty-nine other bridge repair cases that quarter sessions referred to out-of-sessions justices. The very futility of bridge and road repair, joined with the considerable burden of work entailed, must have made this duty one of the most frustrating of all the many tasks that fell to the justices out of sessions.

Three other duties of an administrative nature performed by the justices must be mentioned. The licensing and control of alehouses, the regulation of wages and settlement of disputes between masters and servants, and the enrollment of deeds were minute matters in comparison to the labor that poor law, bastardy, and road and bridge repair entailed. Still, they required the expenditure of some time and, with the exception of deed enrollment, they too rested almost wholly on the justices out of sessions.

[46] PRO, P.C.2/40, p. 68, PC order, 9 July 1630.

[47] SRO, QSOB, 1627/8–1638, Epiph. QS 1631/2, no. 20; Eas. QS 1632, no. 2; Mich. QS 1632, no. 8; Epiph. QS 1632/3, no. 4; Eas. QS 1633, no. 1; Sess Rolls, 67 pt. i, no. 5, mids. QS 1632.

By 5 & 6 Edward VI, c. 25 two justices were given power to allow the keeping of an alehouse and were to take bond of the publican for the good order of his house. The most comprehensive code that early Stuart legislation enacted on any subject concerned alehouses, and six statutes extended the justices' control over them. The culmination of this spate of legislation was 3 Charles I, c. 4, which decreed that no man was to keep an alehouse without first entering surety before and receiving a licence from at least two justices of the peace.[48] As in bridge repair, quarter sessions relinquished its control over alehouses to the justices out of sessions, and most alehouses were licensed by two neighboring justices. The total number of alehouse recognizances certified to three 1630 quarter sessions was two hundred and ninety-seven,[49] and it is impossible to estimate the number of illicit houses that remained in business. What burden the control of alehouses imposed on the justices out of sessions grew mostly out of the steps required to suppress unlicensed houses and licensed houses that disobeyed any of the elaborate articles demanding good order which publicans were bound in sureties to observe.[50] Complaints of vicars, parish officers, and others of the ill-keeping of houses were not all figments of puritanical imaginations. Bawdy houses, headquarters of marauders, receivers of felons and stolen property were terms too often applicable to too many alehouses. The justices, both in sessions and out, attempted to suppress disorderly establishments, but the devolution of the licensing function to justices out of sessions allowed the publican once suppressed to get a licence from another pair of justices. A general order of a 1629 sessions which required the consent of the justices nearest the house to any relicensing of a suppressed publican[51] was the first move in a sustained effort to prevent abuses in licensing and to regulate effectually the county's ale-houses. Since the consumption of ale caused an appreciable drain on

[48] This act was to reverse resolutions of the judges in 1625 which held that justices could suppress an alehouse once opened but could not prevent it opening, see Richard Hutton, *The Reports of* (1682), pp. 99–100. Interestingly, the sole vestige today of the justices' former administrative dominance in county government is the licensing of public houses.

[49] SRO, Alehousekeepers' recognizances, box 1, roll for Eas.-Mich. QSS 1630. No other recognizances are extant for the period, save mids QS 1626. Undoubtedly a number of licenses were certified into Epiph. QS 1630/1. John Symes, JP, alone sent up 23 recognizances to Eas. QS 1633—and unnecessary alehouses were under strict interdict then, SRO, Sess Rolls, 69 pt. ii, no. 94.

[50] SRO, Sess Rolls, 61 pt. i, no. 35. These articles are almost identical to those used in Herts. about the same time, *Hertford County Records* (1905), I, 47–48.

[51] SRO, QSOB, 1627/8–1638, Eas. QS 1629, no. 23.

corn, the government's orders from 1629 to prevent the dearth of grain called for a general reduction in the number of houses. As we shall see, these orders and another experiment in the regulation of alehouses during the "personal rule" had the effect of making onerous to justices out of sessions what before had been only mildly tedious routine.

Since the fourteenth century the justices had exercised control over the relations of master and servant. A succession of statutes erected a complicated structure for the magisterial fixing of wages, the punishment of masters and servants who broke covenant, and for the payment of servants whose wages were unlawfully detained.[52] In the Elizabethan and Jacobean statutes the hearing and determining of disputes and the punishment of offenders were vested in two justices out of sessions. The most common complaints were those of servants whose masters had died without paying their wages or who otherwise detained them. Such complaints were invariably directed to quarter sessions, and from there referred to two justices out of sessions. The law in the matter was not too complex and the hearing a matter of routine. This duty was, however, just one more task that fell to the justices out of sessions.

The enrollment of sales of land was the only administrative task of the justices that in effect devolved from the justices out of sessions to justices in quarter sessions! The Statute of Enrollments (27 Henry VIII, c. 16), intended to prevent the secret conveyance of land, required contracts of bargain and sale of freehold to be enrolled either at Westminster or before a justice and the clerk of the peace. Enrollment took scant time, and the great number of enrollments at Westminster meant that the justices were little troubled by this Tudor statute.[53] What is interesting is that at least as early as Elizabeth's reign the enrollments were increasingly made before a justice attending quarter sessions rather than at a justice's house. This reversal of the process of devolution of administration from quarter sessions to justices out of sessions was undoubtedly done in deference to the clerk of the peace. It did not grow out of any desire to ease the burden of out-of-sessions work on the benighted justice of the peace.

---

[52] 5 Elizabeth I, c. 4, consolidating act. Maximum wages for laborers, artificers, and servants were settled at Eas. QS. Most of the wage assessments for Somerset, 1604–1641, are extant in the SRO.

[53] The enrolled deeds in the SRO are amply calendared in *Somerset Enrolled Deeds, 1536–1655* (1936). There appears to have been only 49 enrolments, 1625–1640, though there were many more conveyances, enrolled at Westminster as the statute allowed.

The Tudor and Stuart statutes which transformed the justices of the peace into administrators as well as judges had one thing in common. They tended to place upon the justices out of sessions the main responsibility for county administration. The effective implementation of the statutes concerning poor law, bastardy, road and bridge repair, alehouses, masters and servants, and numerous other matters relied on the devotion to duty of one or more justices out of sessions. Even where statute decreed that the whole power of the bench be employed, the labor of enquiring and even of determining was readily delegated by quarter sessions to the justices out of sessions. Quarter sessions could have done nothing else. The Crown's concern with lawlessness, manifest in the multitude of new misdemeanors, ensured that quarter sessions would retain its traditional character of a court for the disposition of Crown cases. Save for the most minor misdemeanors, the criminal law rigidly required trial before the court of quarter sessions, and these trials monopolized the time of that court, limited as it was to a duration of three to four days, four times a year. Cases unheard could not be left to justices out of sessions. Administrative matters could be, and were. At the Epiphany 1630/1 quarter sessions—the last before the issue of the Book of Orders—fifty-nine miscreants were tried at the bar and sentenced by the bench. Of the thirty-three administrative orders of this same sessions, twenty-seven referred matters to or confirmed orders by, justices out of sessions. Only six orders had the hearing of the whole bench behind them and three of these were brief matters of course. Law and circumstances limited the duration of quarter sessions—but the time of justices out of sessions seemed infinite. It was on this false presumption that quarter sessions readily delegated its administrative functions to the justices out of sessions. It was on this false presumption that the Council would issue its Book of Orders in January 1630/1.

Emphasis on the declining role of quarter sessions in the administrative business of magistracy must not be allowed to obscure the preeminent place that this court still enjoyed in county administration. No seventeenth-century justice would have deprecated either the importance or the power of quarter sessions; he would have stood in no little awe of the former and in fear of the latter. Quarter sessions remained the essential body of the justices in action. It was the coordinating organ of the whole of the justices' work, legal and administrative, in quarter sessions and out of sessions. It alone possessed a sufficiently mature bureaucracy to support and give effect to the justices' orders and requirements. In most cases, quarter sessions had unquestionable authority to regulate its component members in the discharge of their duties out of sessions.

The court of quarter sessions was the traditional meeting of the justices for the discharge of the duties appointed them in their commission. The statute 12 Richard II, c. 10 (1388) was the consolidating act of the piecemeal legislation of four decades that had set the justices on the road to becoming administrators of the county, for it decreed that the justices should hold their sessions in every quarter of the year, there to enquire "diligently" of the local officers as to their execution of the Statutes of Labourers. This was the statutory sanction for the mixed judicial and administrative body which was the court of quarter sessions for exactly five centuries more. Likewise, both in its procedure and its composition, the court was long to retain its medieval flavor. The charge to the sessions read by the chairman, the receiving of presentments, the indictment and trial of criminals were firmly rooted in medieval practice. Indeed, the greatest changes in the two hundred and fifty years following the 1388 statute were not in the court's procedure or composition, but in its power and its responsibilities.

The 1388 statute had fixed the minimum length of quarter sessions at three days, and Somerset's sessions in this period were never less. In fact, the Epiphany sessions at Wells were, with but one exception, never less than four days; the Epiphany sessions of 1635/6, which lasted five days, being the longest. The calendars of prisoners at Epiphany sessions were usually longer and the administrative orders more numerous than for other sessions. There is no apparent explanation for this. No business was handled then that was not handled at other sessions. In any event, it is clear that Lambarde's criticism was not applicable to Somerset: "And yet in these daies of ours, wherein the affaires of the Sessions be exeedingly increased . . . many doe scantly afford them three whole houres. . . ."[54]

Four towns had the profits of accommodating the justices, sheriff's officers, constables, jurymen, litigants, barristers, attorneys, and hangers-on who attended quarter sessions. The Epiphany sessions were at Wells, where accommodation in inns appears to have been most satisfactory.

[54] Lambarde, p. 606.

Since the Wells sessions usually lasted four wintery days as against three milder days elsewhere, it was well that quarters were comfortable. Just the reverse was true of Ilchester's amenities. Justices who attended the Easter sessions there found few suitable hostels and a fetid town still showing signs of recent floods. The gaol town, the justices might well have echoed a description then current: "all Ilchester is gaol say prisoners there."[55] The midsummer sessions were held at Taunton, and the natural pleasantness of this prosperous town combined with summer provided no grounds for complaint. Bridgwater, the scene of the Michaelmas sessions, provided fair accommodation even if the town itself was unexceptional.

The attractiveness or unattractiveness of a sessions town undoubtedly had an effect on attendance of justices at quarter sessions. Generally, fewer justices attended at Ilchester and Bridgwater than at Taunton, and attendance was greatest at Wells. The figures of attendance are inexact despite a list of attending justices for each sessions in the order book; from signatures to some orders, justices (perhaps late arrivals) appear to have been present who are not listed as attending. There was nothing to compel the presence of a justice at sessions, and a few justices never attended. While the sessions towns formed a convenient quadrilateral in the center of the county, poor traveling conditions tended to discourage any but the most dutiful magistrate from attending the sessions furthest from his seat. (See map on p. 41.) The normally heavy attendance at Wells (as many as nineteen being present on two occasions) resulted from the regular attendance of the three ecclesiastical justices of Wells and the many justices who resided within a ten-mile radius of that city. Colds, gout, "extraordinary occasions," and trips to London account for the absence of many justices who were most conscientious in attendance—and afforded convenient excuses for those who were not.[56] By law, only two justices, one of them of the quorum, were necessary for a quarter sessions, and only eight were to be allowed the 4s a day stipend for expenses authorized by statute. However, the attendance from 1625–1638 was considerably higher, averaging twelve justices with never less than eight.[57] Only three sessions failed of the presence of at least one barrister-at-law on the bench, and at these three an experienced

[55] J. S. Cox, *Ilchester Gaol and House of Correction* (1949), p. 92.
[56] SRO, Sess Rolls, 58 pt. ii, no. 37; 67 pt. i, no. 80; 69 pt. ii, nos. 80, 94.
[57] Average attendances for the same period in Warwickshire were fourteen, *Warwickshire County Records*, I, xxvi.

justice attended who had taken the chair before in the absence of the chairman. Quarter sessions was never in danger of being unable to function properly for want of either numbers or talent.

With the exception of John Coventrye, the custos rotulorum was conspicuous by his absence from quarter sessions. There was no need for him to attend. Sessions could be held without him, and his statutory functions were executed by deputation: the chair was taken by a "deputy custos," and the preservation of the court's records was the duty of the clerk of the peace.[58] Sir James Ley of Beckington, later first Earl of Marlborough, an active magistrate when first appointed custos in 1615, relinquished the post in 1625 soon after his appointment as Lord Treasurer. Henry, his heir and successor as custos (until 1636), never attended sessions, and save on two known occasions performed no magisterial duties. For obscure reasons, probably not unconnected with his financial encouragement of his Beckington tenants' contemptuous refusal to move the parish's communion table into the sanctuary, he ceased to be custos in 1636.[59] He was succeeded by John Coventrye, second son of the Lord Keeper, who served until August 1641. Residing at Barton Grange near Taunton, he was indefatigable in out-of-sessions work and missed only two quarter sessions in this period.

The principal justice at Somerset's quarter sessions was not the custos, but his deputy. The deputy custos was chairman of the court. Even after the custos became locally resident and regularly attending in the person of Coventrye, the deputy custos retained the chairmanship. Since James' reign the pompous and waspish Hugh Pyne of Curry Mallett and Lincoln's Inn was deputy custos. He was removed at the instigation of John Poulett in 1626, having used the chair as a soapbox from which to attack royal policy. He gave in charge to the grand jury at the Easter sessions 1626 that the county rate to pay officers sent to instruct the militia was an extortion, and that they were to make presentment of it.[60] Though Poulett desired that the Duke of Buckingham promote Edward

[58] "Deputye custos" was used by Poulett in a letter to Nicholas (PRO, S.P.16/36, no. 46) in referring to the chairman of quarter sessions, and it will be used throughout this study. It must not be confused with the clerk's of the peace office; the clerk was the statutory deputy of the custos in the sense that he fulfilled the custos's responsibilities in keeping the court's records.

[59] *VCH Som*, II, 44. At Bath in 1630 Ley and Sir Ralph Hopton examined corn rioters— an affair with grave overtones and the most notable of the two occasions upon which Ley acted as a justice, SRO, Sess Rolls, 64 pt. ii, nos. 200–205.

[60] PRO, S.P.16/40, no. 58.

Tynte of Chelvey for the vacant chair, the custos's father (Lord Treasurer Marlborough) accomplished the appointment of his son-in-law, John Harington of Kelston and Lincoln's Inn.[61] Harington remained chairman into the Commonwealth; a comment both on his ability and his politics.

Harington retained the chair even after Coventrye became custos in 1636 because he was a barrister-at-law and an experienced presiding officer. Both Pyne and Tynte (Poulett's nominee for the office) were barristers and it would have been most unlikely that a nonbarrister would hold the office. The increasing bulk and growing complexity of the law demanded a more profound legal knowledge than a year at an Inn of Court could provide. There was in 37 Henry VIII, c. 1 statutory authority for the appointment of a barrister to exercise the custos's duties at quarter sessions. But experience was an even more valuable asset in a chairman than a bar call. At the nine sessions from which Harington was absent, either John Farwell or Robert Cuffe—neither of them barristers—took the chair, even though at six of these sessions a practising barrister was present. Cuffe and Farwell, justices of commanding prestige and high esteem among their brethren, had been active magistrates since at least 1613. By 1636, Harington was indisputably the most experienced justice. This and his legal qualification retained for him the chairmanship. Coventrye, neither a barrister nor an experienced justice, could have been chairman had he so desired. That might, however, have been a mistake.

At the commencement of quarter sessions the chairman read to the whole court, jurors and onlookers, the charge to the sessions. A tediously lengthy composition, it outlined those matters into which the grand jury was to enquire. The charge by a man of Harington's temperament—a theologian—began with a lengthy exhortation on sin and ended, probably two or three hours later, with the enunciation of the final offence that was to be presented.[62] Once the court got down to business, the chairman signed the sworn informations of the common informers,[63]

[61] PRO, S.P.16/36, no. 46, John Poulett to Edward Nicholas, 24 Sept. 1626. Poulett stated that Sir James Bagge (an obsequious place-seeker and unscrupulous protegé of Buckingham) recommended Tynte to the Duke, though obviously Poulett had initially suggested Tynte to Bagge.

[62] Harington's commonplace book (BM, Eger. MS 2711) contains draft texts for three charges delivered by Harington, c. 1640.

[63] Attestation of informers' oaths on informations and certificates of composition appears to have been done in most cases by the chairman at Somerset quarter sessions, and thus such attestation will usually indicate who was chairman in the absence of the deputy custos.

perhaps while the grand jury was deliberating. At the trial of criminals, he ruled on points of law, directed the jury, and rendered the judgment of the court. When the court turned to administrative affairs, the chairman assumed the role of speaker. The evident oratorical ability exhibited by some of the justices in Parliament doubtlessly needed curbing as much at quarter sessions as in St. Stephen's Chapel.[64] When sessions had ended, the chairman and the clerk sorted out the orders and arranged the record. Conscientious though he was, Harington must have been very happy to get back to Kelston. The ignorant might address their petitions to "the Judge" of the sessions,[65] but the chairman was very much *primus inter pares*. He was just another justice despite the custos's accolade. If quarter sessions was to function at all, the chairman had to possess extraordinary tact and masterfulness. Harington had both in good measure. Eschewing politics, his quiet dignity gave offence to no one. His immense learning and practical ability claimed the allegiance of his fellows. Harington more than any other single man sustained the routine of Somerset's magistracy when in the 1630s factionalism threatened to disrupt it. He accomplished this by his personality—not by his office.

Besides the chairman there were only three other magisterial officers of quarter sessions. They were the treasurers of the only two standing funds the county possessed. Appointed yearly, they were strictly accountable to two justices delegated to audit their accounts at the end of their terms. The two treasurers of hospitals (one for the fund for the eastern half of the county, the other for the western half) received and disbursed the "county stock," which has been described already. Between 1621 and 1630 these treasurers were, with but one exception, justices. The exception was a gentleman named William Combes. Combes was appointed treasurer for the eastern half in 1626—an experiment not wholly satisfactory as it took a year and a special audit to get in his account.[66] Nonetheless, after 1630 the exception became the rule, nine of the sixteen treasurers from 1630 through 1638 being gentlemen not in the commission then, or in most cases, later. A fleeting glimpse is caught of a "deputy treasurer" for the eastern division in 1635/6, but

[64] One petition was aptly addressed to Harington as the "chiefe speaker" of the sessions, SRO, Sess Rolls, 63 pt. iii, no. 11.
[65] SRO, Sess Rolls, 63 pt. ii, no. 66.
[66] SRO, Sess Rolls, 58 pt. i, no. 43; QSOB, 1627/8–1638, mids. QS 1628, no. 29. In James' reign, before 1621, quarter sessions regularly appointed annually one nonmagisterial treasurer, who soon afterwards was a justice—training purposes probably.

he was a temporary phenomenon. The treasurers for 1635 had been ordered to carry on an extra nine months so that the appointment of hospital treasurers might coincide with that of treasurers for the maimed-soldiers' fund at the Easter sessions.[67] The deputy treasurer appeared for a principal (a nonjustice treasurer) who had found one year of unremunerated labor enough. There was also a treasurer for the unitary maimed-soldiers' fund. This fund was to provide pensions for deserving and properly recommended veterans. The experiment of appointing a nonmagisterial treasurer here occurred only once, and the man appointed was a former justice of the peace.

The responsibilities of these three treasurers ended when they had received the money collected by the constables, disbursed it on the court's order, and reckoned up and submitted their accounts. As annually rotating offices, they were not particularly onerous. One thing, however, served to make them vexatious and an assignment to be avoided if possible. The funds the treasurers administered remained almost static while the demands upon them increased constantly. The "county stock," as we have noted, was often insolvent, never affluent. The maimed-soldiers' fund was larger, but demands on it were increasingly heavy, and its abundance invited the raiding and misapplication of its monies that characterized the justices' handling of their financial affairs. The general resistance to all forms of taxation in this period prevented any increase in the hospital funds and allowed no more than a slight increase in the maimed-soldiers' fund. The £50 rated on the county by midsummer sessions 1631 to swell the maimed-soldiers' fund was an easily detected subterfuge to provide the £50 annual salary of the universally unpopular muster master. When renewed, it raised a storm of protest.[68] Certainly, there are few things more frustrating to a treasurer than to preside over an insolvent fund, unable to pay to order and besieged by demands for payment anywhere up to ten years in arrear.

The pivotal figure in magistracy was the clerk of the peace. It is conceivable that quarter sessions could have functioned without a permanent chairman or treasurers. Without the clerk of the peace to undertake the onerous paperwork involved there would have been no quarter sessions and likely no magistracy by amateur country gentlemen. The clerk of

[67] SRO, QSOB, 1627/8–1638, Epiph. QS 1635/6, no. 18; mids. QS 1635, no. 1.

[68] SRO, QSOB, 1627/8–1638, mids. QS 1631, no. 2; Sess Rolls, 69 pt. ii, no. 99, Eas. QS 1633. The order's preamble plausibly though deceitfully cited the augmented number of maimed soldiers due to increased pressing.

the peace was both the chief channel and the chief instrument for co-ordination of the justices' work. This function became more important than ever before in a period when the work of quarter sessions rapidly devolved upon the justices out of sessions, and by this function alone the clerk amply justified his existence.

At least as old as quarter sessions itself, the clerk's of the peace office fulfilled a twofold service in seventeenth-century magistracy: the preservation of the quarter sessions' records and the drafting of indictments, processes, and other legal instruments. The former duty the clerk discharged as the deputy of the custos rotulorum, and the latter as the clerk to a court of law. In his capacity as the keeper of the records he produced the documents upon which a court of record depended and which, incidentally, make this study feasible. As a law clerk, he bore the primary responsibility for the easy functioning of a court meting out justice under a code of increasing complexity and fastidious formalism. He was both the memory of the court and its right hand too. If deficient in either capacity, his masters, the justices, were liable for his errors to the law and the King's government. It behoved them to choose wisely the man entrusted with this office.[69]

Throughout this period, the clerkship of the peace in Somerset was a joint office. The senior clerk was far less active in the office than the junior clerk, who did most of the work, though they divided the fees evenly. It should be noted that the junior clerk was not a deputy of the senior, and the senior clerkship was not yet a sinecure. All three of the men who held this joint office in the period were gentlemen, albeit of the lesser gentry, one (Edward Wykes, clerk c. 1611 to c. 1637) boasting "Esq." after his name. As such, they enjoyed the confidence and even the affectionate regard of their superiors of the bench, which made for an intimate sense of partnership among all engaged in the conduct of magistracy. All three were learned in the law, Mr. Wykes having been called to the bar by the Middle Temple, and Christopher Browne (joint-clerk c. 1612 to 1640s) and Matthew Hopkins (1638 onwards) apparently being attorneys. Browne, who bore the greatest burden of office throughout, impresses one who reads his scribbled marginal notes as a knowledgeable administrator of incisive mind, un-

[69] The clerk was appointed by and held office during the tenure of the custos. However, it was unlikely that the custos would appoint a clerk not acceptable to the whole bench. For a more detailed discussion of Somerset's clerical establishment in this period, see the author's *The Clerk of the Peace in Caroline Somerset* (1961).

usual ability, and singular devotion to duty. To a lesser or greater degree, he appears to have instilled these qualities into his assistants.

The clerk's staff was of considerable size—hardly a "scanty clerical staff" as Professor Holdsworth has termed it.[70] Besides the joint clerks, there was a deputy clerk of the peace, who not only served for the clerk in his occasional absences but supplemented him in his ordinary duties. Moreover, there were two to four attorneys who handled correspondence with the justices and doubtless rendered advisory service in court. Finally, there were no less than five others serving in a wholly clerical capacity who remain anonymous but whose hands become increasingly familiar as one goes deeper into the clerks' records. In the early 1630s (and probably at any time in the period) there might have been as many as six members of the clerks' staff, including the joint clerks, at a quarter sessions. Both in numbers and legal talent, the clerks and their staff were well equipped to serve the county's justices.

The same service that the clerk of the peace rendered to the justices as a whole, the clerk to a justice rendered his master in particular. The names of twenty-two of these somewhat elusive individuals can be discovered principally by handwriting comparison collated with letters over their signatures. Their names will not be found in registers of admissions to the Inns of Court, nor were they even attorneys. Nonetheless there can be no doubt that they knew all the law that pertained to their job. The justices' clerks appear to have been private secretaries handling their masters' private business, perhaps resident in their masters' houses. They were expected to attend quarter sessions whether their masters did or not in order to hand to the clerk of the peace the various documents produced by their principals between sessions. With the exception of letters written directly by the justices to the clerks of the peace, they handled the clerical work arising from out of sessions business including the drafting of examinations, certificates, recognizances, bastardy orders, and the accounting for financial affairs. This demanded an intelligence above the ordinary. In nearly every case, they served their masters—and ultimately, the county—dutifully and ably.

The clerk of the peace was the recipient of virtually every communication directed to the court's attention by individual justices, subordinate officers, and private persons. Since all such business passed through his hands

[70] Holdsworth, IV, 150. The Somerset sessions rolls have yielded an invaluable mass of evidence concerning the bureaucratic element in magistracy.

and before his eyes, he served the court as its chief informant. As clerk of the court he saw to it that the court's findings and orders were made of record and notified to interested parties. In this twofold service, the clerk of the peace through his associates at the lower level, the justices' clerks, knit together the whole of the county's administration centering on magistracy. A professional serving nonprofessionals, he saw local government in its total aspect, not only during sessions, but before and after as well. The travel of the clerk and his staff throughout the county between sessions about their own private business as attorneys, stewards of manors, etc., allowed the clerk an appraisal of between-sessions administration that the justices, working within the confines of their divisions, could not obtain. It was the clerk of the peace who bridged the rapidly widening gulf between the work of quarter sessions and the work done out of sessions.

The clerk of the peace, his staff, and the justices' clerks were the sole professional element in magistracy. While the correspondence amongst themselves seems preoccupied with fees and the justices appear to have been always solicitous of the clerks' financial interests, it was the money possible and the prestige inherent in these offices that built up a professional *esprit* conducive to a high measure of efficiency. Any of these offices were valuable; the holder's income and his prestige advanced with the volume of business he undertook. All of these clerkships were sought after, and the bench had its choice of the ablest men in the county to fill its secretariat. Throughout, the men chosen gave full service for their hire. The student who has wended his way through the clerks' records can only come away impressed with the efficiency and the purposefulness with which these men discharged their offices. Had not the offices been profitable, there is reason to believe that the impression would have been far different.

The contrast between the efficiency of the clerks which was the strength of magistracy with the inefficiency of the subordinate officers, which was its greatest weakness, is marked. The reason is not hard to find. The constables, tithingmen, and parish officers (churchwardens and overseers of the poor) were unpaid and unprofessional. They had no interest in an office forced upon them for one unpleasant year. The constables, many of them illiterate, were expected to produce careful accounts and remain on the right side of the very narrow line that separated legality from illegality. When they stepped over this line they found themselves in court for false arrest or unlawful distraint. If through a constable's negligence the putative father of an illegitimate child escaped, he maintained the child. If he omitted to arrest a wanted man, he forfeited 40s. If he withheld rate money collected, or failed to collect it, he might even find himself before the Privy Council. And if he did his duty assiduously he might well find himself maliciously sued, assaulted, or his house covered with excrement.[71] The calendar of nearly every quarter sessions contains a substantial list of constables fined for nonattendance and a few committed for negligence. Evildoers did not respect them because they were ignorant, timorous, and powerless; the justices did not respect them because they were lazy, disobedient, and negligent. The troubles and the shortcomings of the parish officers were the same in degree, only different in kind. Obstinacy in settling a pauper meant a summons to quarter sessions to answer their contempts. Careless disbursements of parish funds could mean a substantial sum out of pocket. Failure to render a proper accounting at the end of their term occasionally resulted in committal to gaol. The constables and tithingmen, churchwardens and overseers were the sole executors that the justices possessed with which to suppress lawlessness and administer the poor law. The constant oversight of these imperfect instruments only added to the justices' difficulties. In great part, the Council's intention in issuing the Book of Orders in 1630/1, was to obtain a greater measure of efficiency from these unpaid and unwilling subordinate officers. Their lordships hardly foresaw the magnitude of endeavor necessary to accomplish that worthwhile end.

This section opened with the warning that the importance of quarter sessions should not be undervalued. Despite the advent of definite petty sessions, this admonition is still valid for the period after 1630. The functions of quarter sessions in administrative matters, other than in the few cases where the court still chose to hear and determine the whole affair, can be broadly classified as coordinating and appelate. These two functions enabled quarter sessions to retain its grasp on magistracy and to circumscribe petty sessions when occasion required.

Coordination of all administrative actions of the justices, both in and out of sessions, was accomplished by the general order of quarter sessions. Sixteen such orders appear in the order book for the period 1625–1638.

[71] SRO, Sess Rolls, 64 pt. i, no. 9; 77 pt. ii, nos. 117–118. Devon assizes 1636/7 found a Devon hundred constable unfit for service because of illiteracy—he was not the only one, PRO, Asz.24/20, f. 142.

They were general in that they laid down a policy that was to be followed in all cases and not merely in a particular case then before the court; they were orders in that they were binding with the full force of the law on all justices and subordinate officers. Many of these orders were issued to give effect to a specific directive from the Privy Council. Thus, the two general orders of Epiphany sessions 1630/1 suppressing all unnecessary alehouses and allowing limited transportation of corn to Bristol were intended to implement the Council's letter of June and the proclamation of September 1630 for ameliorating the effects of the corn dearth.[72] The use of the general order to implement conciliar orders became more common in the 1630s. The ordinary and more humble use of the general order was to give effect to policies that the justices themselves initiated. General orders were promulgated requiring constables to account at least once a year to justices out of sessions, imposing a £50 annual rate increase for the maimed-soldiers' fund, and requiring divisional justices to enquire if pensioned veterans were yet living.[73] The rate increase could have been imposed only by quarter sessions; by the other two orders, the court required information to enable it to control better the administration of the county. It was by general order in 1625 that the court brought into action the county-wide machinery for the relief of plague-stricken Bridgwater and the containment of the infection.[74] This particular order was intended to coordinate the work of the local justices with the resources of the whole county. At the same time, it was an assertion of the sessions's control over justices out of sessions. The last general order recorded (Easter sessions 1638) recited that some had procured badger's licences from justices out of sessions and ordered that henceforth no licence was to be granted save in quarter sessions.[75] This was the strongest assertion of the court's power, and it was patently necessary.

Quite aside from the general order, quarter sessions by its very nature facilitated coordination. "The government of the counties was done very much by discussion,"[76] is a verity too easily obscured by the mass of written sessions material. Quarter sessions had no diarists, and what was

[72] SRO, QSOB, 1627/8–1638, Epiph. QS 1630/1, nos. 28, 33; PRO, P.C.2/40, pp. 25–26, PC to JPs, 13 June 1630; *Foedera,* XIX, 195, proclamation 28 Sept. 1630.
[73] SRO, QSOB, 1620/1–1627, Mich. QS 1626, no. 2; 1627/8–1638, mids. QS 1631, no. 2, and Mich. QS 1637, no. 8.
[74] SRO, QSOB, 1620/1–1627, mids. QS 1625, no. 16. See p. 60.
[75] SRO, QSOB, 1627/8–1638, Eas. QS 1638, no. 15.
[76] G. S. Thomson, *Lords Lieutenants in the Sixteenth Century* (1923), p. 78.

said there is almost completely lost. Yet, the occasional reference to a hearing in open court with counsel representing both sides to a dispute indicates a discussion which might well have helped to clarify principles as well as points of law in the justices' minds. The amount of formative debate behind each general order, concerning each letter from the Council, and over many of the certificates of examining justices out of sessions must have been considerable. It could not fail to have been influential in shaping the approach that individual justices out of sessions would take to like problems arising within their divisions. It was by this process, more than by the general order itself, that conciliar policy was broadcast throughout the county's government, and only by this process could expert information be traded among all the men engaged in that government. Nowhere save in quarter sessions was this very useful means of coordination possible.

In the readiness of quarter sessions to entertain appeals against orders made by the justices out of sessions reposed the greatest safeguard to the individual's right to a fair and exhaustive hearing, and the court's greatest weapon to control the justices out of sessions, to whom, perforce, it was required to delegate so much of its function. The system of appeal was crude and ill-defined. Appeals were possible only in bastardy and those cases where the finding and order of the justices out of sessions was on referral from the court. Where statute conferred the power of hearing and determining on justices out of sessions, the court was powerless to overturn their finding and could at most attempt persuasion. Since, however, so much of the hearing and determining the justices did out of sessions was done on referral from the court, provision for appeals against orders in these cases and in bastardy left very little of the justices' work that was not subject to an appeal to quarter sessions.

Appeals against bastardy orders made by two justices out of sessions have already been mentioned.[77] The justices in this period did not attempt to discourage such appeals. Paradoxically, one of the successful appeals was brought by the appellant at the instigation of the two justices who made the order that formed the basis of appeal.[78] The fact that most appeals were dismissed does not lead to the suspicion that the court

[77] See p. 61. Allowed by 18 Elizabeth I, c. 3.
[78] SRO, Sess Rolls, 71 pt. ii, no. 89. The two justices recited in the order that there were many reasons why the putative father might have been wrongly accused—but the parish had to be freed of the child's charge, SRO, QSOB, 1627/8–1638, Eas. QS 1634, no. 18; *Som Asz Ords*, nos. 99, 185.

4+

was intent on covering up mistakes or injustices done by the magistrates. Sufficient evidence remains to show that the court reached honest decisions on the evidence placed before it.

Virtually all referrals from the court that allowed justices out of sessions to make an order upon hearing concluded with an explicit clause requiring the parties to abide by the order "unless very good cause be shown to the contrary" at the following sessions. Other referrals implied as much. Appeals were brought particularly against orders settling paupers and orders fixing rates. As in bastardy most appeals were disallowed.

An appeal was ostensibly to be heard in open court, preferably with counsel present. There was, however, a growing tendency under the pressure of sessions business to re-refer the hearing of the appeal to the justice or justices who had acted in first instance. In one exceptional case, it was obviously done in the appellant's interests. One Doble had brought a bastardy appeal denying paternity, but on a technicality in law the judge at assizes had decided quarter sessions could not hear the appeal. That might well have ended it, save that sessions by re-referring it to the justices who had made the order to "reexamine" the matter conveniently got around the judge's prohibition.[79] Though Doble was not exonerated, at least justice had been done, and it had been seen to be done. In other cases of re-referring appeals to justices who had acted at first instance, there was an imminent danger to the cause of justice. Such treatment of appeals was an unfortunate selfabnegation on quarter sessions' part of one of the most potent weapons it possessed to control the growing power of the justices out of sessions.

The ultimate control of magistracy, then, still rested with quarter sessions. Despite the tendency of Tudor legislation to place responsibility for administration on the justices out of sessions, almost all petitions, complaints, and the other instruments requisite to initiate action were addressed to the traditional court. From this court emanated the authority to deal with matters so presented, and it retained the power to review the use made of that authority. The justices out of sessions worked as the servants of the court; they were still very far from being their own masters.

Local government saw no institutional development in the five centuries

---

[79] SRO, QSOB, 1627/8–1638, Eas. QS 1634, no. 19; Sess Rolls, 71 pt. ii, no. 96; 73 pt. ii, no. 58.

that intervened between the establishment of quarter sessions and the creation of county councils so important as the advent of petty sessions. Petty sessions could not be eclipsed by the county council, and they may yet outlive quarter sessions. In the three hundred years that have elapsed since they first essayed existence, petty sessions have grown in stature and usefulness until now they are, with the County Courts, one of the two maids-of-all-work in the nation's legal mansion. Their history has been one of vicissitudes, of expansion and contraction of power. Today, petty sessions are again under attack, though a hardy growth that has sustained internal strife, corruption, and professional jealousy will not easily succumb. Petty sessions are a truer representative of an ancient and traditional ideal of government than any other institution, central or local, that England now possesses—the judgment and punishment of the evildoer by his neighbors.

The advent of petty sessions occurred in the early 1630s, the result of a tendency in local government solidified into permanence by a demand from the central government. Here it will suffice to depict that tendency leaving the catalyst to its proper place in a later chapter.

The tendency was the concomitant of the increasing reliance on the justices out of sessions for the administration of the county. The mounting number of administrative matters delegated from quarter sessions required some areas of limited size from which referee-justices could be chosen to undertake a particular matter. From this requirement evolved those areas of increasing definition within which justices out of sessions discharged the burden of administration left to them by sessions. The boundaries of these areas (like most boundaries in the development of England's political landscape) followed familiar, even mapped, limits. In Somerset, the boundaries of the hundreds were found convenient, and a group of two to five hundreds (depending on size and irrespective of detached tithings in other hundreds) formed a magisterial division. Such divisions were found expedient in practice for the referee justices and the parties required to attend hearings. Two justices, in a finding upon a dispute between hundreds, put it succinctly: "hundreds be joyned together to make upp divisions and limitts for order and ease in government. . . ."[80]

It is likely that divisions in a rudimentary form were already in existence before the county's records commence in 1607. Cases referred

[80] SRO, Sess Rolls, 56 pt. i, no. 7, certificate of Sir Edward Rodney and Robert Hopton, Mich. QS 1626—a most statesmanlike document.

from quarter sessions immediately after this date went usually to two justices near the place concerned. The earliest demand by the government for the establishment of divisions had been 33 Henry VIII, c. 10, but this act was repealed in 1541. About that same time, however, the commissioners for subsidies—usually justices—began to act within divisions, which by this period were practically coterminous with the magisterial divisions. The Council revived the abortive Henrician statute almost verbatim in an order of 1586/7. The justices were to "devide them selves into sondry companies and take amongst them into ther chardg by severall divisions all the hundreds" for the execution of the Council's directions dealing with the corn scarcity of that year.[81] The scarcity plagued England throughout the 1590s, while these measures to combat it appear to have been shortlived and doubtless the divisions with them. The successful impetus for the creation of divisions had to come from the justices themselves and short bursts of activity at the Council's behest left no imprint unless the routine work of the justices required such divisions. By James I's reign the justices had probably realized the need for an orderly arrangement of magistrates to deal with the increasing amount of out-of-sessions work delegated by quarter sessions. A conciliar order of June 1605 came at an opportune moment. The judges of assize were ordered to make convenient divisions and assign justices to each so that "none be driven to travel above seven or eight miles" to attend meetings in the division.[82] These orders were not directed at any particular problem, but were for the "better preservation of his Majesty's subjects in peace, order, and obedience." The divisions as they first appear in 1631 fulfilled the requirements laid down in the 1605 order. (See map on p. 41.)

There was a growing awareness and increasing definition of magisterial divisions in the period from 1605 to 1630. Virtually all referrals to justices out of sessions were implicitly made on a divisional basis. Early in the reign of Charles I (though not before) most petitioners to quarter sessions prayed reference to two named divisional justices—an indication that referral from quarter sessions was a commonplace as well as an indication of a universal awareness of divisions. The first general order

[81] E. M. Leonard, *The Early History of English Poor Relief* (1900), pp. 319–326, draft of PC order 4 Jan. 1586/7 printed *in extenso*. There are no reports for Somerset extant in the State Papers Domestic.

[82] A. H. A. Hamilton, *Quarter Sessions from Queen Elizabeth to Queen Anne* (1878), p. 68, PC letter of June 1605 in the Exeter Record Office, printed *in extenso*.

of quarter sessions referring to justices "in their several divisions" occurred in 1616, and within ten years the mention of "justices of the division" in the records had become commonplace.[83] The definition of these divisions was spurred on by the Council's use of divisional justices in capacities other than as magistrates, especially as commissioners for the forced loan of 1626–1627. Without exception, these commissioners were justices and the returns extant are from groups of hundreds that corresponded exactly with the divisions as they can first clearly be seen in 1631. The Council's directions to implement the abortive privy seal loan of February 1627/8, addressed to the justices, ordered them as of course "to divide" and settle the business.[84] By 1631 at the latest the divisions were fully established as defined areas for the exercise of magisterial functions out of sessions. (See map on p. 41.)

The black boundaries of these divisions were not in fact so formidable as they appear on the map. It is a mistake to think of the divisions then as strict and settled jurisdictions of the justices, as they are today. Quarter sessions could and did refer cases to two justices of different divisions if more convenient for them and the parties concerned. Justices in one division were willing to grant a licence to keep an alehouse to a man in another division, occasionally with results injurious to good government.[85] Constables arraigned miscreants for examination before justices in other than the immediate division. As the commission of the peace empowered a justice to exercise his authority throughout the county, so it took no account of the *ad hoc* areas established by the justices for their own convenience. When the justices found it desirable to alter a division they did so without recourse to any higher authority; perhaps without even the sanction of quarter sessions. Sometime shortly before May 1634, the large division (no. 10 on the map) in the northeastern corner of the county was divided into two. No mention of this occurs in the sessions records, and only the reports of the justices as to the execution of the poor laws indicate it. Division no. 10 was unwieldy; three justices resided in the southern half and only one in the northern. Bifurcation was not possible until William Bassett of Claverton was added to the commission in November 1631, thus providing two justices for the northern half;

---

[83] SRO, QSOB, 1613–1620, Mich. QS 1616, no. 26, JPs in their "several divisions" to take order for levying the purveyance composition rate.

[84] *Acts PC*, 1627–1628, p. 284, PC to Lords Poulett and Ley, 12 Feb. 1627/8.

[85] SRO, QSOB, 1627/8–1638, Epiph. QS 1636/7, no. 14. A disorderly publican, suppressed the previous year by justices of one division was relicensed by justices of another.

Bassett and John Harington of Kelston became the justices in the new division. For other purposes, however, the two halves were joined again, four justices from both halves reporting to the Council in January 1634/5 as to the market spinners "in that division."[86] In the one division (no. 7) which throughout the period had only one justice, William Capell of Wrington was assisted by Sir Edward Rodney of Rodney Stoke, just across the line in division no. 11.

Divisions were the prerequisite of the growth of petty sessions, but the establishment of divisions did not in itself produce petty sessions. The 1605 order required the justices to meet in their divisions midtime between quarter sessions to enquire of crimes and see to the due execution of the poor law. Like all Jacobean attempts to spur the justices to increased activity, this one was shortlived in Somerset, though in Norfolk it apparently had commendable effects, petty sessions there appearing at least as early as 1607.[87] No ripple from this rock stirred the Somerset justices two years later when the county's records commence. The twenty-five years preceding the Book of Orders were years of routine activity on the justices' parts, broken only by an unsustained burst of endeavor during the corn scarcity of 1622–1623. Yet in these years, the justices out of sessions for their own convenience tended to meet at definite places to transact the business that quarter sessions referred to them. Division no. 9's justices found Pensford a central meeting place; those in division no. 10 for the same reason chose Frome. Such meetings were not petty sessions by any definition of the term. In that day, as in ours, a petty sessions was a regular meeting, fixed in time and place, to transact regularly appointed business. Referrals from quarter sessions were by their very nature extraordinary. A petty sessions, then as now, had an entity and a function distinct from that of quarter sessions. Referral from quarter sessions was the denial of such a separate existence, and no amount of examinations of felons or occasional meetings of justices to make a bastardy order, bind a few apprentices, or license a handful of alehouses could constitute such meetings petty sessions. The establishment of permanent petty sessions as a distinct institution with regular times and meetings could only be accomplished by a sustained force so strong that the

[86] PRO, S.P.16/268, no. 44, Harrington and Bassett, JPs, to PC, 20 May 1634; 282, no. 8, John Horner and 3 other JPs to PC, 24 Jan. 1634/5.

[87] Mr. A. Hassell Smith has called to my attention a number of references to Norfolk petty sessions at this time which he has found in the papers of Nathaniel Bacon in the Folger Library.

justices could never return to their former unevenness of out-of-sessions administration. For Somerset that force was the Book of Orders which the Council published and distributed to all the counties of England in January 1630/1.[88]

After 1630/1 the term "petty sessions" appeared in the mouth of justices and constables alike.[89] It was, and remained throughout the 1630s, the description of a monthly meeting of the justices attended by all the subordinate officers in the division, primarily to put in execution the laws for the relief of the poor. It hardly had any broader definition. However, as we shall see in Chapter VII, this meeting was convenient for so much other business of the justices that it passed into the realm of permanent local government institutions. This permanence justifies the historian in designating 1631 the birth year of petty sessions.

The vast mass of statutes which bore so heavily on the justices were executed by them on order of the Privy Council. The minuteness in detail of conciliar direction left very little room for the exercise of the justices' discretion and made reasonable the Council's demand for a strict accounting by the justices for their execution of the law. The implicit sanction behind every conciliar order was punishment by the Council, its satellite, Star Chamber, or the judges of assize. Under James I and during the first five years of Charles' reign, both the issuance of directions and the application of sanctions were spasmodic; the routine of the county's administration went on largely undisturbed save for occasional demands by the Council, particularly for the justices to raise extraparliamentary revenue. It was the 1630s that saw the implementation of Tudor legislation by conciliar direction and the severe reprimand of inefficient justices made almost as regular as the passage of time itself.

While the Council was the justices' master—and an increasingly strict master at that—it relied on them not only for the governance of the county but also for the extension of its power in the shire as occasion demanded and for the intelligence without which central government by any body is impossible. After 1630, these last two functions were enhanced as the Council took increased interest in all facets of county life.

[88] Mr. H. C. Johnson ascribes equal influence to the Book of Orders on the growth of petty sessions in Wilts., *Wiltshire County Records* (1945), p. xii.

[89] PRO, S.P. 16/220, no. 48, "At a pettie sessions at Castle-Carey," 10 July 1632; SRO, Sess Rolls, 77 pt. ii, no. 117.

The justices were a convenient and knowledgeable instrument for the extension of the Council's power into the county when extraordinary occasions required it. Matters which the justices at law or by virtue of their commission had no power to treat were referred to them by the Council. Disputes between private persons brought to the attention of the Council and in which the Council was vitally interested were easily assigned to the local justices for examination and certification to the Council. The odd seditionist, Roman priest, and defrauding attorney were readily examined by justices on the Council's order. In all, there were a score of such referrals from the Council. The most trivial and time-consuming was that to Bishop Pierce, Dr. Godwyn, and Sir Robert Phelips, JPs, to investigate the ghost of the late Mrs. Leakey of Minehead. Their twelve-page report (summarizing the examinations of a great many witnesses) concluded that there was no poltergeist but only an "imposture" framed for unknown ends.[90] At the particular time that poor Mrs. Leakey's "apparition" came to the Council's attention, Bishop Pierce was already deeply involved in settling disputes arising out of ship-money rating. Indeed, it was in the use made of the justices in the settlement of ship-money rating disputes on conciliar reference that the justices rendered greatest service to the Council. The Council bared its motives in using the justices as referees most concisely in the referral to Bishop Pierce of the Bruton hundred rating dispute: "Wee have thought good (in regard the truth of the allegacions may better appeare ... [at] the place where witnesses may be produced with lesse charge and trouble then heere) to ... [refer it to you.]"[91] This shows a commendable concern for the witnesses (and incidentally for the Council's time), but it placed yet another and particularly exacting burden on the justices of the peace.

As the justices were an arm of the Council in the county, so too they were ultimately its most useful eyes and ears there. The Council of the Stuarts, dealing with a greater volume of business, was less free than the Tudor Council to gain a firsthand knowledge of the impact of its policies on the life of the county. The difficulty was heightened in Somerset's case because no councillor had his seat in the county; there was no one who, like Burghley in Hertford at an earlier date, could feel the county's pulse. The function of the justices as informants was en-

<hr />

[90] PRO, S.P.16/383, no. 5, report of Bp Pierce, Godwyn, and Phelips to PC, 24 Feb. 1637/8.

[91] PRO, S.P.16/357, no. 5, and P.C.2/47, p. 436, PC to Bp Pierce, 21 May 1637.

hanced after Charles sent home his last stormy Parliament in 1629, thus denying his government its most convenient source of intelligence. Perhaps never before was intelligence so crucial as it was to be in the eleven years that King and Council set afoot experiment after experiment in domestic affairs, experiments not likely to be popular in the country.

The nexus of communication between the local governors and the Council was tenuous. Save where a messenger of the Chamber was sent down by the Council, usually with a warrant for arrest, the Council employed the common post. Crewkerne, in the southernmost salient of Somerset, was an important post station on the main road to the West. The post was notoriously inefficient and slow, and under the stress of increased conciliar activity in 1640, it went completely awry, disrupting preparations by the county's deputy lieutenants for sending troops northwards.[92] The local governors in communicating with the Council found it convenient to entrust one of their own number or another gentleman of repute (such as the muster master) who happened to be going to London to carry up urgent and important messages.[93] The system after 1631 by which the monthly reports of the justices as to the execution of the poor law were given to the sheriff, who in turn handed them to the judge at assizes, was slow but at least sure. Even when the post operated efficiently, letters were often delayed indefinitely between the time they reached the recipient and the time they were made generally known to the justices or deputy lieutenants. Only once did the Council send a number of letters to different justices. Usually, a single letter addressed to the "justices of the peace for the county of Somerset" was sent to a particular justice well known to the Council who was to inform the others.[94] Regardless of a letter's urgency, it might well have sat on a magnate's table two months before finally being passed around at quarter sessions. Letters to the deputy lieutenants were circulated more rapidly, the receiving deputy endorsing the letter with his name and the date and passing it on to the next deputy who did the same. A characteristic note of despair at the post's slowness also conveys the urgency of lieutenancy communications: Pembroke and Montgomery endorsed on the muster orders for 1631 readdressed to his Somerset deputies, "hast, hast, post

[92] PRO, S.P.16/459, no. 7, Wrothe, Luttrell, and Symes, DLs, to Lds Lts of Somerset, 1 July 1640.
[93] PRO, S.P.16/40, no. 30; 16/53, no. 88; 16/525, no. 33; 16/526, no. 5; 16/528, no. 8.
[94] The same was true of letters to the deputy lieutenants, SRO, Phelips MSS, vol. A, f. 97.

4*

hast."[95] Such a vague address as the justices "nearest to Mells"[96] might have resulted in a strayed letter. Though the logical addressee of a letter to the justices was the clerk of the peace, only once was the clerk addressed directly and the matter had to do solely with him. If the Council had addressed its letters to the clerk of the peace, the whole process of communication would have been accelerated and made considerably more certain. There can be no doubt that many of the difficulties of administration in this era, when rapid communication was more than ever essential, arose from the delay of letters in reaching their proper recipients.

For a brief period in the previous reign, the justices had appointed annually two of their number to answer all letters from the Council. This worthwhile experiment was begun in 1610, abandoned by 1614, taken up again in 1618, and finally dropped by 1623.[97] Afterwards, individual justices most interested in the matter at hand answered the letters. This was a poor substitute for the regular committee of correspondence which, regardless of the magnitude of its task, had brought some semblance of regularity into the dealings of the justices with the Council.

Did the Council really know what was going on in the county? In the case of the routine administration undertaken by the justices and the deputy lieutenants, the answer is an unqualified "yes." In so far as the Council or any committee or member of it were interested, the information was readily available from the judges of assize and in the generally frank answers of the magistrates themselves to letters from the Council. The monthly reports by the justices as to the execution of the poor law commencing in 1631, with the corollary of increased surveillance by the judges, meant that the Council was better informed as to the routine administration of the justices than at any time in the preceding thirty years.

But in matters that were of greatest import to the Council—the political state of the county, the reaction of the county to governmental policy—the answer to this question depended on the reliability of the informant and the Council's evaluation of the information received.

While the formal reports of the justices and deputy lieutenants might honestly state the number of apprentices bound and a bit less candidly, the conditions of the trained bands' weapons, any general views as to

[95] SRO, Hippisley MSS, PC letter, 31 May 1631, dorse.
[96] PRO, P.C. 2/50, p. 402, PC to JPs "nearest to Mells," 31 May 1639.
[97] SRO, QSOB, 1620/1–1627, Epiph. QS 1620/1, no. 1.

the state of the county were all too similar to the curt "omnia bene" of a hundred jury presentment. The judges of assize were shrewd men and what they saw and heard was valuable. They were never, though, resident in the county, and their sojourn there was limited to three days on two formal occasions a year. Their usefulness as informants suffered accordingly. For the whole truth, the Council had to rely primarily on the information that came to its individual members and the clerk of the Council from informal sources within the county itself. Secretary Conway's private secretary, George Rawdon, appears to have tapped a valuable source of information in one Francis Egiock, a man about whom little is known other than that he lived in Somerset.[98] Doubtless, it was Endymion Porter, a gentleman of the King's bedchamber, who passed on to the clerk of the Council the letters that a servant of his named Richard Harvey received from a brother in Taunton during 1638. Recusancy and other affairs in Somerset of interest to the Council loomed large in these otherwise purely private letters.[99] Such humble men as Egiock and Harvey were useful, but their information was not based on a thorough and profound knowledge of affairs. Only the local governors could approach omniscience. Although no evidence is available, it may be assumed that those justices of Somerset who were also actively engaged in the royal service in London upon occasion enlightened members of the government with the happenings in the county. Sir Edward Powell, Bart., a master of Requests, evidently attended the King at Greenwich in 1631, as a referral to the bench of the King's wishes concerning a maimed soldier's pension was through him.[100] Serjeant Thomas Mallett, solicitor-general to the Queen, was as active in magistracy as his official duties and legal practice allowed, and it is unfortunate that there is no record of conversations that might well have taken place between him and individual councillors.

None of these scraps of information can compare with the voluminous correspondence that Lord Poulett carried on throughout the period with Edward Nicholas, intensively for a few years with Secretary Lord Dorchester, and sporadically with Secretary Lord Conway. Even though this correspondence is magnified in importance by its inclusion in the State Papers, it was undoubtedly the chief source of the government's knowledge of Somerset affairs. Conway, Dorchester, and especially Nicholas

[98] PRO, S.P.16/316, no. 78, Francis Egiock to George Rawdon [20 March 1635/6].
[99] PRO, S.P.16/387–390, 1638.
[100] SRO, Sess Rolls, 78, nos. 26–27.

(holder of various clerkships at Whitehall) were the three men in the government who were most directly concerned with county affairs during this period. They served Poulett as friends at Court, and he served them as informant. Poulett regularly apprised his correspondents of the state of the county. His detailed letters treating Somerset's reaction to extraparliamentary financial exactions, the enforcement of the Book of Orders, and other concerns, afforded the Council a measure of the impact of these programs on county life and the local governors. At the same time, they also misled the Council. Poulett's single overriding motive in penning these letters was to embarrass his opponent, Sir Robert Phelips. Any fault that could be found with Phelips was inordinately stressed, any disquiet in the county traced to him. Poulett might not have been far wrong on occasion, but since he was the most constant informant of the Council the picture he painted, no matter how lurid, could not easily have been corrected by other information. This was a dangerous kind of intelligence for a government to rely upon.

Nor was the Council over critical of the information that came to it. It had the human failing of hearing what it wanted to hear and believing what it wanted to believe—a perilous practice for individuals, a calamitous one for governments. There was no better example of this than the Council's and particularly Laud's conduct in the churchales affair of 1633. Laud preferred the opinion of three justices who for their own political advantage professed the "King's interest" and attested to the desirability of these revels to the vehement objection to them of the Lord Chief Justice and over one-half of the county bench.[101] The reissue of the Book of Sports was the result. The Book and the punishment of puritan clergy who would not read it to their congregations probably did more to outrage puritan sensibilities and turn Somerset against Laud, Pierce, and the whole ecclesiastical establishment than any other single act of the King and his advisers. The Council was too ready to listen to those who professed the "King's interest" and too willing to forget the personal motives that actuated them. It was too ready to discount information it did not wish to hear and ascribe ulterior motives to those who advanced it. The Council, limited in the sources of its intelligence, increased its difficulties by not critically evaluating the sources it possessed.

[101] Sir Robert Phelips and his adherents favored churchales in opposition to Richardson, CJKB, and 25 justices including Poulett, Sir Ralph Hopton, and Sir John Stawell, T. G Barnes, "County Politics and a Puritan Cause Célèbre: Somerset Churchales 1633," *Trans RHS* (1959), 5th series, IX, 103–122.

It knew little of what the county thought; when it did, it would not heed what it had seen and heard.

It is difficult to imagine county government by local gentlemen without the judges of assize. The local governors were subject to all the limitations that beset an authority with insufficient power tied to too small an area of activity. The Council was a central organ with ample power, but equally circumscribed in depth of treatment by too large an area of activity. The gap was bridged by the learned judges who twice a year carried the power of the King and his Council to the local governors. With the judges came the orders of the government, instruction in law and governance, and full power to call the justices to account for their administration. The judges were not only the instruments of the law; they were also the King's stewards, overseeing the governance of his realm.

The judges rode their circuits in the Lent and Trinity vacations by virtue of four commissions issued under the great seal before each assize.[102] Two judges were named in the commissions which authorized them to hear and determine all criminal cases, and to hear those civil cases commenced before the common-law courts at Westminster and delegated to them under *nisi prius*. Only the judges could deliver the county gaol by proclamation. Usually the judges were judges of the three common law courts, though a King's serjeant-at-law might be put in commission.[103] The judges for the Western Circuit had the counties of Hampshire, Dorset, Devon, Cornwall, Wiltshire, and Somerset committed to their care. The winter assizes for Somerset were held almost without variation at Chard; the summer assizes at Taunton, occasionally at Bath. The justices of the peace were required to attend assizes, and they as well as the subordinate officers could be fined for absence. The clerk of the peace was also present to hand in the record of those cases remanded from quarter sessions to assizes, and the justices presented the examinations of the suspected felons they had bound to assizes for trial. Once the ceremonial opening was completed, the charge was read to the whole court by one of the judges. Following the division of the court into the

---

[102] Commissions of oyer and terminer and of gaol delivery, patents of assize and of association, PRO, Index 4211–4213 and C.181. The judges, also on the commission of the peace, very occasionally acted as justices out of sessions.

[103] Sir Robert Heath, a King's serjeant-at-law, judge on the Western Circuit, winter 1637/8 and summer 1638 assizes, had been CJCP until removed in 1634, perhaps (?) for suspected sympathy with the puritan faction.

Crown side (one judge hearing criminal cases) and the *nisi prius* side (the other judge hearing civil cases) the real work of assizes began. Sometime during the criminal proceedings the Crown side judge turned to the administrative business of the court. It was this function that brought assizes into the closest relationship with the justices of the peace.[104]

Essentially, the whole of assizes was directed at supervision of the justices of the peace. The charge of the judges was an important means by which the Council communicated its demands to the justices and alerted them as to the provisions of new legislation. The charge had been delivered to the judges by the Lord Keeper before their departure from Westminster. By its tone it could convey the Council's greatest displeasure. Having behind it the forcefulness and dignity of the judge who delivered it, the charge could be an effective condemnation of the justices' shortcomings, a public pillorying of misfeasance before the eyes of the justices' inferior countrymen. It was also a powerful vehicle of propaganda acting through both the justices and the multitude attending assizes. Lord Keeper Coventrye's charge before the summer assizes 1635 heralded the issue of the second writ of ship money, the first to impose the tax throughout the whole kingdom.[105]

Supervision of the justices was at the heart of the judges' entertainment of appeals against quarter sessions' administrative orders. There were not a great many such appeals, and they appear without exception to have been dismissed. Still, the appeals served as a constant reminder to the justices that they were strictly accountable at law for the exercise of their authority. The justices turned to the judges for advice on difficult points of law, especially in pauper settlement and bastardy. The justices' readiness to call upon the judge "to whose better opinion in poynt of lawe we humbly referr the consideracion thereof" was more than modesty.[106] The knowledge of the judges—at the justices' as well as an appellant's disposal —was a welcome increment to that provided by justices learned in the law. If nothing else, the presence of the justices at assizes afforded them some instruction in legal procedure. All this worked to make magistracy both more efficient and more just.

[104] I have treated this relationship in considerable detail in the introduction to *Som Asz Ords*, pp. ix–xxxvi.

[105] *Historical Collections* (1721), II, 294–298. See *Som Asz Ords*, nos. 180–182 for three charges, 1620, 1630/1, and 1632/3, and T. G. Barnes, "A Charge to the Judges of Assize, 1627/8," *Huntington Library Quarterly* (1961), XXIV.

[106] SRO, Sess Rolls, 58 pt. ii, no. 21, Epiph. QS 1626/7.

It is a mistake to look too closely for exclusive powers exercised by the judges in county government. The law of seventeenth-century England was little troubled by any other jurisdictions than those of area; two or more courts might exercise concurrent jurisdiction over the same case, applying the same law. This was true of the judges and the justices in the administration of the county. The assize order book is almost indistinguishable from its counterpart at quarter sessions. The same variety of matters, the same remedies were the common property of both courts. None the less, assizes had a definite role to play in county government besides the supervision of the justices. Where the power of the justices could not by law or did not in practice extend, the judges filled the hiatus. In so doing, the judges were less the justices' masters and more their senior partners.

The fact that the commission of the peace allowed for the exercise of its power only within the confines of a single county necessitated the judges' authority to extend that power to other counties. Difficulties occasionally arose in the repair of intercounty bridges and in settlement of paupers and illegitimate children between parishes in two counties. Where the justices of the two counties could not iron out the difficulties, the judges were called upon to make final and binding end. Their commission knew virtually no limitations of area. The power they enjoyed could be delegated to the justices however. In a dispute between a Somerset and a Gloucestershire parish concerning the settlement of a pauper, assizes ordered the next Somerset quarter sessions to hear and determine the affair after first giving notice to the Gloucestershire parishioners to attend. The final order in this case was a quarter-sessions order—not an assize order.[107] The jurisdictional limitations of area, that seem to have been nearly insurmountable until very recent times, were easily overcome by the power of the judges reinforcing and extending that of the justices.

There was a yet more subtle limitation to the justices' power with which only the judges could cope. The justices were local gentlemen, and as we have noted, the meanest husbandmen were wont to insult, abuse, and contemn some of them.[108] The King's commission enhanced the squire's authority, but it did not in itself make him respected among the common folk of the county. What was true of the single justice at the

---

[107] For assizes's referral to QS, see *Som Asz Ords*, no. 97; for the quarter sessions order, see SRO, QSOB, 1627/8–1638, Mich. QS 1636, no. 4.

[108] See pp. 29, 94 n. 109.

parish level was to a lesser extent true of the whole bench of justices at
the county level. Quarter sessions was always ready to bind a refractory
party to assizes and the awe-inspiring presence of his lordship there must
have operated as a strong deterrent to those who would emulate the
accused. The judge's greater power was not a product solely of the law
but a result of his status and his personality as well. It was the practice of
quarter sessions to make full use of that greater power and forcefulness
in those cases where the bench felt it might be required. Rating, always
the source of difficulty, was often left to the judges to order, and there
were rates made by the sessions or justices out of sessions that were
confirmed by assizes.[109] It was intelligent practice to have an order confirmed by the greater court. Enrollment in the assize order book gave it
binding authority on all future quarter sessions and certainly no little
persuasive authority for judges at future assizes. Those who would contemn such an order did so at grave peril.

In some administrative matters, the judges and the justices acted as
coequal partners. Occasionally an assize order of unusual importance and
general in nature was made with the justices of the peace "present and
consenting."[110] Such an order had behind it the full authority of both
the commissions of assize and the commission of the peace. It gave the
justices a stake in the order's enforcement while serving notice on the
county that the judges and justices were in full agreement, distinct advantages over an order made merely by one court or the other.

It is difficult to imagine local government by the gentlemen-magistrates
without the judges of assize, it is impossible to imagine assizes without
the gentlemen-magistrates. Not only was the *raison d'être* of assizes the
supervision of the justices' governance; the administrative work undertaken by assizes reposed ultimately on the justices. It is no exaggeration
to say that assizes bore very much the same relation to the justices out
of sessions as did quarter sessions. The justices were required to attend
both and to examine criminals preparatory to committal for trial to either.
Assizes, like quarter sessions, were limited in duration in an era of

[109] For example, assizes confirmed a poor rate made by Robert Henley and James Rosse,
JPs, and ordered one Knight (who had apparently contemned the justices and their rate)
to make a public submission to the two justices at the next quarter sessions, *Som Asz Ords*,
no. 154. Henley and Rosse had their troubles!
[110] Such was the rate on the whole county to reimburse Minehead's constables who had
deported Irish vagrants—an unprecedented rate, justified only by royal proclamation and
the judges' sanction, *Som Asz Ords*, no. 3.

increasing business and responsibility.[111] Therefore, assizes like quarter sessions delegated the hearing of most cases of an administrative nature to the justices out of sessions. Besides matters of bridge and road repair, bastardy and pauper settlement, apprenticeship, and rating disputes so commonly referred by assizes as well as by sessions, the judges imposed an added burden in appointing the justices mediators in civil disputes brought to the court's attention by petition or suit. The full weight of assizes on the justices out of sessions is apparent when one remarks that of the one hundred and sixty-six Somerset orders in the 1629–1640 assize order book, exactly ninety-nine involved the justices out of sessions in some considerable labor. To the justices of the peace, assizes were just two more "quarter sessions" a year, presided over by a more exacting and infinitely more fearsome "chairman."

The court of King's Bench exercised a jurisdiction superior to both quarter sessions and assizes. By writ of *certiorari* it could call up the record of any inferior court for review in the King's Bench or elsewhere by its direction. In practice, Somerset's justices (and judges of assize for that matter) were little troubled by King's Bench; there was an average of less than two writs a year directed to the justices of the peace for the removal of indictments, presentments, and very occasionally, convictions before them. Two-thirds of the total were for the record of rather serious misdemeanors involving or likely to involve a breach of the peace (riot, forcible entry, assault, barratry, etc.), and the rest were concerned with the most petty contraventions of statutes such as selling ale under measure, erecting cottages with less than four acres attached, and ill-order in tippling houses. It is fairly evident that most of these writs of *certiorari* were secured without sound basis in law by the defendants involved in order to avoid or to mitigate punishment. One, however, for the record of conviction of a couple who had insulted a vicar, was doubtless connected with the concurrent prosecution of the same vicar, Anthony Erbury of Weston Zoyland, in the High Commission.[112] The paucity of writs of *certiorari* issued by King's Bench and the circumstances

---

[111] Ld Kpr Coventrye exhorted the judges to spend most time on business concerning the public good as assizes were "very short and expireth in a few days," *Historical Collections,* II, 294.

[112] PRO, K.B.9/806/386–387. Not all writs of *certiorari* and records returned thereon are extant in this series. Removal of indictments to avoid conviction was an open scandal which King's Bench (Mich. 1639) attempted to stop by enforcing the statutory requirement that he who secured a *certiorari* enter bond either to traverse the indictment in King's Bench or have it quashed there for defect, *March's Reports* (1675), p. 76.

surrounding the issuance of most of them indicate that the supervision of the justices in their judicial as well as in their administrative function was almost exclusively the responsibility of the judges of assize.

On balance magistracy was ill-prepared for the onslaught of the Book of Orders in January 1630/1. To its advantage, the institution had evolved the machinery for out-of-sessions work and the technique to use it. The growth of divisions and the increasing tendency of the divisional justices to handle out-of-sessions tasks at certain places provided an organizational foundation onto which the duties required by the Book could slip readily without commotion or the impetuous creation of a novel structure. The referral of sessions business to the justices in their divisions, ordinary procedure by 1630, educated the justices in divisional work and psychologically prepared them to undertake added responsibility in groups of two or three. To its advantage, too, was the development of a capable and diligent professional clerical staff; the justices' own clerks were likewise prepared to undertake the added clerical work which was the concomitant of the January orders. The clerks' function as coordinators of the whole work of the justices would prove of inestimable value in the 1630s.

Against these advantages must be ranged overwhelming disadvantages. First and foremost was local government's congenital weakness: the ultimate reliance of the justices on the unprofessional and unwilling subordinate officers for the execution of any program. With tools so feeble as the constables and parochial officers, administrative efficiency was exceedingly difficult to obtain. The justices' efforts to secure efficiency from those tools meant added labor, often in vain. Yet the greatest disadvantage of all lay in the fact that the justices were already amply burdened by the accretion of Tudor enactments and the imposition of many other duties by their Stuart masters. Tudor legislation, pressing upon the justices both in their judicial and their administrative capacities, had already shifted the heaviest mass of administration from the traditional court of quarter sessions to the individual justices out of sessions. Added to this were the exacting tasks which resulted from the Council's readiness to use the justices as its arm and ears in the county and the very weighty duties that stemmed from the nearly complete dependence of the judges of assizes on the divisional justices for the handling of assizes's administrative business.

There could be no mistaking the quickening effect of Charles' accession on the county's government. Despite the growing breach between king and nation, the first five years of the new reign were years of faster tempo and crisper efficiency—in marked contrast to the less vigorous governance of the county under James I.

But the fact was that by 1630 the justices were already working at very near their maximum capacity, unless they were to become full-time servants of the state.

Chapter IV ⋊⋉ *Lieutenancy*

The office of the lord lieutenant was wholly a Tudor creation. Tudor concern for the preservation of internal order and Elizabethan embroilment in endemic war with Spain demanded an efficient instrument in the counties for the containment of rebellion and the defence of the realm. Elizabeth established, finally, the lord lieutenant as that instrument. At first more intimately connected with the central government than the sheriff had ever been, the lord lieutenant possessed infinitely greater power than could be bestowed safely upon commissioners for musters. As the commissioners for musters had superseded the sheriff as the military commandant within the county, so the lord lieutenant superseded the commissioners for musters. By the time of the accession of Charles I, the lord lieutenant had attained a position of permanent preeminence in county government that he has retained in form though not in substance to this day.

Internal security had become a reality by 1625, and it was no longer the dominant theme in the institution of lieutenancy. But the peace of two decades was already at an end when Charles succeeded his pacifist father. The next sixteen years were a time of alarums and excursions, threats of invasion, real and supposed. The defence of the kingdom through the agency of the counties received new emphasis, at times equal in intensity to that when the Armada came, far surpassing the years of the Armada in its prolongation for over a decade and a half. The full weight of this emphasis fell on the institution of lieutenancy, still young and immature, foredoomed to perpetual weakness. The terrible climax came at the end of this period, when the Scots' invasion put lieutenancy to the test.

This chapter will depict the institution of lieutenancy, its personnel, functions, organization, and its weaknesses. The history of lieutenancy in Somerset in those sixteen years, the toll that a demanding King and

Council and lieutenancy's own inherent weaknesses took on its personnel and the whole fabric of local government, will be left to later chapters.

The lord lieutenant was intended to be truly the King's personal representative in the shire. The creation of a lord lieutenant was the considered, individual act of a monarch who, especially after 1628, assumed a dominant role in the activities of government. The lords lieutenants were chosen usually from among the small group of noblemen who were also members of the Privy Council. Thus, the preamble to the commission of lieutenancy, though common to most commissions, possessed real meaningfulness: "Knowe yee that for the greate and singuler truste and confidence wee have in your approved fidelitye, wisedome, and circumspeccion . . . [etc.]."[1]

The commission issued from Chancery under the great seal. It named the lord lieutenant, outlined his jurisdiction, charged him to muster the county's forces and lead them against invaders and rebels (both within the county and without), gave him authority to execute martial law and appoint provost marshals, and required him to appoint deputy lieutenants who were to act in his absence. All other officers were commanded to aid and assist him and his deputies. He held office at the King's pleasure or until the King's death terminated the commission. Many lords lieutenants had more than one county committed to their charge, and commissions of joint lieutenancy were not uncommon.

Four men served as lord lieutenant of Somerset in this period. The first, William Herbert, third Earl of Pembroke, Lord High Steward, was lieutenant of Somerset, Wiltshire, and Cornwall from 1621 until his death in 1630. His younger brother, Philip, Earl of Montgomery, succeeded him as fourth Earl of Pembroke and as lieutenant of Somerset, Wiltshire and Cornwall, retaining as well his own lieutenancies of Kent and Bristol. In 1639, William Seymour, second Earl of Hertford, was joined with the Earl of Pembroke and Montgomery as lieutenant of Somerset and Bristol. This was probably occasioned by the appointment

[1] PRO, C.66/2583, dorse, no. 3, commission of lieutenancy to Philip 4th Earl of Pembroke and Earl of Montgomery, tested 12 Aug. 1630. The three other commissions of lieutenancy for Somerset in this period are also enrolled on the dorse of the patent rolls: 9 May 1625, renewal commission to William 3rd Earl of Pembroke; 26 March 1639, commission to Philip 4th Earl of Pembroke and Earl of Montgomery jointly with William 2nd Earl of Hertford; 30 July 1640, commission to William 2nd Earl of Hertford jointly with Philip Lord Herbert. The warrant to the Lord Keeper for a commission of lieutenancy to be drafted and to pass the great seal was always *per ipsum Regem*.

of Pembroke and Montgomery as captain-general of a regiment of horse composed of royal retainers which was to be the King's personal body-guard on his expedition to the North.[2] In the senior lieutenant's absence, Hertford would be able to prepare the county's forces for service against the Scots. In the next year, Pembroke and Montgomery relinquished entirely his lieutenancies of Somerset and Bristol, his fourth son and heir, Philip Lord Herbert, joining the Earl of Hertford in a commission issued 30 July 1640. It was precisely at this time that Pembroke and Montgomery had begun to feel the cold wind of royal suspicion that later drove him into the arms of the Parliamentarians. However, too much political significance must not be attached to his withdrawal from these counties' lieutenancies in the summer of 1640. He remained Lord Chamberlain, an active (if not completely trusted) privy councillor, and lieutenant of Kent, Wiltshire, and Cornwall. Although suspect, he was not yet out of grace. Moreover, his withdrawal appears to have been his own choice. The summer of 1640 was a season of political intrigue in both Court and country, and the Earl was in the thick of it at both levels. While his multiple lieutenancies afforded this foremost of parlia-mentary manipulators a ready influence in a number of counties with which to lever his supporters into Commons, they were also (almost for the first time) a considerable responsibility at a moment when the militia was being sent *en masse* to war. It is not insignificant that the two lieutenancies that Pembroke and Montgomery abandoned on the eve of the Long Parliament were in two counties where neither he nor his predecessor (the third Earl of Pembroke) had been able to exert much if any influence in past elections.[3] Too, Lord Philip, who saw eye to eye with his father, could be counted on to preserve any interests that the Herberts had in Somerset and Bristol.

It is difficult to believe that a Herbert or any other lord lieutenant undertook his office primarily from sentiments of *noblesse oblige* or a deep-rooted concern to fulfill his oath as a privy councillor. His object was largely power. There could be no doubt of the power of a great peer in his own county, but the extension of his influence outside his county

---

[2] PRO, S.P.16/414. no. 155, King to Pembroke and Montgomery (draft) [20 March?] 1638/9. Philip Earl of Montgomery was styled Earl of Pembroke and Montgomery after succeeding to William's earldom of Pembroke.

[3] Miss Rowe did not uncover any indication of Herbert influence in Somerset elections, "The Influence of the Earls of Pembroke on Parliamentary Elections, 1625–1641," *EHR* (1935), L, 242–256. It was unlikely that there was any, for the county's seats were largely in the hands of the county's magnates.

was most conveniently effected through the office of lord lieutenant. Somerset, large, populous, and prosperous though it was, possessed no resident peer of Privy Council rank after 1629. Henry Ley, second Earl of Marlborough, was a litigious squire who found London and Wiltshire most to his liking, but possessed none of the qualities that had made his father a trusted councillor. John Lord Poulett was too newly-risen a star, of little value to the government save in the county. Besides, the Herbert standard had already been placed firmly on Somerset's soil, and no Herbert could forego even the slightest possibility of gaining some of the county's sixteen seats in a forthcoming Parliament, provided always that the office did not interfere with the more important tasks around Court in which both Earls of Pembroke were engaged. This assured that Somerset's lord lieutenant throughout the period would be a nonresident nobleman seated at Wilton House in Wiltshire. Even when Pembroke and Montgomery relinquished the office in 1640, leaving his son as caretaker of the Herbert interest, the senior lieutenant was a Seymour who took up once again that family's traditional influence in Somerset, exercised as late as James' reign by Edward Seymour, Earl of Hertford, lord lieutenant of Somerset.

Whether resident or not, the role that the lord lieutenant played in county government was primarily supervisory. As a privy councillor, his days were full with matters of state. The intimate control of a county's lieutenancy by councillor-lieutenants, which was a marked feature of the institution at its inception, was wanting in Charles' reign,[4] due perhaps to the increased magnitude of the councillor's tasks or to the fact that Stuart councillors might not have been so able as their Elizabethan predecessors. If, as in the case of Somerset's lieutenants in this period, the lieutenant was a non-resident councillor, his personal acquaintance with the county's government and its other governors would be even more limited. Nonresidence robbed the lord lieutenant of the part he might have played as an informant to the Council of events in the county. Granted, Pembroke and Montgomery (though not his predecessor) took a keen interest in all aspects of Somerset's lieutenancy. Yet he could not avoid the limitations of time and space that prevented him from ever attending a muster of the militia. The sole recorded meeting between

---

[4] Burghley, despite his labor as Elizabeth's chief minister, exerted a remarkable degree of control over Hertfordshire's routine lieutenancy affairs, *Calendar of the Manuscripts of the Marquis of Salisbury*, pts. 4 and 5 (1892).

him and his deputies was not accomplished under auspicious circumstances. It was to settle a grave dispute that had hopelessly divided his deputies and had disrupted completely the administration committed to his care. In that dispute he played the arbiter, which was the only role a man so far removed from his subordinates could play. Nonetheless, ultimate control of lieutenancy was his responsibility and the Council expected him to discharge it. To his subordinates, however, he was essentially a one-man committee of the Privy Council to whom they reported as the spirit moved them the actions they had taken in a manner to their own liking. The lord lieutenant served as a convenient secretary of state who relieved the Council at large of the oversight of the minutiae of lieutenancy administration. But so far had he lost contact with that administration that he had ceased to be a county officer at all. He was no longer the bridge between the Council and the county which was the *raison d'être* of his office.

By default, the actual administration of lieutenancy fell to the deputy lieutenants. Early the government of Elizabeth had realized that the lord lieutenant would need deputies in each county of his commission to exercise his authority and discharge his duties in his absence. The power to appoint the deputies had been retained from the start by the monarch, and was not relinquished generally until the accession of Charles I. In the authorization to the Lord Keeper in May 1625 to renew all commissions of lieutenancy, it was ordained that the choice of deputy lieutenants be left to the lieutenants themselves.[5] This practice was followed thereafter, though occasionally Whitehall nominated a deputy and enjoined the lieutenant to appoint him.[6] The deputies held office until the lieutenant's commission terminated, or until he chose to discharge them.

By the reign of Charles I the government had recognized the lord lieutenant's virtual withdrawal from direct activity in local government and its corollary, the exalted status of his deputies. The routine orders of the Council for holding musters, disarming recusants, and the like were addressed to the lord lieutenant who was expected to return the

[5] PRO, C.66/2350, dorse, no. 5, commission to the Ld Kpr, 9 May 1625. A *liber pacis* of Oct. 1626 stated, "The names of the lo. lieutenants who are all to appoynt their owne deputies," PRO, E.163/18/12. Commissions of lieutenancy for all England and Wales were renewed to the incumbents "for appointing their deputies in the same commission," tested 13 June 1623, PRO, Index 4211, p. 307.
[6] For example, the Earl of Bedford wrote Secretary of State Dorchester that as lord lieutenant of Devon he had appointed Sir James Bagge a DL in obedience to the King's command, PRO, S.P.16/147, no. 39, 25 July 1629.

deputy lieutenants' report on the matter. In matters where speed was essential, the Council dealt directly with the deputies, and expected them to reply directly in return. Every Council letter routine or extraordinary, regardless of the addressee, leaves no doubt that the Council held the deputy lieutenants responsible for the performance of the task assigned.

Increased responsibility, increased duties, and the establishment of the deputy lieutenants as permanent officers in local government demanded an increase in their numbers. Originally, the deputy lieutenants had numbered two. As early as Elizabeth's reign, however, the number of deputies in each county had tended to increase. In Somerset's case the increase was modest; there were only three deputies in 1597 and no more a decade later.[7] Since after the accession of Charles the deputies were not named in the commission of lieutenancy and because there is a paucity of routine lieutenancy records, the exact number of deputies at any one time is difficult to determine for the Caroline period. From reports submitted by them, we may hazard the statement that about 1629 there were ten men executing the office of deputy lieutenant in Somerset.[8] Though this was a significant increase over the original number of deputy lieutenants, it was far from sufficient to undertake the preparations for the kingdom's defence at the augmented tempo that the government of Charles I demanded.

In practice one deputy lieutenant took precedence over the others, and it was upon him that the lord lieutenant relied for the execution of the commission. There was no legal sanction for such reliance, which was virtually a self-abnegation by the lord lieutenant of the commission he had undertaken. In Somerset, the "chief deputy" was Lord Poulett.[9] He attended musters, and there commanded and reviewed the trained bands. He, more than any other deputy, had the lieutenant's ear. Commanding by nature, preeminent in rank, on close terms with the powers

[7] Thomson, *Lords Lieutenants*, p. 65; PRO, Index 4211, p. 79, commission of lieutenancy tested 5 Nov. 1597, and S.P.16/33, *liber pacis* of c. 19 April 1608.

[8] The ten deputies were: Sir Charles Berkeley, Sir Nicholas Halswell, Robert Hopton, Sir Robert Phelips, Edward Popham, Sir Francis Popham, Lord Poulett, Sir Edward Rodney, Sir John Stawell, and William Walrond, PRO, P.C.2/39, p. 194, PC to DLs Somerset, 17 April 1629. Interestingly, both Halswell and Edward Popham, long before outlawed for debt and expelled from the commission of the peace, still continued to act as deputy lieutenants on this and other occasions. Of all the deputies in this period, only Sir Charles Berkeley was not also a justice or former justice.

[9] Sir Robert Phelips, writing to Pembroke and Montgomery's secretary, spoke of Poulett as "chief deputy," SRO, Phelips MSS, vol. A, f. 95, 7 July 1636 (draft).

at Westminster, and leader of a faction in the county's political life, Lord Poulett could hardly have been excluded from that place. But the very fact that he possessed it and used it to advance his own position in the political battle for supremacy in the county was sure to evoke from Sir Robert Phelips, deputy lieutenant, a sustained and forceful counterattack.

Thus, it was inevitable that Somerset's lieutenancy would become the principal cockpit of county political strife in the 1630s. The deputy lieutenants were the chief magnates in the county. As in magistracy, such men had so strong a claim to office that even the most authoritative and perceptive lord lieutenant could not deny them it. A deputy lieutenancy, more than any other office, allowed a Poulett and a Phelips the maximum opportunity for the show of power and the exercise of influence that marked the county political leader and gained him adherents from among the substantial classes of rural society. The deputy lieutenant was not expected to sit in judicial silence, curbed in the arbitrary exercise of his power by a bench of two-score colleagues, nor was he much restricted by the requirements of due process of law. Closer than any other officers in the county to the ear of the government at Westminster, the deputy lieutenants were, through the withdrawal of the lord lieutenant from county life, furthest from the government's strong hand.

With the withdrawal of the lord lieutenant from active participation in county government, lieutenancy had come full circle from the days when it had superseded the temporary commission of musters composed of the sheriff and some leading justices. The deputy lieutenants, vested with all the powers and duties of the lord lieutenant, differed from the commissioners of musters only in the absence of the sheriff from among their number and in their permanence in local government.[10] Lieutenancy, as other institutions that the Tudors committed to the charge of one man, was transformed by the Stuart tendency to place offices in commission and govern by committee.[11] In Admiralty or the Treasury such transformation was hardly justified; in lieutenancy nothing but ill could come of it. The loss of the lord lieutenant as a county officer forestalled the

---

[10] In fact, Poulett and two other deputies signed a warrant as "commisioners appointed to take musters," SRO, Phelips MSS, vol. A, f. 44, 19 July 1636. Nottinghamshire as late as 1626 was the last county to have commissioners instead of a lord lieutenant, *Acts PC*, 1625–1626, p. 476.

[11] Even the archbishopric of Canterbury went into commission: when Abbot was suspended for his opposition to royal policy, five diocesans were commissioned to exercise the metropolitical jurisdiction, PRO, S.P.16/84, no. 4, King's instructions, 2 Nov. 1627.

jealousy of his power that affected some Elizabethan gentlemen, but it was the loss of the one officer in local government who might have prevented that crucial institution from becoming the arena of political strife in the 1630s. The withdrawal of the lord lieutenant from county life meant that the real lord lieutenant would emerge from among his deputies. The usurper, though, would not have that intimate tie with Whitehall and the profound understanding of the King's interest which only a privy councillor could attain. He would be a man not above county faction but a fomenter of it.

The traditional duties of the lieutenant and his deputies were the preservation of order and the preparation of the county's might to repel invaders. Miss Thomson has ably though briefly described these functions as they were discharged by Elizabeth's lieutenants.[12] All that must be done here is to alter her picture to accord with the somewhat changed circumstances prevailing in the reign of Charles I.

The period of calm preceding the storm that was the Civil War was very calm indeed for Somerset. For her neighbors the same was not true. Wiltshire and Gloucestershire were in a state of upheaval at the end of the 1620s because of the precipitate disafforestation of royal forests, and in those counties the immense power that lay in the deputy lieutenants' hands was used to restore order. Somerset was not affected. Save for the efforts of Somerset's deputy lieutenants to curb the restlessness of the soldiers billetted in the county in the later 1620s, the normal processes of law executed by the justices were sufficient to deal with riot there. In only one case of forcible entry did the Council direct the deputy lieutenants to employ the force of county to retake possession of a house, and there is no indication that the trained bands were in fact called out.[13] The Council did order in July 1626 that provost marshals be appointed by the lords lieutenants in every county to punish vagrants who, as a source of rumor, might cause unrest in the countryside.[14] Once appointed, however, the provost marshals appear to have become an instrument for

[12] Thomson, *Lords Lieutenants in the Sixteenth Century.* The principal sources for Somerset's lieutenancy in this period are the Phelips MSS and the Hippisley MSS in the SRO. The latter collection, as yet uncataloged, provides valuable material on the routine organization of the militia, being the papers of Capt. John Preston.

[13] PRO, P.C.2/39, p. 194, PC to DLs of Somerset, 17 April 1629.

[14] *Acts PC*, 1626, p. 72, PC to Lds Lts, 10 July 1626. The two Somerset provosts were both justices, one of them also a deputy, PRO, S.P.16/32, no. 76, DLs of Somerset to Ld Lt, 29 July 1626.

the justices' use, particularly helpful later in directing the police efforts against vagrants required by the Book of Orders.

The close connection between Roman Catholicism and disorder in the minds of Elizabethan councillors had early in the lieutenant's history caused him to be made responsible for repressive action against recusants. In Elizabeth's reign the deputy lieutenants had hunted out and examined recusants. Twenty-five years later their only dealings with them were in the disarming of such and the binding over of wilful nonattenders at church. The pitiful collections of antique weapons confiscated by the deputy lieutenants in 1625 indicates how little the power of the deputies was needed to control recusants in Somerset, and the Council's explicitly stated motive in requiring the deputy lieutenants to bind over nonattenders was that they might furnish a proper example for the rest of the justices.[15] Both orders were part of the extraordinary circumscription of the Roman Catholics in the autumn of 1625 by which Charles hoped to placate the Commons and so secure supply.[16] All other repressive measures, when enforced at all, were left to the justices of the peace.

Feeble though they were the ordinary instruments for the preservation of the King's peace, composed of sheriff's officers and constables directed by the justices, were able to deal effectively with breaches of the peace in an era when internal commotion and subversion were more bad memories than current realities. The justices as investigators and police-men had, as against the deputy lieutenants in the same role, the advantages of greater numbers and the power to dispose judicially of the matters they uncovered.

The aggressive policy of Charles and Buckingham assured, however, that the deputy lieutenants would fulfill a more martial function than suppressing the odd riot and harassing recusants. The first five years of Charles' reign were years of war that saw two unsuccessful expeditionary forces launched against the nation's enemies. Even when 1630 brought peace, the seemingly interminable conflict on the Continent and Charles' diplomatic intrigues with Continental powers presented a threat of war. Invasion was no actual peril, nor was it likely that the King at any time until the end of the 1630s believed that it was. But the mere possibility of invasion gave him and his ministers an excuse to prepare the nation's power to serve his own ends.

[15] *Acts PC*, 1625–1626, p. 188, PC to Lds Lts, 4 Oct. 1625; PRO, S.P.16/10, no. 60 [PC to Lds Lts England, Nov.] 1625, no. 48, DLs of Somerset to PC, 28 Nov. 1625.
[16] Jordan, II, 172–173.

Regardless of what those ends were, the preparation of the nation's strength to serve them was basically the responsibility of the deputy lieutenants in each county of England and Wales. A government that possessed no standing army—and could not have raised the money to pay one—had to rely primarily on the manpower of the counties for its military raw material. The main duty of the deputy lieutenants was to take this very rough material, composed of husbandmen and petty squires, and fashion it into a weapon fit for war. A traditional function of the office, this was emphasized so strongly in these sixteen years that it promised to overshadow all other duties connected with lieutenancy.

"For home defence the military system was based on the duty of every man to serve when the country was invaded."[17] This had been the underlying concept of the subject's obligation to defend the realm from the days of the Anglo-Saxon *fyrd*. But characteristically, the Tudors expanded this medieval concept to suit the requirements of a modern state by demanding that the subject prepare himself for this service before the country was invaded. An act of Mary's reign (4 & 5 Philip and Mary, c. 2), which consolidated medieval legislation, minutely detailed those upper classes of society who were to "keep in readiness" various arms and equipment for war. An act immediately following provided sanctions against those of all classes who failed to attend, or attended improperly armed, the annual musters of able-bodied men. Elizabeth gave final definition to the subject's duty to prepare himself for war. Instructions of February 1572/3 directed that a convenient number of able men be organized into units and trained. Trained bands, the backbone of the county's might, had been born.[18] The threat of the Armada hardened the trained bands into a definite organization, and the endemic strife that followed made plausible their continuation. While all subjects from sixteen to sixty remained obligated to serve when called, what power the county possessed rested in its *trained* forces, both horse and foot.

The primary task of the deputy lieutenants was to see that the trained forces were in fact trained. It was a difficult task. To trim a country yokel into the barest semblance of a soldier required hours of drill and infinitely patient explanation. Simple though the arms of that age were, the proper handling of them was crucial in hand-to-hand combat. Drilling to instill discipline and instruction in the use of arms were the two

[17] C. H. Firth, *Cromwell's Army* (1921), p. 5.
[18] *Ibid.*

essentials of a soldier's training that were supposed to be most assiduously attended to by the deputy lieutenants and the trained band officers.

That drilling and instruction in reality received so little personal attention from the deputy lieutenants was in great part the result of the administrative work connected with the office. Even the crude military establishment that was the seventeenth-century militia required considerable attention to administrative detail. The need for ready money to meet the increasing expense of arming and equipping the militia necessitated hundred rates. These the deputy lieutenants ordered, and they supervised their collection. Resistance to the "trained soldiers" rate was not great,[19] but rating meetings and the constant prodding of the constables to collect the money consumed the time the deputies might have given to more martial activities. Paper work, too, took its toll. Lieutenancy had no central bureaucratic agency, such as magistracy possessed in the clerk of the peace and his staff. The work of scheduling musters, notifying the unit officers to require their men to attend, commanding the hundred constables to procure powder and produce the arms, wasted the precious time of the deputies themselves. Far too much of their time at the muster was spent in sending out warrants for the arrest of absentees and in arranging the trained band rolls. The before-muster chores had their counterpart in after-muster paper work. The return of muster rolls and the drafting of the detailed reports the Council increasingly demanded in answer to its enquiries accounted for a large share of the time that the deputies could be expected to give to lieutenancy. With the added load of normal magisterial duties to which all but one of the deputy lieutenants were required to attend, the administrative work of the deputy lieutenants at musters and between musters left little time for instruction. Even if the deputies had been moved by the Council's exhortations to pay greater attention to militia instruction, the demands on their time made by administrative encumbrances would have prevented them doing much about it.

One other duty of truly formidable proportions, emphasized from 1625 to 1630, also militated against the deputy lieutenants being able to expend the time and energy necessary to train an effective militia. Charles, requiring great numbers of men for the expeditions of these years, resorted

---

[19] The only reference to a refusal to pay the trained soldiers' rate which occurs in the sessions rolls was under date 1626/7, SRO, Sess Rolls, 58 pt. ii, no. 44. Sooner or later most rating matters—including rates for lieutenancy—came before quarter sessions. If there had been other difficulties over this rate they would probably have appeared in the sessions rolls

to impressment and this distasteful task fell to the deputy lieutenants and their subordinates. Without variation the Council's orders for the impressment of a specified number of men were addressed to the lord lieutenant who required his deputies to supply the men, properly clothed, to the conductors who would take them to the port of embarkation.[20] The men were chosen by the hundred constables, each hundred being required to supply a set proportion of the total according (in Somerset's case) to a rate established in 1569.[21] The money to supply every man with a good coat and eight pence per day for food while being marched to the port was rated on the county by a hundred rate, the county to be repaid later out of Exchequer. Besides their labor in executing the Council's orders, two attendant difficulties plagued the deputy lieutenants. Desertions of the pressed men were frequent, and required the deputies' vigilance both to prevent escape and to apprehend those who had fled. Also, the county's increasing reluctance to pay the coat and conduct money rate threw on the deputies the added duty of coercing the constables to collect it. The period was ushered in by pressing and coat and conduct money. When it ended sixteen years later, pressing and coat and conduct money saw it out.

If it was indifferently trained, the militia was at least organized and—on paper—not badly armed. The continuing emphasis on military preparedness arising from the endemic war of Elizabeth's last years had caused some attention to be paid to the organization of the militia's component units. The tremendous conflict on the Continent which had raged since the defenestration of Prague turned the eyes of all governments, belligerents and neutrals alike, to the state of their weapons. Thus, though the ferment for modernization and rearmament of the counties' forces was often more apparent on paper than real in practice, it is none the less worthy of treatment. Especially is this true in the absence of satisfactory printed accounts of these two important aspects of militia, save those contained in contemporary theoretical works of varying merit and Professor Firth's illuminating though brief summary.

[20] Elizabeth had made frequent use of the deputies for pressing men, though during the peaceful years of James' reign the deputies had not been much troubled with this.
[21] Ammerdown House, Hylton MSS, "A proportion devised at Henton . . . 13th of July [1569] . . . for levying of one hundred men to be imployed in servise for Ireland." This rate was used thereafter for almost all county rates, both for men and for money, though it underwent slight modification; it was the key to many of the ship money disputes.

It is difficult to determine exactly how mighty the county's host was. Seventeenth-century statistics must be approached with caution, and the numbers of those enrolled in the trained bands are no exception. However, a general census of the trained bands in England and Wales was arranged from muster returns for the Council in 1637/8, probably by Thomas Meautys, muster master-general and clerk of the Council.[22] There is no indication that the returns for Somerset were incomplete and the total number of both horse and foot for the county was given as 4300. The horse totalled 300, of which 82 were cuirassiers and 218 were harquebusiers. The foot stood at 4000; musketeers, 2403 and pikemen, 1597. These figures do not appear excessive; from what is known about the county's population, a shrewd appraisal would confirm the total.

There is some value in contrasting these figures with those resulting from a survey taken by Somerset's commissioners for musters in 1569 and those from the muster returns for some year between 1605 and 1614.[23] In 1569 the total of the county's able-bodied and armed (though not trained) foot soldiers stood at 5855; the horse, however, numbered only 145. In the early years of James' reign, the total number of able-bodied foot soldiers still stood at 5850 and the horse at 150. The markedly greater number of foot in 1569 and 1605–1614—almost 6000—as against 4000 in 1637/8 was accounted for by some 4000 simply armed archers and billmen. Indeed, the Jacobean return candidly listed only 2000 men as "armed," that is, equipped with muskets and pikes, weapons which by then were requisite to warfare. Somerset's 4000 foot in 1637/8 were all more or less armed in the modern manner. Taking into consideration the fact that the trained soldiers of Charles' reign were better armed and better organized than had been their untrained grandfathers, the decreased numbers in the intervening years did not mean that the effective strength of the county's forces had diminished. On the contrary, there had been an appreciable increase in foot armed in the modern fashion and a doubling of the horse strength since the first decade of the century. But measured against the advances made in Continental armies during the same period, it was not enough that there had merely been no diminution or even an "appreciable" increase in foot and "doubling" of horse strength.

The horse were the "senior service" of the militia. Both by virtue of

[22] PRO, S.P.16/381, no. 66, "The trayned bands of the severall counties of England and Wales," 9 Feb. 1637/8; S.P.16/372, no. 45, notes by Nicholas of PC orders, 25 Nov. 1637.
[23] *Certificate of Musters in the County of Somerset* (1904), done in pursuance of a PC letter, 26 March 1569; BM, Add. MS 47713.

their function in the military machine and by the distinction of the class from which they were recruited, the cavalrymen were set apart from the rest of the trained forces. In the event of war the horse by their mobility were expected effectively and expeditiously to carry the war to the enemy. The cuirassiers, armed with a four-foot long sword and a brace of pistols, "armoured cap-à-pie," and mounted on a stout horse,[24] were intended primarily to combat the enemy's horse; secondarily, to attack his supply trains and harass his foot. They were the heirs of the mounted knights of the Middle Ages and the immediate successors of the demilances of the sixteenth century. Tactically, their task in battle was the same though they appear to have been capable of faster movement if for no other reason than that by this time they had been shorn of the encumbrance of a lance.[25] The harquebusiers, armed principally with a heavy smoothbore gun of about seventeen bore (gauge) lightly armored and mounted on a lighter horse, were a new development in warfare. They had supplanted the militia light-horse which as late as the time of the Armada had formed the basic cavalry force. The harquebusiers, not intended for reconnaissance and harassing (the basic function of the light-horse), were in fact highly mobile infantry.[26] Moving with considerable speed to a strategic point far beyond the distance a contingent of foot could march in the same time, they dismounted and opened fire with their heavy smoothbores supported on a forked rest. They were the first military force created primarily to exploit the potentialities of gunpowder. The carabineers, a still newer development of Continental origin, had not yet been introduced into the militia. Armed with very light and short smoothbores and mounted on light horses, they were the essence of the cavalry forces that both Rupert and Cromwell used so effectively for reconnaisance and skirmishing.

The horse had the social distinction of being recruited ostensibly from the gentry class. As the gentry were obliged by their social position to serve in the superior unpaid offices of local government so, too, they were required to serve in the superior unpaid branch of the militia. The value of the gentleman's estate determined the contribution he would make; generally, larger estates, one or more cuirassiers; smaller estates,

[24] PRO, S.P.16/404, no. 138, notes on perfecting musters [Dec. 1638]. The description of all the forces' arms is taken from this document.

[25] There were still a few demilances in some counties as shown by the 1637/8 census, PRO SP.16/381, no. 66.

[26] These were dragoons. There were a few light-horse in some counties in 1637/8.

5+

one or more harquebusiers.[27] The contribution entailed the man, the mount, and the material. It was not expected that the gout-ridden squire should accoutre himself and ride to musters to exercise with his troop, but he was required to send his son or another kinsman of quality. The fact that a horse and equipment to supply its rider cost so much, combined with the superior position that a mounted soldier occupied, was intended to keep the horse as a domain of gentry privilege. Unfortunately for the King's service, many of the gentry were all too willing to relinquish their share of this privileged domain to the "baser sort."

There was nothing privileged about being a foot soldier. The advent of gunpowder ruled out the armoured knight and established the infantry-man as the backbone of the army. He has retained that onerous distinction ever since, performing the most menial tasks that warriors have ever been required to do. Still, the foot soldier of the trained bands was expected to be a man of some substance. One of the numerous "proposi-tions" for perfecting the militia that was advanced in this period rather optimistically intended to enroll in the bands only freeholders, "able [men] . . . of living" and not men decayed in estate, loose idle persons artificers, and cottagers.[28] Too often, the foot soldier came from among the latter categories and not from among the staunch yeomen. Burghley had confessed quite candidly his recognition of the shortcomings of the yeoman-soldier when he wrote his Hertfordshire deputies in 1589/90 that the substantial householders had been so "daintily fed and warm lodged," they were not fit for duty, and that in their places their sons or other "able men" should attend musters.[29] The Lord Treasurer's definition of "able men" would only with difficulty have encompassed many of those classes from which Somerset's foot appears largely to have been drawn a half century later.

Paradoxically, the increased military activity of Charles' first five years made more simple the recruiting of the militia's foot than it had been at any time in the previous reign. A trained band soldier was immune from the press-men. From occasional references to them, hus-bandmen and laborers desirous of staying at home appear to have formed

---

[27] The minor gentry were not required under 4 & 5 Philip and Mary, c. 2 to furnish more than some armor and arms for foot. Even after the repeal of the act in 1603, this as well as the other proportions for contributions of arms and armor remained in force.

[28] PRO, S.P.16/13, no. 43, proposals for more effectively arming and exercising the trained bands [1625].

[29] *Calendar of the Manuscripts of the Marquis of Salisbury*, pt. 4, p. 17.

a generous proportion of the county's foot. Though pressing served inadvertently to fill the militia, it certainly did not fill it with the most desirable persons. Substantial farmers and their sons, because of their economic value to the nation and through the connivance of the local constables who were the press-men, were virtually exempt from impressment. Even though they, as well as all men sixteen to sixty, were liable for enrollment in the trained bands, the effective limitations on the size of the number of men that could be armed and drilled exempted them at a time when the bands could be made up more readily with meaner persons. True, there were stout men like one George Clarke, a "jovial fellow," who enjoyed part-time soldiering. But far too many militiamen were like Roman Spracklinge,[30] who enthusiastically attended musters with borrowed arms while the press-men worked, not to attend again once the levies had been completed and his less fortunate countrymen sent to Ré.

The foot were composed of musketeers and pikemen (integrated in all units) who had replaced or absorbed completely in every county the older archers and billmen. The musketeer carried a heavy firearm, having a four-foot barrel, of about the same calibre as a modern twelve-gauge shotgun though of considerably greater weight.[31] A forked rest, bandoliers, and possibly some light armor completed his equipment. The pikeman carried a heavy-hafted weapon, eighteen feet long, surmounted by a sharp-pointed tip called a Dutch head. For protection he wore an iron corselet. Both musketeer and pikeman wore headpieces and carried a strong sword adapted for either striking or thrusting. This was the ideal that the government aspired to in arming the foot, based on the equipment of the French and Dutch armies.

Reality approached but probably never attained the ideal. As late as 1638, Devon's muskets were of assorted calibres and designs,[32] even though in the years immediately preceding there had been tremendous agitation in Whitehall for the standardization of arms. It is unlikely that Somerset's muskets were much better. The pikes must have been a queerly assorted lot, too, many resembling agricultural implements more than weapons. The armor to a large extent was aged, rusty, and seldom complete. The

[30] SRO, Phelips MSS, vol. A, f. 66. The Spracklinge affair was the catalyst of the last great Poulett-Phelips dispute, see pp. 269–270.
[31] SRO, Phelips MSS, vol. A, f. 3, draft bill for Parliament for perfecting the militia. Though no act was passed, this bill (perhaps presented to the 1627/8 Parliament) was incorporated substantially in later Council orders.
[32] PRO, S.P.16/407, no. 25, memo by Nicholas [1638].

reason for such indifferent equipping is not hard to find. The arms were rated on the tithings according to their supposed corporate values, and on the county's substantial persons, lay and clergy alike, in proportion to the value of their estates.[33] However, once provided—and this was seldom done gracefully—there was no adequate provision for their maintenance Replacement required even more effort. If the trained soldiers' rate yielded any surplus funds, the deputies purchased new weapons. Arms, though, were difficult to obtain and, to judge from numerous complaints, the private armorers were prone to overcharge for shoddy weapons. The arms confiscated from recusants during the sporadic and short-lived periods of severity towards them were to be given (with compensation to their owners) to the trained bands. The obsolescent coats of mail, the carbine, the pocket pistol, the "bastard musket," and the other odds and ends taken from Somerset's papists in 1625,[34] while not impressing the deputies as being worthy of purchase, might have been all too typical of the militia's weapons.

As the trained bands were to be used solely for home defence their supply and constructional machinery (necessary for offensive forces) was crude even for that date. In Continental warfare, pioneer units had proved their worth as service and logistic elements, and by James' reign the government desired that they should be an integral part of the trained bands. In 1626, the Council ordered that a hundred pioneers be established for every one thousand foot;[35] *i.e.*, one company of pioneers attached to a regiment of foot. For engineering work, the pioneers would be provided with spades, picks, and axes, and for supply and transport purposes, with carts and horses. They would constitute the regiment's supply train, bringing up food, weapons, armor, and ammunition. Though the deputies made return in 1626 that they had provided pioneers according to instructions, it was unlikely that these forces ever existed in the proportion demanded.

An approximate picture of the organization of Somerset's militia—assuming the verity of the 1637/8 estimate of 4300 horse and foot—would show a total of six regiments, horse and foot. One of these, the regiment

[33] The troops themselves were furnished on this basis. Thus, John Preston's foot company consisted of 100 enlisted men (not counting non-coms), they and their arms being furnished one-half by tithings and one-half by individuals, SRO, Hippisley MSS, muster roll of Preston's company, 1636.
[34] PRO, S.P.16/10, no. 48, DLs of Somerset to PC, 28 Nov. 1625.
[35] *Acts PC*, 1626, p. 72, PC to Lds Lts, 10 July 1626. In the period 1605–1614, Somerset had a total of 46 pioneers, BM, Add MS 47713.

of horse (consisting of 82 cuirassiers and 218 harquebusiers) might have been put into the field in a desperate emergency, though it is doubtful whether so many mounted men were ever seen at a muster. As for the foot, we have it on Sir Robert Phelips' word as regimental commander that his regiment numbered 800 men, as did that of Edward Popham. Also on Phelips' word, he had six company commanders, whose units with his own company included, gave his regiment seven companies of something over a hundred men each. John Preston's foot company (in Lord Poulett's regiment) consisted of himself as captain, a lieutenant, an ensign, two sergeants, three corporals, two drummers, forty-one pikemen, and fifty-nine musketeers. These figures accord with the national company strength of one hundred other-ranks plus officers.[36] So, including a company of pioneers to each regiment but not including officers commissioned and noncommissioned, the county's 4000 foot comprised five regiments in all, each consisting of eight companies. This is credible.

Except for the county-wide regiment of horse, the various units of the militia were based on and recruited from particular locales. The regiments, the principal organizational and tactical components in the seventeenth-century military establishment, evidently together covered the whole county, each taking a large area for its particular domain. Sir Robert Phelips' regiment was called the "Bath regiment," and was centered on that city, doubtlessly drawing its men from a large area comprising the northeastern section of the county. Lord Poulett's regiment was centered on Ilchester in the southeastern section; Sir Edward Rodney's, on Wells, in the northcentral section east of Sedgemoor and south of Mendip. The companies of the regiments were centered in yet smaller areas which were further subdivided into three squadron areas. John Preston's company covered the major part of South Petherton hundred, the lower half of Kingsbury hundred, and a tithing of Tintinhull hundred geographically in South Petherton hundred; no two points of the company area were more than seven and one-half miles apart. The three squadrons (each under the control of a corporal) were the Chard (south), Whitedown (centre), and Dinnington (north).[37] The files

[36] SRO, Hippisley MSS, muster roll of Preston's company, 1636. The Ré army was based on a regiment of foot consisting of ten companies of 100 men each, *Acts PC, 1627–1628*, p. 292. Gervase Markham, a contemporary author (overly-theoretical) set a company at 200—too large for effective field use, *The Souldiers Grammar* (1626), p. 15.

[37] SRO, Hippisley MSS, muster rolls and list of musketeers called to target practice.

of ten men or so each, which were the smallest units, were probably based on single hamlets. Besides making feasible between musters drill, such local basing of military units was expected to create *esprit* and local pride, valuable factors in raising militia morale.

Despite this, the militia's morale appears to have been very low. That this was so owed much to the want of capable officers to lead it. Service as the commissioned officers of the militia was as obligatory upon the gentry as their attendance at musters. There were no difficulties encountered in securing regimental commanders; the deputy lieutenants played at being colonels.[38] Difficulties arose in procuring suitable company commanders and subalterns. Doubtless many gentlemen, especially those who were not of magisterial status, accorded it an honor and a mark of social distinction to undertake the captaincy of the local company. The equestrian-minded squires of the seventeenth century were particularly susceptible to the age-old ambition to act the soldier. Yet against these attractions weighed one sobering reflection which in many cases may have robbed the trained bands of a prospective officer of merit: an officer's place entailed a great deal of unremunerated work, especially in this period. Thus, the men who would undertake these commands would be drawn primarily from two groups. They would be either young, inexperienced, and often undisciplined minor gentlemen or heirs of good families, or else already amply burdened magistrates who could not easily ignore the deputies' invitation. All Somerset's junior officers whose names can be discovered fit into one of these two categories, save the occasional retired veteran from the Continent. There was no reason why a young gentleman might not become a sound officer. The trouble lay in his being placed in immediate command of men neither more nor less experienced than himself. Seldom was he of such social distinction as to enable him to retain the respect of his men during the agonizing period during which he learned to command and his men to obey. Prestige of place and name in county society alone could cover up mistakes done under the eyes of the never-too-respectful countryman. The magistrates who served as company commanders (such as William Every) suffered from no social disability, but they were already too preoccupied with magisterial duties to give adequate attention to soldiering. Regardless, Somerset did manage to keep its militia officered even if the quality of the officers

---

[38] Sir Charles Berkeley, DL, commanded the regiment of horse. Lord Poulett, Sir Robert Phelips, Sir Edward Rodney, and Edward Popham, DLs, are known to have commanded foot regiments.

might have left something to be desired. It did not have to resort to the
heavy expense of paying its trained band officers £20 a year as did
Staffordshire, nor did its deputies ever report that they were unable to
take an exact muster for want of captains, as did Wiltshire's deputies in
1627.[39] It was not one of the counties from which gentlemen who refused
to be captains were to be brought before the Council for punishment, as
their "contempts in such a matter of this importance deserve."[40] However,
that did not necessarily mean that Somerset's militia was satisfactorily
officered.

The noncommissioned officers in part supplied the martial experience
so often wanting in their gentlemen superiors. Many of the squadron
corporals and file leaders were veterans of the Continental campaigns, for
the deputy lieutenants had had one very powerful argument with which
to persuade these old soldiers to contribute their talent to the local companies. The acceptance by a returned soldier wounded overseas of a
pension extended by quarter sessions obliged him to serve the deputy
lieutenants if called upon. A veteran reluctant to serve would have found
his pension reduced by the court. The deputy lieutenants appeared most
solicitous of the rights of the returned maimed soldier, and there are a
number of letters by them (and even two by the lord lieutenant) to the
sessions endorsing requests for pensions.[41] This indicates that the deputies
were awake to the usefulness of these men who had seen war at first
hand. Despite their injuries, which were not necessarily disabling, such
men could make the valuable contribution to the militia that has always
been the unique gift of an experienced non-com.

Returned veterans of even the greatest experience and devotion to duty,
serving as underofficers could never have been a sufficient substitute
for truly martial superior officers. Lieutenancy's greatest weakness lay
in the fact that virtually all its officers from the deputy lieutenants to the
ensigns were rank amateurs. Sir Ralph Hopton (deputy lieutenant from
about 1630 until the Civil War) was the only deputy who had tasted

[39] PRO, S.P.16/294, no. 38, DLs of Staffs. to PC, 23 July 1635; S.P.16/80, no. 12, DLs of
Wilts. to Ld Lt, 2 Oct. 1627. At the Wilts. winter assizes 1636/7, a colonel, three captains,
and other militia officers pleaded—unsuccessfully—their commands as grounds for exemption from grand jury duty, PRO Asz.24/20, f. 136.
[40] PRO, P.C.2/39, p. 398, PC order, 31 July 1629.
[41] SRO, QSOB, 1627/8–1638, Epiph. QS 1629/30, no. 5, mids. QS 1632, no. 10; Sess
Rolls, 61 pt. ii, no. 8. Somerset militiamen were paid 8d per day for each day (two in all) of
musters, SRO, Hippisley MSS, DLs' warrant to constables, 26 Sept. 1627. This was more
than many of them would have earned as wages.

battle.[42] An able regimental commander in both Bohemia and the Low Countries. Hopton was to become one of the King's most renowned generals in the Civil War. But, he could not train the county's militia singlehandedly. While martial experience had never been the main consideration in choosing a deputy lieutenant, it was a quality of increasing importance as the government pressed for a better militia. The defects of the deputies could have been supplied if even a portion of the captains and lieutenants had done more soldiering than riding to musters. It was anomalous that Sir Robert Phelips should have written that the captains and lieutenants were "commonly such as have been in the wars," when he twice secured a captaincy for a friendly magistrate's strictly civilian son, and when the six captains of his own regiment were lesser gentlemen, apparently without military experience.[43] Far more candid were the anonymous veterans who said, "Commanders in the country are chosen rather according to their estates then otherwise."[44] A nation whose only line of defence was its militia could not afford to have that militia directed, trained, and commanded by amateurs—certainly not in the face of enemies whose professional armies were effectively laying waste to half of Europe.

It was the government's intention that the muster master should supply the martial experience so evidently lacking in the rest of the militia's officers. Recurring conciliar orders enjoined the lord lieutenants to appoint a muster master in each county, whose duties the Council defined as: attendance at musters to ensure that the militiamen were able-bodied and their arms serviceable; instruction of the men, both at musters and at other convenient times, in their duties and the use of their arms; residence in the county to assist the deputy lieutenants when they required his services. He was to be a "practick souldier" experienced in the wars abroad.[45] Both of Somerset's muster masters fulfilled this requirement and one of them, Sir Edward Hawley, was killed at Ré.[46] The

---

[42] At *aet*. 22, Poulett had been colonel of the militia's horse—this and the later command of a foot regiment were the sum of his military experience, GEC, X, 616.

[43] SRO, Phelips MSS, vol. A, f. 1. Phelips' exalting of the company officers in this instance was due to his desire to prove the muster master superfluous. *SANHS Proc* (1910), LVI, pt. ii, p. 24; SRO, Phelips MSS, vol. A, f. 17; Hippisley MSS, captain's commission to John Preston, 12 May 1617, in which Phelips had written in the first name (left blank in the commission) of his good friend, the new captain.

[44] PRO, S.P.16/376, no. 64, proposals by unnamed veterans to drill militia horse [1637?].

[45] PRO, P.C.2/39, p. 554, PC to Lds Lts, 21 Dec. 1629.

[46] Taunton Castle, Brown MSS, vol. 5, p. 116.

muster master was to be a paid, full-time professional, usually, the only paid officer in lieutenancy.[47] The potentialities of his office must not be underestimated. The muster master might well have raised the efficiency of the county's forces to a remarkable pitch. Though subordinate to the deputy lieutenants, his knowledge of things military so overbore theirs that he could have exercised virtual command of the militia, trained and arranged it to produce something approaching a fighting force. This was not to be. In Somerset as elsewhere the constitutional struggle raging in the Commons, when translated into county ferment, effectively sapped his authority and ultimately destroyed his usefulness. The muster master, who might have been lieutenancy's strongest pillar, became instead its heaviest millstone.

The whole of the militia's activity, all the labors of its officers were centered on the summer musters of the various regiments. The muster of the local regiment and the neighboring horse troops was intended to be the "grand review." Mass movements on a regimental front were to be executed, battle lines formed, horse troops wheeled in attack, muskets fired at mark, and pikes brandished in deadly array. The multicolored uniforms, each company with its individual colors, and the fine dress of the gentlemen-cavalrymen were to be a brave and inspiring sight. Companies were to vie with each other in marksmanship, disciplined maneuvers, completeness of arms and equipment.

This was a summer's dream. The summer muster was far from being either an inspiring sight or a useful employment of the soldiers' time. Though the Council made a determined effort to have the musters held in early summer, too often they conflicted with the countryman's first duty, which he owed to his harvest.[48] This consideration, combined with a dislike of the musters on constitutional grounds, from just ordinary laziness, and from a desire to avoid a compulsory duty, assured that absenteeism would be prevalent. Except for a few zealots, those who did come to musters came through fear of the deputy's summary punishment

[47] In 1631, one Sam Whetcombe was to be paid £10 from the maimed-soldiers' fund "for his service in this county," doubtless as the muster master's assistant, SRO, QSOB, 1627/8–1638, Mich. QS 1631, no. 12. The order preceding (no. 11) was for £50 to Capt. Carne, the muster master's annual salary. In 1628, the Suffolk muster master was permitted to execute his office by deputy while he was on active duty—the deputies were also ordered by the same signet letter to pay him his arrears of two years' salary, PRO S.O.1/1, p. 332.

[48] The 1627 orders for summer musters directed that they be held in Whitsun week in order to avoid harvest time, *Acts PC*, 1627, pp. 131–133.

5*

or the more terrible experience of appearing before the Council.[49] Yet even these sanctions, thanks to sporadic application and upon one occasion the connivance of a deputy (as we shall note later), were insufficient to prevent a great many militiamen, gentlemen and farm laborers alike, from avoiding the musters. Absenteeism made massed movements impossible; indeed, made impossible any useful drill at all. It had the more terrible effect of destroying the morale, which can come only from a unit of men proud to serve and keen to match their ability against other units.

The summer muster of each regiment, usually lasting two days, was held in a large open field in the area from which the regiment was recruited. Before the muster the hundred constables served the deputies' warrants upon the various captains, summoning them and their troops to attend the muster fully armed. Doubtless, the summonses provoked a flurry of worried activity on the part of the officers as they attempted to collect together the men, their arms, and ammunition. More or less armed, at three-quarters' strength if lucky, the company set out on the appointed day. The "grand review" commenced when Lord Poulett rode onto the field in his coach after the other deputies, officers, gentlemen-cavalrymen, and foot soldiers had dribbled into the area.[50] Nothing could begin until the constables (usually tardy) had brought the arms and armor from the various village repositories in their hundreds. After some hours spent in waiting, and probably a few more in forming the units, the clerks of the bands[51] called the roll and checked the attendance in the muster rolls. Further delay followed, occasioned by the deputies' absence while they issued warrants for the appearance on the following day of absentees. Probably then the muster master or his deputy walked along the files, perfunctorily checking men and arms. If there was any time left that day, there might have been some drill. The whole process was repeated the second day after absentees had come in or had been brought in. There were no massed movements, no brave show of arms. The muster ended with the hurried exit of Lord Poulett, intent upon getting home to Hinton in time for dinner.

[49] The deputies could impose a summary fine of 40s and, in default of the fine, commit to gaol for ten days those who absented themselves from musters or came improperly furnished, 4 & 5 Philip and Mary, c. 3. It was usual in this period, however, for the names of muster defaulters to be certified to the Council, which then (upon occasion) took action.

[50] This description is composed from a number of documents in SRO, Phelips MSS, vol. A, and the Hippisley MSS.

[51] These were probably the deputies' private clerks, justices' clerks. Lieutenancy had no other clerical staff, unless the muster master could handle a pen as well as he was to handle a sword.

In fact, better than any other aspect of the militia, the musters illustrate two basic weaknesses inherent in lieutenancy. One was the complete absence of vigor, the total want of intelligent purposefulness in all those charged with the defence of the kingdom and their county. The fault rested ultimately with the deputy lieutenants since they were responsible for that defence. They were to blame for those ills so apparent in the summer musters: wasted time, the inane routine of inspection, and the perfunctoriness of all officers, especially of themselves. These ills smothered any spark that might have fired the average militiaman's imagination or aroused in him some pride in his work, some deep sense that this was important for the safety of his home and his loved ones. For the average soldier, the only reality in soldiering was that it was obligatory, boring, and unpleasant. No one attempted to show him that the real object of soldiering was its importance to the nation and to him. Little wonder, then, "that the soldier doth rather seem to act a Maygame."[52]

The other weakness illustrated by musters was the reliance that the deputy lieutenants perforce placed on the constables. As a justice of the peace, the deputy lieutenant had to contend with the inefficiency of the constables. As a deputy, he was further hampered by their carelessness. The delay of the constables in bringing arms and armor from local repositories was matched by their tardiness in transporting powder, match, and lead from the four magazines in the county. The constables were indispensable in all aspects of lieutenancy, both before, during, and after musters. The execution of warrants of arrest for absentees, and the subsequent execution of the *mittimus* to gaol fell to the constables. They were responsible for the construction and maintenance of the warning beacons as well as for the enrolling of all men between the ages of sixteen and sixty, and the collection of the trained band rate.[53] They were saddled usually with the invidious duty of impressing men for overseas service. They were no less indispensable in lieutenancy than they were in magistracy. Nor were they any more efficient.

If musters occupied in lieutenancy the place occupied by quarter sessions in magistracy, between-musters drill of trained band units can be likened to out-of-sessions meetings. The period 1625–1640 was marked

[52] SRO, Phelips MSS, vol. A, f. 1.
[53] PRO, S.P.16/442, no. 128, PC to JJ assize, Western Circuit, 27 Jan. 1639/40, for a Somerset constable who built a beacon on the deputies' orders months before and had not yet been repaid by the hundred. SRO, Goodford MSS, w/55, DLs to hundred constables of Chewton, 9 Aug. 1635, ordering enrollment be made.

by the Council's increasing emphasis on regular drills of files, squadrons, and even companies throughout the year as well as at the muster. The Council ordered in no uncertain terms that the deputy lieutenants oversee personally the drilling of these units in their "several divisions." In fact, lieutenancy like magistracy was becoming increasingly a matter of administration at the divisional level. And like magistracy, lieutenancy had evolved established divisions. Since in Chapter IX divisional work by the deputy lieutenants will be treated, it is well to describe these divisions here.

The records of lieutenancy provide no source for the discovery of its divisions, such as the reports under the Book of Orders allow for magisterial divisions. Thus, the lieutenancy divisions can be recreated only by guesswork, albeit guesswork based on a knowledge of the county's political and geographic boundaries in other instances. The county was divided into an eastern half and a western half, and certainly these were divided on the same line provided by quarter sessions to separate the areas of the eastern and western hospital funds. From the statesmanlike report to quarter sessions of two deputy lieutenants-justices concerning a dispute over beacon-watching in the eastern half, that half appears to have contained three divisions: north, middle, and south, respectively.[54] Paying attention to the magisterial divisions in the same area and taking into account geographical limitations, these three divisions can be determined with some assurance. The western half's divisions must remain suppositional, save that the easternmost division in this half appears to have been wholly Sir Robert Phelips' lieutenancy division; his strong objection to Lord Poulett drilling his regiment within it indicates that its boundary should be drawn between their two seats, just west of Ilchester. Since the seats of the known deputy lieutenants in 1629 when imposed on these divisions show that in all but the north division of the eastern half there was resident at least one deputy, the divisions as here supposed are at least credible.

Charles had not been many months on the throne before the first directives were sent into the counties with the intention of activating the rusty machinery of lieutenancy. The demands of war—the demand for troops and the demand for defensive preparedness—pressed on the

[54] SRO, Sess Rolls, 56 pt. i, no. 7. The unit divisions—regimental, company, etc.— while arranged by area did not necessarily correspond to these organizational divisions.

King and his ministers. They turned to the deputy lieutenants to fulfill these demands. In so doing, new life was breathed into an institution which for twenty years had lain dormant, had suffered a premature aging through inactivity.

King and Council could hardly have recognized the magnitude of their task in revitalizing lieutenancy. Inactivity had aggravated the basic weaknesses of the institution. The deputies and their subordinates in the militia had rested comfortably at home while their counterparts on the Continent had fought across the face of Europe and learnt the art of war. For two decades the English citizen-soldier had not even acted the "Maygame" with much earnestness. The deputy lieutenants had grown lax, and the constables who were the administrative backbone of the institution had troubled themselves even less with the deputies' orders than they had with the justices'. No one had been trained for war, for there had been no war. Morale, the basic stuff of any fighting force, had seeped out of every militiaman from the lord lieutenant to the humblest pikeman. Morale lives on purposefulness, and there had been no purposefulness in militia for twenty years.

In 1625 it remained to be seen whether Charles and his Council could revive purposefulness in the institution of lieutenancy. It remained to be seen whether the spur they applied to the deputy lieutenants would be transmitted through the militia's officers to the common soldier and the constables. It remained to be seen whether a military force commanded by and composed of flaccid amateurs could be welded into a fighting force, trained and armed sufficiently to safeguard the kingdom against invasion.

In 1640 King and Council were provided a tragic opportunity to determine with what effectiveness their task had been accomplished.

Chapter V ∽ *Shrievalty*

The decline of the sheriff was the concomitant of the rise of the justices of the peace and the lord lieutenant. The long process of attrition of the sheriff's powers that had begun with the inquest of 1170 reached its culmination in the century when Tudor monarchs groomed the justices and the lord lieutenant to assume the principal responsibility for county government. The death blow to the sheriff's judicial powers had been 1 Edward IV, c. 2, which removed all indictments before the sheriff in his tourn to quarter sessions for trial. Tudor legislation was concentrated on giving authority to the justices to control the sheriff in the exercise of the few powers left him. A statute of the first Tudor required the justices to oversee the sheriff's county court and to punish summarily the sheriff and his officers for malpractices connected with it. A statute of the last Tudor authorized the justices to swear in the undersheriff and the other sheriff's officers, and to fine them for executing office before taking the oaths.[1] These and other Tudor statutes reinforcing earlier legislation gave the justices considerable power under the law to punish an erring sheriff and his subordinates. The sheriff's military function when the realm was invaded, which in the Middle Ages had been as considerable as was the lord lieutenant's in the seventeenth century, suffered at the Tudors' hands in two progressive stages. Commissioners of musters, of whom the sheriff was to be one, had become the military authority in the county by the middle of the sixteenth century; thus, the sheriff's power over the county's forces became a matter of partnership. The second and final stage came with the permanent establishment of the lord lieutenant and his deputies. With the loss of his judicial and his military powers, the sheriff was left as an administrative agent of the central government and those local officers who had supplanted him. If the office of lord lieutenant was a Tudor creation and that of the justices of the peace a Tudor

[1] 11 Henry VII, c. 15 and 27 Elizabeth I, c. 12.

124

augmentation, then the office of sheriff was a Tudor demolition. However, the structure which was the institution of shrievalty as a local
authority of importance had been undermined over a period of four
centuries. The Tudors merely completed its destruction.

To describe in detail the mass of administrative duties discharged by
the sheriffs of Somerset in this period would be to repeat what can be
conveniently found elsewhere.[2] Nor would it be germane to this study.
This chapter will outline briefly the routine of the sheriff and his officers,
the organization which handled that routine, and the position of the
sheriff in county government. More fully, it will concentrate on the
weaknesses of an institution whose chief officer was catapulted suddenly
into a position both important and invidious. For six years the office of
sheriff would receive unwanted emphasis—the six years during which
the sheriffs were required to collect ship money.

Dalton, in his admirable handbook for sheriffs, *Officium Vicecomitum*,
outlined all the functions of the office under eleven heads, revealingly
entitled "ministerial duties." Michael Dalton was a practical lawyer who
wrote practical books for practical justices and sheriffs. He conceived of
the sheriff as a minister, a servant to government, rather than a governor
himself. He advanced no exorbitant claims for the office. He did not
hide from the reader that his term as sheriff would be a personally
restrictive year as a nominal authority over professional and not always
honest or efficient subordinates who discharged their duties in a manner
that might have unpleasant repercussions upon him. Dalton made no
pretence that the gentleman would receive either political, pecuniary, or
social benefit from his year as the King's sheriff.

The eleven "ministerial duties" of Dalton can be condensed into five,
which together include virtually all the duties that in practice the
sheriff's office entailed.

First and foremost was the sheriff's services to the common law courts
at Westminster. The original writ to commence a civil action before any
of those central courts was sent to the sheriff whose officer then served
and returned it. When a court required a jury in a case, the sheriff impanelled one at Westminster or assizes on the day appointed. Once the

[2] Two contemporary works are particularly valuable: Michael Dalton, *Officium Vicecomitum* (1623), and John Wilkinson, *A Treatise . . . concerning . . . Coroners and Sherifes*
(1628). A recent study of great usefulness is C. H. Karraker, *The Seventeenth Century Sheriff:
A Comparative Study of the Sheriff in England and the Chesapeake Colonies, 1607–1689* (1930).

case was determined, the process upon judgment went to the sheriff for execution. All this involved considerable work for the sheriff's officers, and an intimate knowledge of a complex substantive and adjective law. Dalton felt constrained to give ninety pages to this that his reader might not be in ignorance of so important a subject. "The office of a Sherife consisteth chiefly in the execution and serving of Writs and Proces of Law; and to doe this, he is the immediate Officer of the King and all his Courts . . . and hee is sworne that hee shall truely doe this, and hee must . . . without any favour, dread, or corruption."[3] "Any favour, dread, or corruption" laid open the sheriff and his officers to criminal sanctions or civil damages to the injured party.

No less important was the second duty incumbent upon the sheriff: the collection and payment into the Exchequer of the Crown's established income. This was an ancient duty of the office, and the elaborate machinery developed in the twelfth-century Exchequer had been intended to ensure the sheriff's diligence in discharging it. The established income consisted of the traditional "King's Rents, Fermes, Debts, Issues, Amerciaments, Fines and Forfeitures"—in short, the profits arising from the King's estates, grants of franchises, and the administration of his justices as well as other casual revenues.[4] These were to be collected by the sheriff or his officers, paid into, and strictly accounted for before the Exchequer.[5]

The sheriff's third ministerial duty centered upon his relations with other bodies of local government. In this, he functioned most as a county officer. Food, heating, and housing for the judges of assize when they visited the county twice a year were provided by the sheriff. He attended assizes and quarter sessions, and was the chief executive officer attached to both. He presented the calendar of prisoners held in gaol or bailed preparatory to their arraignment in court.[6] He or his officers impanelled the grand jury, the hundred juries, and the petty juries, and served pro-

---

[3] Dalton, *Officium Vicecomitum,* f. 41v.

[4] *Ibid.,* f. 18v. Among the casual revenues, deodands and suicides' goods were no longer collected by the sheriff, but by the King's Almoner's elaborate organization in London and the counties, the Almoner having received a patent under the great seal to take such and to apply them towards poor relief.

[5] While there are no sheriff's accounts extant for Somerset in this period, the final account as accepted in Exchequer was enrolled on the Pipe rolls (PRO, E.372). I am indebted to Miss Mabel H. Mills for considerable guidance in coping with the mass of Exchequer material touching the sheriff.

[6] The calendars for quarter sessions are in the sessions rolls. None are extant for assizes, though the Essex (Home) Circuit has an excellent series including *nomina ministrorum* (the names of justices and other officials) from 1559, PRO, Asz. 35/1 *et seq.*

cess upon jurors who did not appear on the summons. His men executed the precepts of both courts; levied the fines, gaoled the prisoners, branded the rogues, whipped the petty thieves, and hanged the felons. His officers also impanelled juries for the coroner's inquest and the escheator's inquisition post mortem, and executed the precepts of these officers as well as the orders of the commissioners for sewers. Nowhere was the sheriff's former glory more mimicked and mocked than in his humble attendance upon judges and justices, coroner, escheator, and commissioners, there to do their bidding as the errand boy of those with whom he had once sat in the seats of the county's mighty.

Preservation of the King's peace was the fourth and least exacting ministerial duty of the sheriff's office. Seldom did the sheriff perform even the most elementary police tasks. The few riots that appear in the sessions rolls were apparently handled by the local constables, probably under the direction of the justices. The days when large armed bands of retainers threatened the countryside were in the distant past, and consequently, the elaborate provisions of 13 Henry IV, c. 7, for the sheriff and the justices to move against rioters with the *posse comitatus*, were not likely to be much employed. The trained bands under the deputy lieutenants were a far more potent and reliable instrument to express the power of the county, and they had in fact superseded the *posse*. In Wiltshire, during the agrarian disorders of 1631, the trained bands were called to the assistance of the sheriff.[7] In Somerset in 1640, after a particularly brutal murder of a subaltern by his troops while marching to the North from Devon, the Council ordered the lieutenants to use the trained bands (if necessary) to arrest the murderers; there was no mention of the sheriff.[8] Vagrants were to be driven from the county's roads not by the sheriff, but by provost marshals appointed by the deputy lieutenants and directed by the justices. The sheriff as a peace officer was obsolescent.

Lastly, it is significant that Dalton gives as a "ministerial duty" the requirement that the sheriff "Duely ... keepe his Courts."[9] The bare remnants of the sheriff's once expansive judicial power was the miniscule jurisdiction of the emasculated tourn and the archaic, though still useful, county court. The sheriff had always been the judge in his tourn held twice-yearly in every hundred. However, 1 Edward IV, c. 2, by removing

[7] PRO, S.P.16/202, no. 6, PC to Ld Lt of Wilts., 21 Oct. 1631 (draft); no. 18, Ld Lt of Wilts. to DLs, 23 Oct. 1631.
[8] PRO, P.C.2/51, p. 649, PC to Lds Lts of Somerset, 17 July 1640.
[9] Dalton, *Officium Vicecomitum*, f. 19.

to quarter sessions the hearing of crimes and offences against administrative statutes presented in the tourn, left it at best an insignificant
court of presentment. Even in this it had been largely superseded by the
grand and hundred juries at quarter sessions. Dalton wrote, "this Court
[the tourn] . . . is now almost growne out of use" due to the corruptness
of the sheriff's officer who presided over it.[10] There is nothing in the
quarter-sessions records, either in the way of an indictment made in tourn
or a presentment before that court, to support any other conclusion than
that the tourn had by then quietly expired. On the other hand, the county
court held monthly at Ilchester was still a vital institution. Heir to the
oldest tradition in English jurisprudence, that of judgment by suitors, it
had never been a court of record and the sheriff's function in it was
purely ministerial. The sheriff's officer who presided merely voiced the
judgment independently (in theory) arrived at by the suitors. The county
court's survival was due less to its utility as a court adjudicating civil
actions than to its usefulness as an ostensibly representative body of the
freeholders in the shire. The limitation of the court to hearing causes in
which the maximum damage or debt claimed was £2 had long before
driven most litigation of importance to the courts at Westminster.[11]
However, since freeholders were to attend, proclamations (both statutory
and conciliar) read there would receive wide dissemination. For the same
reason, the process of outlawry and the proclamations under writ of
exigent, both directed against defendants who could not be found, was
performed most conveniently in the county court. The representative
nature of this court of freeholders (whose ranks on election day were
sometimes illegally swelled by meaner citizens) retained for it the privilege
of electing the knights of the shire in Parliament and for the sheriff the
politically advantageous position of returning officer. It is worth noticing
that if the county court's function as a judicial organ was in decline, it
did enjoy a renaissance of importance between 1635 and 1640: those who
refused to pay ship money and had replevied (retaken) their cattle
distrained for the tax were bound to prosecute the replevin in county
court.

[10] *Ibid.,* f. 157. The tourn was a court of record though the record had to be certified into
quarter sessions.
[11] Dalton, *Officium Vicecomitum,* f. 160. From occasional references in SRO, Sess Rolls,
the actions before the county court appear to have been largely concerned with stray cows
and the replevin of distrained goods. By writ of *justicies,* cases involving damages or debt
in excess of £2 might be heard in the county court.

Considering only the sheriff's duties within the scheme of local government, he can no more be entitled a local governor than the coroner or the escheator. Indeed, at their respective inquests, these two officers performed a function far more nearly judicial than did the sheriff in his tourn and county court. Like them, the sheriff was largely the agent of central government departments; in his case, Exchequer and the law courts. Like them, his work was primarily ministerial, cut and dried, leaving little room for local initiative.

Three considerations however, differentiated the sheriff from the coroner and the escheator, and gave him a claim to a place in the "triarchy" and consequently makes him a fit subject for this study. First, the sheriff was usually chosen from among the same class of men who filled the other two premier offices in local government; generally he was a justice, and occasionally a deputy lieutenant. Both the coroner and the escheator were drawn from among the nonmagisterial lesser gentry.[12] Secondly, the sheriffwick, unlike both the coroner's and the escheator's places, was an unprofitable office for its principal. The charges on entering and leaving the office were heavy; the fees and perquisites of the office were absorbed by the charges and the sheriff's subordinates who performed the labor.[13] These two considerations alone were sufficient to accord the sheriff the status of a local governor. However, the third consideration drew him even closer to his brethren of the county bench and the militia. His office, like theirs, received novel emphasis and underwent a heightened burden of work in this period, with the accompanying conciliar supervision that was a feature of Charles' "personal rule."

The most marked characteristic of the tasks involved in these five basic ministerial duties of the sheriff was that they were performed not by the sheriff personally, but by his officers. From an early period, the sheriff had had the assistance of an undersheriff. By the seventeenth century, the undersheriff had become functionally the sheriff. From a profit motive he undertook wholly the organization and operation of the sheriff's office. By warrants in his own name, the undersheriff directed the "bailiffs errant" (those attached to the sheriff's office) and the bailiffs of the

---

[12] Of the 17 sheriffs, Mich. 1624 to Mich. 1641, 14 were justices, and 5 of these, deputy lieutenants; 8 can be termed magnates. See Table on p. 317.

[13] The fees required by Exchequer officials for passing the sheriff's account amounted to almost £100, PRO, E.112/285/1388, and Hodges' collectors of the greenwax were promised £40 for their labors in collecting the casual revenues amounting to about £1000, E.112/285/1383.

hundreds who performed the menial tasks connected with the office.[14] He received the original writs, issued warrants to the bailiffs to execute them, and afterwards returned them to the court from whence they came. Impanelling juries, service and return of process before and after judgment, were handled in the same way. *Replevin* of distrained goods was assigned statutorily to four sheriff's deputies in the county.[15] The monies received from the royal rents, farms, debts and forfeitures were collected by the bailiffs and paid to the undersheriff. Collectors of the greenwax (the warrants for levying fines, issues, and amerciaments went out under a green wax seal of the Exchequer) were appointed by the sheriff especially to garner this casual revenue. It was the undersheriff who accounted before Exchequer for the revenues received (save the greenwax), and who might pass some unpleasant moments if the account was not in order.[16] The commissarial arrangements for the judges of assize, the summoning of assize and quarter sessions juries, and the execution of the judgments of these courts were all the responsibility of the undersheriff working through the agency of the bailiffs. The safe keeping of prisoners was left to the common gaoler, another sheriff's officer. The undersheriff (or any sworn sheriff's officer) on the sheriff's warrant could call forth the *posse comitatus*. The tourn, if it yet functioned, was under the stewardship of the undersheriff. The president and spokesman of the county court was the county clerk. In short, nothing that can be discovered about Somerset's shrievalty in this period differs from Dalton's final analysis of the sheriff's office: "These Undersherifes have at this day to them committed by the high Sherife the whole, or most part, of the exercising and executing of the office of the high Sherife, and may bee called the Sherifes generall deputie."[17] The qualification expressed in "or most part" left just room enough to except the

---

[14] By statute, the sheriff was to have only one "bailiff errant." The sessions rolls indicate that in Somerset in this period there were at least three, probably many more. These sheriff's bailiffs must not be confused with the hundred bailiffs, who were not appointed by the sheriff and who held office for life, though they too served the sheriff in their respective jurisdictions.

[15] 1 & 2 Philip and Mary, c. 12. These ought not be confused with his accounting deputies in Westminster. One or two of the deputies for replevin were also appointed collectors of the greenwax.

[16] In Somerset, the undersheriff was also responsible for paying in the money to aid poor prisoners in the Marshalsea prison—a statutory levy. He was reimbursed by quarter sessions out of the county stock. Richard Mogge, as undersheriff 1633–1634, was summoned by the CJKB for failing to pay it, SRO, QSOB, 1627/8–1638, mids. QS 1634, treasurer for Western division hospital fund accounts.

[17] Dalton, *Officium Vicecomitum*, f. 176v.

sheriff's personal attendance at assizes and quarter sessions and his never-deputized function as returning officer for the county elections to the Commons.

Despite what social prestige the office conferred and the effectiveness with which the sheriff's subordinates shielded him from its routine, the sheriffwick was seldom sought after, and never by any gentlemen of already established status in the county. To the sheriff personally, the office was expensive, hazardous, and disagreeable. The profits the office brought were largely consumed by the subordinates, and the sheriff went to great personal expense in his lavish semiannual entertainment of the circuit judges and for the accoutrement of the ceremonial retinue his office demanded. The sheriffwick was hazardous because ultimate responsibility affixed by Exchequer, law courts, and the Privy Council rested upon him. In so far as responsibility entailed financial loss he was in most cases indemnified. The undersheriff entered bond to the sheriff for the proper passing of his account in Exchequer, and bond was required also from the other sheriff's officers. Even with contractual indemnity, in order to recover from his officers the money exacted from him by Exchequer for an improperly submitted account the sheriff was obliged to put the bond in suit at common law. Such suits were lengthy and uncertain affairs, and even if the sheriff recovered, the proceedings took considerable time and money.[18] The same was true in cases of abuse of power, extortion, and dereliction of duty by the sheriff's bailiffs. That bailiffs were for the most part men of low degree and little substance meant that recovery by the sheriff was difficult on the occasions when the bailiffs' malpractices made it necessary.[19] Records of amerciaments of sheriffs for the faults of their subordinates are numerous on the Exchequer King's Remembrancer memoranda rolls, though it appears that Somerset's sheriffs were by and large better served than some, for fewer amerciaments were levied on them than on sheriffs of a number of other

[18] Henry Hodges (sheriff 1634–1636) put in suit in King's Bench the bonds of his two collectors of the greenwax, who promptly countersued him in Exchequer. Hodges alleged that they had failed to collect monies assigned to them to collect and had made no account, thus causing him to pay Exchequer over £400 from his own pocket, PRO, E.112/285/1383, Coplestone and Barker *vs.* Hodges and Crewkerne. Hodges' allegations are unconvincing, though the suits do illustrate the difficulty encountered by a sheriff who put his subordinates' bonds in suit.

[19] The bailiffs were criminally liable for their own acts, but the sheriff was civilly liable as well. In SRO, Hippisley MSS, there is a copy of the elaborate bond entered into by a bailiff errant with sheriff John Hippisley (1640–1641) which enumerates the various malpractices of which bailiffs were capable and from which the sheriff was indemnified.

counties.[20] Nor could a bond protect the sheriff from the Council's wrath when his subordinates failed in their duty. The Council held the sheriff strictly accountable for the execution of its orders. Never was this plainer than in the collection of ship money; a duty imposed by the Council, for the execution of which the sheriff was personally answerable to King and Council.

The sheriff's was a disagreeable office, because for one whole year he was tied to the county, barred from acting as a justice of the peace, and excluded from an active part in national politics. During the sheriff's one year term (commencing in November) he was required to reside continuously in the county and he might leave it only with royal licence.[21] If a justice, though he was not dropped from the commission, he was prohibited from exercising that office during his shrievalty.[22] Since supposedly his presence was required in the county, the sheriff could not sit in Parliament.[23] Such restrictions on one's personal liberty hardly affected sheriffs like John Lach, Henry Hodges, and John Hippeslye, lesser gentlemen who had little cause to leave the county, were not justices, and took no active part in politics. Of the seventeen sheriffs in this period these three were the only nonjustices; of the fourteen who were justices, over half were magnates, and four were actively embroiled in politics. Even when the gentleman did not aspire to parliamentary fame, or when from 1629 to 1640 there were no Parliaments, the disability of the sheriff from acting as the local magistrate largely cut him off from an active part in county politics. The county arena required the exercise of magisterial authority to retain for the politician the "good opinion" of his

[20] Such penalties on Somerset sheriffs seldom number more than one per year, if any at all. For improper execution of writs of Exchequer and other courts including Star Chamber the penalty was £5 to £10 for the first failure, doubling for the next and each subsequent failure. William Every (1638–1639) was amerced the exceptionally heavy sum of £50 for inadequate service of a writ, PRO, E.159/479, Eas. 15 Chas. I, rot. 65. The Exchequer's bark was usually worse than its bite—it was common practice to permit sheriffs to compound amerciaments at 5 per cent or 10 per cent of the face sum.

[21] Sir Thomas Thynne of Longleat, Wilts. (sheriff of Somerset, 1629–1630) was given permission to reside in Wilts., PRO, S.P.16/152, no. 44. John Mallett (1636) was given license to come to London or any other place out of the county as often as necessary, PRO, S.O.1/3, p. 9. Such dispensations are to be found in PRO, S.O.1/1–3; there is no perceptible decrease in their numbers during the ship money years.

[22] There was no such prohibition with respect to lieutenancy; Sir John Stawell (1628–1629), William Walrond (1632–1633), and Sir Thomas Wrothe (1639–1640) were especially active deputies during their terms as sheriff.

[23] Walter Longe was fined 2000 marks and imprisoned by Star Chamber for sitting as MP for Bath in 1628 while serving as sheriff of Wiltshire, Lincoln's Inn, MS. "Starr-chamber" in press C.4, f. 91v.

countrymen. The sheriffwick was the sole office of county government's triarchy which was not sought after by such magnates as Phelips and Poulett and their adherents for the advancement of their factions' power in the county. The patronage in the sheriff's hands was not inconsiderable, but it was of limited political usefulness. Only Sir Francis Dodington (1630–1631) found the office advantageous for the exercise of influence, and that of a minor sort unconnected with factional advancement.[24] The politically-inclined sheriff's only consolation was that he might juggle the county election to Parliament, as did Sir John Horner in 1614, to work to a friend's advantage.[25] That was the maximum of the sheriff's political power.

To the magnate tied to the county and largely excluded from politics, the sheriff's office was doubly disagreeable. None of these men undertook the office with any delight and all were happy to relinquish it when their year was up. John Poulett revelled in accepting local office and performing the "King's service." But in a letter from Hinton St. George addressed to Secretary Carleton in 1617, he wrote with unusual acerbity and a marked lack of courtliness that he was tied to that "dull durty place" by the sheriffwick.[26]

The unpopularity of the office condemned it to be a curse imposed, not a benefit desired, and thus the gentry did not aspire to it. The Lord Keeper, or perhaps a Secretary of State, appears to have drafted a list of names of three or more substantial gentlemen (knights and esquires) for each county, which was submitted to the King in Michaelmas. With the Lord Keeper and others in attendance, the King then made the picturesque "prick" with the stylus beside the name of one gentleman for each county. The sheriff took office in that same term, and by a deputy opened his account in Exchequer. It is difficult to discover any particular criteria for the routine selection of sheriffs. Seldom was a sheriff chosen who had served before in the same county. That the sheriff was usually a justice was because the justices' names were most readily available to

[24] As a justice, Dodington had tried unsuccessfully to obtain an alehouse license for a suppressed tippler near his seat; Sir John Wyndham, JP in the same division, had blocked his efforts. As sheriff, Dodington obtained a license for the alehousekeeper from the judge of assize, *Som Asz Ords,* no. 39.

[25] E. Farnham, "The Somerset Election of 1614," *EHR* (1931), XLVI, 579–599. Sir John played the same trick at the county elections for "recruiters" in 1645 during his second term as sheriff, 1644–1645, D. Brunton and D. H. Pennington, *Members of the Long Parliament* (1954), pp. 29–30.

[26] PRO, S.P.14/94, no. 19, 10 Nov. 1617.

the Lord Keeper. Service to the King in a paid capacity which would make difficult the attendance of the gentleman in his county if chosen was sufficient grounds for exemption. Many attempted to avoid the office by being sworn "servants extraordinary" to the King and the Queen, but Charles put a stop to this in 1636.[27]

The lack of impetus from the county to procure the sheriff's office appears to have been matched by an equal want of concern on the government's part as to who was chosen. Under normal conditions, so long as some gentleman was selected and took the oath, King and Council were satisfied. Twice in this period, however, the appointment of the sheriff became a matter of the utmost concern to the Council. The first was in Michaelmas 1625 when, on the eve of Charles' second Parliament, the government desired to exclude malcontents who had so effectively disrupted the first. This the Council accomplished by having six former members pricked for sheriffs. Included were Sir Edward Coke, Sir Thomas Wentworth, and, as sheriff of Somerset, Sir Robert Phelips. The original list of nominees for sheriffs throughout the realm comprised the names of three Somerset justices, Sir Robert Phelips' not among them.[28] The final list of sheriffs shows Phelips chosen for Somerset, Coke for Buckinghamshire, Wentworth for Yorkshire, and the other three excluded members for their respective counties.[29] This was a rather negative concern on the government's part in the choice of the sheriff, actuated not by any regard for securing a fit sheriff but rather for excluding an "unfit" member of Parliament.

On the second occasion, the Council's concern was quite positive. In 1636 the judges of assize of all circuits had been ordered by the Council to send to the Lord Keeper a list of four or more "ablest, most serviceable, and wel affected persons" in each county of their curcuit, fit to be sheriff.[30] What action the government took on this information is unknown. In 1639, however Edward Nicholas, clerk of the Council, drew up a series of observations based on reports of the judges as to suitable nominees in

---

[27] PRO, P.C.2/46, p. 370, declaration of the K in Council, 18 Sept. 1636.

[28] PRO, S.P.16/9, no. 43, list of three from each shire [10 Nov.] 1625. John Symes and Sir John Stawell, named in this list, became sheriffs soon afterwards. See Gardiner, VI, 33.

[29] PRO, S.P.16/43, no. 16.

[30] PRO, P.C.2/46, p. 347, PC to JJ assize, Sept. 1636. The judges usually informed the Lord Keeper following the summer assizes of gentlemen able to be sheriffs, which names would be used to supplement the names of nominees carried over from the previous year's sheriff rolls who had not been appointed, Jean Wilson, "Sheriffs' Rolls of the Sixteenth and Seventeenth Centuries," *EHR* (1932), XLVII, 37–38. In the ship money years it behoved the Council to charge the judges to take particular care.

four counties, including Somerset. Two Somerset gentlemen were noted as being very refractory and disaffected, two others as of good estate but unknown affections, one as "unfitt," and the sixth, Thomas Smith (JP), as a man of £2000 annual income and son-in-law of Lord Poulett.[31] The Council desired that the sheriffs for the coming year be men well-affected towards the government so that they would collect ship money zealously, and prosperous so that they would be able to pay it out of their own pockets if they did not collect it. The emphasis then was wholly on appointing a fit sheriff.

The marked contrast between the government's concern in 1625 and its concern in 1639 as to who should be the county's sheriff is the most striking testimony to the impact of ship money on the office of sheriff. The alacrity with which the government filled that office in 1625 with a gentleman who was patently its enemy leaves no doubt that the sheriff's office had become politically unimportant and functionally routine. In fact, it was the place in which the ill-affected gentleman could do the least harm to the King's service. Fourteen years later, it was evident that the ill-affected sheriff could do the greatest damage to a King and his ministers striving to avoid bankruptcy.

Shrievalty suffered from two great weaknesses. The first was that the sheriff did not exercise a sufficiently close control over his subordinates to ensure efficiency and to prevent corruption, and his undersheriff, who was charged with the supervision of the subordinates, was in no position to control them. The second weakness was that even if the sheriff had exercised such control his choice of subordinates was limited and his short term in office with the resultant lack of continuity in administration was sufficient in itself to vitiate the most sterling efforts on his part.

The fact that the sheriff took little part in the working of his office placed his undersheriff in an invidious position *vis-à-vis* the other sub-ordinates. No matter how capable and honest the undersheriff was, he had neither the time, the inclination, nor ultimately the authority to oversee the bailiffs and other subordinates in the discharge of their duties. The undersheriff's place entailed an administrative routine consisting

---

[31] PRO, S.P.16/432, no. 34. Some notes by Nicholas of a Council meeting c. 10 Nov. 1639 indicate the Council's concern about "ill-chosen" sheriffs of recent years, S.P.16/432, no. 33. Sir Thomas Wrothe, of good estate but unknown affections, was selected. William Strode and Sir John Horner were noted as refractory, William Bull "unfitt" (doubtless, in estate), and Sir [Henry] Berkeley of good estate but unknown affections.

almost wholly of paper work. His office was, in effect, an immobile central clearinghouse for the routine business of shrievalty. Of necessity, he placed absolute reliance on the bailiffs for the execution of that business, the amount of which made it impossible for him to exercise a sufficient degree of oversight. The undersheriff did not appoint the other subordinates and they were not answerable to him, but to the sheriff; they were not in bond to him, but to the sheriff. In the appointment of all sheriff's officers there was a considerable play of favoritism, largely however within the confines of a pool of sheriff's subordinates inherited from preceding sheriffs. It was unlikely that any other sheriff was as deceitful as Henry Hodges (1634–1636) who ousted the gaoler in order to sell his place for £60 and removed his collector of the greenwax in favor of two others.[32] But all the sheriffs had a vested interest in their appointees no matter how restricted they were in their choice, if not for financial gain then at least for county political advantage. Against the sheriff's appointees the undersheriff was helpless. Only the sheriff himself could apply the threat of loss of office that might bring into line an inefficient or corrupt man.

This threat was seldom feasible for the simple reason that the sheriff's term was so short, corruption and inefficiency became apparent only when his year was nearly ended—it was too late by then to correct the damage done by corruption and inefficiency. Threat of loss of office even when carried out was not likely to be more than temporarily efficacious because the sheriff was limited in his choice of subordinates to that pool of sheriff's officers who, if cast off by him, would for want of anyone better be accepted in his successor's service a few months later. The fact was, the sheriff and his undersheriff were the victims of an "establishment" strong enough and cohesive enough to withstand the mightiest efforts of either to reform it.

The problem was made more indissoluble by the ambivalent position of the undersheriff. He served as the bridge between the "establishment" and the sheriff. Some undersheriffs did, contrary to statute, serve two or more terms under successive sheriffs.[33] While they were always dependent on obtaining the favor of the incoming sheriff, they were also dependent on retaining the cooperation of the "establishment," the pool of subordinates from which the sheriff would be bound to select the greatest part of

---

[32] See p. 234.
[33] Dalton indicates that this was common practice by then, *Officium Vicecomitum*, f. 176.

his staff. A sheriff bent on reform—none of Somerset's sheriffs in this period appears to have been much inclined that way—could expect the undersheriff to cool perceptibly if reform meant straining his relations with the county clerk, the collectors of the greenwax (who were also deputies for replevin), and the bailiffs upon whom he depended for the execution of the office then and doubtless in the future when he became undersheriff again. This last consideration is worth emphasizing; one attribute which recommended a former undersheriff to an incoming sheriff was his ability to control and direct the subordinates of the "establishment." Even if the undersheriff was a man without ambition to serve again, he was in a difficult and uneasy position from the first in relation to the "establishment," and he would tend to attempt little without its approbation. Christopher Browne, undersheriff of Thomas Luttrell (1631–1632) was such a man. Clerk of the peace, he appears to have agreed to serve Luttrell as a personal favor. A stickler for efficiency as clerk of the peace, Browne as undersheriff appeared no more willing to cross his subordinates than was Richard Mogge, virtually an undersheriff by profession.

By and large, the undersheriffs appear to have been both capable and honest.[34] The sole exception was Henry Hodges' undersheriff, Henry Crewkerne, who was evidently as inept and as devious as his master.[35] Most of the undersheriffs were attorneys and, indeed, as was mentioned before, Christopher Browne was clerk of the peace. Richard Mogge, who served at least three different sheriffs in this period, two in succession, served all well.[36] The undersheriffs of the ship money years stand in bolder relief than their predecessors. One of these, William Cox, escheator 1630–1631 and undersheriff to John Mallet, 1636, was exceptionally capable and industrious. Though they were a peg below the social status of their masters, Somerset's undersheriffs were certainly not as Dalton contended, "most commonly . . . persons of small worth and account."[37]

Dalton's uncharitable characterization is apt enough when applied to

[34] The most convenient source for the names of the undersheriffs is the Lord Treasurer's Remembrancer's memoranda rolls, PRO, E.368.

[35] PRO, E.134/15–16 Chas. I/Hil. 11. William Cox, undersheriff 1636, was as town clerk of Wells accused by Recorder Baber in 1631 of corrupt support of alehouses, PRO, S.P.16/194, no. 19. He was an honest undersheriff, apparently.

[36] Mogge was also John Preston's undersheriff in 1647–1648, SRO, Hippisley MSS, John Buckland to John Preston, 18 Dec. 1648.

[37] Dalton, *Officium Vicecomitum*, f. 135v. Cox, for example, was a lesser gentleman rated at the moderate sum of £10 to the privy seal loan, 1625–1626, PRO, E.401/2586, ff. 257–265. Later, he was a burgess of Wells.

most of the subordinates below the undersheriff, the men drawn from the "establishment": collectors of the greenwax, deputies for replevin, and the bailiffs errant. Only the county clerk and the gaoler can be excluded from the characterization, both being at least a step above the rest in terms of responsibility and ability, the clerk an attorney and the gaoler an Ilchester burgess who held the office for life by letters patent.[38] The majority of the rest of the subordinates were yeomen, petty townsmen, and husbandmen who found (or expected to find) the sheriff's employment more remunerative than other toil. The sheriff's service was moderately profitable to the servant, but it put a premium on unscrupulousness and insensitivity. The work was dangerous and brutalizing—the records of Star Chamber abound in instances of violent treatment of sheriff's bailiffs and violence offered by them in turn. In an age when the noose was so prodigally employed, the habitual criminal about to be arrested felt he might as well be hanged for murdering the bailiff as for stealing a sheep. In a society where resistance to taxation was almost instinctive, revenue gathering was a hazardous occupation, and one that was most successfully followed by disregarding the law and employing every tool available, no matter how devious it was. The very protection of the Englishman's rights assured by the law tended to drive the law's agents into illegality. The sporadically applied punishment, heavy when it came, for their illegal acts was one more hazard of the trade. The number of men in the county who could be found willing to do the sheriff's work was limited, and they were likely to be the least desirable types in rural society. This explains the cohesiveness of the "establishment," its relatively low caliber, and its indispensability to successive sheriffs—consequently, its durability. Like ministers of the Fourth Republic, the subordinate officers of shrievalty were never out of office for long (granted, though, for a somewhat different reason). They served successive sheriffs in one capacity or another and many of them served all badly. Recruitment for the more lucrative and prestigious positions—collectorships of the greenwax and deputyships for replevin—was largely confined to promotion of bailiffs already in the "establishment." New men were admitted to the "establishment" only under the greatest pressure from the sheriff; the sheriff desirous of peace and quiet in his office family was well advised to employ exsheriffs' men before he in-

---

[38] PRO, P.C.2/45, p. 166, PC order 21 Oct. 1635. Richard Browne, the gaoler, was a "gent."

truded any new appointees. The "establishment's" personnel exhibited that discreditable magnanimity in adversity (that is, loss of office) and that spirit of give-and-take characteristic of the closed corporation. John Light, collector of the greenwax in at least the years 1627–1628, 1629–1630, 1631–1632, allowed Sheriff Hodges to sack him without a murmur and appoint his two sureties in his place as collectors in 1634 in order to receive preferment in that job the next year. As if this compliance was not enough, he undertook to serve his usurpers as "deputy collector" and to make Hodges' account for the casual revenues in Exchequer without remuneration. In 1636, Light was collector again; two of his sureties for his bond to the sheriff were the two who had displaced him with Hodges' connivance two years before![39] John Light was all too typical of nearly all his fellows.

The "establishment's" durability was matched only by its inefficiency and indolence, its personnel's resiliency only by their corruptness. A suspicion of this is furnished by the most cursory glance at the schedules of fines, amerciaments, and issues annexed to the long writ under the greenwax and sent to the sheriff for levying and the returns of the juries impanelled to find the lands to be extended for the debts due the Crown.[40] The frequency with which the returns indicate that parties had no lands, no goods points to the failure of the collectors of the greenwax to search out the property of indebted parties—the jury could make a return only on the information furnished it by the sheriff's officers. William Bassett, the able and patently honest sheriff 1636–1637, put in suit the bond in which John Light, his collector of the greenwax, stood bound in £1000, because the latter had failed to gather the revenue for which he was responsible and with which the sheriff was charged.[41] A flagrant dereliction of duty in failing to levy Crown debts was sometimes accompanied by fraudulently levying the debt on both the party indebted and his tenants, the extra revenue taken from the tenants probably never reaching the Exchequer but ending up in the collector's pocket.[42] Complaints against sheriff's officers for refusal to arrest dangerous men, allowing prisoners to escape, failing to serve process, invading other

[39] PRO, E.112/285/1388, and E.159/468, Mich. 4 Chas. I, rot. 8; 480, Trin. 16 Chas. I, rot. 51; SRO, Sess Rolls, 62, nos. 88–89; 69 pt. ii, no. 8; 78, no. 57; *Som Asz Ords*, no. 148.
[40] PRO, E.143.
[41] PRO, E.159/480, Trin. 16 Chas. I, rot. 51.
[42] PRO, E. 159/475, Trin. 11 Chas. I, rot. 88—John Light levied £18 10s on the tenants of William Palmer over and above the £200 fine on him imposed by Star Chamber which he had paid himself.

jurisdictions, and other irresponsible acts are so numerous as to cause one to wonder how the sheriff ever discharged his responsibilities.[43] This seems especially incredible in view of the fact that not only the lower ranks of collectors, deputies, and bailiffs were guilty of misfeasance and corruption, but also such supposedly respectable officials as the county clerk, Walter Gould, and the gaoler, Richard Browne, fell from grace. The former was brought into Exchequer in 1632 to answer for misfeasance and the latter was prosecuted in Star Chamber by the commission on fees upon solid evidence of his oppressive extortion.[44] Not surprisingly, the depredations of the bailiffs were the most obvious and the most corrosive of the efficiency and reputation of the sheriff's office. Instances of extortion, intimidation, illegal arrest and seizure, assault and battery, larceny, and receiving bribes by bailiffs errant appear time and time again in the sessions and assize records.[45] Bailiff William Marshall was complained of to quarter sessions in 1626 by a woman whose house he and his disorderly (unsworn) assistants had broken into and whom he had vilified obscenely; in 1631 he was fined £20 in Star Chamber for bringing false suit; in 1635 he was accused of multiple extortions in partnership with an attorney of the Common Pleas; in 1636 he was shot dead—paid in kind—by a householder whom he had come to arrest on civil process and into whose house he had broken without a color of legality. That the coroner's jury bowed their heads to a stiff fine rather than find against the man who killed Marshall was indicative of the countrymen's sentiment; that the judge of assize mitigated their fines and the judges of the King's Bench vindicated the defendant's right to protect his house against the bailiff's illegal entry reflected law, not sentiment, but it was a condemnation of a practice indulged in by many other bailiffs besides the late and unlamented William Marshall.[46] It is not difficult to ascertain the opinion that the countryman had of the bailiffs. It was justifiably low. One Leonard Higgins of Hatspen put it rather nicely. Seeing a sheriff's bailiff riding to assizes, he remarked that the bailiff was out to get a new suit of

[43] PRO, E.134/15–16 Chas. I/Hil. 11; SRO, Sess Rolls, 61 pt. i, nos. 57–58; 73 pt. i, no. 59; 73 pt. ii, no. 16; 78, no. 57; *Som Asz Ords*, no. 148.

[44] PRO, E.159/472, Hil. 8 Chas. I, rot. 96, and E.215/16/1582, 1585, 1586.

[45] SRO, Sess Rolls, 57 pt. i, nos. 56, 58, 61, 62; 60, no. 48; 62, no. 10; 68, no. 27; 69 pt. ii, no. 31; 72 pt. ii, nos. 138–139; 73 pt. i, no. 79; 73 pt. ii, no. 87; 75, nos. 25–26; QSOB, 1627/8–1638, Eas. QS 1637, no. 32; PRO, S.P.16/53, no. 48; *Som Asz Ords*, nos. 31, 35.

[46] PRO, S.P.16/232, no. 43, and 287, no. 79; SRO, Sess Rolls, 56 pt. i, no. 51; *Som Asz Ords*, no. 107; *March's Reports*, pp. 3–5.

clothes, for should the hangman claim a well-dressed felon, the bailiff "will cutt the rope to have them."[47] The minimum of respect for the agents of the law requisite to their effective implementation of the law was, understandably, missing.

Even had the sheriff actively supervised his subordinates and ruthlessly cashiered them for dereliction and corrupt practices, the mere fact that he was in office for only a year meant that his successor could have undone all his good work. It was paradoxical that although the annual accession of a new sheriff had been intended originally to prevent the sheriff from becoming too powerful and too corrupt, it had succeeded by then in ensuring corruption among his subordinates. The complexity of the matters with which the sheriff's office dealt and the multitude of such dealings necessitated the large, professional, near-permanent staff which had grown up under the undersheriff. The control of that staff to ensure its integrity and efficiency, the responsibility of the sheriff and he alone, could not be exercised by a gentleman who would need his whole year merely to learn the essentials of his office. Any sheriff might have echoed John Buckland's plaintive call for assistance from his predecessor in office: "beeinge a stranger to this kinde of employment, I am much to seeke and cannot take my ayme soe confidently from any freinde as yourselfe."[48] But one sheriff's experience, no matter how faithfully imparted to his successor, was not enough to relieve his successor of the difficult and time consuming task of learning the intricacies of the office for himself. Consequently, a premium was placed upon the attitude "trust your undersheriff," with not always satisfactory results. The contrast between the efficiency and honesty of the clerk of the peace and his subordinates and the inefficiency and questionable integrity of the sheriff's officers is worth remarking upon. When due allowance is made for the different nature of the tasks of the two offices and the heavier and more dangerous responsibilities resting with the sheriff's officers, the basic distinction between the two resulted from the uninterrupted existence of quarters sessions and its long-tenured chairman as a continuing overseeing authority. Shrievalty possessed no such permanent authority, and the institution's master, the sheriff, paid the price for the lack of it, when his master, the King, demanded efficiency.

[47] SRO, Sess Rolls, 70, no. 65, mids, QS 1634. Prof. Willcox in *Gloucestershire: A Study in Local Government, 1590–1640* (1940), p. 46, speaks of a "modicum of bribery" among sheriff's bailiffs as inevitable—in Somerset's case, "modicum" is an understatement.

[48] SRO, Hippisley MSS, John Buckland to John Preston, 18 Dec. 1648.

So long as the duties connected with the sheriff's office consisted mainly in serving writs and processes and collecting fines and traditional rents and revenues, these weaknesses were not crippling. If the subpoena was served, it mattered little that the sheriff never saw it and his bailiff assaulted and ground out of the summoned party an extra piece of silver. So long as the undersheriff collected the various rents, or at least perjured himself gracefully enough to receive a *quietus est* from a slack Exchequer,[49] it mattered little whether the sheriff held office for one year or twenty. But ship money, which suddenly exalted the sheriff, compelled him to take an interest in his office and in the minutiae connected with it. Ship money forced him to demand efficiency, for he was not dealing in this with a careless and ponderous Exchequer. The answer to his demand could not be satisfactory. The subordinates sworn to serve him had acted too long in their own devious and lax ways, in their own time. No sooner had the sheriff responsible for ship money started his cumbersome machine for its collection than his year was up and his machine closed down. Only, the sheriff's personal responsibility for the collection of ship money did not end with the expiry of his year in office.

[49] PRO, S.P.16/306, no. 30, memorial to Sec. Windebank concerning inefficiency in the Exchequer, c. 1635. The anonymous author speaks, without much exaggeration, of the large arrears in the Crown's revenues occasioned by the decline of efficiency in Exchequer, especially in the Auditors' and King's Remembrancer's offices, those offices which played a major role in controlling the sheriff in his fiscal responsibilities. Dr. G. E. Aylmer, in "Attempts at Administrative Reform, 1625–1640," *EHR* (1957), LXXII, 229–259, makes clear the sorry state of the Exchequer, as well as of other central organs.

Chapter VI ❧ *Other Tasks*

The historian is too often the victim of the distrust, cynicism and hatred with which the Long Parliament summed up the history of the preceding sixteen years and the motives of the King and ministers who made it. Or, conversely, he succumbs to the mellifluous romanticism of Charles' posthumous apologists. Either failing does no justice to the King, nor to his opponents, nor to the cause of scholarship. The local historian buried among his sessions rolls will, like the men about whom he writes, have an eye on Parliament and national politics, and like them he must have the same confused approach to the King's and ministers' motives. In losing the pungent contrast that is the parliamentary historian's gift to scholarship, the local historian might still gain a truer view of the history of the period and the motives of the chief actors. For if the first sixteen years of Charles' reign were to end in a Parliament that destroyed him and his two chief ministers, at least they were sixteen years in which King and Council had ample opportunity to lay bare their motives to the gentlemen in the counties.

Few kings who have sat on England's throne and few ministers who have counselled them appear to have been more genuinely desirous of the subjects' good than were Charles I and his principal counsellors. It is incredible that the preamble to every royal letter and conciliar directive was a barefaced lie to make acceptable some new oppression by a charlatan and his henchmen. Almost every domestic policy of this period was inaugurated apparently with a sincere desire to better the commonwealth and the people who composed it, in the largest sense. There were charlatans and jobbers in the Council, but after 1630 at least government was so firmly in the hands of the King and Laud, whose motives were pure and in whom sincerity was dominant, that the government's programs cannot be condemned simply because they were framed in part

6+

and concurred in by a Heath or a Portland. The disafforestation and drainage schemes, the Book of Orders, the revitalization of the militia, and even the ship money fleet were all aimed at securing benefits for the nation, benefits which both King and Council felt had been in too little evidence under his late majesty, James I.

Tragedy lay in the means by which many of those benefits were to be obtained. Money was the prerequisite, and for reasons well known to every student, the government's demand for money was met by hostility, fast mounting to rebellion. As the government's finances shrank, the thirst for money tended to become the end in itself and to obscure the motives which desired the commonwealth's greatest good. Though the ultimate end was perhaps never completely lost sight of, the constant reiteration of the commonwealth's and subjects' benefit began to sound a little hollow and unreal.[1]

Regardless of which end the government desired most—the common-weal or money—the method by which the government sought to attain it was efficient administration. "Thorough," which is forever linked to the names of Laud and Strafford, was ordinary procedure before either rose to dominance and was the factor that made 1 Charles I contrast so markedly with 23 James I in many areas of local administration. Expressed at the lowest and most vital level, it was the government's intention to make maximum use of the justices, deputy lieutenants, and sheriff.

This and the following three chapters will trace the government's demand for efficient county administration throughout the years before the Long Parliament as it affected each institution of the "triarchy" in Somerset. Behind each demand, the unjaundiced eye can see a sincere desire for the subjects' good and in most a ferocious quest for money. In each demand can be seen an added and often novel burden of work laid upon one or more of these institutions of county government and the unpaid gentlemen responsible for them.

Special commissions[2] illustrate more clearly perhaps than any other of the government's directives in this period, its desire both for the

---

[1] Dr. G. E. Aylmer arrived at this conclusion from a study of central government organs: "The change of emphasis from reformatory to fiscal purpose in its use of the commission on fees was typical of early Stuart government." "Charles I's Commission on Fees, 1627–1640," *Bulletin of the Institute of Historical Research* (1958), XXXI, 67.

[2] The term "special commission" is used throughout in a strict sense: a formal instrument issued under the great seal or the Exchequer seal, commissioning specified persons of the

commonwealth's benefit and a full Exchequer. Some of the commissions, such as those for the forced loan (1626–1627) and composition for knighthood (1630–1631) were patently royal money-making propositions. However, those for the improvement of Sedgemoor, Aldermoor, and the river Tone, the disafforestation of Neroche, Selwood, and Petherton forests, and the investigation of depopulating enclosures were intended for the county's good as well as for the Crown's enrichment. In the ameliorative programs envisaged in these latter commissions, it was not merely the urgent need of the government for money that can account for the demand for efficient and rapid implementation, but the King's and Council's sincere belief that the resulting success would work for the county's weal.

Precedents from previous reigns can be found for all these special commissions, both fiscal and ameliorative. The dorse of the patent rolls from early Tudor times had become sprinkled with progressive liberality with commissions directed to gentlemen in the counties for the execution of a particular program or duty. The same phenomenon is discernible in Exchequer records. Tudor government, intruding as it did into more aspects of the nation's—and thus the counties'—lives, had reposed most of the resultant administrative duty on the established institution of the justices of the peace. However, the commission of the peace was at law and in practice an authorization of limited usefulness. Programs of an exceptional nature, not countenanced by common law nor of such permanence or importance as to require enabling legislation, were delegated by prerogative power to special commissioners named and empowered in letters patent under the great seal or in commissions out of the court of Exchequer.[3] Besides, neither Tudor nor Stuart monarch readily left

_____

locale to carry out certain clearly defined tasks and according them sufficient power to do so, other than the commissions of the peace and lieutenancy and the sheriff's patent. However, two projects—the privy seal loan of 1625 and the free gift of 1626—which imposed tasks on the justices by means of less formal authorization are treated here because of their dissimilarity to routine magisterial tasks and their affinity to duties under special commissions.

[3] Some, though not all, of the commissions under the great seal are on the dorse of the patent rolls (PRO, C.66); all are noted in the Crown Office docket books (Index 4211–4213) and entry books (C.181), save commissions for charitable uses which will be found in the Crown Office miscellaneous fiats (C.192/1)—none of these three latter records will provide more than a note of the powers given the commissioners (if that) though the latter two sources give the names of all the commissioners appointed. The commissions out of the court of Exchequer are in the King's Remembrancer's special commissions (E.178) files of commissions and returns. The commission under the great seal carried more weight than the Exchequer commission, even though both might be initiated by the same official and the great seal commission require return into the court of Exchequer.

to the vagaries of Parliament a cherished project which involved the prerogative, as did the forced loan, the King intent on taking by prerogative power what Parliament refused to give. The result was that by Charles' reign, the special commission had become an instrument of wide applicability, unquestionable in Parliament, for the carrying out of a particular policy for an immediate end. Not all of the half-hundred or so commissions issued to Somerset gentlemen in this period fit within this definition. Two types of commissions, those for sewers and for charitable uses, had statutory authority and were intended primarily to confer powers supplementary to those contained in the commission of the peace. Another type was commissions for subsidies. These were strictly grounded on statutory authority, and though of short duration were recurring on the few occasions during this period when Parliament saw fit to cooperate with the King.[4]

One thing that all the special commissions here treated had in common was the commissioners, or at least a good part of them. The leading members of all these special commissions were, without exception, justices of the peace. In nearly all, the justices were in the majority, and in the commissions for sewers, which specified members of the quorum, the justices were invariably named to the quorum. There can be no doubt that in every commission the government expected the justices to lead and if necessary accept full responsibility for the fulfilment of its terms.

The government found definite advantages in using the commission of the peace as a reservoir of names for making up the special commissions out of Chancery and Exchequer. Because the Council was in most constant communication with the justices, the reliability of those gentlemen was well known to the government. The fact they were justices meant that they had an intimate knowledge of the county at

[4] Another type of special commission is worthy of mention: commission of oyer and terminer. Special commissions of oyer and terminer could be issued to local justices of the peace (invariably afforced by the judges of assize of the circuit and sometimes by non-magisterial gentlemen) to deal with a particular and immediate outbreak of crime—the only one issued for Somerset in this period was in 1640 to deal with martial disorder, see p. 277, n. 89. Special commissions were issued for other counties in the West, particularly to suppress piracy in the later 1620s. Such special commissions must be differentiated from the regular commission of oyer and terminer issued twice yearly to the judges of assize, the custodes rotulorum of all counties on the circuit, and a number of other justices from each county on the circuit, which will be found in PRO, C.181. This latter was one of the four commissions by virtue of which the judges of assize sat; save for the Northern Circuit commission only the circuit judges were of the quorum, the local magistrates being included merely in an honorific capacity.

all levels of society and commanded the respect of the rural society, both by their innate social status and the abundant power that the commission of the peace provided them. They had far more experience of government than any other members of the community. At the same time, they possessed in quarter sessions and divisions a ready-made administrative machine. Propaganda was required implicitly in some of these special commissions, and quarter sessions provided an excellent sounding board. And one commission, that for the forced loan, placed total responsibility on the magistrate-commissioners working at a divisional level. Undoubtedly, though, the most appealing advantage to a government in extreme financial straits was that justices did not cost anything—no fees, no share of the profits. Special commissions composed largely of justices permitted inexpensive administration by capable and generally well-affected administrators of long experience, profound local knowledge, and high status.[5]

As in magistracy, though he did not pay for their services the King demanded that the commissioners serve him diligently and without question. Unlike in magistracy, the tasks incumbent upon the commissioners were often wholly strange, sometimes infinitely difficult. Not a few of them were repugnant to the sensibilities of those gentlemen charged with carrying them out.

Both commissions for sewers and commissions for charitable uses were standing commissions, issued at regular intervals under the great seal. Both were based on statute, and in both the county's justices were in the majority although there were other commissioners, some of them borough magistrates. Clearly, these two standing commissions were issued to supplement the powers conferred by the commission of the peace. Neither imposed a serious burden of labor on the commissioners for the simple reason that the total business under both commissions was small.

Commissions for sewers were issued quinquennially and the proportion

[5] These considerations resulted in justices being used by those central courts employing examination procedure. Both the courts of Chancery and Exchequer commissioned one or two justices (along with others) to examine witnesses, etc., in the county. The court of Wards on those occasions when it employed commissioners usually appointed one or two justices among the five or six commissioners, and noted them as "justices" on the feodary's certificate. However, justices were seldom appointed to bankruptcy commissions; nor was it Star Chamber's practice to employ much justices as commissioners for examination in the county. These commissions out of the various courts invariably required one or two days' service.

of magisterial to nonmagisterial commissioners was roughly equal.[6] The commissioners' duties, imposed by a multitude of statutes, were basically the removal of impediments to the free flow of water in ditches and the upkeep of the walls and banks of such watercourses. Six commissioners (three to be of the quorum) had full authority to enquire by jury of twelve men and other lawful means, order removal of an impediment or improvement of a bank, tax persons for the repair, and fine and imprison at discretion those who refused to comply with their orders. In short, their powers were equal and their duties akin to those of the justices in bridge and road repair.[7]

In practice, the commissioners of sewers were indistinguishable from the justices. One half the commissioners were justices; fully three-quarters of the justices were commissioners. The active commissioners were the justices. In fact, the "sewers sessions" in Somerset by this time appear to have been merged often with quarter sessions,[8] and the clerk to the commissioners was probably the clerk of the peace. This was a natural development. The hundred juries, attendant at every quarter sessions, could as easily present a ditch bank in disrepair as a highway. Since the personnel of both commission of the peace and commission of sewers was largely the same, as a matter of convenience the administration of both commissions should have become the same. Evidently, though, this was a very recent development. In James' reign, quarter sessions in asserting its exclusive jurisdiction to order a bridge repaired, "rather than it should be repaired by the Commissioners of Sewers,"[9] indicated that there was then a division in practice as well as at law. However, by the 1630s, the merger appears to have been complete, and matters involving ditches were recorded in the sessions rolls, though all referrals for out-of-sessions treatment were to justices who were also commissioners for sewers.

Indeed, most of the repair of ditch banks, etc., was undertaken by

[6] PRO, C.181. Commissions for sewers were issued in 1625, 1629, 1634, and 1639 for all counties much as commissions of the peace were issued, PRO, C.66.

[7] Dalton in *The Countrey Justice*, p. 24, notes that two judgments in cases before the Common Pleas requiring commissioners for sewers to act according to "le rule del ley & reason" were also binding on the justices of the peace—an indication of the similarity of the two commissions. See Rooke's Case, 1598, in Edward Coke, *Quinta Pars* (1605), f. 99, and Keighley's Case, 1609, in Edward Coke, *La Dix[ie]me Part des Reports* (1614), ff. 139–140; also, John Herne's *Reading* (1659) on sewers.

[8] The Bridgwater "sessions of sewers" corresponded in time and place with the Michaelmas quarter sessions, SRO, QSOB, 1627/8–1638, Epiph. QS 1636/7, no. 15.

[9] SRO, QSOB, 1620/1–1627, Eas. QS 1622, no. 4.

justice-commissioners in their divisions. As nearly all justices were commissioners, there was no difficulty in referring the matter to commissioners out of sessions. It would be wrong to claim that the work involved under this special commission was onerous either by magnitude or frequency. Yet the duties were the same as those of the justices in bridge repair, and the great number of water courses, especially in the north-central portion of the county, did demand recurrent attention. The justice-commissioners had one more duty to perform by virtue of their special commission, one more duty added to many on justices out of sessions.

Commissions for charitable uses were issued almost annually by virtue of 43 Elizabeth I, c. 4, which was concerned with the misapplication of lands, goods, and money given in charitable trust.[10] The commissioners (or four of them) were, upon complaint, to enquire by jury and other lawful means, hear, determine, make order to correct the abuse and return the record of their proceedings into Chancery. By bill of exception out of Chancery the order of the commissioners could be reviewed in the court of Chancery and there upheld, modified, or overturned. The order, even if not reviewed, was confirmed in Chancery. Thus, the commissioners were in a sense an extension of the court of Chancery into the county. In contradistinction to the referees often appointed from among the justices by various other Westminster courts, the commissioners for charitable uses were not only a fact-finding body but a tribunal of determination as well.

Like the commissions for sewers, these commissions were composed of a nearly equal number of justices and nonmagisterial gentlemen. Unlike the commissioners for sewers, these commissioners had no connection with quarter sessions, and they held their enquiries independently in the locale involved in the matter. The hearings appear to have been of long duration. Though largely involving questions of fact, the law applied was equity, which, in that day even more than in ours, held many pitfalls for the layman. At least, these commissions meant little added work for the commissioners, for there seem to have been only three enquiries held in this period concerning Somerset charities.[11]

---

[10] For 1629–1642, the names of the commissioners for charitable uses can be found most readily in PRO, C.192/1.

[11] PRO, C.93/13, no. 1, 14, nos. 10, 18. I am obliged to Miss Carol Czapski for having observed that the justices acting as commissioners for charitable uses were in essence governing those aspects of poor relief otherwise outside their control.

The reason there were so few cases dealt with by the commissioners was because the majority of complaints concerning charitable uses apparently were brought by petition to the court of quarter sessions. There were a half-dozen such complaints, most of them connected with almshouses. It is not difficult to understand why such complaints were not brought before the commissioners, but it is difficult to discover by what authority the justices entertained them. There were two obvious procedural advantages in petitioning the justices. In the first place, they could reform the abuse more quickly by the informal method of investigation by justices out of sessions, coupled with final order of sessions. Moreover, the final order was not reviewable in the court of Chancery. Yet every one of these cases fitted exactly within the statute of charitable uses. In all the cases, the matter was referred to out-of-sessions justices for investigation, and in some, for final order as well. Quarter sessions did not even trouble to refer it to justices who were also commissioners for charitable uses. Such ready usurpation of the authority of another body was characteristic of all Tudor-Stuart legal institutions, and this was probably only a counterpart at a lower level of the overlapping jurisdiction in law that caused so much acrimony in Westminster Hall. Since the composition of both county bodies was largely the same, and since neither enjoyed any monetary gain from increased jurisdiction, there was no rivalry.

If these two standing commissions of sewers and charitable uses were far from imposing much more work upon the justices, the same was not true of the commissions issued in connection with four improvement schemes in Somerset that Charles and his ministers saw fit to undertake in this period. These four schemes had parallels in other counties. In fact, the most notable attribute of the Somerset schemes was that they did not result in the complete disruption of law and order as did similar projects in Lincolnshire, Wiltshire, Dorset, and Gloucestershire. But opposition there was, though it never reached such bounds as to require issuance of commissions of oyer and terminer and the intervention of the trained bands. In its very subtlety lay the strength of this opposition, and in the case of the great enclosing scheme for Sedgemoor, it was just as effective as the lawless efforts of the fenmen of Lincolnshire. It was with this opposition that the commissioners had to cope. It was to this opposition that the commissioners capitulated in the end.

Of all these projects, that for enclosing and draining of King's Sedgemoor was the greatest in magnitude and the most complete in failure. The vast watery wilderness comprising 14,000 acres in the central portion of the county had been the Abbot's of Glastonbury along with twenty-five manors adjacent, and on the Dissolution had passed to the Crown.[12] The Crown granted the manors to various gentlemen, but the swamp continued as a no-man's land in which the countryside round about and neighboring counties pastured their stock and its own amphibious folk made a living by netting ducks and fishing. James, with a mixed concern for the county's good and a desire to turn to royal advantage this not unproductive wasteland, first entertained the idea of undertaking the "religious" work of enclosing and draining this vast area.[13] Proceedings were begun in the court of Exchequer to prove the King's title to the moor against all those who claimed right of common in it. This had the intended effect of bringing to terms the twenty-five adjacent lords of manors; his Majesty was graciously pleased to allow to the lords and others who "pretended" commons rights 10,000 acres of the enclosed moor to be held in fee-simple, retaining for himself 4000 acres.[14]

It is likely that the speculators were in the scheme from the beginning; it had doubtless originated with them. The most active was one Adam Moore, and it was he who actually undertook the "negotiations" with the lords of the manors. In an apology written by himself and two associates there was no lack of mention of the county's and commonwealth's good.[15] But another argument that could not have failed to carry great weight with his Majesty was that the King's 4000 acres would soon produce an expected annual income of £2000. Naturally, Moore and his associates did not work for nothing and they intended to receive the fee farm of 1000 of the King's acres.[16]

The actual division of the moor and the laying out and draining of the King's portions was the responsibility of special commissioners. The

[12] Bodl, MS North, b. 26, ff. 50–51, survey and petition for draining King's Sedgemoor, *temp.* James I. I am indebted to Miss Nancy Briggs of the Essex Record Office for bringing this useful document to my attention.
[13] BM, Royal MS, 17A XXXVII, ff. 17–33. "Religious" was James' own epithet, and quite characteristic!
[14] PRO, C.66/2858, dorse no. 7, commission for the enclosure of King's Sedgemoor, tested 16 May 1639.
[15] BM, Royal MS, 17A XXXVII, ff. 17–33, "An apology of the King's agents for the enclosure of Kinges Sedgmoore in the county of Somerset." [*temp.* James I], by John Shotbolt, William Burnarde, and Adam Moore. This is a most able and persuasive argument for enclosure, containing a rather too colorful account of the deplorable state of the unenclosed moor.
[16] Bodl, MS North, b. 26, ff. 50–51.

6*

first commission was issued under James. Charles issued seven under the great seal and a number under the seal of the Exchequer.[17] Every commission was directed to a dozen or so local gentlemen, of whom no fewer than two-thirds were the most active justices of the peace. They were to meet, by the oath of lawful men and other means determine the size of the moor and divide it (according to directions) among the King, the bordering lords, and the freeholders and tenants who claimed rights of common. Then, with the cooperation of the commissioners of sewers, they were to supervise the draining of the King's portion. The commission was to be returned into the court of Exchequer within one or two terms following its issue, upon which the court would make a final decree.

Exchequer never made a final decree. The successive reissue of commissions for the enclosing and draining of Sedgemoor (largely to the same commissioners) were all in vain. Though there are no records of proceedings extant, there can be little doubt that each successive group of commissioners met, heard some evidence, perhaps advanced the division somewhat, but definitely did not settle the business. Just how little they did was evidenced by a signet letter to the judges of assize (who were made commissioners in the latest enclosure commission) complaining of the "many delayes and neglectes" in the prosecution of the Sedgemoor scheme, a "great cause" of which was the failure of the commissioners to attend sittings of the commission. Conceiving "that the best effect of the designe wilbee wrought by the countenance and carefull industrye of our commissioners," the King directed the judges to summon both the commissioners and the lords of bordering manors before them at assizes and declare to them the King's will. The commissioners were to be warned not to fail of "theire carefull attendaunce and execucion of the same effectually according to theire chardge therein expressed, whereof wee shall take both a due accompt and royall notice of each mans particular meritt and loyall demeanor towardes us."[18] This letter had no noticeable effect, anymore than a very plaintive letter to the newly appointed commissioners under an Exchequer commission of 1631/2. In this, the King took pains to allay the fears of the commoners:

[17] The commissions issued by Charles under the great seal were: 1625 (2), 1628, 1630, 1637/8, 1639 (2). I have found only the 1632/3 and 1633 Exchequer seal commissions. The commissions varied little either in commissioners or in terms of reference.

[18] PRO, S.O.1/2, pp. 13–14, 25 Feb. 1629/30. The commission referred to was that tested 2 April 1630, directed to Richardson, CJCP, and Denham, B, and other (magisterial) commissioners—the late *teste* date on the commission does not preclude the probability that this was the commission referred to in the signet letter.

"And you shall let the commoners knowe that the parte of the moore which shall thus be left to them shalbee absolutely conveyed by us in trust for theire use and behoofe and that we will take that course that they shalbe eased of such as pretend common there and have none." In the next sentence, Charles made a clearer statement of his intentions: "But if they [the commoners] shall neglect this our grace then they must knowe that we will make the best of our owne."[19] The King had already begun to make "the best" of his own. By privy seal of 25 January 1631/2, he conveyed to trustees all his interest in King's Sedgemoor. Some two years later, he directed the trustees to make over all his interest in the moor, including his 4000 acres set aside but not yet bounded, to a number of grantees, notable among them Sir Cornelius Vermuyden of the Fenland scheme fame and Jeffery Kirby, a London merchant and a promoter of the Fenland scheme. Kirby had paid £12,000 to the King as a fine for the conveyance and had agreed to an annual rent of £100 for the King's 4000 acres—a far cry from Charles' expected annual income of £2000 from the enclosure. Following Kirby's death, on the petition of Vermuyden and Kirby's widow, Margaret, the King agreed to issue letters patent under the great seal releasing them from the payment of all rents and charges for the 4000 acres.[20] Margaret Kirby never received the benefit of the lands. In 1637, she petitioned the King for another commission under the great seal for the division and draining of the moor and the setting out of her 4000 acres.[21] The commission was duly granted, but it was no more effectual than its predecessors in terminating the project. Over one hundred freeholders who claimed commons petitioned Charles II for the division of the moor according to the agreement made a half-century before by the King's grandfather.[22] Not until an act of Parliament in 1791 was the whole business essayed in the 1620s finally brought to fruition.[23]

[19] PRO, S.O.1/2, p. 171, signet letter to Sir William Portman, Bart., *et al.*, 21 Feb. 1631/2.

[20] Bodl, Bankes MSS, bundle 51, no. 65, petition of Vermuyden and Margaret Kirby, and warrant on the same, 2 Jan. 1634/5. It is evident that by 1631 Vermuyden was the moving force behind the Sedgemoor scheme.

[21] PRO, S.P.16/323, no. 166, petition of Margaret Kirby, and reference to A-G Bankes to prepare commission, 12 Oct. 1637. The commission was tested 3 Feb. 1637/8, PRO, C.66/2763, dorse, no. 2.

[22] BM, Add. MS 35251, f. 21, petition of freeholders, etc., adjoining King's Sedgemoor [*temp.* Charles II].

[23] 31 George III, c. 91. The award, of 1795, is in the SRO; the area comprised was 4000 acres more than in the Jacobean scheme.

The main responsibility for the failure of the Sedgemoor scheme must rest with the justice-commissioners. The lords of the manors were compliant though lukewarm, and the speculator Moore had laid the necessary groundwork. The trouble was that the commissioners came up squarely against the opposition of the small tenants who had nothing to gain in the exchange of extensive commons for minute parcels of fenced-in, seasonally water-logged sod. The small commoners recognized that the lion's share of an enclosed Sedgemoor would go to the Earls of Pembroke and Northampton, Sir John Stawell, John Mallett, and the other adjacent manor lords. So, they initiated an obstructive campaign which buzzed continuously for over fifteen years. And in the end the buzzing sapped the vitality of the whole program. The commissioners were in the invidious position of deciding between the claims of their powerful peers, the lords of manors, and the claims of the multitude of small freeholders. On the one hand, the commissioners had to serve the King's and manor lords' interests, and on the other, they had to avoid offending the mass of smaller men who in the final analysis formed the "good opinion of the country" on which those commissioners relied for their power in the county. It is too easy to underestimate the pressure that these freeholders might bring to bear upon their masters of the rural bench. Though inarticulate and brave only when drunk or safely beyond their betters' ears, these were the "wealthy and substantiall men though none the best bred" who elected the knights of the shire. It was because the justices were not acting in their accepted position of county magistrates but as the agents of the Crown for the execution of a widely unpopular program that they were incapable of acting with decision and finality. It was too much to expect that commissioners like Sir Robert Phelips, Sir John Horner, and Sir Henry Berkeley, their eyes on a seat in Parliament, always in pursuit of the country's good opinion, would take the calculated risk of offending a goodly portion of the county. Yet, it was also too much to expect that these men would patently oppose a project which the King appeared determined to perfect. The course the commissioners took was the line of least resistance, the policy of do-nothing. They merely drifted until the commission was returned into Exchequer. Then all breathed easily again. The lack of enthusiasm among the lords of the manors and the King's growing indifference after he had sold his interest made the act of drifting infinitely easier under the commissions of the 1630s. Even drift, though, required some show of effort, and for men actively engaged in magisterial duties, the show was tantamount to a very real expenditure of time and energy.

Unlike Sedgemoor, Aldermoor near Glastonbury did not have to wait for the more ruthless and less sensitive methods of eighteenth-century parliamentary enclosure.[24] The marked success that attended the commissioners for the enclosing of Aldermoor provides additional confirmation as to the Sedgemoor commissioners' responsibility for the conspicuous failure of that project. The fourteen commissioners (half of them also Sedgemoor commissioners at the same time) named in a commission out of the court of Exchequer in 1630/1[25] appear to have carried out their tasks with celerity and thoroughness. They too encountered opposition, on one occasion certifying the seditious words of a recalcitrant commoner to the Council—they were saved from the weightiest opposition of all, that of William Strode (who distinguished himself as an opponent of ship money) for that obstreperous gentleman and claimant of rights in Aldermoor made his stand in the court of Exchequer some five years after the commissioners completed their labor.[26] Three circumstances vitiated the effects that opposition might have had on the commissioners. The first was that Aldermoor was a very small area, the enclosing of which involved only two adjacent lords of manors, four neighboring villages, and consequently a fraction of the number of freeholders and small tenants concerned in Sedgemoor's enclosure. Thus, the commissioners ran little chance of forfeiting the good opinion of any appreciable portion of their countrymen. Secondly, the commissioners were required only to set out and delimit the allotments of the moor on the basis of a settlement already reached by the King's farmer (who moved the enclosure) with the lords of manors and others holding rights of common in Aldermoor. The commissioners were not charged with the responsibility of obtaining the agreement or for undertaking all that was demanded of the Sedgemoor commissioners.[27] The commissioners were, therefore, not subject to the same

[24] For a lively account of an attempt to enclose King's Sedgemoor in 1775 and the near-success of the methods employed, see J. L. and B. Hammond, *The Village Labourer* (1948), I, 59–65.

[25] PRO, E.178/5616, commission to Sir Robert Phelips *et al.,* 15 Feb. 1630/1.

[26] PRO, S.P.16/198, no. 37; 533, no. 44, Sir Robert Phelips to the Earl of Holland, August 1631. Phelips urged action against the commoner, especially since other designs of that nature "are generally beset with bold oppositions"—a sly strike at his enemy Poulett's battle against the disafforestation of Neroche, see p. 222. For Strode's action, see PRO, E. 159/477, Eas. 13 Chas. I, rot. 37.

[27] PRO, E.178/5615, commission of 15 Feb. 1630/1; E.159/477, Eas. 13 Chas. I, rot. 37, Exchequer order 15 May 1637.

pressures which beset the Sedgemoor commissioners, who bore the major responsibility and so most of the blame for enclosure there.

Of even greater significance was the third circumstance. It was decidedly in the interests of the chief commissioner, Sir Robert Phelips, to dispatch the King's business. As the new decade opened, Phelips like others of his outspoken parliamentary brethren found himself in the wilderness, the Commons House darkened, and an angry monarch resolutely embarked on his "personal rule." Unlike Eliot, Selden and Holles, Sir Robert had reason for hope. Phelips' voice having been somewhat muted in that last great debate, the King perceived within him the seeds of redemption. Sometime before the Aldermoor commission was issued, the King in referring to the project exhorted Phelips to "rather use your best endeavours and care for the preservation and increase of our . . . inheritance then for the favour of the multitude, and doubt not but what benefitt wee shall receave by your service we shall thankfully accept."[28] To Phelips, painfully climbing the road to the royal favor that his two years out of the commission of the peace and the loss of his deputy lieutenancy indicates he had forfeited, these words must have sounded very sweet. It was worth the calculated risk of offending a few of his countrymen to regain in part the royal favor that constituted the other foundation of the magnate's power in the county.

No less success than that enjoyed by the commissioners for Aldermoor attended the efforts of the two bodies of commissioners for the disafforestation of Neroche and Frome Selwood forests, respectively. Charles, evidently on the advice of Attorney-General Heath, who appears to have had a personal interest in the disafforestation of Neroche, decided in 1627 to disafforest these royal forests in the county. The income that would be derived from the surrender of his forest rights the King intended should go towards defraying the charges of the Ré fleet upon its return. This disafforestation was not an isolated attempt to procure revenue, for similar projects were undertaken at about the same time in the forests of Gillingham (Dorset), Braydon (Wiltshire), and Dean (Gloucestershire), though with far unhappier and probably less remunerative results than in Somerset.

Accordingly, two commissions, one for Neroche and the other for Frome Selwood, were issued under the great seal in July 1627. The commissioners (mostly justices) were to compound with all landowners, great

[28] PRO, S.P.16/427, no. 51, King to Sir Robert Phelips, draft [30 Aug. 1629]. See Gardiner, VII, 319.

and small, within the forest for the conveyance of a portion of their lands to the King in return for which the King would be pleased to relinquish all rights to the forest. Three other sets of commissions, directed to most of the initial commissioners, authorized them to set out highways, enclose the lands laid out by them, and sell the King's portion of the settlement.[29] From the sale of his portion of the two forests—one-third of each—the King expected £20,000.[30] What money remained would go towards paying the cost of the disafforestations, the greatest item being the fee of Sir Sackville Crow who, like Adam Moore in the Sedgemoor business, negotiated the agreement with the landowners and represented the King's interests in the affair. Charles' sanguine hopes, that £20,000 would be forthcoming by Hallowstide 1627, were not realized. The commissioners for both forests were still busy in 1640. As late as 1638, £1000 of the King's expected share was outstanding, and it is unlikely that Crow ever collected the £2800 still owed him for his pains.[31] None the less, this was a marvellous success compared to the paltry returns that Sedgemoor ultimately yielded.

As in the division of Sedgemoor, there was no lack of opposition to hinder the commissioners. The disafforestations in the three neighboring counties carried on at the same time as that for Neroche and Frome Selwood called forth a reaction so violent that it amounted almost to civil war.[32] Opposition in Neroche, though, was of the same quiet variety that brought the division of Sedgemoor to a halt. The smallholders and tenants realized that the diminutive tracts allotted them could never compensate for the loss of the commons they had enjoyed when the King's forest law prohibited enclosure. As the commissioners for Neroche began their work, the rumor campaign was under way.[33]

[29] The commissions (all on the patent rolls) for each forest were issued the same days: 25 July 1627, 17 Nov. 1627, 24 Dec. 1627, 21 April 1628. Unfortunately, the State Papers Domestic are largely silent on the actual proceedings of the Frome Selwood commissioners. The fullness of the evidence concerning Neroche is due to Poulett's involvement and consequently his correspondence with Secretary of State Dorchester.

[30] PRO, S.P.16/290, no. 78, notes by Sec. Coke of financial business, 12 June 1635; E.403/3041, p. 5, warrant of 13 Dec. 1634.

[31] PRO, S.P.16/44, no. 92, state of accounts for disafforestation of Frome Selwood and Neroche [1638]. Demands, including Crow's, amounted to £7849, and there was only an expected £1264 to meet them.

[32] See D. G. C. Allan, "The Rising in the West, 1628–1631," *Econ Hist Rev* (1952), series 2, V, 76–83. Mr. Allan pays tribute to the local governors of Dorset, Wilts., and Gloucestershire who put down the insurrections.

[33] The commission to Lord Poulett and others of 24 Dec. 1627 was principally "for examininge upon oath and discovery of such practizes as have ben used by any person to the hinderance" of the Neroche disafforestation, secondarily for the enclosure, setting forth of highways, etc., PRO, Index 4211, commission tested 24 Dec. 1627.

The little people of Neroche had one powerful friend on their side. From the beginning, John Lord Poulett appears to have fomented trouble and resistance. Poulett had been the keeper of Neroche forest since 1619, and by right of that office had in that privileged area indulged to satiation his passion for the chase. Disafforestation meant for Lord Poulett the end of his hunting and (this was probably a lesser consideration) the termination of a royal office which provided him with close, sociable contacts at Court. His numerous letters to Conway and Dorchester concerning the disafforestation reached the zenith of vituperation when he wrote of the commissioners who "turned [me] out of my pleasure."[34] Although some among the commissioners, such as John Symes, JP, had long been on poor terms with Poulett, their repeated complaints to the Lord Treasurer of Poulett's obstinacy and sullen opposition ring true. There can be no doubt that the meeting of two hundred malcontents at Ashill in January 1628/9 had been organized by Poulett's ranger, perhaps with Poulett's privity.[35] If he was not in collusion with the opposition, Poulett was far from circumspect, and took no pains to place himself above suspicion. By 1631, his activities had almost brought about his disgrace at Court.[36]

That such opposition and its powerful though not wholly vocal ally were unable to vitiate the Neroche project was due to a number of reasons. In the first place, the King was far more directly concerned throughout in the disafforestation of Neroche than he had been in Sedgemoor. Attorney-General Heath, too, had secured a manor within the forest, and was intent on enclosing it and selling off its timber, Sir Robert Phelips having conveyed Broadway manor to him in return for Muchelney manor from the Crown.[37] On at least two occasions a word at Court from Heath had meant severe regal reprimand for Poulett. Sir Robert Phelips, striving to regain his place on the rural bench and in royal favor and delighted to embarrass Poulett, cooperated fully. Nominated by a royal letter to be an "assistant" to the Neroche commissioners, he was in a position to flay Poulett but in no position to lead the potential malcontents. But above all, the commissioners did their job with gusto.

[34] PRO, S.P.16/530, no. 58, Poulett to [Sec. Dorchester] 20 May 1629.
[35] PRO, S.P.16/131, no. 16, minutes of events in Neroche by two of the commissioners, 4 Jan. 1628/9.
[36] Poulett appears to have been fined, or threatened with fine, in connection with the Neroche business—he showed unusual firmness in writing to Dorchester, refusing to pay it, PRO, S.P.16/210, no. 33, 15 Jan. 1631/2.
[37] PRO, C.P.25(2)/479 Mich. 5 Chas. I, Heath *vs.* Phelips.

In the case of John Symes and Thomas Brereton, both justices, personal dislike for Poulett gave added zest to the discharge of their assignment. Two other active commissioners of lesser status saw in the business a way to royal favor, and they were particularly diligent.[38] Again, as in the Aldermoor enclosure, the opposition was not so great in numbers as to provide a serious threat to the commissioners' reputations in the county. Not least, the commissioners knew that the interests of the King and the Attorney-General were involved to an exceptional extent. It behoved them to act with more than ordinary dispatch and care.

If the opposition was not successful it had at least made infinitely more difficult the task of those commissioners engaged in the Neroche disafforestation. The two most assiduous, John Symes and Thomas Brereton, were as well two of the most active justices. Though there is insufficient evidence on the progress of the disafforestation of Frome Selwood to draw any definite conclusions concerning it, the fact that the first agreements made with those claiming rights in the forest were not drawn until 1631 indicates that the commissioners there had also encountered opposition. Their work was not wholly completed until the eve of the Long Parliament. Following 1631, the commissioners for both forests continued the piecemeal task of concluding agreements with landholders in the two forests; there was a spate of agreements entered for confirmation in the Exchequer in 1639/40.[39] For all the justice-commissioners involved in these two projects the four or more years of regularly recurring meetings required before they completed the bulk of their commissions had been years of increasing tempo in their other duties as magistrates. The commissions had been issued just as the justices were most busy with the collection of the forced loan. They demanded the greatest effort at the moment of greatest activity invoked by the Book of Orders.

Two other disafforestation projects were essayed, one for the disafforestation of Exmoor (mostly in Devon) and the other for Petherton Forest near Bridgwater. About 154,000 acres was involved in the former scheme and the King hoped that £100,000 in fines for conveyances and a large annual rent could be secured. There is, however, nothing to

[38] Poulett had some particularly hard words for William Dyneley (not a JP) who was obviously in the scheme for what he could get out of it, PRO, S.P.16/195, no. 12, Poulett to Sec. Dorchester, 27 June 1631. Dyneley was the most active of the commissioners in both forests, and doubtless the Crown's principal agent, Bodl, Bankes MSS, bundle 6, no. 26.

[39] PRO, E.159/479, Hil. 10 Chas. I, rots. 39, 51-56.

indicate that this project, mooted in 1629/30, was ever put into operation, perhaps for want of "some great person" to undertake the responsibility of the business as the original discussion seemed to indicate would be necessary.[40] Nor was the Petherton scheme brought to fruition. In Trinity term 1638, a commission under the Exchequer seal was directed to John Coventrye and nine others (in all, seven of them justices) to survey Petherton Forest, to treat with all claiming rights, and to disafforest the soil of the King and the soil of other owners willing to come to terms.[41] A local jury of enquiry—including, evidently, three jurors with extensive holdings in the forest—found that the forest was not a royal forest! The commissioners dismissed the hostile jury and refused to treat with any claimants for disafforestation. The commissioners' understandable reluctance to run the risk of suit for proceeding to disafforest an area which a jury had found was not a forest halted the project. Sir Thomas Wrothe, the neighboring magistrate, offered to contract for disafforestation of his 1400 acres within the forest,[42] but he appears to have been alone in his readiness to come to terms. The Exchequer court does not appear to have made any order in connection with this project.

Three other improvement project commissions were issued which for want of evidence can only be mentioned. A commission under the great seal, tested 6 March 1637/8, was directed to eighteen Somerset gentlemen, twelve of them justices, directing them to compound with owners of mills, etc., on the River Tone between Taunton and Bradford Bridge (about two miles west of Taunton) for recompence to be made by them to John Mallett, JP, who had undertaken at his own expense to make this stretch of river navigable.[43] For Somerset as for almost all other counties, commissions for the investigation of depopulating enclosures were issued in the middle of the 1630s. Two commissions for Somerset, tested 4 April and 8 July 1635, were directed to six men (three of them justices) and seven men (two of them justices) respectively. There is no record for Somerset of compositions for depopulations on the only surviving composition roll; neither will any warrants for compositions by Somerset landholders be found in the registers of issues, Auditor's warrant books,

[40] PRO, S.P.16/161, no. 80, note of the King's intentions concerning Exmoor and Dartmoor Forests [c. Feb. 1629/30].

[41] Bodl, Bankes MSS, bundle 51, no. 5, warrant to A-G to draft a commission, 30 June 1638. The ubiquitous Dyneley of the Neroche and Frome Selwood schemes was also a commissioner here.

[42] PRO, S.P.16/406, no. 47, minute of application by Sir Thomas Wrothe [c. fall 1638].

[43] PRO, C.181/5, p. 197, and Index 4212, commission of 6 March 1637/8.

warrants for depopulations, 1636/7–1639/40.[44] One thing is certain: any time expended by the commissioners in execution of these three commissions was time which at that juncture they could ill-afford to spend away from the more pressing duties of magistracy and lieutenancy.

The heaviest of the "other tasks" which devolved upon the local governors occurred when the King and Council chose to use them as agents for the collection of revenue. In the brief span of the first eight years of Charles' reign they were so employed on nine separate occasions. Four times they acted in the accustomed duty of commissioners for subsidies.[45] Five times they were required to collect revenue, the legality of which was in all but one instance highly questionable, the opposition to which in all instances was mighty. Compared to the enormous opposition raised by the free gift of 1626 and the forced loan of 1626–1627, the heeldragging rumor campaigns in Sedgemoor and Neroche were hardly more annoying than the mosquitoes which inhabited the former.

The revenue projects bore with far greater weight on the justices than did the other special commissions. While the commissions for improvement were directed to a dozen or so justices, the revenue projects, with one exception, required the labor of almost all the justices at the divisional level. Above all, the pressure of a king and his ministers striving to avoid bankruptcy was applied to the justices undertaking the revenue programs in such liberal doses as most of them had never felt before, nor would feel again until the Book of Orders and the writs for ship money came forth from Whitehall.

Charles' first financial experiment was deceptively easy for the justices. Having secured only two subsidies with no fifteenths from the first session of his first Parliament, Charles fell back on the well-worn expedient of demanding a loan by letters under privy seal directed to wealthier yeomen and the higher orders of society. Consequently, in September

[44] PRO, C.181/5, pp. 3, 43; C.212/20; E.403/3041–3042. A commission of swans for the counties of Hants., Dorset, Somerset, Devon, and Cornwall and the Isle of Wight was issued to gentlemen of those counties, including the lord lieutenant, a deputy lieutenant, and eleven justices of Somerset, tested 20 May 1629, PRO, C.181/4, ff. 2–3. The duties of the commissioners could not have been onerous, though nothing remains of their proceedings to determine what labor was required of them.

[45] Four grants of subsidies were made, two in 1625 and two in 1628. The commissioners for the subsidy were appointed for divisions corresponding to the magisterial divisions (see map on p. 41) and were, with very few exceptions, justices. They were responsible for adjusting rating, supervising the collectors, etc., PRO, E.179/171/361–367, and 172/371–408.

1625 the King informed the Council that he had sent letters to the lords lieutenants of all English and Welsh counties requiring them "with ye advice of their deputy lieutenantes, as persons best acquainted . . . with the state of the countries where they dwell," to certify to the Council those able to lend and what sum they could lend.[46] The Council was thereupon to direct the dispatch of privy seal letters to all those named requesting them to lend the specified sum, to appoint a collector in each county, and to stand ready to make rating adjustments in particular cases. There was nothing novel in this procedure, for as early as Elizabeth's reign the deputy lieutenants had acted as rating officers for privy seal loans.[47] More justices than those who were deputies were involved in the rating. The deputy lieutenants (apparently of their own volition) relied on the divisional justices for the actual information necessary to make the rate. Since one hundred and forty persons were returned as being able to lend, it is unlikely that the deputies had a personal knowledge of all their estates sufficient to fit them with any degree of accuracy within the broad scale of rates specified by the Council.[48] This, however, was the sum total of the local governors' duties in connection with the loan, save those incumbent on the collector, who happened to be a justice. There does not appear to have been any opposition, and if there was the Council evidently dealt with it directly and effectively. The privy seal loan was deceptively easy—but the justices in 1625 had not yet felt the effects of the nation's growing disillusionment with the new King and increasing hatred of his chief minister. That disillusionment set in only after the stormy second Parliament.

There was nothing easy about the free gift that was to take from the nation at large what its representatives at Westminster in the second Parliament had refused to give. On 7 July 1626, the King ordered all the justices of England and Wales to exhort their countrymen to freely give the equivalent sums of money that the four proposed subsidies in the last

---

[46] PRO, S.P.16/6, no. 70, King to PC, 17 Sept. 1625. The names of the "lenders" and the sums involved are in PRO, E.401/2586. The net income expected from Somerset was £2219 13s 4d. Some of the privy seal letters—printed forms with names and sums filled in by hand—are in PRO, E.401/2590.

[47] G. S. Thomson, *Lords Lieutenants,* pp. 120–125. The 1589 and 1596 loans were raised by the deputy lieutenants, as was the 1611 loan, PRO, S.P.14/67, no. 114.

[48] Two Somerset deputies, moving for a reduction for one gentleman, confessed that they had been misinformed as to his estate by the divisional justices, PRO, S.P.16/540, no. 9, Robert Hopton, DL, to Sir John Horner, collector, 25 Jan. 1625/6. In SRO, Phelips MSS, vol. B, f. 171 there is an assessment by Sir Robert Phelips, JP, of all in his division able to lend.

Parliament would have brought in had the Commons acquiesced.[49] Perhaps no other financial expedient that Charles resorted to was so devoid of political reality. The careful preparation for this naive request had been the discharge of unreliable magistrates from some counties' commissions of the peace. In Somerset, Sir Robert Phelips and Edward Kyrton were stricken from the commission at the moment the free gift was demanded, and three other Somerset justices followed them shortly afterwards.[50] The opposition in Somerset to the free gift was led by four of these men. Without giving undue emphasis to John Poulett's implication of Phelips in the opposition, there can be no doubt that Phelips and Hugh Pyne, in particular, agitated with great forcefulness against the free gift. It did not take long for a vast rumor campaign centering on the expected convocation of a new Parliament to make impossible the work of the divisional justices busily cajoling their lesser neighbors to give. The justices might well have proceeded "temperately and discreetlye" in their divisions, and many of his Majesty's subjects might well have expressed their "dutiful affections."[51] But in Somerset, as elsewhere, the free gift was a colossal failure. There were no efforts to spur the justices to great activity, for by September even the Council realized how hopeless was the justices' task. By then, too, the Council had hit upon a far more fruitful means of obtaining revenue.

The *enfant terrible* of a financially embarrassed King and his ministers was the forced loan of 1626–1627. Of all the unparliamentary financial expedients (save ship money) that the first two Stuarts resorted to, the forced loan was the greatest in magnitude of demand and the greatest in magnitude of accomplishment.[52] That the result was so nearly

---

[49] PRO, S.P.16/31, nos. 30–31, King to JPs Eng. and Wales, 7 July 1626. There were historic if not legal precedents for the free gift. The justices had been required to collect a "benevolence" in 1614. On that occasion, the slowness of the justices in many counties, Somerset included, had resulted in the Council summoning justices in droves. There, the Somerset justices pleaded that 1 Richard III, c. 2 prohibited such exactions; the Council informed them that the statute was not directed against "any guift or contribucion," *Acts PC*, 1613–1614, p. 629. In 1622, the justices of the kingdom raised a "voluntary contribution" for the Palatinate.

[50] Phelips and Kyrton were struck off the commission solely on the Council's initiative along with thirteen justices of other counties for their opposition in Parliament, BM, Harl. MS 286, f. 297, fiat of Ld Kpr Coventrye, 8 July 1626. From the next commission (tested 9 Sept. 1626) Hugh Pyne, John Symes, and Thomas Lyte were omitted, evidently at John Poulett's instigation, in order to embarrass Phelips, SRO, Commissions of the peace, box 2, commission of 9 Sept. 1626.

[51] PRO, S.P.16/36, no. 46, John Poulett to Edward Nicholas, 24 Sept. 1626; S.P.16/37, no. 5, John Poulett to Sec. Conway, 1 Oct. 1626.

[52] The forced loan of 1626–1627 produced somewhat less than £300,000 according to Gardiner, VI, 143n1.

satisfactory to a King and his chief minister, who with singular stupidity had taken the nation to war against France as well as Spain, owed nothing to the nation's willingness to finance the extended war effort. The refusal of supply by the nation's representatives in the Parliament that had been dissolved a few months earlier had been a clear condemnation of the government's prosecution of the war against Spain. The result of the forced loan was satisfactory because the King's ministers did not scruple to use coercion of unprecedented forcefulness against those who opposed the loan and pressure of comparable forcefulness upon those local governors who were responsible for its collection.

The forced loan was a loan in name only. The money, ostensibly to be repaid within eighteen months, was never repaid, nor is it likely that it was ever the government's intention that it would be. It was a subsidy without parliamentary sanction. The actual rate was fixed on the basis of five subsidies (a heavy rate of taxation) and the procedure to collect it was the same as that used to collect a subsidy. In fact the only particular in which the forced loan differed from a parliamentary grant was that it taxed more people. Besides the gentlemen and freeholders who appeared in the subsidy rolls, all others of "ability" were to be rated as well—a precedent for the future, for ship money rating also took account of "ability." The manifest illegality of the levy was condemned by inference in the refusal of the judges to extend legal sanction to it. They were willing to subscribe to it merely to please the King, but not as an indication of their approval of its legality.[53] Charles was not satisfied with this, and Lord Chief Justice Crew paid the price for incurring the King's displeasure by loss of office. If the government would brook no defiance from the judges, even less would it brook defiance from the justices of the peace.

Despite the judges' refusal to give legal sanction to the forced loan, it had considerable success during September 1626 in Middlesex and a few other counties under the Council's eye. The government was encouraged to enlarge its grasp. Accordingly, on 13 October commissions for all the remaining counties of England and Wales passed under the great seal, the commissioners for Somerset being all local governors with the exception of one peer.[54] Any two or more of the commissioners were

---

[53] *Ibid.*, VI, 148–149.

[54] PRO, C.66/2376, dorse, no. 1. Besides privy councillors, the first Somerset commission included the lord lieutenant, one deputy, and sixteen justices—the second commission, tested the same day as the first (13 Oct. 1626) apparently included all the justices in the county. Recently appointed justices were added to the loan commissions in Dec. 1626.

"att such and soe manie tymes and places as yee shall thinke fittest call before you all such persons"[55] able to lend and acquaint them with the King's will and see the commission "speedily" performed and returned, according to the instructions sent them. As conciliar directions, these twelve pages of instructions were unparalleled for completeness and attention to minute detail. All the commissioners were to meet together and themselves subscribe to the loan. Then they were to divide, and rate all who appeared in the subsidy books and others of ability who did not. The commissioners were to urge the necessity of the loan and make very clear that it would not be a precedent. One half of the sum rated was to be paid within a fortnight to the collector for each division (appointed by the commissioners) and the other half within three months. Those who would not subscribe were to be examined on oath to discover if any had persuaded them to defy the royal will. Everything was to be done in the utmost secrecy, and discussion of the loan was to be discouraged. Finally, the names of all refusers and other refractory persons were to be certified to the Council along with the names of any commissioners who absented themselves from the service.

These detailed instructions containing the implication of strong retribution set the tone for the whole business. In a further letter from the Council, the commissioners were directed to bind over collectors who would not serve. Unlike some counties, in Somerset there do not appear to have been any commissioners or collectors who did not set-to with exceptional diligence.[56]

The opposition to the loan in Somerset was sizable and it was widespread. Nowhere did it manifest itself in direct refusal to pay the loan, nor did it express itself in any high-sounding espousal of rights and liberties. It lacked leadership among the magisterial class itself and the "powers, favours, and creditts"[57] which the magistrates had in the county were turned to the King's service. Lord Poulett did not fail to note the significance of the fact that when the business began, Sir Robert Phelips "took his journy to London."[58] Indeed, it was the opposition's want of such leadership in Somerset that made the loan go more smoothly

[55] PRO, S.P.16/36, no. 43, instructions to commissioners for the loan [Sept.] 1626.

[56] On Buckingham's order, three Cornish justices were ousted from the commission of the peace for opposition to the loan, PRO, S.P.16/48, no. 16, Buckingham to Edward Nicholas, 27 June 1627.

[57] PRO, S.P.16/36, no. 43.

[58] PRO, S.P.16/53, no. 88, John Poulett to Edward Nicholas, 12 Feb. 1626/7. Phelips and the four other Somerset justices dropped before or during the free gift were still out.

there than it did in some other counties where even peers of the realm agitated against it. But opposition there was, and though never as strong or as serious as that in Lincolnshire and Essex it required the constant attention of the commissioners and collectors to combat it successfully.

Inevitably, the opposition held up the progress of the loan and it required eleven months of nearly constant activity to overcome it and bring the loan to its final, fairly satisfactory conclusion. In proportion as the commissioners' efforts were retarded by the effects of opposition, the Council demanded even greater effort. In January 1626/7 various privy councillors visited every shire, three of them sitting as commissioners at Bath and there summoning before them the recalcitrant and the slow to subscribe to the loan under their gaze.[59] Doubtless, this extraordinary, brief extension of the Council *in propria persona* into the county had the desired effect of coercing the gentlemen and freeholders, previously reluctant, into subscribing. Moreover, it had the broader effect of quickening the work of the commissioners. The kind words of the Council, reconvened at Westminster, that followed the visitation of the councillors[60] were sound tactics, and combined with the not so kind words heard at Bath a few days earlier, left the commissioners with no misunderstanding of what was expected of them. To judge from their reports, for the next three months the commissioners worked hard. However, the opposition slackened but little in its struggle, and when the three months were up in May, many had still not paid. This called forth a new round of very sharp Council letters which by demanding that the collectors pay in all monies by Easter term[61] stirred up the commissioners and collectors to added effort. Again, the opposition took its toll—generally as well as in Somerset. In June, when the monies had not been paid by Easter term, further Council letters of harsher note than any that had gone before demanded concerted action against those who had not yet paid. At the same time, the clerks of the peace of all the counties appear to have been summoned before the Council,[62] undoubtedly

[59] PRO, S.P.16/53, no. 48, commissioners of loans for three hundreds to PC, 8 Feb. 1626/7. The three councillors were: Earl of Pembroke (Lord Steward and Ld Lt Somerset), Earl of Montgomery (Lord Chamberlain), Sir Richard Weston (Chancellor of the Exchequer).

[60] *Acts PC,* 1627, p. 43, PC to commissioners in ten counties including Somerset, 31 Jan. 1626/7.

[61] *Acts PC,* 1627, p. 272, PC to commissioners in most counties and boroughs of Eng. and Wales, 12 May 1627.

[62] *Acts PC,* 1627, p. 387, PC to commissioners in most counties and boroughs of Eng. and Wales, 30 June 1627—"His majesty imputes the fault rather to you . . ." than to those who are to lend. PRO, S.P.16/89, no. 1, persons summoned before PC [c. 30 June 1627].

so that a report on the activities of their masters could be wrung from them. This alone might have accounted for the burst of effort displayed in progress reports from collectors and commissioners in the ensuing weeks. Finally in August, with the opposition reduced to a small hard core—albeit a hard core fast softening—the last Council letter ordered the commissioners to take the accounts of the collectors in their divisions and report within ten days on the state of the accounts.[63] The final series of reports, though meagre, indicate that virtually all the money in Somerset had been collected and paid in. The Council was satisfied, the commission terminated, and the commissioners became once again merely justices involved in the normal round of magisterial duties.

Certainly, the justice-commissioners returned to their routine duties of administration. But, unknown to them, in the eleven months they had executed so diligently the commission for the forced loan, they had taken the first step along the road that led to the Book of Orders on the one hand and ship money on the other. By the end of these two great programs of the 1630s, the very complexion of county government had been changed. Though the change was not apparent to the justices themselves until the Book of Orders and ship money came to dominate all of county government, it had been heralded unobtrusively in the forced loan of 1626–1627.

The forced loan was the unintentional prelude to the program inaugurated by the Book of Orders. In the execution of the commission for the forced loan can be found all the elements which made the administration centering on the justices of the peace so vastly different and so much more difficult after 1630/1 than it had ever been before. Divisional meetings, reports, the continuous application of pressure upon subordinate officers and, above all, the relentlessly recurring demand of the Council for speed and efficiency—all can be found in the minute instructions of October 1626 and their embodiment in practice during the following eleven months.

Of even greater significance, the forced loan marked the end of the justices as officers of government above the constitutional struggle that had disrupted the relations of the King and Parliament in a crescendo of acrimony. Charles' second Parliament bore witness to how wide the gulf was which separated the King and his ministers from the nation's

---

[63] *Acts PC,* 1627, p. 492, PC to commissioners in most counties and boroughs of Eng. and Wales, 20 Aug. 1627.

representatives. That division was carried down to the level of every justice of the peace when Charles sent home Parliament and turned to the justices to obtain from the country what he had been unable to get from the country's representatives. In so doing, he propelled every single justice into the struggle in which hitherto only a few of them as individuals had been involved. With the forced loan, so manifestly illegal that the learned judges would not give sanction of law to it, the individual justice faced clearly for the first time the terrible choice of either serving the King or respecting the interests of his countrymen and the law as he conceived it. This was the choice posed by the widespread opposition on the one side, and the pressure of the government to overcome that opposition on the other. Both opposition and pressure were so considerable in intensity that the issue could not be avoided as, time and again, the justices had avoided it before.

We can only guess, three centuries after, what conflicts were raised in the mind of the ordinary justice when faced with his King's demand and his neighbors' sincere opposition to that demand. Never before had he been presented was so clear-cut a choice as in those eleven months. Yet, the 1630s was an epoch in which that choice was recurrently posed. Each time it became more difficult as the chasm between his King and his neighbors widened. As the individual justice valued his office and the prestige it conferred, as he honored his sacred oath taken upon assuming that office, so he chose outwardly to serve his King. As he valued his neighbors' respect, as he cherished his own deep and impelling reverence for the sanctity of the law, so he repudiated inwardly his King and his King's program. Ship money was the last great moment of choice. The first moment had come in 1626. The forced loan had been the point of no return.

Between the first moment of choice and the last, Somerset's local governors were required only twice more to gather unparliamentary revenue. Those of them who served as commissioners for the composition for knighthood had the unpleasant task of levying what was in effect a fine for no crime committed upon members of their own class, indeed, upon associates of the rural bench.[64] Pecuniary punishment to gain revenue from gentlemen who had not taken the degree of knighthood

[64] Three commissions were issued for Somerset, the first in July 1630; little was accomplished under this commission, and the real work was done under the commissions of 12 Feb. 1630/1 and 29 June 1631. Of the seven commissioners in each of these latter two commissions, six were justices, one of whom was also the collector, PRO, E.178/5614–5615.

as befitted their estates was undoubtedly legal, but very poor policy in seventeenth-century England. The labor required of the commissioners was considerable. They had to search the subsidy and rate books, conduct hearings, issue warrants for attendance of parties to compound, assess composition sums, and direct payment of the composition, all in accordance with a complicated set of fifteen instructions annexed to the commission. The hardest job was to press the victims to pay the assessment. The task could not have left a pleasant taste in the commissioners' mouths. Thirteen of those fined (that is, forced to compound) in Somerset were justices—the instructions quite explicitly directed that no justice of the peace was to be allowed to compound for less than £25, and most of them were forced to pay considerably more.[65] The commissioners were in no position to ease their colleagues. In Somerset and six other counties the second group of commissioners had a nasty warning of what would befall them if they favored any of their friends and associates. Sir Thomas Thynne, Bart., sheriff of Somerset 1629–1630, was one of three sheriffs amerced £200 apiece in Exchequer (four others were amerced £100 apiece) for their negligence and contempt in omitting names of many who should have been returned as fit for the order of knighthood, "which ommission the courte [Exchequer] conceyveth to be in favor of the severall persons soe omitted to the apparant prejudice and damage of his Majesty and contrary to the oathes and dutyes of the said sheriffes."[66] These amerciaments, levied on the eve of the issue of the second commission, implied a distrust of the commissioners which might well have been deserved in some cases but which was not calculated to move them by force of affection to do the King's service. By the same token, it was too much to expect that the use of the justices to collect money for the reedification of the cathedral church of London would fill them with enthusiasm for the King's interest.[67] In a county which had made abundantly clear its preference for the "reformed way" this unprecedented

[65] PRO, E.407/35. Francis Baber, JP, compounded for £77, apparently the largest sum assessed on a magistrate in Somerset.

[66] PRO, E.159/470, Hil. 6 Chas. I, rot. 15, order of the Exchequer, 29 Jan. 1630/1. Since 1626 annual writs had gone out to sheriffs to return the names of those fit for the order of knighthood and to warn the parties to appear for knighting. Thynne was *not* one of the two sheriffs amerced who was later allowed to compound the amerciament for a nominal sum.

[67] PRO, Index 4212, p. 92, 72 commissions tested 29 Sept. 1632 directed to counties and boroughs for collection of benevolences from persons "of abilitye" for the repair of St. Paul's. Further commissions were tested 31 Oct. and 2 Dec. 1632. The commissioners comprised all the justices of the county.

levy for the refurbishing of St. Paul's according to the "Popish" lights of William Laud would hardly sit well with husbandmen or justices. The opposition to it was the measure of the county's hostility, and for two years at least it appears to have made difficult the task of the divisional justices in collecting the money.[68] Again the choice had had to be made. For all the justices the decison—as before, as later—was for the service dictated to them by the King and his ministers. But it was hardly a free choice.

With the exception of the improvement schemes and two of the revenue projects, the events related here largely took place in the first five years of Charles' reign. Thus, save for the increased duties incumbent on those justices who were also deputy lieutenants during these five years,[69] the tasks of the special commissioner-justices were the exceptional features in the working hours of men yet unencumbered by the programs begun during the "personal rule." Nonetheless, these duties were additional to the normal routine of the justices as commissioners of the peace. As has been stressed in Chapter III the intensity with which the justices applied themselves to their routine work had quickened almost from the moment the new King ascended his throne. Undoubtedly, this increased tempo owed much of its sustainment to the Council's pressure exerted upon the justices as special commissioners, particularly as commissioners for the forced loan. While imposing new and added tasks, these extraofficial programs had had the wholly beneficial effect of shaking the justices out of their accustomed lethargy.

Unfortunately, the programs had another, deleterious, effect. The opposition in the county, outwardly expressing itself in resistance to the enclosure and disafforestation projects and the financial expedients, seems infinitesimal against a background of mounting strife in Parliament. In a very profound sense, though, the covert antagonism of the Sedgemoor commoners, the inimical agitation of the little people of Neroche, the apologetic though adamant refusal of the yeomen and gentlemen arraigned before the commissioners for the forced loan, was

[68] As late as 1635, sheriff Henry Hodges in answer to a Council letter stated that he had received reports from only two divisions, PRO, S.P.16/300, no. 56, 29 Oct. 1635. Laud sanctioned a payment to the repair fund by a South Petherton churchwarden who had violated a tomb for its lead, as a composition for his offence, PRO, S.P.16/383, no. 3, 24 Feb. 1637/8.

[69] See pp. 245–258.

a facet of the struggle concurrently raging at Westminster. Insofar as that struggle affected the governance of the county, it was this local expression that bore with the greatest weight upon the local governors. Throughout the years to come, in every program of the King and his ministers, that weight remained, indeed, increased. Each program evoked a greater or lesser degree of opposition of the same kind, to the same end, as the opposition portrayed here. It was this opposition that demanded of the local governors greater effort than ever before they had been called upon to expend. Too often in the coming decade, their effort would be two-fold: to overcome the resistance from without, to overcome the reluctance within their own minds and hearts.

Chapter VII ❧ *The Book of Orders*

It was a vigorous young man who on a March day in 1625 became King of England. Not yet twenty-five, "he had already discover'd an Activity, that was not like to suffer him to sit still."[1] In the next quarter-century this "Activity" was to find its outlet successively in oversea war, a constitutional dispute of terrible proportions, "personal rule," and, finally, civil war. It was stilled only upon the scaffold. Yet war and death were far in the future when Charles ascended the throne vacated by his unlamented father. To the new King, confident in his ability, it was an opportunity to govern with forcefulness, govern as his father had never governed. There was nothing radical in Charles' character and there was little radical about any program that he undertook, be it an expedition to Cadiz or the more effectual enforcement of the poor law. The novelty brought by the new King was vigorousness, and compared with the pedantic cautiousness of James it was a strikingly potent factor in the governance of the realm.

Vigor alone was not enough to account for the grand program in local administration begun by the Book of Orders. Charles required direction and his vigor required channelling. So long as the guidance came from the Duke of Buckingham, it would hardly be towards the prosaic matters of the local administration. Buckingham was too busy with diplomatic intrigue and grandiose expeditions against Spain and France to be interested in local government, beyond a spasmodic concern to prevent sworn enemies from gaining power in the counties and to reward with local office those who manifested their regard for his person and his projects. Even when the Duke was compelled to direct his energies into domestic affairs, the constitutional struggle which was to a very great extent a personal feud between himself and Parliament caused him to keep his eyes on Westminster. The Parliament House effectively blotted out the

[1] Clarendon, I, 24.

countryside beyond. It was not until an assassin removed Buckingham from authority that any program concerned primarily with matters of domestic import was possible.

William Laud probably never filled the place in Charles' affection that Buckingham had occupied. Nevertheless, his influence upon the King after the Duke's death was greater than that of any other minister, and during the "personal rule" it was Laud who above all others directed the King's trenchancy in matters of state. True to his own principles and his own peaceable (though far from conciliatory) character, Laud was intent upon reform within the kingdom's two spheres, church and state. Thus, the King's "Activity" was channelled into paths of domesticity, and Laud's own administrative penchant supplied for eleven years the greatest defect of that "Activity," which was Charles' unconcentrated and vacillating application to affairs of state. It is difficult to fix responsibility for any single project upon any single minister or indeed upon the King himself, but there can be little doubt that the spirit infused into the Council and Court by William Laud nurtured the ideas culminating in the Book of Orders.

This is not to say that before the rise of Laud, in the time of Buckingham's absolute ascendancy, the King's and Council's attitude towards local administration was wholly one of indifference. 1 Charles I was indeed very different from 23 James I so far as county government was concerned. The new King's reign was marked by a quickened tempo, the cause of which was largely the government's demands on the counties' lieutenancy in time of war. The urgency explicit in the Council's letters to the lord lieutenants transmitted itself to the rest of the justices, with concrete results when the forced loan appeared.

In fact, it was the army of runaway soldiers who had swollen the normally substantial ranks of England's vagrants that called forth in 1627 and 1628 two directives from the Council demanding their suppression.[2] These were the first attempts of Charles' government to make magistracy more effectual. There is no evidence extant either in the public or the county records to indicate that either directive caused much of a stir in Somerset. However, the sessions records afford ample evidence, especially in the fields of apprenticing, alehouse regulation, and even highway and bridge repair, that the justices were moving with greater

[2] *Acts PC*, 1627, p. 185, PC to JPs Eng. and Wales, 31 March 1627; *Foedera*, XVIII, 967, proclamation of 16 Feb. 1627/8.

dispatch and more effect than they had been wont to do a few years previously. It is no exaggeration to say that the period from 1625 to the issue of the Book of Orders in January 1630/1 saw a steadily augmenting efficiency in magisterial administration—the concomitant of both conciliar interest and the justices' own (probably unconscious) awareness that greater efficiency was the order of the day. As evidence of this, the proclamation of May 1629 for the relief of the poor and the binding out of pauper apprentices left at least one visible trace in the sessions records and not a few inferences that in poor relief the justices were applying themselves with greater effort.[3] Moreover, this directive signaled a more marked interest on the Council's part in local administration.[4] While recognizing this, it should be recalled that the forced loan of 1626–1627 was the sole program before 1630 which exhibited any strongly applied and mightily sustained demand for efficiency from the justices of the peace. Then, it was money to prosecute war, not the reform of lax local administration, that the government wanted.

If by 1630 the cessation of war, the absence of the distractions of parliamentary opposition, and the arrival of Laud to preeminence in government meant that Whitehall was more attuned to matters of domestic import, there was no lack of problems to engage its attention. The arrest of overseas trade during the five war years, combined with the refusal of the merchants to export in protest over tonnage and poundage, contributed greatly to the sudden virulence of the endemic depression that afflicted the cloth industry. For a county like Somerset, a large proportion of whose people gained their livelihood by clothworking, the glut of unsold worsteds and coarser stuff in Blackwell Hall meant widespread unemployment. As in the recession of the early 1620s, nature looked with disfavor on the artisan, for the corn harvest of 1629 was far below requirements. When September 1630 brought an even more meagre harvest and prices of the poorer grains as well as wheat doubled, unemployment spelt starvation for the clothworker and high corn prices

---

[3] *Foedera,* XIX, 71, proclamation of 17 May 1629. The sessions rolls contain a note by the overseers of Haselbury of children fit to be apprenticed there "accordinge as your worshipps [the divisional justices] did appoynt us . . . to certifie you at this time" dated just eight days after the proclamation. The local justices had lost no time in complying with the Council's orders, SRO, Sess Rolls, 61 pt. i, nos. 85–87.

[4] Even before this directive, the Council had requested the judges' opinions on a number of legal points connected with the suppression of Irish vagrancy and poor relief, PRO, S.P.16/141, no. 75, notes of the JJ opinions by Heath, A-G and the PC's proposals concerning Irish [April–May 1629].

meant half-filled stomachs for all the lower orders of society. Action on the Council's part was imperative, and that action could be implemented only by the justices of the peace. The efficient cause for a complete overhaul of magistracy—the Council soon came to feel that nothing less was sufficient—presented itself in the stark reality of starvation.

The preservation of order was of greatest urgency in 1629 and the first half of 1630. When, in the spring of 1629, it became evident to the county's folk that the harvest of that year would be poor, some stout men took the law into their own hands. In April, a riotous crowd caused a commotion in Langport in an attempt to prevent exportation (probably abroad) of corn.[5] The proclamation of 2 May prohibiting exportation[6] was promulgated not only to prevent the drain of the nation's corn reserve, but as much to remove provocation for riotous action by men and women who remembered the great hunger of seven years before. Yet, the restrictions placed on the movement of grain within the realm by overzealous magistrates soon had to be relaxed if cities such as Bristol were to survive. The authorized transportation of grain from Somerset and through the county from Wiltshire to that center of "conspicuous consumption" provoked a number of incidents. The worst took place at Midford Hill, near Bath, in November 1630.[7] By that time people were very hungry, and violence, always just below the surface in seventeenth-century England, bubbled out in threats and occasionally in action. In every case the justices moved with celerity, and considering the difficulties of dealing with large groups of desperate men, the King's peace was preserved remarkably well. The government, by treating such law-breakers with understandable leniency,[8] did not perhaps make the justices' task any easier.

[5] SRO, Phelips MSS, vol. A, f. 162, PC to Sir Robert Phelips, 30 April 1629. Phelips was instrumental in suppressing the riot and received the Council's thanks. The Council also ordered him to publicize the proclamation that would be issued 2 May.

[6] *Foedera,* XIX, 64, proclamation of 2 May 1629.

[7] The Midford Hill riot, directed against carriers licensed by Wilts. justices to transport corn to Bristol, involved over 100 hungry and desperate people. The custos, Henry, 2nd Earl of Marlborough, spent two days taking examinations; his sudden interest in Somerset magistracy is an indication of the seriousness with which such outbreaks were regarded, SRO, Sess Rolls, 64 pt. ii, nos. 200–205, examinations taken 17–18 Nov. 1630.

[8] After warrants had been issued against a dozen men and women who had attempted to stop corn transportation, the King (upon their petition) referred the examination to three Somerset justices; besides preventing the execution of the warrants, this indicated to the magistrates that their justice should be tempered with mercy. At the following sessions, the rioters were dealt with very lightly, most being fined only 3s. 4d, SRO, Sess Rolls, 63 pt. ii, no. 25, warrant to constables upon a *supersedeas*, 24 Feb. 1629/30.

7+

Second only to the preservation of order, the Council was most concerned to husband the grain remaining and to see that it was equitably distributed. The directions to this end sent to the justices throughout the realm in June 1630 had been anticipated in the case of Somerset by two general orders at Easter sessions restricting the number of alehouse keepers and tightening controls on badgers and maltsters, three types of businessmen who it was felt most prevented proper distribution and needful use of grain.[9] All that the Council's letter required in addition to the measures already effected in Somerset, was that the justices visit the granaries of "noted" corn hoarders and see that the markets were being supplied. The sessions records leave no doubt that many alehouses were shut down. The prosecutions of hoarders and exporters of foodstuffs were more than double those for 1629. The sudden increase in the number of badgers and maltsters licensed by quarter sessions (from four in 1629 to twelve in 1630) indicates that the old haphazard method of licensing by two justices out of sessions had fallen before the Easter sessions' order.

Such efforts, while having a momentarily alleviating effect, were not sufficient to cope with the scarcity that followed the failure of the 1630 harvest. In September, the gravity of the situation impelled the Council to reissue a book of instructions to the justices, promulgated in 1586/7, revised and reissued in 1608 and again in 1622.[10] These instructions required strict curtailment of maltsters, badgers, and alehouses, and equitable distribution of grain stores without regard to private interests. The justices in each division were to attend every market held in the division, take notice of prices of corn, and by "all good meanes and perswasions" compel the merchants to distribute the corn equitably and at reasonable prices. The divisional justices were to report their actions once a month to the sheriff, who in turn would inform the Council.

Somerset's justices and borough magistrates from the outset applied themselves with energy. The first divisional meetings in the market towns began at the latest in November, and the first reports commenced in December. Little did the justices then realize that they would still be meeting together every month a decade hence. For the instructions of

[9] The Council's directions, PRO, P.C.2/40, pp. 25-26, PC to JPs, 13 June 1630; QS's orders, SRO, QSOB, 1627/8-1638, Eas. QS 1630, nos. 3-4. A badger was one who bought victuals in one place and transported them to another for sale.

[10] PRO, P.C.2/40, p. 97, PC order 9 Sept. 1630, followed by proclamation of 28 Sept., *Foedera*, XIX, 195. The instructions as issued in 1586/7 are printed in Leonard, pp. 319-326.

September 1630 were incorporated in the Book of Orders, issued four months later, and were in fact the first step in the revitalization of magistracy by the King and Council in the era of "personal rule."

We shall probably never know exactly when the government decided to undertake the sweeping reform of magistracy explicit in the Book of Orders. As Gardiner pointed out, "perhaps the experience gained in this struggle with famine . . . suggested to the Council the propriety of more permanent intervention on behalf of the poor."[11] Only a few months before the Book's publication, though, the intention of the Council was restricted to something less. Doubtless by the summer of 1630, the Council had come to recognize that the effects of the famine were so widespread and so deep, that to preserve order and to prevent starvation of the unemployed and submarginally employed, special emphasis would have to be placed on the poor law. The Council's awareness manifested itself in a special committee of ten councillors appointed in June 1630, which was to deal specifically with matters relating to poor relief that came to the Council's attention.[12] This committee was evidently created merely for the Council's convenience, and in itself advanced the position of the country pauper not at all. By September, however, when the Council ordered the justices to oversee strictly the supply of corn in the markets, it had probably decided that the full application of the poor laws was a matter of proximate urgency. On 5 January 1630/1 a commission under the great seal nominated almost the whole of the Privy Council as commissioners for the poor.[13] Significantly, the commission enjoined them to inquire how "other public services for God, the King, and the Commonwealth" were put into practice as well as to inquire into the execution of the laws in "any way" concerned the relief of the poor. The die had been cast. Reform was clearly the government's intention, and the area in which the reformers could roam was virtually limitless.

Within a matter of days the commissioners had subdivided themselves, allotting to a group of six or seven councillors the oversight of one assize circuit, in every case the one most familiar to the commissioner by virtue

[11] Gardiner, VII, 163.
[12] Leonard, p. 156; PRO, P.C.2/40, p. 7.
[13] PRO, C.66/2535, dorse, no. 4, commission to Abp of Canterbury *et al.*, tested 5 Jan. 1630/1.

of residence or office held in the counties comprising it.[14] With the conciliar machinery for oversight ready, the government waited only for an opportune moment to commence operations. That moment was 31 January 1630/1, the height of the corn scarcity and the peak of the justices' fervor to combat it. Three hundred and fourteen printed books, each accompanied by a Council letter, were distributed among the sheriffs of all the counties of England and Wales; enough for a copy to each county and borough magisterial jurisdiction.[15] The Book of Orders had been issued and the most concerted effort, almost until our own times, to make the statute book an effectual reality was under way.

As an executive instrument, the Book of Orders was very nearly perfect in its blending of matters of great scope with minuteness in treatment. It enjoined the strict enforcement of most of the statute law within the cognizance of the justices of the peace, especially of the justices out of sessions. At the same time, the directions as to the means to effect enforcement were set out with extraordinary care. The attention paid to the smallest matters of administration made this the veritable epitome of conciliar directives in an age when detailed instructions were considered a positive virtue. Its twenty-nine octavo pages of bold print contained the commission of 6 January in its entirety, eight "orders" and eleven "directions" of the commissioners. The commission, obviously included to remind the justices by what authority the ensuing instructions were issued, also served as an effective expression to them of the government's reasoning behind the new program and the effort expected of them. It was the commission which portrayed the whole range of this project for reform. The eight "orders" established the method to realize the desired ends by extending the already existing machinery of monthly meetings and monthly reports by the justices and quarterly reports by the sheriff. The eleven "directions" stressed the particular features of the program with which the justices were to be most concerned, and reiterated for

[14] PRO, S.P.16/183, nos. 60–61, orders of commissioners for the poor [Jan.] 1630/1. This order mentioned, however, that all commissioners had power in all counties. The commissioners for the Western Circuit were: the Lord Chamberlain (Earl of Pembroke and Montgomery), Earl of Danby, Earl Morton, Bishop of Winchester (Richard Neile), Lord Newburgh, Chancellor of the Exchequer (Sir Francis Cottington), Master of the Rolls (Sir Julius Caesar).

[15] For the title of the Book, see p. 179. For convenience it was soon shortened to Book of Orders. The copy cited throughout is in BM, Add. MS 12496, pp. 243–271. The accompanying Council letter is PRO, P.C.2/40, p. 327, 31 Jan. 1630/1. The charge before the winter assizes given to the judges by Ld Kpr Coventrye within a fortnight of the Book's publication dealt with every aspect of its contents; see *Som Asz Ords*, no. 181, for the charge.

their benefit their unquestionable authority to effect the same. Houses of correction, petty constables, watch and ward, leets, masters and servants, apprentices—the law, both procedural and substantive, concerning nearly the whole field of local government, was subjected to a most unambiguous abridgment. Even a very ignorant country justice after reading the last page could have made no mistake as to what he was supposed to do. The Book of Orders was as clear and simple as a child's primer.

Save for the requirement contained in the "directions" that houses of correction should henceforth be built adjoining the common gaol, there was nothing novel in the government's demand, nothing which had not appeared in one order or another during the preceding thirty years. What was novel about the Book of Orders was the inclusiveness of the program contained in it, the intensity with which the program was executed subsequently, and the duration of that intensity. Inclusiveness, intensity, and duration were elements lacking in every previous attempt to spur the local government centering on the justices of the peace into more effective activity. The historian seeks in vain for antecedent parallels to the program commenced by the Book of Orders. If he would discover anything comparable, he must look to his own times and the course of local administration stretching from the great landmarks of Victorian legislation through recent practice in local government.

To equate the Book of Orders with the enforcement of the poor laws would be to deny it the inclusiveness signified by its title:

> *Orders and directions, together with a commission for the better administration of justice and more perfect information . . . how and by whom the lawes and statutes tending to the relief of the poor and . . . the reformation of disorders and disordered persons are executed. . . .*

This equation has been the failing of the few who have accorded the Book of Orders any considerable treatment.[16] It is only natural that the poor law aspect of the program should catch the historian's eye and hold his gaze to the exclusion of its other aspects. Indeed, the implementation of the poor law was of most immediate concern when the Book was

---

[16] This is an understandable failing in Miss Leonard who restricted her pioneer study in this complicated field to the poor law. As an economist, interested in the economics of the poor law, Mr. Lipson stressed the Book's poor law aspect to the exclusion of all else, *The Economic History of England*, III, 449–455. Prof. Willcox, while devoting an entire chapter to the poor law in his excellent study, *Gloucestershire: A Study in Local Government, 1590–1640*, failed to mention the Book of Orders.

issued, and it was the efficient cause of the Book's existence. In bulk, too, the poor law loomed large. The duties of the justices in implementing the poor law can be summarized conveniently under four main heads: provision for the relief of the impotent poor, provision of work for the unemployed of able-body, the binding of poor children as apprentices, and the suppression of vagrancy. All other poor law matters mentioned in the Book were ancillary to and corollaries of these four categories, which quite naturally received the greatest initial emphasis.

It would be a great mistake, however, to overlook the injunction of the councillor-commissioners that the justices in their monthly meetings punish offenders against those statutory misdemeanors triable out of sessions. As we shall see, this latter demand, while rather lost among the congeries of poor law which dominated the Book, had a more lasting effect of greater importance to institutional development than any other element in the program. When the emphasis on punishing offenders is ranged side by side with the poor law, it is evident that there was hardly any area of magisterial endeavor left untouched by the Council in its campaign for reform. This is the clearest proof that it was a general reform and not the mere implementation of this or that statute which was the government's intention in publishing the Book of Orders.

The intensity inherent in the Book of Orders pervaded the conciliar directives to the justices throughout the 1630s. Every letter, every proclamation, every extant charge to the judges before assizes sounded a note of earnestness usually absent from the Council's communications before the scarcity crisis of 1630. This intensity was grounded on the proposition that the good laws of the kingdom had not been executed "especially from the neglect of dutie in some of Our Justices of the Peace and other Officers, Magistrates, and Ministers of the Peace. . . ."[17] The intensity was intended to correct this neglect at each level among the "Ministers of the Peace." The hierarchy of control was organized with the commissioners at the top, who directed the judges of assize to oversee the justices of the peace, who in turn were to oversee the hundred and petty constables, churchwardens, and overseers of the poor. In a very real sense, this machinery was an echelon of successive inquisitions. The Lord Keeper's charge to the judges before their circuit and the commissioners' interrogation of the judges afterwards was the highest inquisition. The charge to and interrogation of the justices by the judges at assizes

[17] The Book of Orders, BM, Add. MS 12496, pp. 243–271.

was the middle inquisition. At the bottom was the direction and interrogation of the subordinate officers by the justices in petty sessions. The Council's intensity was transmitted downwards, and it lost nothing in its descent through the hierarchy; what began as a complaint to the judges became a sharp criticism directed at the justices and ended probably as a crushing reprimand to the constables. Without the machinery enjoined by the Book, the Council's intensity would not have been conducted to the level where it was most needed, the level of the unpaid and refractory subordinate officers. The establishment of the monthly meeting where the justices of each division took the presentment of the various subordinate officers as to their activity during the previous period, followed by the quarterly report to the judges via the sheriff, was absolutely essential. It was the petty sessions that ensured that both instructions and punishment would strike with the greatest force the lowest and weakest element in county government.

Though both the inclusiveness and the intensity of the program were decidedly novel, that alone is not sufficient reason to devote a chapter to the Book of Orders. It deserves full treatment because in its entirety the program lasted for almost a decade with remarkably slight diminution of intensity in its application. During that decade the Council never lost sight of the goal formulated in 1630/1 and in one way or another never failed to remind the justices of it. During that decade the machinery established in 1630/1 continued actively throughout, and the program was applied with enough effect to ensure permanence for part of its machinery and all of its ideal despite the disorder of war and revolution.

The program got off in quick step. Sir Francis Dodington, the sheriff, made his first quarterly report to the judges of assize (as required by the Book) on 10 May 1631.[18] The divisional reports annexed to it indicate that the justices were concerned largely with the measures for the preservation of grain and the supply of the poor with corn, which was true of most divisional reports during the early months. The corn scarcity was at its height and quite aside from setting the poor on work, it was necessary to provide them with food for their money. Nonetheless, the Book was put into execution immediately in conjunction with the corn controls. These initial reports were extremely detailed, occasionally verbose. In most cases they convey a note of crisp efficiency and zeal.

[18] These reports are in the State Papers Domestic. From Somerset, there were a total of 49 divisional justices' reports (36 from county justices and 13 from borough jurisdictions) from 21 Feb. 1630/1 until 27 May 1635. Dodington's first report is PRO, S.P.16/187, no. 36.

The divisional justices lost no time in increasing parish poor rates; even doubling or tripling them. To the aid of parishes which had so many paupers that they could not support them alone, were rated wealthier neighboring parishes.[19] The augmented funds at the disposal of parish officers provided pensions for more of the impotent poor and purchased "stocks" of materials to set the able-bodied poor on work. "Masterless persons"—able-bodied men and women with no visible means of support—were enjoined at petty sessions to enter paid employment at once. Those who proved recalcitrant were summarily committed to a house of correction. It was not long before they were joined there, in ever increasing numbers, by the sturdy vagabonds "that will abide nowhere." Probably for the first time since the reign of Elizabeth, these troublesome citizens felt the full weight of the law. Their number was likely greater, too, than in Elizabeth's day, for besides the professionally indigent and the army of veterans, depression had forced many honest men onto the road. Particularly in Somerset's case, the horde was swelled by unwanted immigrants from Ireland, landed surreptitiously in inlets along the Bristol Channel by unscrupulous shipmasters.[20] Under the continuing prodding of the justices in petty sessions, the constables succeeded in clearing the roads, sending the Irish home via Minehead and Portishead, and the native product to the houses of correction. In fact, so effective was the program of law enforcement against masterless persons and vagrants that a very heavy and suddenly imposed strain was thrown on the county's three houses of correction. Even in 1629, the keeper of the Taunton bridewell had stated that the numbers in his charge had recently increased. Through overcrowding and lack of proper maintenance, conditions in all these houses were terrible. Despite the fact that the Shepton Mallet house had been constructed as late as 1625, by the 1630s it was in the endemically ruined state of the Taunton and Ilchester

[19] The provision in the Book that wealthier parishes should be rated to help poorer ones was not so novel as Miss Leonard suggested, Leonard, p. 158. Occasionally since James' reign, such rates had been made by Somerset quarter sessions; this had statutory authority in 43 Elizabeth I, c. 2, so it was hardly a "new regulation."

[20] One Keyson, master of a bark, landed between fifty and eighty poor Irish near Portishead (Avonmouth) in May 1630. He said that "as longe as there were English in Ireland hee would bring Irishmen into England." But this Hibernian patriot had mulcted his miserable compatriots 4s apiece for the passage and defrauded them of their food and belongings by blarney about the richness of England obviating the need for them to take anything ashore with them, SRO, Sess Rolls, 62, nos. 38–42. The repatriation of Irish cost the county £250. As late as 1633/4, the Council noted that the kingdom—especially Somerset—still swarmed with Irish, PRO, P.C.2/43, p. 463, PC order 29 Jan. 1633/4.

bridewells.[21] Just prior to the issuance of the Book, Lord Poulett proposed to quarter sessions that he build another house of correction at Crewkerne.[22] It does not appear to have been constructed, though with the increased number of petty offenders, vagrants, and masterless persons committed in the flurry of law enforcement launched by the Book, it would have been a useful addition to the county's penal institutions.

The rigors of the law also touched the unlicensed purveyors of drink. Although the justices had always exercised more than usual diligence in suppressing alehouses and punishing publicans who would not suffer suppression, seldom had second offenders been sent to the bridewell as the law required. From the beginning of the corn scarcity, the justices out of sessions closed alehouses with alacrity and to judge by the reports after 1630/1 they were equally ready to commit publicans who would not suspend business. First-offending publicans, though they could not be committed, were fined in petty sessions and the fines applied to the parochial poor funds, as were the fines of many other miscreants convicted at petty sessions. Doubtless, the goodly sum of £7 13s 4d raised by the three shillings or so fines levied on unlicensed alehouse-keepers, drunkards, and other petty wrongdoers in one division[23] was fairly typical of fines levied in all divisions. It provides, too, a crude quantitative measure of the energy with which the justices were implementing the Book of Orders in the first half-year of its existence.

The divisional justices' zeal manifested itself also in the better repair of highways. Though it did not deal explicitly with road repair, the Book by requiring the justices to stir all subordinate officers to greater efficiency brought the parochial surveyors of highways within the purview of petty sessions. Thus, the justices of a number of divisions reported that the action they had taken in petty sessions for the repair of highways had been of unparalleled success.[24]

21 The sessions rolls contain much evidence, some of it overly-lurid, as to the deplorable state of the bridewells. The Book enjoined that henceforth the house of correction be built adjoining the county gaol. The Ilchester house, constructed in James' reign, was under the same roof as the county gaol—the poor suffered in fetid incommodiousness with the wicked. The dreaded gaol fever did not distinguish between pauper and felon.

22 SRO, QSOB, 1627/8–1638, Epiph. QS 1630/1, no. 3. Quarter sessions received his suggestion favorably.

23 PRO, S.P.16/192, no. 48, divisional report, 26 May 1631. This was the large division of five hundreds centered on Bridgwater.

24 The justices of the division embracing Ilchester and Yeovil reported that by commanding the surveyors to present defaults in highway repair at petty sessions more had been done in highway repair than for many years before, PRO, S.P.16/192, no. 5, divisional report, 26 May 1631. Justices of five other divisions reported in a like vein during 1631.

7*

That the first six months of the new program went so well was probably due to the justices' readiness to fine negligent underofficers in petty sessions. The Book required that the justices make certain that the subordinate officers were "able" men. There is nothing to indicate that the constables and parochial officers for the year 1631 were any more "able" than their predecessors. If they were not, they were at least readier to do as they were told rather than pay a fine for the previous month's dereliction. So long as the justices were zealous, the subordinate officers could not be otherwise.

The initial fervor was beginning to wear thin by the autumn of 1631. The reports of the justices became more perfunctory and curt, less informative and less detailed—indeed, stylized. As early as July 1631, the county justices for the large division of which Bridgwater was the petty-sessions town wrote the sheriff "that wee shall not henceforth have cause to trouble you or ourselves with longe cirtificates. For at our present meetinge wee finde that the presentments of hundreds within our division affordes noe particulars worthie certifyinge unto their lordshipes. . . ."[25] By the summer of 1632, the reports of some other divisions had become almost stereotyped. Three divisions returned at about the same time exactly the same curt report which was in effect a mere recitation of the various clauses of the Book of Orders preceded by "we have done our best."[26] Henceforth, until a Somerset division sent the last extant report in May 1635, the justices' reports were at best a table of apprentices bound, vagrants punished, drunkards fined, etc., and at worst an *omnia bene* decorated with verbiage.

Zeal was wearing thin not only through the erosion of time and the enervating weight of such a program on all the justices and subordinate officers concerned, but in part through the vitiating effects of opposition to one important aspect of the program. The forced apprenticing of pauper children or children likely to become a charge on the parish rates was both an important relief measure, and with respect to the primitive manufacturing organization of the time, an economic necessity. Along with the suppression of vagrancy, apprenticing received the most marked emphasis in the Book of Orders and in subsequent conciliar and judicial directions. Nobody but the vagabond chafed under the measures against

[25] PRO, S.P.16/196, no. 43, divisional report from the large division centered on Bridgwater, 10 July 1631. They did not in fact send any more long certificates.
[26] PRO, S.P.16/219, nos. 27, 46, two reports from different divisions, 26 and 28 June respectively, and S.P.16/230, no. 55, divisional report [July ?] 1632.

vagrancy, but forced apprenticing evoked a very strong and not un-respectable reaction.

According to Elizabeth's famous statute of artificers, the apprenticing of any youngster was to be done before two justices of the peace. Ante-cedent to the Book of Orders, the enforced apprenticing of children was seldom resorted to except in the case of illegitimate children; only occasionally did the parochial officers, with the consent and aid of the justices, undertake to bind out the child of a parish pauper. Ordinarily, the parents of children, paupers and self-supporting persons alike, were most desirous that their children be placed in service, and they applied for the covenant and provided the covenant money themselves.[27] Nor-mally, there was no shortage of artificers desirous of taking an apprentice, more or less training him and providing for him, in return for his seven years of labor and a considerable sum of covenant money. However, widespread unemployment coupled with the socially disrupting effects of the corn scarcity in 1629–1630 resulted in a far larger number of children who either had to be bound out or be provided for out of the parish funds. The same conditions resulted in a reduction of the number of persons either able or willing to take apprentices. Thus, the justices in giving effect to the urgent injunction of the Book to bind out poor children could not avoid running headlong into a virile, at times almost desperate, opposition.

With the notable exception of clergymen, a practitioner in almost any trade or profession was liable to become an apprentice's master whether he liked it or not. This proposition, though applied by the justices from the beginning, was still disputable at law until the so-called "resolutions of the judges" in 1633 gave it legal sanction. It is not surprising, then, that the more vocal hostility of would-be masters was based on some claim at law, and that in Somerset's case the opposition was led by a lawyer. Thomas Trevillian, gent., a practicing attorney, town clerk of Langport, and an employee of the clerk of the peace, resolutely refused to take an apprentice whom Sir Robert Phelips and the other divisional justices attempted to enjoin upon him early in 1632. He submitted that as an attorney he was not bound to take an apprentice and that if he was chargeable to an apprentice's maintenance, it was only by a common rate.[28] Unfortunately for him, Phelips at this particular moment was most

[27] It appears that the county paid the covenant money for enforced apprenticing, SRO, QSOB, 1627/8–1638, Eas. QS 1638, no. 10.
[28] PRO, S.P.16/239, no. 6, Thomas Lyte, JP, to Sir Robert Phelips, 19 May 1633.

desirous of proclaiming the King's interest and most zealous in executing the Book of Orders, and that worthy referred the matter to Whitehall. In the summer of 1633, Trevillian appeared before the Council,
and since the recent "resolutions of the judges" denied him lawful
excuse for his refusal, he had no choice but to submit.[29] If Trevillian's
opposition had been an isolated instance, little damage would have been
done. However, it was merely the most vocal opposition in one county.
A Hertfordshire justice who was rash enough to state in petty sessions
that enforced apprenticing was illegal—and was brave enough to repeat
it before the Council—was discharged from the commission of the peace
and fined £100 in Star Chamber.[30] Though no Somerset justice assumed
a like stand and none there questioned the legality of enforced apprenticing, many artisans followed Trevillian's example. These were bound to
assizes if they persisted in their refusal.[31] They generally saw fit to recant.

The judges and justices found it far harder to combat the less obtrusive
opposition that expressed itself time and again in devious and fraudulent
practices by outwardly compliant masters. Evidently the most common
method adopted to slough off an unwanted child was to maltreat him so
abominably that he ran away or otherwise broke covenant. The sessions
records following 1630/1 indicate a very sudden and sustained increase
in the number of apprentices released from their indentures because they
were being flogged or starved to death. In such cases the justices in petty
sessions invariably assigned a new apprentice to the master. Far too often
this merely meant further inhumane treatment, such as that persisted in
by one Edward Scriven who viciously maltreated about half a dozen
poor children, one of whom he threatened to flay to death. A justice in
petty sessions might threaten that Scriven "should be whipped if ever he
came before hime again about such business,"[32] but this did not heal the
bruises of children tortured for no fault save that they were unwanted.

[29] PRO, P.C.2/43, p. 71, PC order 31 May 1633. Trevillian had relied on the 1633 "judges'
resolutions" for vindication, but the one touching this point (no. 3) was vague and could
be interpreted to include an attorney: "Every man who by his calling or profession or
manner of living entertayneth and must have the use of other servants of the like quality
must entertayn such apprentices, wherein discretion must be guided upon due consideration of circumstances." *Som Asz Ords*, no. 186 (3).
[30] PRO, E.159/474, Trin. 10 Chas. I, rot. 12—Thomas Coningsby. He was restored to
the commission in 1637, PRO, Index 4212, p. 256.
[31] As late as 1639/40, two Somerset justices bound a man to assizes for refusing to keep
an apprentice they had placed with him against his will, *Som Asz Ords*, nos. 163, 166.
[32] SRO, Sess Rolls, 69 pt. i, nos. 39, 84, depositions, 21 July 1633. The indignant justice
was James Rosse—who was not particularly pleasant at any time.

The common practice of some masters, of assigning the indenture over to another desirous of having an apprentice, was at least more humane even if it defeated "his Majestys directions in that kind."[33] Many times "his Majestys directions" were defeated, and the attendant difficulties in righting the legal wrong doubled the tasks of justices fully occupied in the normal routine of petty sessions work in pursuance of the Book of Orders.

The Council was not ignorant of the decrease in magisterial zeal, evidenced primarily in the perfunctory reports coming in from most counties by the winter of 1631–1632. To stir up activity and impress upon the justices that although the corn scarcity was past the Book of Orders was not *passé*, a particularly sharp letter went out to the sheriff of every county in April 1632. Commencing with a touch of sarcasm—"You cannot but easily recall the Book of Orders"—the letter stated that "whilest ye businesse was fresh it was well putt in execucion, and much good came of it; but now of late [there] is so much slacknesse as all retournes againe to ye former course . . ."[34] The sheriff was to remind the justices of the duties enjoined by the Book, especially in binding apprentices, quickening the constables to catch and punish vagrants, and seeing that the bridewells were well supplied with goods for setting the poor on work. He was to thank the justices who had done well and so encourage them. He was not to fail in returning to the judges an account of the justices' performances of the instructions. In Somerset this letter had the desired effect. The divisional reports immediately following it were considerably more detailed than those immediately preceding. The sessions records also indicate a greater application on the justices' parts. In fact, things were far from returning "to ye former course." The justices had not ceased taking presentments of subordinate officers and severely punishing them when justified. As long as this machinery remained active zeal could not so far diminish that the Book was really in danger of arrant neglect. Nonetheless, the program was operating at a somewhat more reasonable tempo.

If the Council would admit of no relaxation of effort in the county, it

[33] SRO, Sess Rolls, 71 pt. ii, no. 60, order of Eas. QS 1634. In this case the court ordered the recalcitrant master to take any other apprentice the divisional justices assigned him, which was the usual practice.

[34] PRO, P.C.2/41, p. 545, PC to sheriffs, 30 April 1632. A copy of this letter is preserved in SRO, Phelips MSS, vol. A, f. 139, which hints at the importance Sir Robert Phelips attached to it.

desired to take a less active role in the enforcement of the program. A Council order of December 1632 was indicative of the Council's attitude by that time.[35] The clerk of the Council attending at the end of term was to make an abstract of the divisional reports from every county and submit it to the Council. Hitherto, it was evident that the councillor-commissioners had viewed personally the reports as they came from the judges under the justices' hands. Now, an abstract was felt to be sufficient. This is not to say that the Council was losing interest. Rather, it was shifting to the judges the main responsibility for overseeing the Book's enforcement. In line with this progressive transferral was the Lord Keeper's charge to the judges before the winter assizes 1632/3. He informed the judges that they were to see that the sheriffs were more diligent in making poor-relief returns—with the inference that the judges were also to ensure that the justices would be more diligent in executing the orders and drafting the returns.[36] It was the Council's intention that the Book should become a matter of local administrative routine, requiring no more direct conciliar intervention than was necessary to keep the program alive.

It is somewhat ironic that the single most important contribution to the Book becoming a matter of local administrative routine was made by a legal authority of suspect validity. The so-called "resolutions of the judges of assize 1633" were in fact answers to questions put to Chief Justice Heath on the Norfolk Circuit by some magistrates desirous of obtaining authoritative definition of points of law arising from apprenticing, pauper settlement, master and servant relations, and other vexing legal questions connected with magistracy. Some of the questions appear to have come from the Council, or rather via the Council from other justices of the peace.[37] Heath submitted his answers to thirty-eight such questions to his brethren at Serjeants' Inn, but it appears that they refused to subscribe to his interpretations. Notwithstanding this, the thirty-eight resolutions, though they had no more authority than that attaching to the Chief Justice of the Common Pleas minus the strictures of those other judges who would not accept them, soon became in common parlance the "resolutions of the judges." And they exerted a powerful influence

---

[35] PRO, P.C.2/42, p. 325, PC order 7 Dec. 1632.

[36] See *Som Asz Ords*, no. 182, for this charge in full.

[37] *Ibid.*, nos. 186–188, the questions and the resolutions as well as some of the original questions upon which the resolutions were based. The 1727 edition of Dalton's *Country Justice*, p. 231, notes Justice Twisden's denial of the resolutions' validity in 1676.

on all those connected with the enforcement of the Book of Orders (and consequently, the law) for the simple reason that they furnished reasonable and comprehensive answers to long-vexing questions. By universal use—their validity was not questioned until the Restoration—the resolutions settled finally matters which had impeded the enforcement of the poor laws and provoked much needless and time-consuming argument at sessions. Indeed, the resolutions of 1633 effected the final absorption of the Elizabethan poor laws into the routine working of the justices of the peace.

The virtual end of the Council's direct participation in the program was made pointedly clear by the last occasion before 1635 when it had cause to issue a directive in furtherance of the program, and in this it moved through the agency of the judges of assize. In October 1633, after hearing the judges' summary of their findings as to the Book's enforcement garnered from their summer circuits, the Council concluded that the program had not been so well executed as before because the justices did not assemble as often as they should and the sheriffs were remiss in submitting reports. This complaint was hardly applicable to Somerset. The reports from the county survive in good number and there are numerous indications that the monthly meetings in the divisions were being held regularly and the program effectively, if not zealously, implemented. The mildness of the Council's order—the judges on the next winter circuit were to require the sheriff to send up divisional reports at once so the judges could report to the Council before the end of the following term[38]—indicates that the Council was fairly well satisfied with the justices' execution of the Book. Had the remissness been as widespread as the preamble to the Council's order complained that it was, far more direct, drastic, and immediate action would have been taken to correct it.

Indeed, the emphasis in execution of the Book of Orders had shifted imperceptibly from the supervision of poor law enforcement to the punishment in petty sessions of vagrants and other offenders in misdemeanor. This had come about by 1634 with the end of corn scarcity and the consequent reduction in tempo of poor law implementation. While giving a helpful fillip to the divisional justices' efforts in punishing crime, a Council order of January 1633/4 extending the power of justices and peace officers to take vagrants in flight in other counties

[38] This order is printed in full in *Som Asz Ords*, no. 183.

and liberties also accelerated this shift in emphasis.[39] The last reports for Somerset were discursive only when they considered the number of offenders whipped or fined for various statutory offences. Though the records of quarter sessions indicate no diminution in the number of misdemeanors heard before that court, there can be no doubt from the divisional reports that most minor offenders received their "condign punishment" at a monthly meeting.[40]

Though merely from one division, the last preserved report for the county sent in by the justices of the large division comprising the western salient of Somerset and dated 27 May 1635 rather remarkably indicated the course the Book of Orders would take in the last five years of its life. The two magistrates stated that they had held "divers and sundry meetings," commanded strict watch and ward be kept to catch vagrants, suppressed unnecessary alehouses, levied fines on nonattenders at church and on blasphemers, and bound out forty-four apprentices since their last report.[41] It was precisely these aspects of the Book of Orders that received most emphasis in the period from 1635 to 1640, when the absence of divisional reports for Somerset in the state papers forces the historian to turn largely to the county's records for evidence as to the continuation of the program.

Purely by accident, the last conciliar directive (until a final, fruitless proclamation in 1640) dealing with the Book of Orders as such coincided with Somerset's last divisional report. In May 1635, the Council instructed the judges to give timely notice every year on all their circuits for the justices to render full certificates to them for return to the Council.[42] Despite this strict order, Somerset appears to have sent no more reports, and fewer reports after this date came from other counties.[43] The reason

[39] PRO, P.C.2/43, p. 422.

[40] Four justices reported on 16 April 1634 that during the past half-year they had levied fines totalling £54 8s (£7 of which were on subordinate officers for derelictions) and had otherwise punished 78 for offences connected with apprenticeship, vagrancy, refusal to enter employment (20 committed), keeping ill-order on Sunday, neglecting watch and ward, stealing wood, breaking hedges, drunkenness, swearing, and church absenteeism, PRO, S.P.16/265, no. 72. A commendable mixed-bag for a single division!

[41] PRO, S.P.16/289, no. 57, divisional report of the large division in the westernmost extremity of the county, 27 May 1635.

[42] PRO, P.C.2/44, p. 555, PC to JJ all circuits, 7 May 1635. The Council complained again of the justices' neglects in executing the Book.

[43] Reports of other counties are extant until 1639 in the State Papers Domestic, though in ever decreasing numbers. It seems unlikely that if some Somerset divisions continued to send in reports, no trace of them would remain. I believe that the last preserved report from the county was, in fact, the last report made.

for this can be found in the charge to the judges by Lord Keeper Coventrye before the autumn assizes of 1635.[44] The Lord Keeper dwelt earnestly on those matters concerned with the Book, especially the reform of alehouses, punishment of vagrants, and apprenticing. In this, his charge was similar to all those he had delivered since 1630/1. It is the last clause in the charge which is arresting. It required the judges to propagandize the second writ of ship money. Henceforth the Council's attention—and particularly the attention of its clerk, Edward Nicholas, whose collection of state papers affords most evidence both as to the Book and ship money—was taken up by this new tax. For the next five years, the Council's attention could hardly have been elsewhere. Only in three narrow fields involved in the great program did the Council turn from ship money business long enough to write directly to the justices. As a consequence of ship money, Whitehall no longer emphasized the need for justices' reports concerning the Book. Nor were the magistrates, soon engulfed in ship money rating disputes, and the sheriff, who had other, more urgent and more frequent reports to return (those for ship money), loath to forego the paper work required by the Book of Orders. Even those which came in from other counties could not possibly have received more conciliar attention than that required to hand them to the judges of assize for consideration.

The judges of assize had been groomed to accept full responsibility for the program's execution since the gradual transferral of the Council's mantle to them had begun in 1633. For this reason, the withdrawal of the Council's attention did not result in an appreciable lessening of pressure on the justices. The program had become routine, but as the assize order book testifies, the judges saw to it that routine never meant slackness. One among three extant charges to the judges between 1635 and 1640 (that prior to the Lent assizes, 1639/40)[45] indicates that the Lord Keeper's reminder of the various clauses of the Book was sufficient to mobilize the judges' sense of duty and so revitalize the program at the county level. It was no small compliment to the Council's previous forcefulness and the judges' sedulity that the Book was not forgotten. Nor was any less credit due to the justices' power of application in that in those aspects of the program of greatest importance the good work continued without noticeable abatement of efficiency, despite the novel demands on the justices' energies attendant upon ship money.

[44] *Historical Collections*, II, 294, charge of Ld Kpr Coventrye to the JJ, 17 June 1635.
[45] *Ibid.*, III, 985, charge of Ld Kpr Finch to the JJ, 13 Feb. 1639/40.

Though it was unlikely that watch and ward was continued as faithfully after 1635 as it had been in the first flush of enthusiasm, there can be
no doubt that vagrancy as a minor social evil had been subdued far better
than at any time in the previous forty years. If the flow of Irish had not
been staunched, at least it had been lessened considerably and the
wide-ranging domestic vagabond circumscribed. The examinations in the
sessions rolls for 1631 reveal a marked decrease in the number of crimes
committed by vagabonds immediately following a staggering increase
in 1630 caused by the unsettling conditions accompanying famine and
unemployment. No longer were there gangs of "Bethlehem-men" such
as the one which had terrorized Goody Hedges at Tickenham in 1627.[46]
The making of false passes (used by the professional beggar who posed
as a returned soldier) was effectively repressed, and the end of the
"postwar era" resulted in the depletion of the great concourse of veterans
walking, and occasionally thieving, through the country side. The period
after 1635 was marked by no resurgence of vagrancy, but rather by its
continued repression. An order of midsummer sessions 1638 settling an
annual pension of £4 on a subordinate officer who was particularly
zealous in catching vagrants, with the implication that it would continue
so long as he continued his good work, is significant.[47] It indicates that
the justices were still pressing subordinate officers into greater activity
long after they had ceased reporting to the sheriff.

Apprenticing, too, was carried on without apparent slackening by the
justices. The assize order book affords ample proof that after 1635 the
judges still had to contend with opposition to enforced apprenticing, and,
incidentally, that justices in petty sessions were still actively binding
out apprentices. At the winter assizes 1637/8, Serjeant Heath issued a
general order charging the justices to take special care to bind out
apprentices, to send obstinate parents to the house of correction, and to
bind over to assizes those who would not take apprentices or who through
ill usage made the child break the covenant. To encourage subordinate
officers, those who refused to take an apprentice were to pay the expenses
of the officer who prosecuted him to conviction.[48] The sessions records

[46] SRO, Sess Rolls, 60, nos. 88–90. The leader of this band (who had aroused the poor
old lady in the middle of the night) was one Bartholomew Kidly, self-styled "poore gent
of *Comitatus* of Woster," who alleged himself to have been an inmate of Bedlam. If he was
not, he ought to have been.

[47] SRO, QSOB, 1627/8–1638, mids. QS 1638, no. 16. It also hints at remuneration for
an unremunerated and obligatory petty office, surely a rare if not unique instance for this
period.

[48] *Som Asz Ords*, no. 124.

also provide glimpses of justices in petty sessions binding out poor children, just as they had done between 1630/1 and 1635.

To what extent the clauses of the Book that required the able-bodied poor to be set on work were carried out after 1635 it is impossible to say. Save for a brief scare in 1636 that corn would be scarce and save for the endemic difficulties of the county's cloth industry, there were no particularly pressing occasions to take any extraordinary steps for setting the able-bodied poor on work. The sessions records give no hint that this part of the program was still in feverish operation. Neither do they hint that it had ceased altogether. It is likely that it continued; the continuing decrease from 1631 of the number of cases involving poor relief brought before quarter sessions might indicate that the justices in petty sessions were administering this aspect of the program sufficiently carefully to obviate recourse to the higher court.

If after the summer of 1635 the Council did not see fit to intervene directly in the implementation of most aspects of the Book of Orders, in three spheres it did interfere most emphatically. The Council had never been fully satisfied with the justices' activity in controlling maltsters, brewers, and alehousekeepers. Even before the Book of Orders, the justices had shown commendable energy in controlling the latter, and with the coming of the corn scarcity in 1629–1630 all these three types of businessmen had been curbed and their numbers reduced in a most ruthless manner. Yet, the fact that after 1632 no more maltsters' licenses were recorded in the sessions records would seem to indicate that once the corn scarcity was over the justices had ceased to trouble themselves with licensing maltsters. Alehousekeepers, though the pressure upon them by both the justices and the judges never wholly ceased, appear to have grown more numerous by the second half of the 1630s. The control of these small, often fly-by-night entrepreneurs who brewed their own beer and sold it illicitly was always difficult, and when the end of the corn scarcity removed the necessity for strict control, it was quite probable that the justices had grown lax. It is worth remarking, too, that the only recorded instances in which justices of the peace patently exercised a corrupt favor were in the licensing of alesellers.[49] Undoubtedly, the

[49] In 1635, Robert Hopton and his son, Sir Ralph, JPs, allowed their woodward to sell beer to their woodcutters without license. On information, Robert was forced to bind the woodward to quarter sessions, but wrote a letter to the clerk of the peace to have him discharged, SRO, Sess Rolls, 73 pt. i, no. 79. For Sir Francis Dodington, both as a justice and as sheriff, exercising undue influence on behalf of a Stogumber publican in order to gain prestige, see p. 133, n. 24.

Council had very good grounds in other counties as well as Somerset for demanding a tighter control on maltsters, brewers, and alehouse-keepers.

The method chosen by the Council to control maltsters and brewers was to remove the power of licensing from the justices' hands, to punish offenders before the Council, and to leave the investigation and reporting of abuses to the justices. In short, power was taken away from the justices though their labor hardly one whit decreased. This departure from established practice was accomplished by issuing a commission to the clerks of the Council, the clerks of the Signet, and one Captain James Duppa authorizing them to compound with all those maltsters wishing to be "incorporated" and willing to comply with the regulations of the Council.[50] The prime mover of the commission was Duppa. Doubtless, the financial advantage accruing to the Crown was the primary aim of the Council in authorizing the commission, though the Council's continuing involvement in enforcing the regulations was unusual in grants of this kind and points to a very strong secondary consideration in its thinking, namely the proper control of brewers and maltsters for the commonweal. A table of strict regulations was drafted, with which the divisional justices were to acquaint all maltsters, certifying the names of those who would comply. From the one divisional justices' report extant for Somerset, it appeared that a great many maltsters chose rather to give up the trade (or else go underground) than to buy a license.[51] In November 1636, the Duppa patentees were empowered to license brewers as well. The Council set to with fervor to suppress those who refused to obtain a license but continued to brew or malt, and four Bridgwater brewers along with some from many other counties had the unpleasant experience of attending at the Council Board.[52] Complaints by licensed brewers—there were quite a few complaints—were in some cases referred to divisional justices, thus increasing the work required of them. Though the Council through Duppa and company assumed full control, it had still to rely on the divisional justices for the intelligence necessary to exercise it. This is clear from a Council letter of April 1638 requiring the divisional justices to direct the constables to give an account of any

[50] PRO, P.C.2/46, pp. 371–374, PC to JPs Eng. and Wales (four letters to Somerset JPs) 25 Sept. 1636.

[51] PRO, S.P.16/352, no. 34, certificate of Dr. Warburton, JP, to PC, 5 April 1637.

[52] PRO, S.P.16/381, no. 49, application for warrants by Duppa, 7 Feb. 1637/8. Between 1637/8 and April 1638, there were a number of prosecutions before the Privy Council.

who had malted since Christmas (when the new licensing regulations came into effect) and by what authority they malted.[53] But the experiment was ill-founded and the amount of evasion of the regulations so widespread,[54] that in June 1638 the malting regulations were relaxed and the Duppa commission revoked in March 1639. The Council tacitly recognized then that the justices were by far the soundest instrument to enforce summarily the law against these small businessmen who operated at the purely local level; the petty sessional machinery for local control was still functioning and could (when aroused) ensure effective control. If the brief incursion of the Council and its agents into a sphere best left to the justices had had no other worthwhile effect, at least it served to spur the magistrates into greater activity in petty sessions.

No drastic steps were taken to control alehousekeepers. However, both in December 1635 when the clerks of the peace were to return to the Council the names of licensed keepers and whether the justices duly certified to the clerk the recognizances of the same, and in December 1637 when the Council ordered the judges to oversee the suppression of all unlicensed publicans and the reduction in number of licensed ones, the Council applied that direct, strong pressure which the justices could remember from the early years of the Book of Orders.[55] The Council's pressure had the desired effect; quarter sessions showed itself much readier to suppress licensed keepers in the interests of good order,[56] and divisional justices became more wary in granting licenses. Thus the Council, by merely issuing an order, stepped up the tempo of the machine which was magistracy organized and instructed according to the Book of Orders. A decade earlier, it is doubtful whether a Council order would have been a fraction so effective.

In May 1640 a proclamation was issued requiring the poor laws to be duly executed, the justices in quarter sessions to order assistance for those parishes unable to provide for their own poor, and the judges of assize to

---

[53] PRO, S.P.16/408, no. 21, PC to JPs Eng. and Wales [18 April] 1638.

[54] Evasion was inevitable: seventeen brewers and one maltster (only this many were licensed for Somerset) could not supply the numerous publicans in the county, PRO, S.P.16/377, no. 65, note by Duppa of brewers and maltsters licensed [1637].

[55] PRO, P.C.2/45, pp. 322–324, PC to clerks of the peace of Eng. and Wales, 31 Dec. 1635. This letter is preserved in SRO, QSOB, 1627/8–1638, Eas. QS 1636. PRO, P.C.2/48, p. 460, PC to JJ assize, 15 Dec. 1637.

[56] The justices were so touchy that on the false information of a Duppa licencee that Yeovil publicans had broken the assize of beer and ale, quarter sessions suppressed every publican in town, SRO, Sess Rolls, 78, no. 56, draft QS order, Epiph. QS 1638/9.

inquire and report.[57] In itself, this proclamation was not extraordinary. Set in time and seen in the light of later events, it is worthy of mention. This was the last general edict aimed at spurring the justices to greater efficiency in a phenomenal program begun almost a decade before. This was the last directive before civil strife obliterated much of the immediate benefit of that program.

The immediate benefit of the Book of Orders was the end desired by the King and Council in publishing it. In the first place, throughout the 1630s the content of the Book was effectively translated into reality. The impotent poor were better relieved. The masterless poor were set on work. Apprentices were bound out, and if not always well treated, at least taken off the parish rates. Vagrants were, to a far greater extent than before, shown the error of their ways or recurrently locked up and removed from the concern of society. Despite the Council's reluctance to acknowledge it, alehousekeepers were curbed to a remarkable degree considering the difficulties of enforcing the law against such elusive proprietors. The same was true of maltsters and brewers. And there can be no doubt that the whole *corpus* of statutory offences, including blasphemy, assault, church absenteeism, hedge-breaking, drunkenness, and many others, was implemented with a rigor hitherto unknown. In short, taking into account the varying emphases placed on different aspects of the program at different times in this decade, the 1630s saw the poor provided for and the wicked punished to an unprecedented extent. Without exaggerating its benefits, one may say that the Book of Orders accomplished more in vivifying enacted law than the King and his ministers could possibly have hoped for in January 1630/1. Indeed, it accomplished more than any other sovereign and his ministers would even attempt for another two centuries.

Furthermore, the Council's desire that the whole of local government comprising the justices of the peace and the subordinate officers should be reinvigorated was substantially fulfilled. This was by far the most amazing result of the Book of Orders. The marked contrast between the activity of the justices out of sessions in the period before 1630/1 and after that date testifies to the Book's effect. It was possible for a justice earlier to be "not ... at leasure" to hear a referral.[58] After the Book, he

---

[57] *Foedera,* XX, 407, proclamation of 20 May 1640.

[58] In 1628, the clerk of Dr. Barlow, Dean of Wells and a county justice, had informed a defendant in a referred case that his witnesses would not be heard then because the Dean "could not be at leasure to heare them," SRO, Sess Rolls, 65 pt. ii, no. 28, petition to Epiph. QS 1630/1.

would risk his place by such flagrant indolence. Following 1631, far fewer quarter sessions referrals dragged on from sessions to sessions because of the failure of the referee-justices to meet and hear the referral. In this, of course, the creation of regular monthly petty sessions was responsible, for machinery to implement the Book was also ready at hand to justices charged with undertaking a referral from quarter sessions. Even the justices in quarter sessions were not immune from the invigorating effects of the Book. The quarter sessions order book indicates that after the advent of the program the court, hitherto reluctant to give definitive order without first a referral to out-of-sessions justices, began to make settlement orders at first instance. This acceleration of a previously nigh-interminable process might have been accomplished to relieve some of the quarter sessions' burden on the justices out of sessions, but the demand for such acceleration was implicit in the program itself. Also from the stimulus of the Book, quarter sessions for the first time since at least 1604 took the trouble to make the annual wage assessments accord with economic reality. The sudden and sharp increase in the scales of maximum wages for most categories of laborers and artisans occurring at the Easter 1631 sessions indicates that the old practice of merely renewing the previous year's assessments without investigation had ceased. The wage assessments of the 1630s varied one from another; and even more important, they varied with some respect to the prevailing cost of living.[59] The same animating effects of the Book of Orders are discernible, too, in the increased efficiency of the subordinate officers. For the first time, their every act was brought under the minute scrutiny of the local justices who were thoroughly familiar with the locale and often personally acquainted with the officers themselves. Exercised at the regularly recurring monthly meetings that scrutiny was salutary, to say the least. Certainly, the effect of the Book in arousing from its too accustomed lethargy the whole of local government—the greatest justices as well as the lowest petty constables—had one result that King and Council had not foreseen in 1630/1. When a few years later the government turned to the constables to levy and collect ship money and to the justices to settle the innumerable disputes arising from that unpopular tax, these

---

[59] SRO, Wage assessments, 1604–1641. For example, the maximum annual wages (including livery) for an ordinary journeyman were:

1625	£2 5s	1635	£3 0s
1626	£2 5s	1638	£3 0s
1631	£3 5s	1640	£3 0s

officers were working already at a level of efficiency unmatched by that of any of their predecessors. That ship money was attended by any success at all was due in no small measure to the continuing momentum of efficiency in the officials who still felt the spur of the Book of Orders.

The permanent benefits of the Book of Orders were no less remarkable and considerably more important than the immediate ones outlined above. It is likely that the impetus for relieving the poor, which was the concomitant of the decade's work directed by the Book, carried on through the Civil War. This is the view of Miss Leonard, who held, that despite the lassitude and confusion brought by war,

> ... the effect of the execution of the Book of Orders remained. For nine years the overseers had been drilled by the justices ... and that part of [the program] ... continued which was most easily enforced by the overseers, and which seemed to them most urgently necessary. The impotent were still relieved, and children were still apprenticed, though less efficiently than before, but the able-bodied poor were no longer found with work, except in a few isolated cases.[60]

No matter how probable this thesis is, very little evidence can be adduced at this time to support it. The proof lies in the unexplored contents of numerous county record offices, and not until historians turn to a minute search of the local records for the 1640s and 1650s will judgment be possible.

Of far greater future benefit, however, the Book of Orders permanently established petty sessions. True, petty sessions suffered the same fate as most of the great program during the Civil War inasmuch as it was eclipsed by the chaos of the 1640s. But with the more settled conditions of the Commonwealth and Protectorate and the reincarnation of Caroline local government under the later Stuarts, petty sessions reappeared.[61] Certainly by the last decade of the century, that with which the Webbs commenced their invaluable study, the inchoate and weak institution of the 1630s had become a full-fledged organ of local government.

For the period 1630/1 to 1635, there is ample evidence from the

---

[60] Leonard, p. 268.

[61] In 1661, a Westmorland hundred constable, responding to the judge's charge at assizes, reported that the petty constables had given an account of vagrants caught and punished to the justices "at their private sessions," also an account of alehousekeepers (a number of whom the justices suppressed), and that the justices in quarter sessions and "private sessions" took care that poor were set on work and poor children apprenticed, PRO, Asz.47/20. This might as easily have been 1635.

divisional reports in the state papers concerning the existence of and the work done in Somerset petty sessions. Yet there is also proof in the county records that petty sessions were held as regularly during the remainder of the decade although such proof does not exist for every division. It is particularly significant that most of this evidence is concerned with the punishment of minor offenders at petty sessions upon presentment by subordinate officers. The *mittimus* of four divisional justices for two men "this day convicted before us for divers and severall misdemeanors" in April 1637 and the deposition of a tithingman in another division in November 1637 that he was required by the justices of the "limit" to present at a "petty sesses" divers disorders,[62] indicate that by this time petty sessions had become a court in the strictly judicial sense of the word as well as an administrative body. While this function of the new court must not be overstressed in the face of evidence that the poor law aspects of the Book were still performed in petty sessions during the later 1630s, by their number and their nature, the summary trial of misdemeanors must have occupied most of the petty sessions' time.

If the program enjoined in the Book of Orders had been allowed to lapse when the supply of corn and the difficulties of the poor returned to the more normal conditions preceding the crisis of 1629–1631, petty sessions would have withered away, following all the other well-meaning and short-lived attempts to regularize the work of the justices out of sessions. The Council did not allow the program to lapse, and when of necessity it turned its attention to other more pressing affairs of state, the judges' pressure preserved the program and petty sessions intact until the Civil War. The survival of petty sessions once the force of the Book of Orders was spent depended, however, upon the new court proving its worth to the justices themselves. In this it received an invaluable twofold legacy from the Book of Orders. The Book, by stressing the punishment of minor offenders, ensured that petty sessions would never want for business. As well, by enjoining the punishment of negligent underofficers at petty sessions, the Book established that court as the most useful instrument the justices had with which to detect negligence and summarily punish those subordinates whom they had long recognized were the least satisfactory limbs of local government.

The new court proved its worth many times over because of its convenience for justices already fully engaged in the numerous out-of-sessions

[62] SRO, Sess Rolls, 75, no. 103, 77 pt. ii, no. 117.

activities that were routine before the Book of Orders and would be routine long after. Petty sessions was regular in time and place, it was well attended, and it had a more judicial atmosphere than that surrounding a mere meeting of out-of-sessions justices. Thus, the parties and witnesses in a case referred by quarter sessions for hearing by the local justices could be summoned to attend the next petty sessions. There, without the necessity of holding a special meeting, the justices could investigate the matter; the presence of numerous subordinate officers and spectators and the judicial aura surrounding the sessions being more conducive to seeing that justice was done. The quarter sessions order book indicates that many referrals during the 1630s were made to the "justices of that division" in contrast to the practice that prevailed before, when most referral orders named the referee-justices. Here is the clearest proof that the greater court expected its referees to hear the matter at their regular petty sessions. This development was significant. Petty sessions had become a court *de facto* as well as *de jure* on which quarter sessions was beginning to rely for nearly all out-of-sessions work including not only referrals, but bastardy orders and rating as well.[63] Indeed, by 1640, because of its usefulness as a general divisional business meeting for handling most out of sessions matters, petty sessions had become indispensable to the divisional justices. Even though the Book of Orders was forgotten, the machinery it had created was far too convenient to the magistrates themselves ever to pass into oblivion.

No justice could deny that the program enjoined in the Book of Orders and executed in petty sessions had worked to the good of the county and the better preservation of the King's peace. But no justice would have found the novel burden of labor entailed in that program and in its machinery at all agreeable. It was difficult to combat opposition to enforced apprenticing and to stir up constantly each succeeding year's churchwardens, overseers of the poor, high and petty constables, surveyors of highways, and tithingmen into some semblance of efficient administration. It was difficult to meet once a month for nearly a decade in order to execute all the provisions in that abundant source of hard work, the Book of Orders. By the middle of the 1630's, there can be little doubt that the justices were chafing under the load of petty-sessions business.

[63] Examinations of suspected criminals do not appear from the sessions rolls to have occurred at petty sessions, save in a few instances. Such examination had to take place very shortly after the party was arrested, and could not be deferred until a monthly meeting. Moreover, only one justice was required to examine and take evidence.

Moreover, by its very nature, petty sessions weighed heavily on the magistrates. This court laid upon them a far greater personal responsibility than they had ever labored under as justices at quarter sessions. There was no learned clerk of the peace at petty sessions; only accidentally was there a barrister on the bench to steer the little court around the legal pitfalls inherent in the confused and oft-times contradictory mass of statute law applied there. The full weight of the increased bulk of paper work, including estreats of fines, committal orders, and recognizances, fell on the justices and their personal clerks at petty sessions. Hanging over the two or three justices sitting in petty sessions, their dog-eared Lambarde or Dalton open before them, their clerks scribbling away below them, was the very grave threat of a stiff rebuke or even more drastic retribution for any mistake made, any task left undone. If the individual magistrate failed to attend his monthly meeting, he fell prey to the gravest sanction of all—expulsion from the commission of the peace. Before 1631, the individual justice who did not feel disposed to attend a quarter sessions, or who might be touched only by the strictures of his fellows if he absented himself from an out-of-sessions referral, was under no such sanction. In the imposition of this threat lay the new responsibility incumbent upon every justice under the Book of Orders. This responsibility could not be shifted either in 1631 or as late as 1640. Since the absence of even one divisional justice from the regular monthly meeting might mean that the petty sessions could not be held, the King's directions would not have been executed. This the King and Council would never tolerate. Every justice knew it.

Not only was the work of petty sessions in the execution of the Book of Orders far harder and more monotonously recurring than any work the justices had undertaken before. It was a burden that no justice dared avoid.

It is refreshing to treat the one project involving local government during the "personal rule" which proved undeniably successful. The next two chapters will paint a different picture. No contrast is here intended between this and the other programs that ended in failure, in setting down the causes for the unique success of the Book of Orders. If, however, the reader will take the negative of each reason for success given here, he will have a clue to the failure both of ship money and the attempted revitalization of the militia.

The success of the Book of Orders stemmed in great part from the moment when it was issued and from the nature of the demand it made on the county. The dreadful famine and unemployment of 1630–1631 necessitated drastic action, and every decent citizen welcomed it. At the same time, the drastic action was neither unreasonable nor unprecedented. The Book was intended to implement the law as known and practised (albeit indifferently) for many years. The program by its broadness allowed the shift of emphasis within it that adapted it to the changed circumstances prevailing once famine and depression were over. Introduced in a time of great need, the Book was suited to a purpose universally acceptable for more normal times. Therefore, opposition was never abundant, nor could those who opposed the Book secure a large following. Neither was a conflict of loyalties raised in the minds of the justices, no choice was required to be made between obedience to royal will and obedience to one's conscience and respect for the country's opinion. The justices appreciated the need for the program, and though they suffered from the responsibility of executing it, they were unanimous in shouldering it. This raised the Book of Orders above the push and pull of county politics, an elevation possible only because the program threw up no issues which county magnates, intent upon advancing their own power, could grasp and twist to political advantage.

No other program of the "personal rule" enjoyed such unanimous goodwill, and consequently such success.

Chapter VIII ❧ *Ship Money*

In retrospect, no other secular program attempted by Charles and his Council during the "personal rule" appears quite so foolhardy as ship money. In magnitude it was the greatest of all financial expedients, and the opposition to it was of corresponding size. When both the Short and the Long Parliaments attacked the King's financial exactions, the list of their grievances on this score was long, but among them, ship money was preeminent. It was to a nation outraged by ship money that Charles turned in 1639 and 1640 to defend his interest in Scotland. The nation's angry and unwilling response was in no small measure an indication of its hatred for ship money.

Foolhardy in retrospect, ship money did not seem foolhardy at the time. A worsening situation on the Continent and his own grandiose schemes combined in 1634 to impel Charles to prepare a great fleet. The depleted state of the Exchequer directed him elsewhere to secure the money to finance the fleet. The shift decided upon was the not untried device of requiring maritime places of the realm to provide ships for the royal navy. The Attorney-General was moved to shape the writs and letters into correct legal prose and the keeper of the Tower records was sent to his muniments to search out historical precedents for such a course.[1] When the writs were issued and letters of instruction sent to the sheriffs of maritime counties for raising one or more ships singly or in combination with other counties or levying a specified sum in lieu thereof, the Council was most forward to assure the local officers that the demand was founded on law and precedent, as indeed it was.

Sir John Borough need not have searched his records as far back as Edward I, for there were respectable precedents of later date. The Cadiz expedition fleet of 1596 had contained ships provided, equipped, and manned by the maritime places. That the government made no mention

---

[1] PRO, S.P.16/276, no. 63, correction of ship money letter by Bankes, A-G; no. 65, "A briefe of the precedents" by Sir John Borough [Oct.] 1634.

of an even more recent precedent, was probably as well, however. In 1626, coastal shires and towns had been ordered to supply ships for the fleet. Dorset, London, Essex, and Somerset were outspoken in their reluctance to comply. The Somerset justices, directed to join the county with Gloucestershire for the aid of Bristol in setting forth two vessels, demurred softly in a letter sent from Michaelmas quarter sessions. The Council then wrote the deputy lieutenants to gather the money, but without success. When pressed again in March 1627, twenty-three Somerset justices (including three deputies) replied to the Council that they would

> ...undergoe [the charge] ...with great unwillingnes, because wee conceave it will begett uppon us and our posterities the presidente of a chardge which [neither] wee, nor our predecessors did ever beare; ...whereof wee humbly beseech your Lordshipps to take bothe these and our former letters in good parte, and to give them a favourable construction as cominge from a countrie that hath not byne backwarde in publique services when custome and aunciente usage hath byne the grounds of those comaunds. . . .[2]

There does not appear to have been any conciliar reply to this letter. Had there been, it would likely have read as petulantly as the one sent to the Essex justices who refused to join with Colchester in providing a ship. Nor could the letter to Somerset have failed to end, as did the letter to Essex, with a reiteration that "the defence of a kingdome in tymes of extra-ordinarie danger are not tyed to ordinarie and continued presidents."[3] These words had a future, for they were the cornerstone of the Crown's case against John Hampden a decade later. So, too, had the opposition that expressed itself at this first halting resuscitation of a levy which even under Elizabeth had not been popular.

With respect to the royal interest, the autumn of 1634 could not have appeared more propitious for the issue of the first writ of ship money. The demand in 1626 had served as a goad to a countryside hostile to preparations for the Cadiz expedition, angered by having had to pay coat and conduct money as yet unrepaid, and determined not to pay the forced loan. The reluctance voiced by the justices of Somerset and other counties was that of men who were already busily engaged in com-

---

[2] PRO, S.P.16/60, no. 32, petition of the Somerset JPs, Glastonbury, 16 April 1627. The petition is in the hand of Sir Henry Berkeley's clerk and his signature leads all the rest —that he would be the prime mover of such a bold course would certainly be quite in character.

[3] *Acts PC*, 1627, p. 222, PC to JPs Essex, 13 April 1627.

bating a wave of unconcealed indignation raised by the forced loan. The situation was far different in 1634. The nation was quiet, dissidence apparently nonexistent. The dominant theme in local government was the routine enforcement of the Book of Orders. Laudianism, not yet the *bête noire* of the puritans, was in its infancy and had still to evoke on a large scale and a vast front impassioned preaching, polemical pamphlets, and riots in churches. The recent revival of the forest laws, as yet unmarked by any serious disruption, the increasing flow of money from tonnage and poundage imposed with the blessing of the court of Exchequer, and the relative ease with which the commissioners for the composition for knighthood had accomplished their work were encouraging signs. Superficially, at least, the "personal rule" had become accepted by the nation at large as the mode by which government functioned. The bold—albeit secretive and unrealistic—new foreign policy bore witness to the King's pleasure with the state of the realm. As well, it promised the rich satisfaction that the two previous disastrous expeditions had denied him. Ship money was the obvious, easy answer to his need for a powerful fleet to bring that satisfaction within his grasp.

Used once, ship money was certainly the easiest answer. The amount of money demanded by the first writ was moderate, being little more than one-quarter of those which would be demanded in all the subsequent writs save that for 1638. Translated into the burden it imposed on the ratepayer in the maritime counties, it stung far less than an average parliamentary grant of recent years. The legality of the 1634 demand was not open to serious question. The state of the war on the Continent with an imminent threat of Dunkerque falling into hostile hands and the necessity of protecting the fishing fleet from privateers were sufficient to impel most men to look twice at the requirement of "extraordinary danger" before dismissing the writ as an illegal contrivance. Nor was the demand unprecedented in its scope, since only maritime ports and counties were included. Above all, however, there was no hint in October 1634 that the writ was more than a temporary expedient to furnish a fleet for the immediate defense of the realm. The three months which had elapsed between the time the late Attorney-General Noy's suggestion had materialized in a committee to study the matter and 20 October when the writ was issued gave the government no time to propagandize, no time to herald the writ's approach by the judges on circuit as was done the following year. Taking the potentially disaffected and recalcitrant by surprise was half the battle. The disarming spontaneity with which the writ was issued and the long, carefully drafted preamble playing on the buoyant and never quite submerged prides and prejudices of Englishmen and urging preparedness against an immediate—and by implication, nonrecurring—danger allayed all suspicion that tendering a penny might mean subsequently losing a pound. A demand of this moderateness, projected with such spontaneity and an aura of temporary urgency onto a citizenry quieter almost than at any time before in the reign, was not likely to evoke a broadside of opposition.

The favourable impression made by the seemingly temporary nature of the first writ of ship money cannot be overstressed. What raised the storm and lashed it up with increasing fury was the permanence of the levy, a feature which did not become apparent until the second writ. Twentieth-century sensibilities, dulled by monotonously recurring taxation, are incapable of absorbing the full impact that a yearly tax of such magnitude would have on the consciousness of the seventeenth-century Englishman. There was something homely and familiar about the minor annual demands of three shillings here and two shillings there for the parish poor and the hospital fund; although, as the justices could testify, there was enough grumbling about these rates. In magnitude, only a grant of subsidies and fifteenths approached ship money. And the infrequent and irregular nature of parliamentary supply (especially of late) markedly differentiated that revenue from ship money. It was this contrast which struck hardest the average yeoman or gentleman served with a new demand for ship money almost as soon as he had paid on the last one. To these people, ultimately the backbone of the opposition, the unparliamentary quality of ship money was not a matter of overwhelming concern. What was, was that they could look forward in every year of life left to them to paying an unprecedentedly sizable part of their earnings in taxes. The more vocal men of higher place might espouse the rights of Parliament and the liberty of the subject, but if assured to his own satisfaction that he would never have to pay again, the most obstinate countryman would pay once. It had been the impermanence of the forced loan that had assured its success, that to a large extent had vitiated the strongest efforts to keep opposition at a high pitch once the little men had become convinced that it was not in truth going to be a precedent. It was the permanence of ship money, apparent in the 1635 writ, that assured its final and complete failure in 1640.[4]

---

[4] While not giving so much stress to it, Prof. Willcox mentions the importance of the permanence of ship money, *Gloucestershire*, p. 123. Prof. Dietz's contention, that if Lindsey's fleet in 1635 had achieved "some signal and dramatic success . . . [ship money] might have

Doubtless, though the permanence of ship money was prominent in the Council's considerations during the autumn of 1634, the ignoble end of the tax was unforeseen. Indeed, the Council took great pains to construct an administrative machine, operating with a simple and easily regulated procedure, that would minimize the difficulties which had attended the collection of parliamentary subsidies by archaic procedures. The machine centered on the hapless sheriff. The writ was sent to him with instructions of typical minuteness, ordering him to meet with the mayors of corporations and rate the towns involved. Then, he was to send for the hundred constables and by warrant specify the amount each hundred was to supply and require them to convoke raters, "substantial men" from each parish on tithing within the hundred, who would rate the hundred's inhabitants according to an "equal" rate and return the rate to him. The sheriff was to dispatch the rate to the Privy Council at once. Within a specified period (varying from one year's writ to the next), the hundred constables were to collect the money from the other subordinate officers within their hundreds and send it to the sheriff. This he was to pay in turn to the Treasurer of the Navy. Thus, the whole responsibility was thrown on the sheriff and, in years to come, the Council was never backward in reminding him of it.[5]

---

continued to receive . . . little popular opposition," is highly questionable, *English Public Finance, 1558–1641* (1932), p. 267. The permanence of ship money was an effective antidote to the seductiveness of jingoism.

[5] For the reader's information, I tabulate here the ship-money writs, Somerset sheriffs responsible for them, the sums required, final arrears (as of the end of 1640), and percentages of the required sums uncollected by then. These figures are from M. D. Gordon, "The Collection of Ship-Money in the Reign of Charles I," *Trans RHS* (1910), 3rd series, IV, 141–162. I have checked Miss Gordon's figures which pertain to Somerset against the accounts in PRO, E.351/2274–2284, and have found no discrepancies. However, she failed to note that the £6735 originally charged on Bristol, Somerset, and Gloucestershire for 1634 ship money was reduced to £6500—each county to pay one-third of it—and that the final arrears of £68 6s 8d were owed only by Gloucestershire, the Bristol corporation and Somerset sheriff having paid in all required of them by the fall of 1635, PRO, S.P.16/296, no. 58, Nicholas's accounts, 1634 ship money, 31 Aug. 1635.

Writ	Sheriff	Required Sum	Arrears	Percentage
Oct. 1634	Henry Hodges	£2166 13s 4d	None	0
Aug. 1635	Hodges and John Mallett	£8000	£956 2s 1d	12
Oct. 1636	William Bassett	£8000	£146 12s 5d	2
Oct. 1637	Sir William Portman, Bart.	£8000	£270 8s 6d	3½
Nov. 1638	William Every	£2800	£332 10s 0d	12
Nov. 1639	Sir Thomas Wrothe	£8000	£7665 12s 4d	96

Hodges, appointed sheriff in November 1634, remained in office until January 1635/6 as did all sheriffs that year. He issued the warrants for 1635 ship money and was jointly responsible for its collection with Mallett, who served as sheriff from January 1635/6 until October 1636.

8+

The most important feature of the system was that the sheriff's responsibility lay directly to the Council. In the case of the sheriffs charged with the 1634 and 1635 writs, the responsibility entailed less obtrusive oversight by the Council than was the case later. It was as a result of the growing opposition which retarded the sheriff's efficiency in collecting the money that the Council in January 1636/7 demanded fortnightly reports from the sheriff.[6] This demand was never afterwards relaxed. From November 1635, the omnicompetent Mr. Edward Nicholas, clerk of the Council, kept a book of all correspondence and made periodical reports to the Council on the progress of payments.[7] Hardly since the days when Richard FitzNeal wrote of the sheriffs quaking before Henry II's Exchequer had that official been brought under such close and exacting scrutiny. The Council was alive to almost every move the sheriff made, and it had the distinction of not once flagging in its almost day-to-day oversight for the duration of ship money. It was not loath to act upon its knowledge by sending frequent letters of great forcefulness; occasionally by summoning the sheriff, perhaps prosecuting him in Star Chamber, or more degrading yet, putting him in the charge of a sergeant-at-arms who would accompany him day and night about his tasks. A sheriff, followed around the country by a sergeant-at-arms, would be a ludicrous sight to his countrymen, a Don Quixote squired by a menacing Sancho Panza. Ultimately, the feature of his responsibility that loomed largest to each succeeding sheriff falling hopelessly in arrears, was that his responsibility did not cease when his year was up. Until the end of his life, the sheriff was accountable for every farthing levied on his county under the writ for his year. Nor was the Privy Council a lax Exchequer, for ship money unlike the traditional revenues could not be shifted by a bit of perjury and some ambiguous accounting onto the shoulders of a successor. In 1640, four Somerset exsheriffs were trying desperately to collect ship money due for their respective years.

By making the sheriff solely responsible for the collection of ship money, the whole power of the Council was poised to drop with terrible weight on that one official. One man only had to be watched and one man only had to be castigated. Threats directed towards and abuse heaped upon the sheriff were sure, the Council thought, to reach the lowest level of the machine with maximum force and secure the maximum efficiency

[6] PRO, S.P.14/219, no. 140 (Nicholas' letter book) Edward Nicholas to sheriffs of Eng. and Wales, 30 Jan. 1636/7.
[7] PRO, S.P.16/301, no. 38, order of King in Council, 8 Nov. 1635.

of operation. For the collection of ship money no better officer could be found than the vulnerably solitary sheriff.

But the Council made one initial miscalculation and three subsequent mistakes. The initial miscalculation was its failure to recognize that the extent and the power of the opposition were sure to increase as the demand for the tax was repeated. This miscalculation was not corrected until the state of the program had so far deteriorated that nothing could be done about it. Indeed, it is questionable if the Council ever realized how great that opposition had become. Out of this miscalculation grew three mistakes. Briefly summarized, they were: the wide latitude permitted the sheriff in applying his own discretion in rating; the Council's reluctance to visit with swift retribution those individuals who manifestly opposed the sheriff and his subordinates; the Council's belief that the counties' and boroughs' subordinate officers would prove capable and loyal instruments for the collection of the tax despite their neighbors' hostility. Each of these errors allowed a situation to develop in the county which the rapidly growing opposition turned to its own advantage. Each of these errors of judgment on the Council's part was used by the opposition as an effective weapon slowly but surely to bring ship money to a standstill.

The opposition to ship money was akin to that which had made so difficult the work of the commissioners for the forced loan. Geographically and socially, it was broadly based, encompassing finally the whole county with both farmer and householder as its rank and file. Unlike the forced loan in Somerset, however, it found leadership in men of the magisterial class itself. Its principal leaders were magnates. These great men, from motives not always idealistic or disinterested, gave to the inchoate army of the hostile a disciplined form which secured the recognition by the sheriff in 1640 that the opposition was a closely-knit and elusive conspiracy. At the outset the opposition was not so widespread geographically, nor was its aim so undeviatingly fixed on the destruction of a hated tax. In the first expression of the countrymen's hostility to ship money, there was a certain hesitancy discernible, a reluctance to oppose openly the imposition. This early hesitancy was not the sham it later became under the repeated demand for ship money and after the opposition was given organization by clever minds and powerful hands.

Hostility to ship money found its outlet in three successive stages. The first was the complaints of a number of hundreds and towns, tithings and parishes that the particular proportion of the county's charge levied on them was excessive. The most marked characteristic of this expression of obstinacy was its apparent reasonableness, its limited objective, and its careful avoidance of any express objection to paying the levy. The second stage, the outright refusal of individuals to pay the tax, saw for the first time unconcealed antagonism to ship money itself. Here, the merest pretence of a claim to having been excessively rated, discriminated against by a spiteful constable, etc., was considered a sufficient shift by men who felt they could challenge with impunity the power of the King and his minister, the sheriff. The third stage was the most disastrous of all. It was the inactivity and hostility of the constables and sheriff's officers compounded of the by then universal hatred of ship money, fear of their neighbor's fury, and the deep loathing of officials (most of them unpaid) forced to do a task more difficult and more thankless than any their predecessors had been called upon to perform. The constables would not convoke raters, would not collect the money. They and the sheriff's officers would not levy distress—in short, would not discharge those duties which were absolutely essential to the collection of ship money. These three stages were attained by the opposition in the order in which they have been set down here. The latter two were developments in part growing out of the previous stage or stages. But the new developments did not preclude the previous ones. They gave greater potency to the antagonism expressed thereafter at the previous stage or stages. By 1640 the opposition was fighting at all three levels, and that promised the destruction of ship money.

At the three several stages of opposition the corresponding errors of judgment on the Council's part provided aid and comfort for the enemy, even direction of his course of action. As the history of ship money in Somerset—or any other county—is largely a history of the opposition to it, so the unfolding of that history should follow the opposition onto each platform from which it chose to attack the tax. The story cannot help but emphasize how effectively the opposition used the weapons inadvertently placed in its hands by a government that did not or would not realize how completely the nation was estranged from its policy.

Ship money levied under the writ of October 1634 was the only ship money in Somerset fully collected within the sheriff's term of office; in fact, was the only ship money fully collected.[8] In comparison to the era

[8] See p. 207, n. 5.

of disruption ushered in by the 1635 writ, the year of the 1634 writ was tranquil. Nonetheless, already the first murmur of hostility could be detected when the first hundred complained that it had been improperly rated by the sheriff. By the next year, this murmur had become a shout—within two years, a roar.

For the increase in the amount and the intensity of hostility being expressed by complaints of over-rating, the Council had only itself to blame. With a laudable desire to tax equitably every man according to his true wealth, the Council permitted two contradictions to creep into its instructions to the sheriffs. The first contradiction was, that while paying lip service to the existing criteria of county rating, the Council enjoined the sheriff to rate according to criteria in direct conflict to the existing ones. This contradiction arose from the Council's advice that the sheriff was to follow the rates for other "common payments." In virtually the next sentence, the sheriff was strictly enjoined to extend consideration in rating to cottagers who had only their earnings to support them and to take into account personal as well as real property when rating the more prosperous members of the community. The subtle, though very material, contradiction between these two criteria for rating lay in the fact that the rates in other "common payments" were based on the ancient landscot (that is, a tax on land) which took no account of personal property or provided any ease for the less affluent. Consequently, the second contradiction became of tremendous significance. For, though the sheriff was to convoke a meeting of raters within each hundred to assess the tithings and parishes, which were in turn to assess by tithing-raters their individual ratepayers, he was empowered to accept or reject their rate and substitute his own.[9] This sowed the seed of dissension between sheriff and raters. Naturally, the raters generally preferred the traditional rates for the "common payments." The sheriff, on the other hand, might feel (or for his own dishonest ends, pretend to feel) that a particular tithing which usually paid one-tenth of the hundred's proportion for "common payments" had so many merchants of great personal wealth, or so many persons living on marginal incomes that it should pay to ship money in a proportion more or less

[9] For example, the 1635 instructions, PRO, P.C.2/45, pp. 71–75, PC to sheriffs and mayors, 12 Aug. 1635. The machinery for rating is clearly demonstrated in operation by two ship-money rates, one of them for the tithing of Cricket St. Thomas and the other for the hundred of South Petherton (to which Cricket St. Thomas was rated) extant in the Preston papers among SRO, Hippisley MSS.

than one-tenth. He would reject the assessment. Thus, there would be a head-on collision, a conflict between sheriff and raters conducive to the growth of a rating dispute. Even in those cases where the sheriff could win the raters to his way of thinking, an assessment in marked contrast to the traditional one provoked grumbling that a disaffected leader could transform into a community's vehement complaint of over-rating.

In the case of hundreds, only the first contradiction was germane. In apportioning the charge among the hundreds, the sheriff did so usually on his own discretion and never with the advice of local assessors. Here, in following the Council's directions to give greatest weight to particular circumstances of wealth, thereby disregarding its earnest advice to make the rate accord with those for other "common payments," the sheriff was playing the most dangerous game of all. It was the complaints of the hundreds that swelled the volume of expressed hostility from a murmur to a roar.

From a sincere desire to rate according to true value, from ignorance of the rate for "common payments," and not infrequently from cupidity, successive sheriffs played into the hands of the opposition. From one or another of these motives, depending on his character, each sheriff exercised the discretion the Council allowed him to rate ship money on a different basis than that of the "common payments." William Bassett (sheriff for 1636 ship money) fell victim to rating disputes either because he conscientiously attempted to apply the Council's criterion of rating to true worth or because he was ignorant of the normal rate. Henry Hodges (1634 and 1635 ship money) in order to ensure obtaining sufficient money to meet the writ's requirements, assessed at a higher rate those hundreds and tithings which he considered would give most willingly. This evoked a rash of well-deserved troubles. Hodges, and to a lesser extent Sir William Portman, Bart. (1637 ship money) were wont to give preferential treatment to those hundreds in which they, their undersheriffs, or their friends held extensive properties.[10]

While there could be little excuse for rate juggling done from such motives, the sheriffs cannot be wholly damned for it. They were men drawn from and closely linked to the community and in many ways prey

---

[10] Abdick and Bulstone hundred complained that Portman overcharged them in order to reduce the assessment on Milverton hundred, where his undersheriff's estate lay. Portman's defense was not convincing, PRO, S.P.16/389, no. 26, petition of Abdick and Bulstone [c. Jan. 1637/8] and Sir William Portman, Bart. to PC, 2 May 1638.

to the power of the community. They were under constant pressure to procure revenue in the face of formidable opposition. Therefore, they were tempted to misuse the power given them by the Council. Blame must attach to the Council who had given that power, knowing full well from abundant experience that the sheriffs would abuse it.

During the six years of ship money, Somerset appears to have had the distinction of troubling the Council more concerning rating to ship money than any other county.[11] On at least thirty different occasions, one or more hundreds, towns, tithings, or parishes launched an outcry against an assessment that was heard in Whitehall. Exactly twenty-three of these complaints grew out of a divergence between the sheriff's assessment and the assessment for the "common payments"; not a few of these from a difference between one sheriff's assessment and another's. It should be remembered that there were probably a great many more complaints, especially at the parochial level, that never reached the Council's ears and thus escaped being noticed in Edward Nicholas' state papers.[12] Especially for the years in which the 1635 and 1636 writs were levied, these complaints were the dominant mode of expression of an opposition fast stiffening to more direct resistance.

The complaints of the hundreds are of the greatest interest if for no other reason than that among those heard at Whitehall they were the most numerous. Moreover, they were the most damaging to the King's cause because of the size of the area involved. Nine of the towns that complained did so on the basis that they had paid to the "common payments" with the hundreds in which they were situated; complaints which merged inextricably with the complaints of the hundreds. To both town and hundred the rate for "common payments" meant only one rate, the Hinton rate. This was the "most aunciente, generrall, and usuale rates of the countye"[13] that hundred after hundred, town after town, explicitly or implicitly charged had been infringed by the sheriff. This rate, determining the proportion which each hundred was to furnish either of men or money, had been devised by nine commissioners for musters at Hinton St. George in 1569 for levying

---

[11] From a perusal of PRO, S.P.16 and P.C.2 concerning such disputes in other counties.
[12] Sheriff Bassett spoke of the "continual wrangling" between parishes and tithings, and overassessments of individuals, PRO, S.P.16/350, no. 39, William Bassett to Edward Nicholas, 20 March 1636/7.
[13] PRO, S.P.16/312, no. 77, petition of Bruton, Horethorne, Catsash, and Norton Ferris hundreds [c. Jan. 1635/6] copy.

one hundred Somerset men for Irish service.[14] The intervening decades
had caused a goodly number of alterations as magistrates and deputy
lieutenants found that changed conditions had resulted in changed
abilities in some hundreds to pay the sums assessed or provide the
men required under the rate. These alterations, though minor, had
caused a great deal of confusion as to what exactly a hundred was
charged to pay at the present day. There was some justification for
a sheriff finding it difficult to rate ship money according to the "most
aunciente" rate, and there were grounds for the belief that in many
cases it would be inequitable to base on it a tax levied in 1635. Regardless, these were inadequate excuses for infringing the Hinton rate—
or so felt the hundreds. Though the intervening decades had caused
modifications and made urgent the need for more, they had also lent
a sanctity to the old rate that made meddling with it almost sacrilege.[15]
Yet, its popularity must be explained by more than the mere passage
of time. If age had beatified it, it was the opposition's need for an
authority universally reverenced and a traditional usage martyred by
the government's lust for money that had canonized it. The Hinton
rate certainly worked miracles for the opposition.

Despite a ready excuse for complaint present in the sheriff's novel
assessments, despite a rallying point provided by the Hinton rate,
the opposition's plaints might have been stifled by a sheriff moving
against them from a position of power and prestige. However, once
men of equal or greater power had organized the complainants and
had amplified the outcry so that it was heard at Whitehall, a greater
power than the sheriff's was needed to check the wail. Amplification
came from and organization was manifestly accomplished by four
magnates in the county. Sir Robert Phelips, both a justice and a
deputy, placed himself in command of the recalcitrant as early as
the first writ. Sir Henry Berkeley, JP, assumed a like authority during
the second year of ship money, and with the advent of the third writ

14 Ammerdown House, Hylton MSS, "A proportion devised at Henton . . . [1569]."
Through correlation with other county rates of later date and documents concerning ship
money, I am satisfied that this was the Hinton rate which lay at the bottom of Somerset's
rating disputes. I have transcribed and printed it in full with an analysis of it in "The
Hinton Rate, 1569," *SDNQ* (1959), XXVII, 210–213.
15 Quarter sessions had cracked the authority of the Hinton rate in 1619 by directing
that no ancient prescription hold against the rule of discretion and good conscience in
rating for one of the common payments, the composition for purveyance, SRO, QSOB,
1613–1620, Mich. 1619 QS, no. 13.

was seconded by his elder brother and near neighbor, Sir Charles Berkeley, a deputy lieutenant. Sir Francis Dodington, JP, also attacked in
the third year, though more covertly. How many other magistrates
attached themselves to the nascent corps of opposition in their neighbor-
hoods cannot be determined, though suspicion falls on some of them.[16]
In the case of the four gentlemen named, their leadership was restricted
to the immediate locale in which they lived or possessed social preponderance by virtue of large estates. However, the influence of their leadership was not so limited. The map below depicts those hundreds,

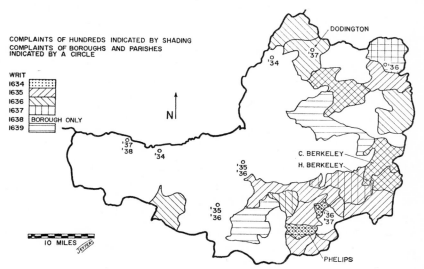

FIG. 3.—*The complaints of over-rating to ship money, 1634–1639 Writs.*

parishes, and towns which complained to the Council of an unequal
assessment in the years of the six writs, along with the seats of these
four gentlemen. The marked pattern of the hundredal complaints, especially for ship money of the years 1635–1637, suggests far more than mere
coincidence of complaint. The influence of one powerful voice in one
hundred on the unquiet spirits of others nearby could be immense. The
example of one successful challenge of the sheriff's authority encouraged

[16] Without the acquiescence, if not the support, of Thomas Luttrell, JP, Minehead could
not have complained against its assessment to 1637 and 1638 ship money. John Coventrye,
custos and intimate of Sir Robert Phelips, had influence in neighboring Taunton and
might have had a hand in that borough's complaints against 1635 and 1636 ship money.

8*

many such challenges. The opposition was alive and it required leadership. Sir Robert Phelips, Sir Henry Berkeley and Sir Charles Berkeley,
and Sir Francis Dodington supplied the demand.

Sir Robert Phelips first rose to the occasion. Sheriff Henry Hodges,
charged with collecting ship money under the 1634 writ, levied £20 on
the town of Ilchester and the other parishes of Tintinhull hundred that
he considered maritime, by warrant of 28 March 1635. Raters from the
parishes met and apportioned the charge. Their assessment received the
approbation of Sir Robert, who as divisional justice, lord of much of
the soil of the hundred, high steward of Ilchester, and the greatest
magnate in that part of the county had good claim to pass judgment
upon the assessors' product. Most of the money was duly collected. However, when proffered to Hodges, he refused it and sent a new warrant
requiring a new rate to be used which specifically reduced Ilchester's
share by one-third. Within twenty-four hours of receiving the new warrant, Phelips and his lesser neighbors petitioned the Council that Hodges
had imposed his own assessment in contradistinction to theirs in order to
ease one George Smith, an Ilchester burgess. Smith, rated at £6, had
peremptorily refused to pay under the first assessment; small wonder, in
light of the fact that he was assessed at nearly one-third of the whole.[17]
Smith was an inveterate enemy of Phelips, and had for a number of years
past repeatedly challenged the steward's (i.e., Phelips') ascendancy in
the borough. The £6 rate on Smith was probably nothing more than an
act of personal vindictiveness on Phelips' part, though Smith's wealth
appears to have been such that he might have deserved to pay so much.
Regardless, the Council upon consideration of both Phelips' and Hodges'
written arguments, found for Phelips and the Tintinhull inhabitants
and ordered the sheriff to receive the money collected under the first
assessment. Obviously, its finding was little governed by the merits of
the case, but was merely an act of policy to the end that ship money
should be obtained with the least fuss.[18] Expediency proved fruitful and

---

[17] SRO, Phelips MSS, vol. B, f. 153, petition of Tintinhull hundred [7 May 1635] fair
copy in Phelips' secretary's hand. The rate as well as this petition (original) are in PRO,
S.P.16/535, no. 69. Even before, in April, Phelips had called Hodges' rating of Martock
hundred as "maritime" wrong, SRO, Phelips MSS, vol. B, f. 192.

[18] PRO, P.C.2/44, p. 577, PC to sheriff of Somerset, 25 May 1635. Phelips had his revenge.
The prosecution to conviction in Star Chamber in Michaelmas 1639 of Sheriff Hodges (for
selling the gaoler's place, fine of £400) and of Smith (for tampering with witnesses in a suit
against Richard Browne, fine of £50) was undertaken by Richard Browne, the displaced
gaoler and Phelips' staunch ally in Ilchester, HLS, L. MS 1128, no. 391, and PRO, E.159/479,
Hil. 15 Chas. I, rot. 12.

the £20 was deposited with the Treasurer of the Navy. But the first gun had been touched off by an able general, and before long a large force had rallied to his colors.

It fell to Phelips' old friend and most constant supporter, Sir Henry Berkeley, to evoke for the first time explicitly the sacrosanct Hinton rate. His was not an untried hand at opposition, for he had apparently led the justices in protesting so forcibly against the 1626–1627 ship-raising. This time his followers were his neighbors of the hundreds of Bruton, Horethorne, Catsash, and Norton Ferris, and the issue was an £80 overcharge for 1635 ship money. With more discretion than he had exhibited before, Sheriff Hodges at the outset called upon the justices of the whole eastern half of the county (including Berkeley) to meet, discuss, and instruct him as to the usual proportions for the hundreds in that area. The justices followed the Hinton rate which set these four hundreds at eight one-hundredths of the total county charge (£640 to this writ of ship money), and in accordance with their finding Hodges rated the four hundreds at that sum. Then, he made the grievous error of superseding his first warrant with a new one demanding £80 more than the proportion under the Hinton rate. Hodges' intent was obvious; the extra £80 would compensate for money uncollected elsewhere, these four hundreds seeming quiet and willing. Hodges had not counted on Sir Henry Berkeley. In a petition drafted by Berkeley's clerk and signed by the magnate himself, the inhabitants with self-righteous indignation protested against the "needles vexacion and chardge Mr Shereiff hath layd upon us...."[19] The petitioners advanced the Hinton rate as the rightful criterion and produced the violation of it as their prime evidence of the sheriff's iniquitous dealing. Bishop Pierce, acting as referee for the Council, ordered Hodges to repay the £80 unless he could prove his authority for having imposed the extra by producing "a sufficient proofe [by which is meant] ... a rate whereunto the deputy lieutenants and all the justices of the county have been called, and unto which the major part there present have subscribed."[20] Hodges was a long time in repaying it, and before the affair was settled the Council was twice again troubled.

It was not Hodges who suffered most; it was his successor. Bruton and Catsash a year later complained that Sheriff Bassett had over-rated them.

[19] PRO, S.P.16/312, no. 77, petition of Bruton, Horethorne, Catsash, and Norton Ferris hundreds [c. Jan. 1635/6].

[20] PRO, S.P.16/330, no. 15, certificate of Bp Pierce and John Mallett, sheriff, 6 Aug. 1636.

The first signatures at the bottom of the petition were those of Sir Henry Berkeley and Sir Charles Berkeley. While the dispute dragged through a reference to the judges of assize, then to the bishop sitting with the sheriff and the exsheriff, the hundreds did not pay ship money.[21] The opposition could hardly have enjoyed greater success.

There is no denying the damage done by Phelips' first attack and Berkeley's first evocation of the Hinton rate. Each had pointed the way for the opposition in other hundreds to pursue. Each had resulted in vindication for the complainants, and so had given the encouragement that only success affords. Yet, other hundreds were slow to follow. It was Phelips who, in the last great battle of a long career marked by conflict, supplied the final impetus necessary to cover much of the eastern half of the county with rating disputes.

The cockpit was again Tintinhull hundred. Sheriff Bassett in levying 1636 ship money disallowed the rate that Phelips and the raters of the hundred had imposed for the assessment within the hundred, intruding his own rate which he claimed was the ancient rate but which Phelips and his neighbors dismissed as inequitable.[22] Sir Robert's son and heir, Edward, took up the lead offered by his father by refusing to pay ship money levied on his estate in the hundred by any other rate than that of the assessors. At this moment, Sir John Stawell, a landowner in Tintinhull and the lifelong rival of Sir Robert, entered the fray. The eyes of the whole county then shifted to Tintinhull to watch the dispute that was sure to ensue. Stawell informed the Council—with a large measure of truth interlaced with malevolent falsehoods—that Sir Robert Phelips was determined to stir up trouble. The King in Council personally heard the adversaries. In delivering the most stinging rebuke that Stawell had ever suffered at the hands of his enemy, Charles found that Edward Phelips had shown his "good affection" to the service and that Stawell's accusations against Sir Robert were frivolous. By implication, King and Council had accepted Phelips' argument that Stawell had insidiously prevailed with the sheriff to impose the new rate.[23] His Majesty admonished both Sir Robert and Stawell to lay aside their differences and join together in the service of the King and the county. This final injunction proved unnecessary.

---

[21] PRO, S.P.16/365, no. 4, Bp Pierce, William Bassett, sheriff, and John Mallett, ex-sheriff, to PC, 1 Aug. 1637.

[22] PRO, P.C.2/47, p. 256, PC to sheriff of Somerset, 22 March 1636/7.

[23] PRO, P.C.2/47, p. 430, order of King in Council, 21 May 1637; SRO, Phelips MSS, vol. B, f. 141, brief of argument by Sir Robert Phelips before the PC [May 1637].

Within a year Sir Robert Phelips was dead. His legacy to the county had been this last great challenge which, in its success and through its notoriety, had plunged the King's service into a tangle of ship money rating complaints from which neither sheriff, judges, nor Council were able to extricate it.

The immediate result was undoubtedly the five other petitions of over-rating presented to the Council by hundreds in the eastern and southern part of the county and referred to Bishop Pierce, the sheriff, and the ex-sheriff.[24] In each, ship money went uncollected while the referees labored to settle the mass of conflicting claims and still the petty objections. The long-term effects proved to be the many other disputes that hampered and exasperated the unfortunate sheriffs charged with collecting ship money in the succeeding years. Phelips' countrymen had carefully watched the Tintinhull dispute, waiting expectantly for its outcome. As Hampden's case the next year was to stiffen personal and individual opposition to ship money, so Phelips' challenge stiffened opposition anonymously and euphemistically expressed by complaints of inequitable rating. A magnate like Sir Francis Dodington, possessed only of a bully's bluster, was emboldened to agitate covertly among his neighbors, disrupting the course of ship money in the northern part of the county.[25] Lesser men than he summoned their courage and, following the example Phelips had set them, added their voices to the murmur that had become a roar.

After a dispute had arisen, the Council was powerless to deal expeditiously with it. It could not summon a whole hundred before the Board. It could hardly punish the more notorious leaders of a cause which appeared to have tradition and one clause or another of the Council's contradictory instructions on its side, and which hid its true intentions in dutiful expostulations. All that the Council could do was to hear the dispute and settle the rate by which the hundred or tithing was to pay. Or, as more often happened, it could drop the whole affair into the laps of first, the bishop, the sheriff, and the exsheriff, or other justices, and if this did not suffice, into the laps of the judges of assize. There were twenty-four such references which absorbed an incalculable

[24] Complaints by Bruton, Horethorne, Catsash, and Norton Ferris; Chewton; Milverton; Frome Selwood; and Wellow hundreds were referred to the bishop *et al.* in May 1637.

[25] The complaints of Portbury, and Hartcliff and Bedminster hundreds against 1636 ship money was undoubtedly the work of Dodington. The complaint of Barrow tithing against 1637 ship money was contained in a petition of Dodington, PRO, P.C.2/49, p. 340, PC order, 15 July 1638. He also complained of an overassessment on his lands in Gloucestershire, 1636 ship money, P.C.2/47, p. 299.

amount of time of these various officials. Had the time lost by these busy men achieved any lasting results, it would have been well spent. However, as fast as the referees determined one complaint, another sprang up to take its place and so start the whole process again. Occasionally, the settlement of the complaint was itself shortlived, for a new sheriff made a new rate and the opposition in the hundred or the parish seized the opportunity to complain once more. There could be no limit to the number of hundreds and parishes that complained; no limit to the damage such complaints could do to the collection of ship money.

One thing only could have removed this weapon from the hands of the opposition. That was the rerating by the justices of the whole county, hundred by hundred and tithing by tithing, and its corollary, a strict injunction binding the sheriff to adhere to that rate alone. This would have proved effective. Though some of the justices, notably Bishop Pierce, had early been identified with the imposition of the tax, none of the opposition had questioned the integrity or the authority of those justices who advised the sheriff as to the rate he should make. Rather, the opposition in its petitions had referred to the justices' advice with respect and accepted it as binding. This might have been cant, mouthed in order to contrast the justices' counsel with the sheriff's practice, thus laying open the sheriff to the charge of inequitable and novel rating. Yet, the justices were too many in number, too preponderant as a bench of composite local powers, to have had their authority questioned by any but a few diehards. Rerating accomplished by the command of the court of quarter sessions would have left those who dared question the new rate naked in intransigence and vulnerable to swift punishment. It would also have forced those magistrates who had furnished the opposition's leadership to relinquish that stand and defer to the act of their colleagues in which, perforce, they had had to concur. Rerating would have snatched the initiative from the opposition in one fell swoop.

Though the Council appears to have been unaware of the motives behind the interminable disputes of unequal rating, it realized full well their immediate deleterious effects.[26] To put an end to the disputes, the Council in May 1637 ordered the judges of assize to treat with the sheriff, the justices, and principal gentlemen of Somerset for the general rerating of the county, taking into account improvements which had

[26] The Council stated that the complaints were not from disaffection to the service, but rather grew from a sense of injustice due to inequality in rating, PRO, P.C.2/48, p. 187, PC to JPs of Somerset, 27 Aug. 1637—this at this late date!

altered the values of various localities.[27] The impetus for this move had come from the county in two conflicting petitions from justices and other gentlemen, one advocating the Hinton rate, the other condemning it as inequitable.[28] In furtherance of the judges' efforts, the Council in August 1637 ordered the justices to make a new general rate for the county. The next quarter sessions gave effect to the order by appointing a special rating meeting of the justices at Wells in Easter Week (1638); the divisional justices in the interim were to evaluate the various hundreds, parishes and tithings.[29] The meeting was held, but the justices unable to reach a decision referred the business to a committee of four who were to report to the Michaelmas sessions. The death of one referee, Sir Robert Phelips, while auguring a better prospect of speedy conclusion, held up the work of the committee, and all that the Michaelmas sessions did was to postpone the matter to the next Easter sessions (1639). What happened after that is obscure. One thing is certain, the county had not been rerated by 1640, and the sheriff in that year was even more troubled than had been his predecessors with complaints of inequitable rating.

In the absence of positive evidence to the contrary, it is safer to assume that the failure of the justices to revise the county's rates was due more to the magnitude of the task than to any unwillingness on their part occasioned by private interest or covert opposition to the tax. The work required was enormous. At a time when every community was intent upon avoiding its share of the burden, there would have been innumerable objections to the divisional justices' evaluation, each of which would have to have been reinvestigated and satisfied before the rate could be promulgated. The Council had committed an error, though, in setting the venture on foot and then omitting to drive it to completion. All that the bold venture resulted in was a complete arrest of ship money payments throughout the county during the spring of 1638, while the hundreds waited to see what would come of the abortive Easter meeting.[30]

---

[27] PRO, P.C.2/47, p. 473, PC to JJ assize Western Circuit, 31 May 1637.

[28] Only the petition favoring the Hinton rate is extant, signed by Sir Ralph Hopton, Thomas Luttrell, and 13 others, PRO, S.P.16/357, no. 140 [May] 1637.

[29] PRO, P.C.2/48, p. 187, PC to JPs of Somerset, 27 Aug. 1637; SRO, QSOB, 1627/8–1638, Mich. QS 1637, no. 19. In October 1637, the King in Council ordered the judges of assize to confer with justices of all counties for a general rerating, PRO, P.C.2/48, p. 295, PC memo, 15 Oct. 1637. Somerset's prior and particular treatment indicates that its rating disputes had proved the most troublesome to the Council.

[30] PRO, S.P.16/381, no. 2, Sir William Portman, Bart., sheriff of Somerset, to PC, 1 Feb. 1637/8.

There can be no doubt as to how effectively the opposition had disrupted the collection of ship money by rating complaints. Each dispute was a sharp blow to the sheriff. It meant that he received no money until the dispute was settled. It meant that he wasted time and effort in settling the affair—so much so, that Sheriff Mallett lamented that the time he should have given to collecting his arrears was spent hearing complaints and certifying the issues to the Council.[31] Such disputes hopelessly undermined the sheriff's authority, not only because his rate was disputed in the first place, but also because (as it usually fell out) the complainants were vindicated by the Council. The apparently iniquitous carriage of the sheriff as evidenced in the disputes further outraged the county's sentiment and gained new adherents to the opposition. Each dispute struck at the constables who bore the unwelcome task of collecting the money. These yeomen and minor gentlemen were caught in the middle of the combat raging between their neighbors and their immediate superior, the sheriff. The constables were saddled with a divided allegiance, two loyalties which were fast become mutually exclusive. Furthermore, each dispute encouraged and emboldened individuals to attack the tax and refuse payment. By enhancing the power and numbers of the opposition, the rating disputes advanced the day when no man would pay ship money or any constable collect it.

In the year 1637, the third of ship money, the opposition attained the second level of its expression, the refusal of the individual to pay ship money. By the end of it, the opposition hardly made any pretence of dutifulness, took few pains to conjure up legitimate grounds for a complaint, and seldom bothered to dissemble its true motive. Resistance was overt. Husbandman, yeoman, and gentleman attacked ship money in the most effective manner that any financial exaction can be attacked: they refused to pay it.

The first Somerset man who adamantly refused to pay ship money was the upstart gentleman, William Strode, Esq., of Barrington Court. He must not be confused with another William Strode of more enduring fame,[32] though the cause he advanced and the vehemence with which he supported it remind one most forcibly of his Parliamentarian namesake.

[31] PRO, S.P.16/412, no. 13, John Mallett, exsheriff of Somerset, to Edward Nicholas, 2 Feb. 1638/9.

[32] The multiplicity of West Country William Strodes has been sorted out by the able antiquarian Thomas Serel, though not without some ambiguities remaining, *SANHS Proc* (1865–1866), XIII, pt. ii, pp. 6–20.

Strode aspired to the county magnate's authority, but his ambition was unable to gain him more than a trained band captaincy. Highly prosperous, he had capped a succession of able purchases by buying the beautiful house at Barrington from an insolvent cousin of Sir Robert Phelips. His connection with Phelips was more solid than this, however, for he had long been considered by the common folk a friend of Sir Robert.[33] His tactics of disruption were certainly reminiscent of those employed by that master of the art, though in the matter here considered he found Phelips to be his implacable foe.

In November 1636, John Mallett's undersheriff, William Cox, complained to the Chancellor of the Exchequer that Strode had refused to pay ship money under the 1635 writ. Upon the distraint of a cow belonging to him, he had refused to receive back the surplus from its sale, and had replevied the beast.[34] Strode and his cow became a Council matter. Their lordships referred hearing of the case to Bishop Pierce, who summoned Strode, the former sheriff who had levied the ship money, and the constable who had distrained the cow. Strode's prime antagonist was a neighboring gentleman, John Preston of Cricket St. Thomas, who with the assistance and encouragement of both Sir Robert Phelips and Lord Poulett (strange allies) gave to the prosecution of Strode a cutting edge. Upon hearing, Strode's argument was adjudged to be pure fabrication. He contended that he had refused to pay the sum assessed upon him because it was excessive, not because he desired to hinder the service; that the whole tithing had been grieved at being over-rated but that he had persuaded them to pay so as not to disrupt the collection, undertaking to act as their champion; that he had waited three months before bringing suit for replevin in the county court so as to cause no disturbance. The lie was given to each of these arguments and Strode did not help himself by baldly informing Pierce that his lordship "did not look upon this businesse with an indifferent eye." The truth of the matter was that Strode had refused to pay ship money in other places and that he was the only man in his tithing who had refused to pay. He had waited so long to replevy in order that the sheriff who had issued the *distringas* would be out of office when the action came before his county court! But a far more terrible truth that came out at the hearing was the statement of the undersheriff, Cox, that Strode was the only man who had

[33] SRO, Phelips MSS, vol. A, f. 66, certificate of four militiamen [1636].
[34] PRO, S.P.16/336, no. 29, William Cox to Lord Cottington, 21 Nov. 1636.

replevied a distress taken for ship money and that many people in his presence upon hearing of the replevin had said they wished they had not paid so soon.[35] Mr. William Strode had set a solid example. The subsequent actions of others who, like him, refused to pay ship money indicate how well it was followed.

In the light of the evidence contained in the bishop's certificate of Strode's conspicuous defiance, the mildness of the Council's retribution is astounding. Before the Board stood a man convicted of the most blatant and disruptive malevolence towards an act of government which King and Council were determined to carry to completion. The Council at last had within its power one solitary individual who could be so stiffly punished as to serve as an awful example of what would happen to any other Somerset man who chose to follow in his footsteps. It was not as if his was the one discordant voice in the county. Somerset, despite its transparent dutifulness, had made it abundantly clear that there were forces hard at work to destroy ship money. Three months before, Sheriff Bassett had not minced his words when he wrote Nicholas: "I cannot but impute this [aversion of raters to make rates] ... to the generall underhand refusall, though they will not let me know it."[36] The Council could have struck a mighty blow at those "generall underhand" refusers by laying strong hands on the first insurgent it caught. Instead, it ordered Strode to apologize to the bishop for his offensive words and to reimburse the unfortunate individual who had bought the cow since replevied from him. Their lordships graciously passed over the "shifts" which Strode had used to free himself from paying ship money, since he had already paid it.[37] The Council's forbearance to strike down Strode was merely part of a policy which allowed greater men, such as Lord Saye and Sele in Gloucestershire, to escape retaliation. In the months ahead the Council would have cause to regret its leniency and the loss of the first and (as it was to prove) the last, opportunity to curb the opposition in Somerset.

Even before Strode had returned home, hardly smarting from his chastisement at the Board, outright refusal to pay had become the dominant

---

[35] PRO, S.P.16/355, no. 54, Bp Pierce to PC, 3 May 1637. Considerable light on this affair, particularly on the issues involved in it, has been cast by Preston's papers in SRO, Hippisley MSS; among them, is a long draft of arguments to be used against Strode at the hearing before Pierce.

[36] PRO, S.P.16/347, no. 23, William Bassett to Edward Nicholas, 16 Feb. 1636/7. A month later, Bassett wrote of the "factious spirits" in the hundreds, S.P.16/350, no. 39, Bassett to Nicholas, 20 March 1636/7.

[37] PRO, P.C. 2/47, p. 457, PC order, 25 May 1637.

mode of expression for the opposition. Sheriff Bassett, whose fortnightly reports hitherto had been calm and unruffled, began to show the strain of combating resistance expressed in a curt "no." On 10 April he sent an earnest letter to the Council asking for instructions as to how to deal with royal wards who refused to pay on the quibble that they had already paid great liveries for their lands.[38] In a tone of desperation, Bassett wrote that most men in the western part of the county had said that if they didn't receive any other punishment they would never pay without distress being taken, "which causes on me an intollerable labour."[39] Intolerable was a strong word, quite out of character with Bassett. Worse yet was in store for him. In June, Bassett's most candid and plaintive letter of all informed Nicholas that he had paid £800 from his own purse, since money had come in slowly and on "troublesome terms," scarcely any of it paid without distress taken or distress granted.[40] So it continued over the summer. When his year was up in October 1637, resistance had left Bassett with arrears totaling nearly £1500. He was destined to undergo a great deal more "intollerable labour" before the Long Parliament's destruction of ship money relieved him of it.

This was the pass to which the opposition had brought ship money when the news came from London that a Buckinghamshire squire prominent in the last Parliament was to be prosecuted in the court of Exchequer for refusal to pay ship money. The impact that Hampden's Case made on the consciousness of even the humblest countryman in the spring of 1638 cannot be adequately conveyed by words written three hundred years later. The more intelligent and more articulate members of rural society had probably become inured to the court case of great constitutional significance in an age which had produced a surfeit of them; the ignorant and inarticulate members of rural society had probably never even heard of them. But Hampden's Case became a *cause célèbre* overnight and remained such for many months. Hampden's Case was absorbed so readily and so rapidly into the consciousness of every man, high and low, just because it dealt with a facet of every man's life which had loomed large in his thinking for the past two years. The homegrown "village Hampdens"—the Phelipses, Strode, the Berkeleys, and the myriad lesser men below the surface of the sea of anonymity—had

[38] PRO, S.P. 16/352, no. 52. The Council told Bassett that wardship was no excuse for not contributing to defense, PRO, P.C.2/47, p. 318, PC to sheriff of Somerset, 19 April 1637.
[39] PRO, S.P.16/350, no. 39, Bassett to Edward Nicholas, 20 March 1636/7.
[40] PRO, S.P.16/361, no. 19. Bassett to Nicholas, 4 June 1637.

cultivated their grievances in the minds of their neighbors, and by
1637 those minds were receptive to the mighty force of John Hampden's
intractable spirit and the intellectual suasion of his counsel, St. John.

The knowledge that one man had become the champion for the nation
solidified the county's resistance while further reducing whatever deference to or fear of royal authority still remained. A Somerset gentleman
sued a constable at common law for distraining his cow; a Somerset
yeoman broke open a pound and drove home his distrained cow.[41] Both
actions were different expressions, appropriate to rank, of the same spirit.
Where men would not pay before, now they would not suffer distraint.
Some were willing to commit violence to prevent distress being taken;
a sheriff's bailiff nearly succumbed to a pike wound inflicted while he
was distraining. The voice of the county spoke in the bold presentment
of the nineteen gentleman of the grand jury at the Bath assizes on
2 July 1638:

> Corne and other provision is growne to an excessive rate, which wee
> doe conceave not to be occasioned soe much by scarcity and want...
> as by other accidents, namely one principall one is the great and heavy
> taxacions by new invented wayes [which causes farmers to sell at
> high prices to meet them].[42]

The economic reasoning of these intrepid gentlemen was fanciful, but
their grievance was all too real. These jurymen might well have provoked
Chief Justice Finch, the most condemnatory of Hampden's judges, to
the "diverse malicious speeches," with which he "inveighed against and
threatened all such as refused to pay ship money," on the Western
Circuit.[43]

Hampden's prosecution having signalled the end of the Council's
leniency, process was issued out of Exchequer against those who had
not yet paid ship money for 1635.[44] How ineffective this punitive action

[41] PRO, S.P.16/341, no. 44, note by Edward Nicholas of direction by PC [May 1638];
379, no. 29, petition of Robert Pope, late constable of Bempstone hundred, to William
Bassett, exsheriff, 20 Jan. 1637/8.
[42] *Som Asz Ords,* no. 184. The jurymen were almost all lesser gentlemen, save for the
stormy parliamentary dissident of the 1620s and former justice, Edward Kyrton.
[43] Finch, CJCP's, advocacy of ship money from the bench on the Western Circuit was
the basis for count 7 in the articles of his impeachment in the first session of the Long
Parliament, as quoted here, *The Harleian Miscellany* (1801), V, 568.
[44] PRO, P.C.2/48, pp. 639–640, PC to sheriffs and exsheriffs of 17 counties (Somerset
included) 28 Feb. 1637/8. The processes were: (1) *scire facias,* requiring a party to show
cause why judgment (here, for not paying ship money) should not be executed; (2) *levari*

proved to be in Somerset may be gathered from a letter to John Mallett (1635 ship money) from his undersheriff, William Cox, dated almost three months after the processes had gone forth. The veracious Cox told his superior that upon rumors bruited about concerning the pending opinion of the judges in Exchequer Chamber in Hampden's Case, nobody would pay arrears for 1635 ship money.[45] When cattle were distrained, their owners let them starve in the pound or wounded them as they were being driven off by the bailiffs making them not worth the taking. With a sincerity born of desperation, Cox concluded that he could see no other hope than death or, what was as bad, perpetual suits. William Cox's plaint portended the final victory of the opposition to ship money in Somerset.

The judgment against Hampden (for what it was worth), the threats uttered by Finch, and the Exchequer processes had only a transitory good effect which helped the sheriff collecting 1637 ship money but afforded scant assistance to former sheriffs striving to collect arrears. In the long run the punitive action served to stiffen the opposition to all ship money for the simple reason it had come too late to produce more than a momentary fear in the recalcitrant, which soon gave way to a doggedly determined refusal to pay. The opposition had been allowed to gather too much strength to be smothered by anything but impossibly brutal repression. The Council had made the irreparable mistake of not proceeding stringently against Strode in Somerset, Saye and Sele and others in other counties when they were discovered in overt opposition to ship money.[46] It compounded its error by taking so long to prosecute Hampden. Too, the six months that had elapsed between the hearing in the court of Exchequer and judgment in the Exchequer Chamber had given plenty of time for the opposition to rally its forces, though neither the Council nor the Barons of the Exchequer can be rebuked justifiably for that delay. Quite aside from the government's desire to secure the

---

facias, requiring the sheriff to levy a debt (ship money) upon lands and tenements as well as goods and chattels—hitherto, the sheriff had been restricted to *distringas* out of his own county court by which he could attach only goods and chattels.

[45] PRO, S.P.16/389, no. 124, 6 May 1638. Cox was a hard-headed professional, not given to extravagant utterances.

[46] Apparently as early as December 1636 A-G. Bankes contemplated large-scale prosecution of ship money refusers—on his warrant to the clerk of the Crown in Chancery (rare) three writs of *certiorari* went out under the great seal (tested 5 Dec. 1636) directing the sheriff of Glamorganshire to return by 24 Jan. 1636/7 the names and assessments of all who refused to pay ship money, PRO, Index 4212, p. 223.

approbation of all the judges, both government and judges were too inextricably ensnared in due processes of law to have hurried on the case once it had reached this stage.[47] Where the Council can be rebuked was that it did not move with dispatch when Hampden had thrown down his challenge to the King two years before he was brought to trial. The cautious canvassing of judicial opinion in Hilary term 1637 as to whether refusers could be legally proceeded against was unnecessary at law even though it had become standard procedure under the Stuarts. If, instead, the bill against Hampden had been entered earlier in Exchequer and the trial brought on in Hilary 1637, even the slim seven-to-five decision for the Crown would have carried far more weight in a countryside that had hardly yet turned to direct refusal to pay as its dominant expression of hostility to ship money. This was true of Somerset, and it might well have been true of other counties. By Trinity term 1638, when the last judicial opinions were filed, the countrymen had travelled too far along the road blazed by their more advanced fellows to be turned back by either legal argument or fear of punishment. The Council could inform the sheriff of Somerset in petulant tone that the dissenting opinions of some of the judges was not to be used to refuse or delay payment of the tax,[48] but by the summer of 1638 no action, let alone words, could make an impression on the opposition.

The opposition had gained formidable victories, but it was not yet victorious. While the constables and the sheriff's officers remained loyal and remained at their tasks, ship money would not be defeated. Some men would pay willingly, and so long as the constables and bailiffs levied distress others also could be persuaded to part with their money rather than their cattle. It was when the subordinate officers, upon whom rested the whole structure of ship money collection, defected to the opposition that ship money was doomed. Perhaps many of these officers

---

[47] See *Cobbett's Complete Collection of State Trials* (1809), III, 826–1316 for Hampden's Case.

[48] PRO, P.C.2/49, p. 283, PC to sheriff of Somerset, 20 June 1638. A manuscript copy of Croke, JCP's, dissenting opinion in Hampden's Case—the most forthright and weighty of all—is among the papers in SRO, Hippisley MSS. Miss Carol Czapski has found the same among the papers of a Buckinghamshire ship money sheriff; Croke took the Buckinghamshire assizes throughout this period. Few documents have left such traces of wide dissemination as this. A copy is printed in *Camden Miscellany VII* (1875). By 1639, the ulterior circulation of literature against ship money was enormous, instanced by an eminent Western Circuit counsellor, Gabriel Ludlowe's, receipt of a manuscript remonstrance against the levy, left in his chambers without his knowledge (?) by a professional scribe, Bodl, Bankes MSS, bundle 19, no. 7, examination of Ludlowe by S-G, 24 Oct. 1639.

did not freely ally themselves with the opposition. That mattered little. By 1640, whether through sentiment or fear, the constables and sheriff's officers had become the enemies of the service they had been sworn to uphold. The collapse of the service was inevitable.

At no time had the constables done their duty with alacrity, though it was not until the third year of ship money that their waning efficiency became patently apparent. Their increasing inactivity was a direct consequence of the innumerable rating disputes which had sprung up on every side. It is significant that over half of the Somerset constables summoned before the Council or its referees for arrears of 1635 and 1636 ship money were the collectors in those hundreds and parishes which have left a recorded complaint against their rates. The reaction of constables caught in such a dispute was one of strict neutrality, and a manifestation of it was their refusal to exert any force whatever in collecting ship money until their arrears had grown so great that they attracted the attention of the sheriff and Council. Another manifestation of neutrality was their refusal to draw up the rate of their hundred or parish for fear of becoming involved in a dispute. Thus, Sheriff Basset was unable to procure from most constables these assessments upon which depended the collection of the tax.[49] Rating complaints had caused the constables to step with caution—to step without the vigor that was necessary to collect a highly unpopular tax.

The constables had stepped too cautiously, however, and by 1637 both the sheriff and the Council realized that the constables had been drifting. It was undoubtedly the absence of assessments from most of the counties that caused Nicholas to take notice of the inactivity of these men. Sheriff Bassett was aware of it sooner. In February 1636/7, he bound a number of constables to appear before the Council (as authorized by his instructions), and those who refused, he gaoled.[50] The results were most salutary. During 1637 a dozen constables went through the uncomfortable experience of answering at the Board for their remissness and were there dealt with gently but effectively. Much of Bassett's relative success in collecting ship money, even in the face of an opposition increasing by leaps and bounds, was due to the greater sedulity of his chastened and fearful constables.

[49] PRO, S.P.16/371, no. 20, William Bassett, exsheriff, to Edward Nicholas, 3 Nov. 1637; S.P.14/219, no. 162 (Nicholas's letter book) Edward Nicholas to sheriffs for 1636 of 27 counties (Somerset included) 8 Nov. 1637.

[50] PRO, S.P.16/347, no. 23, William Bassett to Edward Nicholas, 16 Feb. 1636/7.

Bassett's successors were not so fortunate. Under the impetus of Hampden's Case, what had been in 1637 sporadic outbursts of direct refusal had become by 1638 the dominant expression of resistance, often coupled with violence. The constables charged with collecting the fourth writ were caught fairly between their fear of the Council on the one hand and their fear of their neighbors on the other. But one threat was more real and immediate than the other. A tithingman threatened with arrest if he levied distress upon a man "full of law," a tithingman told by a refuser that if he dared to take a distress he would "scower" him, a constable in dread of threatened suits at common law by gentlemen of "great quality,"[51] could hardly think that the King's service was worth bodily injury or bankruptcy. The Council had no terrors to match those that the constables' neighbors threatened with increasing frequency and, upon occasion, perpetrated, nor could it stem the mounting reluctance on the part of the constables to place themselves in danger to procure the King's revenue. More and more constables were summoned before the Board, and those caught were threatened with stricter punishment—for not a few evaded the sheriff and the pursuivants. The Council tried the softer touch, glibly promising indemnity against law suits incurred in doing the King's service.[52] Nothing availed. Their lordships were too blind to discern that the opposition to ship money had grown so great, encompassed so many, that no one (least of all the timorous constables) would dare face it.

By the winter of 1639, the Council and the sheriff stood alone, confronted by an opposition of such size, strength, and hostility that it had become almost impossible to collect ship money. The course of events in the North had awakened the countrymen to the realization that other of his Majesty's subjects had spoken out in word and action their defiance of the King's authority. As Hampden's Case had stiffened the opposition, the stirring news of the Scots' insurgency confirmed the opposition in a singleness of purpose that the lonely power at Westminster and its lonely

[51] PRO, S.P.16/363, no. 11, Bassett to PC, 2 July 1637; 443, no. 82, petition of Samuel Foy, late constable of Horethorne hundred, to PC [Jan.] 1639/40.

[52] Bassett watched for a week—to no avail—the houses of some exconstables who still owed him ship money. One very troublesome exconstable escaped from an arresting officer; when the officer came again to arrest the "desperate man," he was threatened by him, PRO, S.P.16/369, no. 86, William Bassett to Edward Nicholas, 16 Oct. 1637; 426, no. 75, petition of Richard Hippisley, late petty constable of Chewton, to PC, [July 1639]. PRO, P.C.2/49, p. 308, PC to sheriffs of most counties, including Somerset, 30 June 1638.

agent in Somerset could not deflect. The opposition, now attacking at all three stages, had attained its greatest power.

The Council had been a long time awakening to the fact that there were inimical forces ranged against ship money. As it was, it never fully appreciated their magnitude. The Council's reverie was broken by the storm gathering in the Northern Kingdom, which had not only made more imperative than ever before the continuance of the fleet, but had also made their lordships more attentive to the hostility closer home. By the time the Council decided to send out the sixth writ of ship money, in November 1639, it had resolved that no effort should be spared to overcome all opposition, any reluctance on the part of the sheriff, constable, or individual payer. With a ferocity unparalleled in the previous five years of ship money, the Council moved to crush the defiance in the counties.

Its only weapon and, because it held him solely responsible, its only target, was the sheriff. Simultaneously with the issue of the 1639 writ the new sheriffs of the ten counties which had hitherto exhibited greatest hostility were summoned before the Board, Sir Thomas Wrothe of Somerset among them. This was not merely another round of sheriffs cited to appear for upbraiding for their neglect; these men had been in office only a few days. The Council said no more than that they were to "have a care of the assessing and collecting his Majesties ship moneyes for the yeare ensuing,"[53] but what was left unsaid was evident enough. They were no sooner home than the Council informed them (and all other sheriffs) that not only negligence would bring its just deserts, but diligence its just reward. Upon the full payment of all ship money by the sheriff, he would be allowed six pence in the pound; a novel departure for an office which had ceased to have much if any profit attached to it. It was the Council's intention, shortly afterwards expressed to the sheriffs, that they were to fulfill their part of the bargain by 20 February or else appear at the Board.[54]

When February 20 came, only Devon's sheriff had given satisfaction. The sheriffs were allowed until 1 April to pay the full sum required, or else suffer exemplary proceedings. For Wrothe, as for nearly every other sheriff, that deadline could never have been met. From the moment he had taken up his duties, the interminable rating disputes had erupted.

[53] PRO, P.C.2/51, p. 38, PC minute, 15 Nov. 1639.
[54] PRO, P.C.2/51, pp. 101–104, PC to sheriffs and exsheriffs of counties of Eng. and Wales, 30 Nov. 1639.

Many constables had refused not only to return a rate to him, but even to make one. It required no unusual perspicacity on Wrothe's part to conclude that the refusal of almost one-half the county's forty-one hundreds to make rates was due to communication among them to raise the "same cavill of purpose to confound the service."[55] A week before the deadline, Wrothe managed to return £200 of the £8000 required, but £95 of it came from his own pocket. He received no sympathy from the Council when he informed their lordships that no one would buy a distress taken for ship money. The Council merely told him to offer distresses at "cheape" rates.[56]

By May, the Council was desperate. The intelligence from Somerset was matched by bad news from almost every other county. With a wrath approaching hysteria, the Council struck out wildly at the sheriffs, singly and collectively. The Attorney-General was ordered to institute proceedings in Star Chamber against the sheriffs of eight counties, Wrothe escaping only by a hair. The sheriff of Yorkshire was ordered under close arrest. All the sheriffs were warned to pay one-half of what was yet due by June and the other half by July or else they would feel the "smart and punishment" due their wilful remissness.[57] With the pursuivants already hunting down the unfortunate eight whom the Attorney-General

---

[55] PRO, S.P.16/448, no. 57, Sir Thomas Wrothe, sheriff, to Ld Kpr Finch, 21 March 1639/40.

[56] PRO, P.C.2/51, p. 477, 19 April 1640.

[57] *Historical Collections*, II, 1173, order of King in Council, 7 May 1640; PRO, S.P.16/452, no. 53, minutes of PC business by Secretary of State Windebank, 6 May 1640; P.C.2/51, pp. 481–482, PC to sheriffs of most counties including Somerset, 11 May 1640. The Attorney-General was hard at work during the early summer of 1640 drafting the prosecutions against the eight sheriffs, Bodl, Bankes MSS, bundle 42, nos. 42, 45, 47, the first Star Chamber prosecution being ordered by the Council on 1 April against the sheriff of Oxfordshire. None of the sheriffs appear to have been prosecuted to conviction. The prosecutions were opened in Trinity 1640, ship money was declared illegal (retroactively) by Parliament in the vacation following Hilary term 1640/1, and Star Chamber was abolished in Trinity 1641—in a case of this kind, a Star Chamber action could not be determined in so short a time. Sir Walter Norton, Bart., sheriff of Lincolnshire 1635–1636, was convicted and fined £300 in Star Chamber in Trinity 1639 for extortion, receiving bribes, and scandalizing the Earl of Lindsey, admiral of the ship money fleet, all in connection with ship money, PRO, E.159/480, Trin. 16 Chas. I, rot. 27, and Bodl, Bankes MSS, bundle 43, nos. 41–42. A special commission of oyer and terminer, tested 16 Feb. 1636/7, had been issued to the judges of the Midland Circuit to hear charges of extortion against him and his officers, PRO, Index 4212, p. 230, though it appears that five of his officers were convicted and fined an aggregate of £1750 in Star Chamber with him in Trinity 1639, PRO, E.159/480, Trin. 16 Chas. I, rot. 27. Significantly, the Attorney-General had allowed the Star Chamber proceedings to lapse—doubtless to encourage Norton to get in his arrears—but on order of the Council, 20 Aug. 1638, he recommenced the prosecution, Bodl, Bankes MSS, bundle 43, nos. 41–42.

had summoned, there could be no doubt what the Council meant by "punishment." In one final, convulsive attempt to spur on the sheriffs to greater effort, the Council wrote the Lord Treasurer to authorize the escheators to "advise" the sheriff of negligent or ill-affected subordinates so that the sheriff's dereliction would be more "inexcusable." In reality, the escheators were set to act as political commissars who would report the sheriffs' activities to the Council in return for which they would receive such reward "as theire services respectively deserve."[58] Probably never before had the central government so patently employed the services of a minor, fee-taking, local official to spy on a local governor. Yet never before had the Council been so desperate and so distrustful.

On 17 August 1640, the escheator of Somerset reported that the sheriff had collected only £300 and that the constables and bailiffs threatened with law suits and violence would not distrain because "they had rather fall into the hands of his Majestie then into the hands of resolute men...."[59] The opposition had won.

The opposition killed ship money. Yet it remains to be determined whether or not the sheriff and the Privy Council contributed to its demise by negligence or recklessness, and what measure of responsibility each must bear for allowing the opposition to become so virulent that the tax just could not be collected.

To what extent was the sheriff responsible? As far as his master, the Council, was concerned, completely. The answer though must depend on two considerations: (1) whether the sheriff fulfilled to the utmost of his ability the orders of the Council, exercising an energetic initiative in their execution, and (2) whether the sheriff truthfully informed the Council of the state of the service and the forces intent upon crippling it.

Henry Hodges was wholly responsible for 1634 ship money and jointly responsible with John Mallett for collecting 1635 ship money. His success in bringing the former to a satisfactory conclusion before the issue of the second writ owed little to him, but was due to the almost total absence of opposition. Indeed, in the dispute with Phelips of that first year (in which Hodges had demanded more from Tintinhull that he might ease his crony Smith in Ilchester) he had exhibited that defect of character which,

[58] PRO, P.C.2/51, p. 652, PC to Lord Treasurer, 19 July 1640.
[59] PRO, S.P.16/464, no. 23, John Palmer, escheator of Dorset and Somerset, to Lord Treasurer, 17 Aug. 1640. The situation was somewhat better in Dorset, the sheriff there having collected one-half of the ship money.

in the next year, would provide the nascent opposition with a half-dozen excellent causes for complaint of over-rating. In each case, Hodges made an increased assessment on various hundreds in order to gain revenue that could have been collected elsewhere only with greater difficulty. Though he could not have exceeded the broad powers of rating the Council's instructions permitted, from his selfish and dishonest motives and in the arbitrary manner in which he employed those powers his use had been far from what the Council intended.

For the course of ship money in Somerset, the choice of Hodges as sheriff during the crucial years of the first two writs proved tragic. He was an utter rogue. Indicted for cheating a woman of £60, he defended his action by a plea amounting to a confession to attempted subornation of a judge in Chancery.[60] He failed to appear at a Dorset assizes in 1637 to answer Crown charges against him.[61] He was defendant in three suits in Exchequer in 1638–1639, one of them for his invasion of the Bishop of Winchester's liberty of Taunton and the other two for fraudulently (as it was alleged on good evidence) putting into suit the bonds of his two collectors of the greenwax and their deputy whom he had sacked as collector in order to put them in his place.[62] In 1639 he was fined £400 in Star Chamber for selling the gaoler's place "for threescore pounds and a velvet petticoat to his wife."[63] That he was able to pay off that substantial fine in four installments over nine months hardly bore out the concern that some raters in his home parish who underrated him to ship money (which he didn't pay anyway) showed when they contended that he had lost much in his late shrievalty.[64] It does lend some credence to the exaggerated evaluation of his estate venomously related by Sir Robert Phelips to a privy councillor: "The man [Hodges] is I suppose about as well known to your lordship as he is here, which suer I am he merits no favour or respect being the worst of men and generally known to be the most extorting usurer that ever lived in these parts, by which he hath to the injury of others amassed togither an estate of £20,000."[65] The

[60] SRO, Phelips MSS, vol. B, f. 176v.

[61] *Som Asz Ords*, no. 111.

[62] PRO, E.134/15–16 Chas. I/Hil. 11; E.112/285/1383, 1388.

[63] HLS, L. MS 1128, no. 391; PRO, P.C.2/45, pp. 30, 166; SRO, QSOB, 1627/8–1638, Epiph. QS 1634/5, no. 17; Sess Rolls, 73 pt. i, no. 84.

[64] PRO, E.159/481, Trin. 17 Chas. I, rot. 12; S.P.16/438, no. 104.

[65] SRO, Phelips MSS, vol. B, f. 176v, Sir Robert Phelips to a Privy Councillor [c. Oct. 1635]. This letter was in connection with the ship money rating dispute in Tintinhull. In 1632, Thomas Merrifield complained to the Council that Hodges had extorted money from

evaluation of the estate was an exaggeration—the evaluation of the man was not. Hodges' infamous reputation in the county could not help but contribute ill to the name of the tax which he was charged with collecting. Had he been a capable rogue Hodges might have been an effective agent, his notoriousness nothwithstanding. But Hodges cannot even be credited with this. Of all six sheriffs involved in ship money, only Hodges appears to have wilfully misled the Council, by both innuendo and barefaced lies, as to the state of the service and his own diligence in executing it. His guile was matched only by his incompetence and indolence.

That the arrears for 1635 ship money were reduced finally to twelve per cent of the total was due largely to John Mallett's assiduity. When he became sheriff in January 1635/6 to finish out the second term of Hodges the arrears were over three-eighths of the total, and this five months after the 1635 writ was issued. Mallett was loyal, hardworking, and possessed of business sense. He was wise enough to choose an intelligent under-sheriff, William Cox. Between them they were able to collect over £2000. But they had to struggle for every penny of it. Not only were they caught with the mounting opposition that made so difficult the collection of 1636 ship money (let alone arrears for 1635 ship money), but they had to contend as well with the confusion that resulted from Hodges' laziness and dishonesty. Hodges did not give Mallett the 1635 writ and his rates until the Council forced him to, and he never assisted Mallett in collecting the arrears for which they were jointly responsible.[66] The rating disputes stirred up by Hodges had to be settled by Mallett. Mallett seldom complained. His informative letters were candid, for he was under no illusion as to the extent of the opposition to ship money, and he was too honest to withold from the Council the unwelcome truth.

William Bassett appears the most outstanding of the six. His concise and informative letters to Nicholas make an immediately favorable impression which becomes stronger when the contents are examined more closely. When Bassett erred in rating—and unfortunately for him it was far too often—he appears to have done so through ignorance or too close

---

him; the Council referred the case to common law, PRO, P.C.2/42, p. 51, PC order, 30 May 1632. Hodges appears to have died under mysterious circumstances in 1646—assizes ordered two justices to investigate his death, PRO, Asz.24/21, f. 65v, assize order, 28 Aug. 1646.

[66] PRO, P.C.2/46, p. 59, PC to Henry Hodges, 29 March 1636; S.P.16/412, no. 14, deposition of Robert Rich, 2 Feb. 1638/9.

following of the Council's injunction to rate according to true worth. He was indefatigable, and during the three years it took him to reduce his arrears to a highly commendable two per cent of the total, he had probably seen more of the county than any other sheriff. His energy was complemented by his ability to grasp the realities of an unpleasant predicament. He struck hard against backward constables, and urged the Council to visit assessors who made unjust rates with the "severest of punishment."[67] In all rating disputes, he attempted to adjudicate fairly on the issues presented, while realizing at the same time that his decision could not stifle the hostility behind the complaint. He did not color intelligence he sent to the Council, nor was he afraid to say just how bad the situation had become. When Bassett concluded a letter with "I will not faile to use all dilligence,"[68] their lordships could rest assured he meant it.

Sir William Portman, Bart., received a singular honor in that he was the only sheriff of Somerset commended by the Council for his efforts in collecting ship money. Though harder words were in store for him, he richly deserved the Council's commendation for his "diligence in the generall" in February 1637/8.[69] The 1637 sheriff was latterly the victim of the full force of Hampden's Case, as well as of the confusion caused by the abortive county-wide re-rating project. That he was able within a year after the Council's compliment to pay in all but £353 was indeed creditable. However, Portman's success was due in large part to the momentary softening of the reluctant by the Council's and the Exchequer's punitive actions in the first half of 1638. And alone among the ship money sheriffs, he stood in the premier rank in the shire, was one of the richest men in Somerset, and a magnate accounted by his countrymen an influential man at Court—considerable initial advantages when it came to demanding ship money from his neighbors. Portman was wont to boast overmuch of his not inconsiderable abilities, and he affected a forced optimism which, by underemphasizing the growing opposition, might have misled the Council.

For the course of 1638 ship money too little evidence remains to judge William Every's sedulity. As a magistrate he had for the preceding twenty years proved himself a talented and conscientious divisional justice. His final arrears, however, amounted to twelve per cent of the

[67] PRO, S.P.16/335, no. 141, William Bassett to Edward Nicholas, 8 May 1637.
[68] PRO, S.P.16/392, no. 1, William Bassett, exsheriff, to Edward Nicholas, 1 June 1638.
[69] PRO, P.C.2/48, p. 600, PC to sheriff of Somerset, 14 Feb. 1637/8.

total of £2800 required (approximately one-third only of that required for 1635–1637 and 1639 ship money). The power of the opposition by this year can be pleaded as an extenuating circumstance for his poor showing.

Sir Thomas Wrothe received roughest treatment at the hands of the Council, but this was an outcome of the Council's desperation far more than of his own shortcomings. He was condemned to gather the tax when it had become impossible to collect. Despite the Council's strictures, there is no question of Wrothe's good faith or diligence. Because of its strictures, there is ample proof of his courage in informing their lordships of the terrible pass to which ship money had been brought. Had he not been so frank, he would not have suffered such strong censure at their hands.

With the sole exception of Henry Hodges (William Every must be omitted for want of evidence), the sheriffs of Somerset cannot be condemned for contributing to the destruction of ship money in that county through negligence or lack of affection. Indeed, one may hazard that they cannot be condemned on the grounds of ineptness, again excepting Hodges. These were capable men who served with singular devotion a government that had but one kind word for one of them and which demanded of them all a greater measure of service for a longer period of time than any of their predecessors had been obliged to give. By and large, contributory responsibility for the catastrophic end of ship money must be affixed elsewhere.

Elsewhere can only mean the Council. It alone possessed the ability to see the program as a whole, to comprehend the state of ship money at each moment of its existence. It alone possessed the authority to direct the operation and strike down those who would oppose it. The Council commanded all power, and to the extent that its agents in the county did not blind its sight or abuse its trust, the Council must assume responsibility for contributing to the demise of ship money.

It was the Council's initial miscalculation, the failure to recognize that the magnitude and power of the opposition would increase, that bore the most bitter fruit. It had induced the Council to see in the rating complaints, growing in number and clamor, nothing more than the just claims to fair treatment of a well-affected citizenry. It dulled the Council's perception of the terrible effects of the individual gentleman who stirred up his neighbors and pointed out the manner in which lesser folk might also work to avoid, finally to destroy, ship money. It caused the Council to realize belatedly, if at all, that the constables and other subordinate officers were instruments too fragile and too treacherous in the face of their neighbors' wrath to have ever performed their vital duties once wrath reached its zenith. For this latter error the Council cannot be wholly blamed. There were no other instruments available for the Council's use. But the short shrift given the constables when called before the Board leaves the impression that their lordships might have been wise to have listened with greater respect to the tales of men who had experienced the growing resistance to ship money. Had they, the rude awakening would have come in 1637 instead of 1639. In 1637 it was not too late to correct the initial miscalculation, realize the rating disputes for what they were, perceive the disruptive effects of individual defiance, and act accordingly. This was not to be however. The sheriff suffered no diminution of his power to rate as he saw fit. The Council took no steps to require that a uniform rate be put into effect immediately, but instead began the business and then failed to see it through to a conclusion. Strode went free, no worse for his experience before the Board, a living example of successful resistance for every countryman to emulate. The prosecution of the Buckingham squire and the issuance of penal processes out of the court of the Exchequer came too late. The tragedy was that the Council would not recognize the might of the forces arrayed against ship money. It was this lack of recognition that amounted to the Council's contributory negligence in the destruction of ship money.

The Council's myopia—it was nothing less—can be attributed in great part to the attitude of mind the Council assumed upon saddling the sheriff with the task of collecting ship money and investing him with the authority with which to do it: the sheriff has been instructed in his duties, he has been given the power to fulfill them, therefore, ship money is his responsibility. Every letter of instruction issued with a new writ and nearly every other communication of the Council to the sheriff inordinately stressed his sole responsibility. The Council would assist him by summoning obstinate constables and wilful refusers, but he was informed in no uncertain terms that he had ample power to deal with all others who might prove recalcitrant. The Council never retreated from this position. Thus, if the sheriff complained of extraordinary difficulties in assessing or collecting, so far as their lordships were concerned, he was merely attempting to excuse himself for failing in his duty. As late as March 1640 when the Council had finally realized that there were powerful forces working to destroy ship money, it would not admit that Sheriff Wrothe's letter, which in a spirit of candor spoke of half the hundreds refusing to assess themselves, was to other purpose than "to prepare an excuse for doing nothing, . . . [rather] then to performe your duty."[70] This outward distrust, affected by the Council at the start to impress the sheriffs with their singular responsibility, was dangerous. By constantly reiterating that distrust, the Council had come by 1640 to believe unquestioningly in the sheriff's perfidy. In so doing, the Council lost the ability to evaluate critically the sheriff's intelligence as to the growth of opposition in the county. Even when the Council finally realized that there was a real opposition, it probably never fully apprehended its size. The sheriff could have told their lordships, but his words were lost on men who had convinced themselves that his evidence was merely "to prepare an excuse."

An even more subtle malaise divided the King and Council from the truth. Ultimately, if for no other reason than that it was so deep-rooted in their outlook that it enslaved their thinking in every aspect of governance, this malaise proved most perilous. It was the profoundly held belief of the King and his chief ministers that opposition was limited to a few malcontents who, through the argument of law and reason, could be won to the King's service in company with all the rest of his well-affected subjects. It was this creed that elevated the slim majority opinion in Hampden's Case into a talisman reverenced by King and Council, though despised by an opposition which was far beyond the charms of judicial arithmetic. The will to comprehend reality was not in men who in June 1640 could say of facts vital to the formulation of an intelligent policy to combat the opposition, "wee esteeme them of little consideracion especiallie at this tyme, there havinge bene a publique judgment past for the Kinge."[71] In the same month, during the last days of a universally hated tax, Nicholas subscribed on a candid report by the sheriff of Lincolnshire setting forth the impossibility of collecting ship money the Council's angry reply: "That his excuses are frivolous and he is to execute writt or shall answere for his owne neglect."[72] Allowing that these words were destined for public consumption, they still bespeak an attitude of mind like a dense veil through which could not penetrate a realization

[70] PRO, P.C.2/51, p. 413, PC to sheriff of Somerset, 31 March 1640.
[71] PRO, P.C.2/49, p. 308, PC to sheriffs of most counties (Somerset included) 30 June 1638.
[72] PRO, S.P.16/457, no. 92.

9+

of the increasing strength and extent of the opposition. Never did the King and his Council bring themselves to believe that so many were ranged against the King's will.

Myopia is an affliction common to all those who in any age have been called to a ruler's place. Yet, the historian may count on the fingers of one hand those governments which in the sweep of England's history have so sorely needed clear vision as did King Charles and his ministers in 1640.

The impact of six years of ship money upon the political ferment that led ultimately to civil war need not be mentioned here. Though the animosity unleashed by this tax was not slow to mature and erupt, it reached its greatest potency in a period and expressed itself with greatest vehemence on a stage which are beyond the limits of this study.[73] However, within this study's limits lies the impact of ship money upon the government of the county, a result of the tax no less important and far more immediate. This impact was so strong that it turned the abilities of every official in county government into the service of ship money, and so constant that it kept them there for an unparalleled length of time.

The justices of the peace were far more intimately associated with ship money than would appear at first sight. Their function did not consist in collecting the tax.[74] Rather it was the sheriff's difficulties in collecting which sucked the justices into this aspect of the King's service and left them with some of the most intricate and difficult tasks they had ever undertaken. The use of some of the justices as referees of rating disputes, notably Bishop Pierce, has already been mentioned. Between 1636 and 1640, the bishop convoked no fewer than fifteen hearings in matters connected with rating disputes, sitting usually with the sheriff and exsheriff, though in two of the hearings he was assisted by two other justices.[75] Enough has been said to indicate the amount and kind of work

[73] Mute testimony to the vehemence of the Long Parliament's destruction of ship money is the scratched-through patent roll enrollment of the 1636 writ, in the margin of which is noted that on 27 Feb. 1640/1 Parliament declared ship money illegal, PRO, C.66/2725, dorse. The same treatment was accorded the Exchequer's judgment in Hampden's Case, PRO, E.159/477, Trin. 13 Chas. I, rot. 44, and the King's letter of 2 Feb. 1636/7 touching ship money and the judges' opinion thereon, E.159/476, Hil. 12 Chas. I, rot. 63.

[74] Miss Wedgwood is mistaken in saying that the justices "collected" ship money, *The King's Peace, 1637–1641* (1955), pp. 156, 166.

[75] Emanuel Green held that the use of Pierce as a referee was an "attempt to revive the authority" of bishops, *SANHS Proc* (1884), XXX, pt. ii, p. 48. That Victorian was overly preoccupied with prelates. Pierce was a loyal, able, and hardworking magistrate of preeminent authority in the county, and doubtless these qualities most recommended him to the Council.

these hearings entailed. Moreover, the bishop was not the only justice involved in rating disputes. On three other occasions, either by conciliar direction or on his own initiative, the sheriff enlisted the aid of divisional justices to settle complaints. How many other minor disputes were settled summarily by the justices, we will never know, for unless the Council was in some way concerned with a dispute no mention of it appears in the public records. Given the power of the divisional justices in seventeenth-century society and given the innumerable minor and unrecorded disputes which there is strong reason to believe occurred, it was highly unlikely that the sheriff would not enlist the considerable aid of the local justices. It is of record that once each, quarter sessions and assizes referred for examination to justices out-of-sessions complaints against constables who had made excessive rates for ship money.[76] The rating disputes were productive also of labor for the justices in another way, for besides the special sessions attended by a large part of the county bench to rerate the county and the meetings of the committee of justices nominated there to investigate further, rerating had involved the divisional justices in the complex task of evaluating the personal and real estates of every taxable individual in their divisions. Nor should the two meetings in the fall of 1635, attended by most of the justices of the eastern half of the county to settle the rates for ship money in that area, be overlooked. However, the records of the justices themselves reflect most vividly the weight of ship-money affairs upon them. From 1635 through 1638, there were nearly twice as many rating complaints brought to quarter sessions (usually referred to justices out of sessions) than there had been in the preceding four years.[77] Even more significant, the sessions records show that during these same four years, there were before the court twelve cases of men reluctant to serve as constables or tithingmen, exactly as many as there had been in the preceding ten years. Nine of these cases occurred between Epiphany sessions 1637/8 and Epiphany sessions 1638/9. It is no mystery why men were loath to serve in these offices then. In nearly every case, it fell to the divisional justices to hear the conflicting claims and trivial excuses. Taking into account in

[76] SRO, QSOB, 1627/8–1638, Epiph. QS 1635/6, no. 12; *Som Asz Ords,* no. 115.

[77] The greatest incidence of rating complaints before quarter sessions occurred in 1627–1628—the time of the forced loan, which like ship money was based on the county rates. There were few such complaints, 1629–1634, but a sharp increase occurred in 1635. It was more than mere coincidence that there was a spate of complaints during the two periods of heaviest financial exaction, though in none of the cases was the exaction itself alluded to.

purely quantitative terms the added duties on the justices that grew
out of ship money, regarding it in terms of additional hours spent at
magisterial tasks, ship money had provided more work for the justices
than any other project save that which concerned largely themselves, the
Book of Orders. These new tasks were not only additional to the normal
duties of the country justices, but were additional as well to the duties
still incumbent upon them under the Book of Orders.

Quantitative measurement can hardly indicate how heavy the weight
of ship money lay upon the county's magistrates. This tax, far more than
the forced loan, outraged the sensibilities of men who respected the
sanctity of the law and valued their neighbors' respect. Such sentiments
were not common to all the justices. To county politicians like Sir Robert
Phelips, Sir Henry Berkeley, and Sir Francis Dodington who equated
their neighbors' respect with votes in a parliamentary election and defer-
ential subservience in the community, ship money afforded an unparalleled opportunity to place themselves in the vanguard of opposition and
so gain a greater measure of that variety of respect they most desired.
To the vociferous champions of the "King's interest," such as Sir John
Stawell and Lord Poulett, ship money presented the possibility of striking
at the power of their political opponents by exhibiting their good affection
to the King's service and contrasting it with the animosity of their opponents. These, though, were not all the justices. There were many more
sensitive men, of whom John Harington, Thomas Lyte, Sir Ralph
Hopton, William Capell, and Francis Baber stand in boldest relief. They
felt the weight of ship money on their hearts as well as on their backs.
To these souls even the barest connection with ship money must have
been abhorrent at times. As in the forced loan, they had to make the
choice between the claims of their neighbors and their King, the choice
that was no choice at all. It is easy to undervalue the power of these
sentiments, easy to underestimate the importance of such consciences. But
the nation was on the threshold of an era when men responded to the
dictates of conscience.

The sheriffs were far too busy to have paid much heed to the inner
voice, even if their sensitivity was as acute as that of some of their fellow
magistrates. The reality of ship money to the sheriffs was the labor
demanded and the pressure of their master to provide it. The Cinderella
of county government, the sheriff had suddenly blossomed forth as the
single most important local governor. He enjoyed (though the term is

scarcely appropriate) the unceasing attention of the King and Council for six years. He had been selected as carefully as a prima donna, after full consultation with the judges of assize and a thorough investigation of his financial ability and political sympathies. Then he was sent out to meet the hostility to the service he was ordained to perform and which he knew full well would be the most difficult service he had ever undertaken. He knew, too, that until he performed it there would be no peace for him. He was watched, reported upon, threatened, summoned, and upbraided; seven times a sheriff of Somerset stood before the Board. Innumerable times he was stung by a conciliar letter stronger than any letter he or his predecessors had ever received. And before him always was the realization that the mounting opposition to the tax would require greater and greater effort to overcome if he was to complete his work and secure his liberty. By the end of his year, the sheriff must have despaired of ever seeing the end of his labor.

Chapter IX ∽∾ *The "Perfect Militia"*

The "perfect militia." In these words, which appeared in a royal letter in 1626, there is both irony and tragedy. Irony because despite the King's desire, the militia was never perfect; tragedy because by the sixteenth year of his reign there was nothing that the King needed more than a "perfect militia." The student who traces the history of a county's militia in those sixteen years is haunted by the picture of the King brought to ignominious terms by his rebellious Northern subjects because England's militia could not, would not, fight.

This chapter is not intended to show why the men of Somerset would not fight to the death for the King in 1640. It is intended to show why, even if they had had the will to fight, they could not have fought effectively. The "would" and the "could" were closely related. If the men of Somerset had been disciplined and trained, the inclination to fight might well have been in them when they were marched to the North. Even if the inclination had been wanting, the crust of discipline would have kept them from those mutinous outrages which in any age are the negation of the soldier's training. Thus, this chapter must concentrate on the institution and its principal figures, who during these sixteen crucial years failed to create and harden that crust of discipline in Somerset's militiamen.

The emphasis that the demand for a "perfect militia" received at the deputy lieutenants' hands was conditioned by the exigencies of the moment. For though the demand was first made in the summer of 1626, it was not until 1629 that the deputies could spare the time necessary to implement fully the King's wishes in that particular. The period from 1629 to 1638 was the period when the militia might have been brought to a higher peak of military efficiency than it had ever attained before. The confused years, 1638–1640, were the years of trial, when the deputies' sins of omission and commission caught up with them and with the institution in their care, with disastrous results to the King's cause. One thing, however, all three periods had in common. The deputy lieutenants stood opposite countrymen who were always suspicious of and openly hostile to any action they might take to perfect the militia or discharge other, more invidious tasks the King and Council required of them. This hostility was a constant factor throughout an era when the work of lieutenancy received far greater attention from the central government than at any time in the preceding thirty years. The deleterious effects of this hostility, amplified by the divisions among the deputies themselves and combined with the inherent weaknesses of lieutenancy—lack of purpose, amateurishness, and imperfect conciliar control—were enough to ensure that the "perfect militia" would never exist, save in the wishful thinking of the King and his Councillors.

From 1625 to 1629, the events that determined how much energy the deputies could channel into their primary task of training the militia were the exigencies of war. Defence of the kingdom from sea invasion by Spain was stressed by the Council in 1625 and 1626, and it was the responsibility of the deputies to provide that defence. On the deputies, too, devolved the bulk of the preparations for the two disastrous expeditions sent against Spain and France. On the deputies devolved all the labor required in sustaining and controlling the remnants of the broken armies that returned from Cadiz and Ré.

Behind the urgent orders for the mobilization of coast defences that issued from the Council Chamber on 28 August 1625 was no real fear that the country was in danger of invasion. King and Council knew full well that Spain was in no position to attack, and the fact that they intended momentarily to take the offensive with the fleet's attack on Cadiz belied his Majesty's somewhat equivocal statement that he feared an attempt on "some parte of his dominions." The urgent tone of the demand to muster the trained bands, set watches on the beacons, and put in readiness two of the county's regiments to march at the first alarm to the most vulnerable points on the county's shoreline was undoubtedly meant to make the gentlemen in the counties more receptive to the forthcoming privy seal loan than they had been to the plea for subsidies made by Buckingham at the Oxford Parliament three weeks before.[1]

[1] *Acts PC*, 1625–1626, p. 141, PC to Lds Lts, 28 Aug. 1625, copy of same in SRO, Phelips MSS, vol. A, f. 11. At the meeting of the Council at Woodstock, 14 Aug., it had been decided to issue the privy seals, PRO, S.P.16/5, no. 41. The royal directive for the issue of the privy seals was 17 Sept., S.P.16/6, no. 70, King to PC. It should be recalled that the rating to the privy seal loan fell to the deputy lieutenants.

This was merely the first time that Charles would use mobilization orders to make more palatable a financial exaction by conjuring up the chimera of invasion.

Regardless of whether or not the subterfuge was discovered, neither the county as a whole nor the deputies in particular were thrown into a state of panic. None the less, the latter put the orders into execution with at least some of the "care and sedulity" that the lord lieutenant required.[2] The beacons, long disused, were supplied with fuel and watches set on them. The result was two rancorous disputes among various hundreds as to the responsibility for watching beacons that diverted the most active deputies from more pressing duties to a long and difficult hearing of the rival claims of the hundreds involved.[3] The latent dislike of the county for such needless employment as beacon watching was aroused in 1625, and this made no easier the task of the deputies in preparing the county's defences for the real threat of invasion that came the next year.

The failure of the expedition to Cadiz to render that port inoperative and Sir Edward Cecil's inability to keep his warships at sea long enough to capture the Spanish treasure fleet left Spain free to launch an attack upon England in 1626. During the summer of 1626 transports massed along the Biscay coast of Spain, and to meet them, Lord Willoughby was sent to prepare a leaky fleet in Portsmouth. Prudence dictated the issuance in July 1626 of an extraordinary general order for musters throughout England and Wales and the readying of the nation's defences. The preamble to this order, reciting the preparations in Spain and Flanders of land and sea forces directed at England, was a far truer statement of a real fear than the ambiguous reference to the suspicious arming of "some princes" contained in the order of the preceding year. Certainly the King expected a heartier reception for the increased demands contained in the July order. Besides the provision for watching

[2] SRO, Phelips MSS, vol. A, f. 12, Earl of Pembroke, Ld Lt Somerset, to DLs Somerset, 30 Aug. 1625. This volume of the Phelips MSS, "Musters 1615–1667," with miscellaneous papers in other volumes of that collection provide an incomparable source for the workings of Somerset's lieutenancy at the higher echelons. Sir Robert Phelips copied nearly every document that came to hand concerning those lieutenancy matters in which he was involved —and he was involved in most. The papers of Capt. John Preston of Cricket St. Thomas, now among the Hippisley MSS in the SRO, provide warrants of commission, muster rolls, and other documents disclosing the routine functioning of lieutenancy as related to Preston's foot company. In the absence of more formal lieutenancy papers, the latter has had to suffice to indicate the lieutenancy routine.

[3] Sir Edward Rodney and Robert Hopton were the deputies. The disputes concerned Corton and Dundry beacons. In the case of Corton, one of the parties complained of the "continual watch there now of late," SRO, Sess Rolls, 58 pt. ii, nos. 11–12; 56 pt. i, no. 7.

beacons and other measures for coastal defence, the deputies were to enroll all men between sixteen and sixty to form a reserve for the militia, ready the trained bands to repair to their colors on one hour's warning, take steps to have a good supply of powder and match on hand, and appoint provost marshals to suppress the vagrants who might cause panic by spreading false rumors of invasion.[4] At the same time, a printed broad-sheet—half instructions to the deputies, half exhortation to the county—was issued, dwelling at greater length on those points of the Council's order of immediate concern.[5] Supplementary letters followed in a few days, directed at alerting particularly vulnerable points on the coast. The deputies for the Western and some of the Home Counties were to prepare combined forces, ranging from 11,000 to 17,000 fully armed and provisioned troops, capable of marching to any one of four Channel ports upon the first firing of beacons. In conjunction with this, twenty-four ports of England and Wales, including Bridgwater and Minehead in Somerset, were ordered to fortify themselves under the supervision of neighboring deputy lieutenants.[6] Not since Elizabeth's time had the kingdom been put on so extensive a martial footing.

With far more celerity than they had exhibited before or would exhibit again the Somerset deputies reported to the lord lieutenant on 29 July. They informed the Earl of Pembroke that immediately upon receipt of the letters they had addressed themselves to the execution of his commands. They had completed the mustering of the trained bands, appointing 13 September to draw the whole of the county's forces into one body, enrolled all able men between sixteen and sixty, apprised themselves of the county's supply of powder (which was chronically insufficient), nominated two justices as provost marshals, and executed the other orders.[7] They reported that the beacons were satisfactorily repaired and carefully tended. With unusual crispness they informed his lordship that as soon as they could they would give an account of their preparation of the force for Channel defence. Even more than its contents, the tone

[4] *Acts PC*, 1626, p. 72, PC to Lds Lts, 10 July 1626.

[5] *Orders Appointed by His Most Excellent Maiestie, and Signified by Special Letters [etc.]* BM, Harl. MS 5936, no. 25 (Barford collection). This is a broadsheet, not a proclamation as Steele indicates, *Bibliotheca Lindesiana* (1910), I, no. 1496. It bears a marked resemblance in its form to the Book of Orders. Steele gives the date as Oct. 1626 (query) but certainly the broadsheet was so explicatory of the 10 July order that it must have been sent to the deputies at the same time. That it was undated is evidence of its not being a proclamation.

[6] *Acts PC*, 1626, pp. 87–88, PC to Lds Lts of 9 Western and Home counties, 15 July 1626; p. 60, PC to 24 ports in Eng. and Wales, 19 July 1626.

[7] PRO, S.P.16/32, no. 76, DLs of Somerset to Ld Lt, 29 July 1626.

9*

of this report indicates that the deputies had taken especial pains to follow the Council's dictates. Whether in the event of actual invasion the forces of the county and the other shires would have been sufficient to repel the Spaniards is a debatable point.

The military effectiveness of the trained bands is open to question because they were far from trained. As was emphasized in Chapter IV twenty years of peace had robbed the militia of any sense of purpose. The muster orders of James' reign had laid little emphasis on true military preparedness, and James' Council appears to have considered itself fortunate to possess any organized militia at all.[8] As for instructing that force in the rudimentary use of arms, the Council had rested content to exhort the lords lieutenants to provide some drill for the men. To judge by the pitch of the demand for drilling in the orders of the new reign, James' lieutenants had not taken the exhortation to heart.[9]

True, in 1623 the Council had sent a printed book of drill instructions to the lords lieutenants. However, this erudite textbook, drafted with an eye on Continental military practice,[10] appeared to have made no impression on Somerset's trained bands until Charles' reign. From the outset, Charles' Privy Council and Council of War had entertained a spate of proposals, some practicable and others impossible, all concentrated on perfecting the militia, "which in respect of the curious height to which the militia of this age is brought requires timely, frequent, and orderly practice."[11] Most of these proposals received uncredited recognition in the extraordinary general muster order of July 1626 previously mentioned. While enjoining measures for defence, the order particularly stressed instruction of soldiers in the use of their arms, first at the level of the file and finally at the level of the whole county's forces. The clause requiring the officers to learn the performance of their duties struck at the root problem of militia training. Besides increasing the number of armed trained band soldiers, the deputies were required to place untrained men in units, arm them with recusants' weapons and such other arms as the "best sort" of men would voluntarily furnish, and reduce them

---

[8] Muster orders were issued annually as a Council letter to the lords lieutenants and were enregistered in PRO, P.C.2, transcribed in *Acts PC* up to and including the 1629 order.

[9] The 1625 general muster order, the first of the new reign, complained of the slack performance by the deputies of the previous directions, *Acts PC*, 1625–1626, p. 37, 10 May 1625.

[10] *Instructions for Musters and Armes, and the Use Thereof* (1623), 12 pp.

[11] PRO, S.P.16/13, no. 43, suggestions for more effectively arming and exercising trained bands 1625. For other proposals of same date, see S.P.16/13, no. 49; 522, no. 105.

to discipline. While prescribing in minute detail what the Council expected the deputies to do, the order directed them to the book of 1623 to find out how to do it.

A "hopeful beginning" in revitalizing the militia was already under way before the summer of 1626. In the previous January the Council had sent into every county experienced officers who had volunteered to leave their regiments in the Low Countries in order to spend three months training English militiamen. Four sergeants of unquestionable competency were sent to Somerset to drill the trained bands, company by company, and especially to train cadres of noncommissioned officers for continuing instruction once they had left.[12] The deputies welcomed them, and most of the regimental commanders liked them for their "discreet and sober behaviour."[13] Only Sir Robert Phelips proved an exception. Complaining vehemently that he had not been informed such officers were being sent to the county and alleging that since he was the senior colonel the sergeants ought to have been sent to his regiment first, he refused to accept the services of a sergeant sent him. It took all the tact of the fair-minded deputy, Robert Hopton, to avoid an open rupture with Phelips in this matter, and though he smoothed the ruffled feathers by suggesting that Sir Robert should have the assistance of all four officers for a fortnight, Phelips would still not cooperate.[14] In fact, if the King and Council had not decided that the officers should continue for an indefinite period in all the counties Phelips' regiment would not have had the salutary experience of the sergeants' instruction. Phelips, already shorn of his deputy lieutenancy, was relieved of his command of the Bath regiment shortly after this incident. His successor did not stand on punctilio, and from the summer of that year through the summer of the next the Bath regiment as well as the other regiments were drilled by the four sergeants.[15]

The efforts of the four sergeants, readily supported by the deputies, could not help but have had a marked effect on the trained bands. The sergeants were experts. They knew more about war than any man in the

[12] *Acts PC,* 1625–1626, p. 321, PC to Lds Lts, 24 Jan. 1625/6. The emphasis on the sergeants training cadres was reiterated in the broadsheet sent to deputy lieutenants in July 1626, *Orders Appointed by His Most Excellent Maiestie [etc.],* BM, Harl. MS 5936, no. 25.
[13] SRO, Phelips MSS, vol. A, f. 13, letter of introduction for a sergeant sent to Phelips' regiment, 25 April 1625.
[14] SRO, Phelips MSS, vol. A, f. 103, Phelips to [Robert Hopton, DL, c. May or June 1626].
[15] PRO, S.P.16/170, no. 19, Poulett to Sec. Dorchester, 3 July 1630.

militia, including the muster master and the handful of returned veterans serving as underofficers for fear of losing their pensions. Above all, they attacked the martial ignorance of the militia at its most apparent and most corrosive level—the company. On holidays and other convenient times the sergeants put the local company through a drill, checked the arms, and patiently worked with the countryman to make him look a soldier. Their prestige with all ranks was imposing.[16] They had fought, and like any regular soldier they were not loath to talk impressively about their exploits. Nor did a local captain go away from a drill conducted by the sergeant quite so ignorant of military matters as he had been before. If nothing else, he had at least learned how a command should be given; he might even have visualized himself at Breda, a brave commander. After all, in such dreams as these officers are created, even if they are matured by the terrors of real battle.

Both King and Council were well satisfied with the effect wrought in the kingdom's militia by the sergeants. A letter under the sign manual sent to the lieutenants in June 1626 commended the lieutenants' work in settling a "perfect militia" and spoke of the "hopeful beginnings" which the sergeants had made in training the foot; this, in marked contrast to the querulous letters sent before, full of complaint at the poor training of the militia.[17] Yet, such a cheerful and commendatory letter was never again written by Charles, for the "hopeful beginnings" were to a hopeless end. Once the sergeants had gone the local company ceased its drilling, and the brief excursion into serious soldiering was forgotten by officers and men alike. The sergeants had not had sufficient time to build up the training cadres of noncommissioned officers which the Council, in its boundless optimism, had expected. The activities of the constables in pressing men for the Ré expedition flooded the trained bands with men who took refuge in the local company to avoid the pressmen. Such recruits were beyond the reach of any of the invigorating effects the sergeants had left behind them, and no more sergeants were sent to shape into soldiers the new, reluctant militiamen. When the sergeants left the county (often as conductors of pressed men on their way to embarkation at Plymouth) the art of war went with them.

[16] It was significant that the local companies wanted the sergeants to remain longer, PRO, S.P.16/32, no. 76, DLs of Somerset to Ld Lt, 29 July 1626.

[17] *Acts PC*, 1625–1626, p. 496, King to PC, dated 31 May, signed 11 June 1626, sent to Lds Lts by PC.

The sergeants had been concerned only with the foot. The regiment of horse had not undergone the chastening and beneficial experience of expert instruction. If the foot were far from trained, the horse were in an even sorrier state, for the inactivity of all the militia in the previous reign had had a proportionally greater corrosive effect on the horse than on the foot. The horse were recruited from among the gentry, and gentlemen in James' reign had shown little inclination to emulate the equestrian valor of their fathers of the era of the Armada. Gentlemen could more easily escape their commitment to find men, mounts, and arms than could lesser men avoid mustering with their foot companies. Far too often, the gentleman sent a servant with obsolete weapons on a borrowed nag, and the deputies out of deference to their friends would let the matter rest there.[18] Only occasionally had the Council's pressure on the deputies been transmitted to defaulting squires, as in 1619 when two or three of them had been brought before the Council for reprimand.[19] Certainly, the proper instruction of the horse was a far more difficult task than training the foot. The horse, scattered as they were among the better houses of the shire, could not with any convenience be drawn into a regimental front for systematic instruction. Nor would it have been practical to send a trained officer around two score centers in the county to instruct minute groups of younger gentlemen in the very complicated mass maneuvers which were the essence of cavalry combat. Despite the difficulties, however, the fact remained that under James there had been no attempt to train the horse and little zeal exhibited to reform the abuses that left the militia without much more than the shadow of a mounted force.

In the very first muster order of the new reign the Council commanded the lords lieutenants to return the names of defaulters at musters without respect to their "quality." Somerset's lieutenant was even more specific in his letter to his deputies accompanying the Council's order. Informing them that the mustering of horse had been much neglected of late, Pembroke peremptorily told them to reform the abuse speedily.[20] In the order for musters the following year, the Council called for the muster of all the counties' horse on the same day to avoid borrowing of arms and mounts and set the deputies the nigh impossible task of sending a description

[18] PRO, S.P. 16/522, no. 105, petition of Capt. John Gunter to PC [1625].
[19] *Acts PC*, 1618–1619, p. 455, PC warrant, 9 May 1619.
[20] *Acts PC*, 1625–1626, p. 37, PC to Lds Lts, 10 May 1625; SRO, Phelips MSS, vol. A, f. 12, Ld Lt to DLs of Somerset, 30 Aug. 1625.

(color and stature) of every mount mustered.[21] The July 1626 orders had
called for an increase in the number of horse, but it is unlikely that the
"good effects" of this demand mentioned in the 1627 order applied to
the horse.

The Council did more than merely require that the deputies reform
the abuses. In their returns for the 1625 musters, the Somerset deputies
had complained of four varieties of gentlemen who had failed to attend
musters or who had attended improperly accoutred. The Council lost no
time in acting. The lord lieutenant was informed how his deputies should
deal with each type to enforce the law.[22] Pursuivants were sent for the
defaulters informed against, and four Somerset gentlemen were before
the Board within the month. Obviously the deputies of other counties,
under the stimulus of increased conciliar attention, had not been reticent
in returning the names of defaulting gentlemen, for some Norfolk,
Hampshire, and Kent squires also took a wintry journey to London.
In most cases the Council was satisfied with the defaulter's promise of
future good conduct. This proved sufficient in Somerset's cases, for no
gentleman from this county was among the many defaulters from a
half-dozen counties who appeared before the Council after the 1626
musters. Thus, the Council's pressure on the deputies had overcome
their natural reluctance to place members of their own circle in an uncomfortable position. And the Council's strictures and threats laid upon
the unfortunate gentlemen before the Board had undoubtedly resulted
in a far better show of horse at musters than previously was the case.
But neither benefit in itself advanced the martial ability of the horse
regiment. That the Council had neither availed itself of a proposition
by a veteran cavalryman[23] who had offered to do in any county with
the horse what the sergeants would do later with the foot, nor had
taken any other steps to fashion the horse into a more martial frame,
indicates that as late as 1626 their lordships were still satisfied with a
shiny form, though weak substance, so far as the cavalry was concerned.

Probably under the smart received by the defeat at Ré, the Council
had decided by 1628 that the horse must be put in a better state for war.
Relying wholly on the county to supply its own instruction, either by

---

[21] SRO, Phelips MSS, vol. A, f. 19, PC to Ld Lt of Somerset, 21 May 1626.

[22] The four were: (1) without excuse (2) royal wards (3) colonels and captains of foot
(these the Council excused) (4) those with estates in the county but residences elsewhere,
Acts PC, 1625–1626, p. 277, PC to Ld Lt of Somerset, 19 Dec. 1625.

[23] PRO, S.P.16/522, no. 105, petition of Capt. John Gunter to PC [1625].

the muster master or any other trained cavalrymen resident there, the Council hit upon the ingenious idea of calling a grand review of all the horse of England and Wales. The date set was 21 April 1628, when the King would personally review the Home Counties' horse on Hounslow and Councillors would review the rest of the horse regiments at four other regional centers in the kingdom.[24] The cavalrymen were to appear fully armed, and in the meantime the deputies and other militia officers were to give personal instruction to individuals at their own houses two or three times a week. The troops were to train frequently together to prepare them for more advanced instruction at musters. Considering the magnitude of the demand, the incursion that individual instruction would have made into the time of deputy lieutenants fully occupied with billeting troubles, and the consequent fiasco that a royal review of some thousands of milling country squires would have been, it was as well that his Majesty twice postponed and finally cancelled the review. In 1588 when every man could see that the realm was in imminent peril a popular monarch could call her countrymen to attend her at Tilbury and be assured of a stirring answer. In 1628, after the humility of Ré and under the indignities of billeted troops, the answer to the call so great would have been unsatisfactory if not unprintable. Though the proposed review had done nothing to prepare the horse for war, it had raised the ire of even the best affected deputy lieutenants.

The stated reason of Charles for cancelling the grand review was that it would have been "very chargeable" to the counties at that time.[25] Implicit in this was recognition that the training of the militia was secondary to the deputies' efforts in billeting the defeated army that had returned from Ré. From the moment of the King's accession, when the preparations for the Cadiz expedition were already under way, the government had concentrated on spurring the deputies into an efficient discharge of their duties in conjunction with that and the succeeding expedition to Ré. In so far as the work connected with the expeditions increased, so the time which the deputies could spend on training the militia decreased. By 1628 there was just no time left in the deputy's day to think about drilling the local company or instructing some nearby cavalrymen.

The Cadiz expedition did not make undue demands on the deputies' time either before or after the debacle. From Somerset the reasonably

---

[24] *Acts PC,* 1627–1628, p. 277, PC to Lds Lts, 10 Jan. 1627/8. The Western counties were to muster at Shaftesbury.

[25] PRO, P.C.2/38, pp. 185–187, PC to Lds Lts, 31 May 1628 (general muster order).

small number of four hundred foot were pressed in May 1625 to sail with Sir Edward Cecil's fleet, and in September a further one hundred and fifty were gathered to fill the vacancies caused by disease and desertion in the army still at Plymouth. The constables appear to have had no difficulty in finding sufficient vagrants and village *mauvais garçons* to fill the companies that straggled to Plymouth during that humid and unhealthy summer. The countrymen did not object strongly to the coat and conduct money rate levied to clothe the men and to reimburse some local gentleman for his not inconsiderable pains and expense in conducting the men to the port.[26] Soldiers passing through from other counties committed some few outrages of a minor sort, but the justices and constables dealt with these, there being no need for the deputies to call out the trained bands to keep the peace. Once the fleet and what was left of the army had returned, the county was host to over a thousand of the wretches from January 1625/6 until September 1626 (at least). Yet the hosts were willing and the billeted soldiers remarkably well-behaved, so that there were apparently no incidents to try the deputies and absorb their time. Therefore, 1625 and 1626 were fairly trouble-free years during which the deputies could give their attention to training the men, latterly in concert with the Low Country sergeants.

The two years following were far different. Between February 1626/7 and September 1627 Somerset's constables pressed one thousand men to serve in the army and the fleet sent to Ré. The Council demanded that the men be more "able" than those the deputies had formerly sent, and the men supplied were indeed husbandmen, laborers and artisans, not vagrants.[27] But they did not leave their homes gladly, and the sessions records afford glimpses of men who refused to serve and others who deserted once they had been inducted.[28] Not every man could escape the constables armed with press-warrants by joining the trained bands, and

[26] Coat and conduct money was a general rate levied throughout the county (in Somerset, as a hundred rate) to buy each soldier a good coat and to maintain him on the march to the port of embarkation—figured usually at 8d per day per man. The county was to be repaid from the Exchequer, the money for the Cadiz expedition coming from the 1627 forced loan receipts, *Acts PC*, 1627, p. 344, PC order, 14 June 1627.

[27] *Acts PC*, 1627, p. 271, PC to Lds Lts of Eng. and Wales, 11 May 1627, and PRO, S.O.1/1, p. 65, signet letter of 11 May 1627 to Lds Lts. Three indentures between the Somerset deputies and the conductors of two different levies afford the names, addresses, and occupations of the pressed men, PRO, S.P.16/46, no. 12, indenture of 19 May 1627; 82, nos. 91–92, indentures of 25 Oct. 1627.

[28] At midsummer quarter sessions 1627, two men were committed to the bridewell, one for refusing to serve and the other for desertion after his enrollment, SRO, Sess Rolls, 58 pt. i, no. 94.

the poorer men could not engage others to serve in their places. Connivance by the constables—all too common—allowed some to escape and heightened the sense of injustice in their neighbors who were not so favored. There is only one recorded allegation of a Somerset deputy lieutenant acting partially in the matter of pressing; Sir Robert Phelips charged Sir John Stawell, DL, with having pressed one Rogers, a bailiff to Sheriff Thomas Wyndham, out of spleen to Phelips, Wyndham being an ally of Sir Robert.[29] There is nothing to indicate that in Somerset the deputies extorted money from pressed men to let them off, as did Sir Simeon Steward, a Cambridgeshire deputy fined £50 in Star Chamber for that offence, or that the strictures voiced by the reporter of Steward's Case were applicable to Somerset: "And without question, this crime of Sir Simeon is generally applicable to all the deputy lieutenants of England."[30] The deputies were the final court of appeal for men desperate enough to attempt any artifice in order to stay at home, and they must have been called upon time and time again to right a wrong, real or supposed. On the deputies, too, devolved the task of running the deserters to earth—difficult at any time, impossible when people were all too willing to shelter a fellow countryman arbitrarily condemned to an unknown though terrifying fate. It is indeed amazing that Somerset's levies were up to strength when they left the county under the conductors. It had taken all the vigilance of the two deputies always attendant upon the men at the county rendezvous to see that the required numbers did in fact leave the county.[31] During the spring, summer and fall of 1627 the deputy lieutenants of Somerset labored as they had not labored before. It was only the beginning.

If the expedition to Ré had been foolish from the start, the decision of Charles and Buckingham to retain under its colors the remnants of the shattered army that returned was idiocy. Into the southern and western shires was poured a shamefully disorganized mass of defeated, ill-clothed, diseased, starving, and armed men to be housed and fed at the counties' expenses. Onto the shoulders of the deputy lieutenants was thrown the full responsibility for quartering the men in inns and private homes and raising the money to provide for them.

[29] PRO, S.P.16/72, no. 47, Somerset JPs to PC, 31 July 1627; *Acts PC*, 1627, p. 453, PC to JJ assize for Somerset, 27 July 1627.
[30] HLS, L. MS 1128, no. 48, Steward's Case in Star Chamber, Mich. 1628.
[31] PRO, S.P.16/61, no. 91, draft notes by Edward Nicholas of regulations to be sent to deputy lieutenants concerning pressing and conducting [April 1627].

Money was the crux of the billeting troubles that beset the Somerset deputies until sixteen hundred soldiers ended their half-year sojourn there in July 1628. Had the Council sent the money to pay the soldiers' unwilling hosts, it is probable that murmurings would have been the full extent of the county's opposition to billeting. There was, however, no money forthcoming from Westminster, and the deputies were thrown back upon the communities and neighboring parishes where the men were billeted to collect the cash necessary to keep them in quarters.[32] People who had paid a forced loan a year before (and that only under marked duress) were even less willing to provide out of their own pockets for disgruntled and unwanted men intruded into their homes. In and around every one of the fifteen Somerset communities where soldiers were lodged, people refused to pay the money demanded. By the middle of April 1628 householders in Wells were forcibly ejecting the soldiers, and in many places people threatened to beat the soldiers out of the county.[33] In Taunton, the wrath of the townsmen became more than Sir John Stawell, DL, could subdue, and a very serious disturbance ensued.[34] The deputies, desperate and powerless before the surge of opposition, sent impassioned pleas to Whitehall to send money so that the soldiers could be provided for and order restored.[35] There was no money to be sent. In its stead, the King supplied the lords and deputy lieutenants of the counties within which soldiers were billeted with a promise to discontinue billeting soon and with dulcet words of monarchial grace: "In the meanetyme [until billetted troops are removed] lett not this smale delay seeme greivous to the countrie or to yourselves, but take care as becometh lovers of their prince and country to keep things in peace and due order."[36] A gratuitous reminder of their duty was hardly what the hardpressed deputies required. In Somerset the lie to the King's promise became apparent almost at the same time it was made. Previously, the Council had attempted to relieve the tension in some counties (including Somerset) by drawing men piecemeal from the various billets and sending

[32] Trull, one of the outlying parishes rated to aid Taunton, paid £5, the average assessment being c. 5d per 10 acres of land—not a heavy burden financially, SRO, Trull MSS, box 4 (23/13) rate on Trull, 7 Jan. 1627/8.

[33] PRO, S.P.16/101, no. 35, Thomas Grove to Sir Richard Grenville, 18 April 1628.

[34] PRO, P.C.2/38, p. 246, PC to JJ assize of Somerset, 30 June 1628.

[35] PRO, S.P.16/101, no. 53, Robert Hopton, DL, to John Thoroughgood, secretary to the Ld Lt, 21 April 1628. About mid-April, the deputies petitioned the Council to send aid; an extraordinary form of address by local governors to the Council, and one which short-circuited the lord lieutenant completely, S.P.16/529, no. 110.

[63] PRO, S.O.1/1, p. 227, signet letter to a number of Lds Lts, 19 April 1628.

them to the Earl of Denbigh's fleet at Plymouth. In April, two hundred of these soldiers were returned to Somerset because Denbigh had no means to provide for them. They arrived almost literally with the King's promise to discontinue billeting and just in time to add fuel to the flames of discontent. The Council attempted to brazen out the situation. On 12 June, it directed the lords lieutenants to order their deputies to continue billeting until the first monies expected from the recently granted subsidy came in, for the ill-clothed soldiers could not "in decency" be marched out of the counties until they had been properly clothed![37] Fortunately for the wretched soldiers they did not remain in Somerset until the subsidy returns came to renovate their wardrobes. They were moved to Portsmouth in July, marched at the phenomenal speed of twenty miles per day.[38] By then the temper of Somerset was such that had the troops not been quick they might well have sampled the fury of the countrymen.

There was a direct connection between the debate concerning billeting in the Commons on 2 April and the disorders that swept the countryside a fortnight later. It is worth noting that three of the principal speakers in that debate, both pro and con, were Somerset men. Sir Robert Phelips, still excluded from his deputy lieutenancy, was not content to attack only billeting, but felt that he must "state the question higher then yet it toucht," for as he said,

> I was entreated by our countreymen that what ever we did we would bring securitie against the oppression of deputie lieutenants. . . . This is more dangerous then any thing els, and hath dangerously undermined the fabricke of the government of England; and it containes all our complaints both proprietie of goods and libertie of person. This appeares in sending warrants to rayse money. . . . Billetting of souldiers toucheth us all. We are all commanded to have a garrison on us, even in our owne howses. . . . What need is there of Parliaments; if they may rate 20s they may as well rate £20,000. . . . But now the power of deputie lieutenants is come up to the long robe, and they send abroad their warrants. Let us take some course to reprehend some that so knowingly violate the lawes. Let us apprehend this that the poore countreyman is most sensible of.[39]

[37] PRO, P.C.2/38, p. 209.

[38] PRO, P.C.2/38, p. 303, PC to DLs of counties where troops were billeted, 18 July 1628. The normal speed was 12 to 15 miles per day.

[39] This and the following speeches are taken from BM, Harl. MS 4771, ff. 56v–57. Edward Kyrton, another Somerset man and former justice, spoke briefly against billeting the same day, 2 April 1628, BM, Harl. MS 2313, f. 27.

In vain, Sir Edward Rodney (who as a deputy had been most active in billeting) countered this argument by denying that there were any such oppressions. His plea of "inevitable necessitie"—that the soldiers who came with "weapons by their sides and . . . hunger in their bellies" would have taken what they wanted—fell on deaf ears in Parliament and the county. The words that the countryman harked to, that summed up his own experience, were those of George Browne, recorder of Taunton:

> Every man knowes there is no law for this; we know our howses are our castles, and to have such guests putt upon us, our wives and children, is a violacion of the lawes. . . . Deputie lieutenants came to the towne [Taunton] and asked the souldiers where they would be billetted; they said some with the mayor, some with the recorder; and all the regiment came to our towne. Theis soldiers being thus encouraged come into mens howses by force. All this is not necesitie.

And if the countryman heard these words distorted or never heard them at all, at least his actions inadvertently echoed them in the weeks that followed.

Though the Petition of Right was the final echo of these brave words, they had an humbler future as well. When in the years to come the deputy lieutenants turned to the more mundane tasks of lieutenancy, the odium incurred by their actions in 1627 and 1628 remained attached to their office and to their persons with consequent injury to their usefulness. At the bottom of the warrants that had taken from the ratepayers of Somerset £3370 for the Ré expedition and its sequel were the signatures of Sir John Stawell, Sir Edward Rodney, Robert Hopton, and the other deputies.[40] The indignities suffered at the hands of the soldiers and the invasion of private homes were all laid at the feet of the deputy lieutenants. It did not matter that the deputies were merely servants about their master's business; the master was far removed, the servants were near at hand.

Until its closing years, the era of "personal rule" was an era of peace. Though formal treaties ending the war with France and Spain were not concluded until 1630, the war effort of England had ceased abruptly in the winter before the prorogation of Charles' stormy third Parliament. The assassination of the man who had been the mainspring of England's bellicosity, the irretrievable fall of La Rochelle, and the

[40] PRO, S.P.16/110, no. 47; 16/114, no. 77, accounts of money due the eastern and western divisions of Somerset, July and August 1628.

unexpected military successes of the Stadtholder which diverted all the energies of Spain quenched in Charles and his ministers the last measure of inclination to carry on war. In 1629, the King, freed of both war and Parliament, turned to matters of domestic import, and the era of "personal rule" began.

The orders for musters from 1629 through 1634 reflected the pacific atmosphere that had settled in the Council Chamber. There was no urgent demand for the trained bands to be ready on an hour's warning, no orders for enrolling untrained men between sixteen and sixty, no exhortation to increase the trained bands, no mention of provost marshals or "sufficient carriages" to transport baggage and munitions. The only concession that the Council felt was necessary to defensive preparation was the maintenance of the beacons and an adequate supply of munitions in the magazines.

That which the Council did demand was that the deputies turn all their effort into training the militia, particularly the horse. The 1629 order complained of the general neglect of musters in most counties; an unjustifiable reproach on men who had been totally occupied in other matters for the King's service. The complaint was nothing new, nor was the program enjoined in the order. Reciting almost verbatim the July 1626 order, emphasis was placed on an exact view of the trained bands to ensure full strength and proper arming and instruction of men and officers by "experienced" persons. The injunction to the deputies that they were to persuade the "best sort" to furnish themselves with arms had been a feature of all recent orders. The Council's preoccupation with the state of the horse expressed itself in two clauses: one ordained that the liability of an estate to furnish weapons and horse was not to be diminished by joint tenure or dower but rather was to be increased, and the other that all horsemen who failed to attend musters properly accoutred were to attend personally the King in Council and there show their arms. A sting was reserved for the lord lieutenant and his deputies, for the last clause warned them to return a certificate and muster rolls by 1 October, or else attend the Council.[41]

Somerset's deputies avoided a trip to London by the very full report returned after the summer musters. Even if the King and the Council detected a note of exaggeration in it, they must have been encouraged by

[41] PRO, P.C. 2/39, pp. 226–228, PC to Lds Lts, 30 April 1629. The deputies of Somerset had not made a muster return the previous year.

it. The six deputies reported that the horse were much amended both in arms and furnishings and that the muster master (recently appointed) had performed his duty diligently and had found men, arms, and munitions sufficient. The beacons were well repaired. The deputies' concluding remark—that they had been and would always be diligent in the instruction of the men—was specious.[42] None the less, it was obvious that they had taken some pains to supply the deficiencies wrought in the militia by their previous, unavoidable inattention.

The muster orders for the next five years were brief and did little more than refer the deputies to the 1629 order. The only addition occurred in the 1631 order; the captains were to drill their companies, file by file, on holidays and at other convenient times in accordance with the printed instructions of 1623. With the leave of the divisional deputy, the whole company was to be drilled occasionally in the presence of the muster master.[43] Thus, the salutary mode of instruction (between musters drill) adopted when the sergeants came to the county in 1626 was re-instituted, though with one difference—the sergeants were no longer there, and in their absence such drill lost most of its efficacy. There is nothing to indicate that the captains and subalterns were martially experienced enough to fill the sergeants' boots. Rather, it was a case of the blind leading the blind.

During these years, the Council showed itself well satisfied with the deputies' efforts. Though there are no extant reports from Somerset after 1629, Pembroke and Montgomery twice commended his deputies for their great care in mustering, on one occasion informing them that their good report was second to those of few other counties. The Council paid him a similarly handsome compliment in 1633, which of course was intended for his deputies.[44] However, the strongest proof of the Council's satisfaction reposes in the muster orders from 1630 through 1634, sent without discrimination to all counties. In none was there a preamble full of re-crimination or a conclusion threatening conciliar displeasure and punishment for duties left undone.

In Somerset's case, at least, there is strong reason to believe that the Council's satisfaction was born of ignorance. The bulky volume in the

---

[42] PRO, S.P.16/149, no. 20, DLs of Somerset to Ld Lt, 5 Sept. 1629.

[43] PRO, P.C.2/40, p. 557, PC to Lds Lts, 31 May 1631.

[44] SRO, Phelips MSS, vol. A, f. 24, Earl of Pembroke and Montgomery to Poulett, *et al.* DLs Somerset, 11 May 1632; f. 32, same to same, 25 April 1634; f. 27, PC to Pembroke and Montgomery, 31 March 1633.

Phelips manuscripts entitled "Musters 1615–1667" affords evidence to support this contention. Allowing for the fact that some of this evidence appears in arguments drafted by Sir Robert Phelips to confound his ancient enemy, Lord Poulett, there is sufficient corroboration in the statements of men partisan to neither faction to lend certainty to some and credibility to all the evidence.

Phelips, himself a deputy lieutenant, attended only one muster between 1631 and 1636 and then merely to serve a letter of dismissal on a trained band captain who had offended him.[45] Twice he had failed to appear at a meeting of the deputies called to settle the muster master's pay.[46] The result of Phelips' continuing defection had been to throw upon the other deputies the whole burden of training the militia and handling the weighty administrative affairs of lieutenancy. Moreover Phelips was not alone in shirking his duty. During this period most of the work of the deputies was done by Sir John Stawell, Sir Edward Rodney, William Walrond, and, especially, Sir Ralph Hopton, which meant that three or four other deputies, including Sir Charles Berkeley and Lord Poulett, were far less active than they should have been. There are indications, too, that those deputies who were active were lax in prosecuting muster defaulters. One foot soldier whose name had been called repeatedly at musters was not questioned for his default until Lord Poulett chose to use his absence as a stick with which to belabor Phelips. It is worth noting that no absentees were returned for Poulett's regiment in 1633 and that the muster master's signature did not appear on the return. The lie to this return was given by the fact that the foot soldier referred to above was clearly an enrolled member of Poulett's regiment, that his name was called in 1633, and that he did not answer to the call.[47] This one

---

[45] SRO, Phelips MSS, vol. A, ff. 34–35, Poulett *et al*. DLs of Somerset to Pembroke and Montgomery, 3 Oct. 1636; the officer was John Boyse.

[46] SRO, Phelips MSS, vol. B, ff. 95, 97, Sir Edward Rodney and Robert Hopton, DLs, to Sir Robert Phelips, 13 and 22 Jan. 1629/30, respectively. In a letter to his son, Edward, probably written in 1636, Phelips complained that the other deputies had delayed convening to fix the times of the musters, thus the delay would cause inconvenience for the country-men, i.e. would fall during harvest, Phelips MSS, vol. C, f. 52.

[47] A trained band soldier stated on oath that the soldier in question had been called at many previous musters, and Poulett himself stated that he had been summoned to every muster, SRO, Phelips MSS, vol. A, ff. 67, 49. In 1637, Phelips alleged that the statute against defaulters had not been enforced "till of late"—referring here to Poulett's prosecution of the unfortunate soldier, Roman Spracklinge, merely to embarrass Phelips, f. 85, draft argument of Phelips [c. 15 May 1637]. Phelips made the statement concerning Poulett's return of no defaulters in 1633 in an argument to be presented before the lord lieutenant, f. 101; he was not likely to lie under these circumstances since the return would be available and Poulett, also present, would have been able to refute an untruth at once.

false return gives rise to a suspicion that there were others. That the muster master had not signed the return does not speak well for his diligence. There may well have been a large measure of the truth in the accusation levelled by Phelips against the deputies of the other faction: "[They have neglected] the direction of 26 [1626] for the convening and instructing of the soldiers every holiday by the captains and disciplining them to make them fit for the general muster...."[48] Indeed, in 1637 Pembroke and Montgomery could not have been so contented with the labors of his deputies, for in that year the internecine strife among his deputies came to a head. Before him and two other councillors, Poulett and Phelips presented their arguments. Without doubt, all that is written here—and more—was said there. That the three councillors found the case of Sir Robert Phelips proven argues strongly that his lordship was quickly disabused as to the diligence of his deputies during the preceding six years.

To a great extent, the militia and its masters were suffering from the same purposelessness that had afflicted them in the previous reign. It may appear paradoxical that at the moment when all the efforts of the deputy lieutenants could be concentrated on training the "perfect militia" that responsibility received less emphasis than it had when they were busy with preparations for expeditions and in readying the defences of the county against possible invasion. The paradox is only apparent. The last five years of the 1620s had been years of war which, while demanding preparations for war, had given purpose to the militia and to the deputies in their instruction of the militia. With the end of war had come the end of purposefulness, and all slid back to the easy carelessness of peace time.

More than purposelessness afflicted the deputies and the militia in the 1630s. Opposition to everything connected with the militia, to everybody connected with the institution of lieutenancy expressed itself with increasing intensity as the 1630s wore on. Nothing military had ever been popular, not even in the year of the Armada. Hitherto, however, unpopularity had seldom blossomed forth as direct refusal or overt dilatoriness. The rambunctious deputy custos, Hugh Pyne, had declared in his charge to the grand jury at Easter quarter sessions 1626 that the contribution of the trained band soldiers to the Low Country sergeants was an "extorcion,"

---

[48] SRO, Phelips MSS, vol. A, f. 99. This is a draft argument by Phelips, also intended for presentation before Pembroke and Montgomery.

and in that sense they were "to make presentment of it."[89] Regardless of whether the grand jury responded to these rousing words then, the county at large certainly did not. A grand jury of the 1630s might well have answered in the affirmative. Then, the county from husbandmen to magistrates indicated by its action and inaction just where it stood. An institution and its officers which had been identified with billeting, pressing, and coat and conduct money was weak prey to every fractious countryman whose customary dislike of taxation and soldiering had been stiffened to staunch opposition by the events of 1626 to 1628.

The opposition of the county at large to all things military fell with greatest force on the muster master. The county had always been unappreciative of his efforts, and in 1615 the pay of the muster master was £112 in arrears. Two years later quarter sessions had ordered that his £50 annual salary be raised by a special countywide rate.[50] It was one thing to impose a rate and another to collect it. In 1626 muster master Sir Edward Hawley's pay was £126 in arrears, and part of that sum was still owed him when he fell at Ré. Legally, the muster master's rate was highly questionable, for the muster master was not a statutory officer and there was no statutory authority for his remuneration. In 1619 when the muster master of County Durham petitioned assizes for his arrears, Mr. Justice Hutton had justified the rate by affirming that the office received life from the royal prerogative.[51] In the 1630's, such an argument would carry very little weight with the countryman. Anyway, it was insufficient to secure a regular income for the muster masters of Somerset and a dozen other counties.

Captain Thomas Carne, gent., a cousin of both Somerset's lords lieutenants in this period, caught the full force of the county's antagonism. Sir Robert Phelips had attacked him obliquely by holding that the muster master was unnecessary for instructing the militia and directly by stating that Carne was remiss in his duties.[52] If Phelips' attack reached the ears

[49] PRO, S.P.16/40, no. 58, depositions against Hugh Pyne [Nov.] 1626.
[50] SRO, QSOB, 1613–1620, mids. QS 1615, no. 4; Mich. QS 1617, no. 10. Sam Norton, the muster master, was also a justice.
[51] G. S. Thomson, "The Bishops of Durham and the Office of Lord Lieutenant in the Seventeenth Century," *EHR* (1925), XL, 355.
[52] SRO, Phelips MSS, vol. A, f. 1. "An office itt is newly invented and kept upp to serve the lord lieutenant by giving him meanes to oblige some one or other neare him out of the purses of the poore people . . .," an arrow which hit the mark in Capt. Carne's case! This document can be dated between the appointment of Carne (Jan. 1627/8) and the readmission of Phelips to his deputy lieutenancy (c. autumn 1628) it being unlikely that he would so openly attack the lord lieutenant's cousin if he were a deputy.

of his countrymen, the objection in it which made the most profound impression was that concerning the great expense of a muster master. It was through the pocketbook that the county at large expressed its dislike for this officer in particular and lieutenancy in general. Nor was such expression confined to Somerset. The refusal to pay muster masters had become so widespread in England that in December 1629 the Council wrote all lords lieutenants requiring them to ensure that the muster master was an able man and to certify within two months the best pay he had ever received in his county.[53] In July 1631 the Council took the direct course of ordering that a general rate should be made in every county for paying the muster master.[54] Already a committee of four Somerset justices (including one deputy) had hit upon the deceptively easy method of funding Carne's salary by adding a £50 increment to the rate for the maimed soldiers' fund and then paying him from that fund. Consequently, at the midsummer quarter sessions 1631 this increment was ordered on the pretext that the money was needed to provide for the greatly increased number of disabled veterans.[55] It was not long before the subterfuge was pierced, and the justices were soon busy adjusting the complaints of unequal rating which the county found (as later in ship money) was the safest and most effective method of opposition. Despite the new imposition, Carne was no better paid than before because, either through poor management on the justices' part or through a real increase in the number of maimed soldiers, the £50 increment was devoted in time to the true purposes of the fund. The last glimpse that the records give of Captain Carne is an order at the midsummer sessions 1634 for a stopgap payment from the hospital funds to meet his arrears— this provoked by a particularly sharp letter from Pembroke and Montgomery to his deputies, castigating them for their indifferent treatment of his kinsman.[56]

More than any other expression of opposition, the refusal to pay the muster master tended to frustrate the King's hopes for a "perfect militia." Despite the shortcomings of Carne (if we are to accept Phelips' strictures) and the profession of deputies in other counties that the muster master

---

[53] PRO, P.C.2/39, pp. 553–554, PC to Lds Lts of England, 21 Dec. 1629. Upon the certificate of the deputies, the Council confirmed the £50 *p.a.* stipend for Carne, P.C.2/39, p. 721, PC to DLs and JPs of Somerset, 25 March 1630.

[54] PRO, 2/41, p. 133, PC to Lds Lts, 29 July 1631.

[55] SRO, QSOB, 1627/8–1638, mids. QS 1631, no. 2.

[56] SRO, QSOB, 1627/8–1638, mids. QS 1634, no. 3; Phelips MSS, vol. A, f. 32, Pembroke and Montgomery to Poulett *et al.* DLs, 25 April 1634.

was superfluous, that officer was the sole professional element in most county militias. With the Low Country sergeants only a memory, the instruction of the militia had devolved on the muster master. He might not have been efficient, but he never had a chance to be. And an officer whose livelihood depended on the salary the county accorded him could hardly be damned if his efforts corresponded to his pay.

In Somerset, opposition was not confined to the refusal to pay the muster master rate, nor did it fail to express itself at the highest level of the militia. Sir Robert Phelips, ever receptive to the opinions of his lesser neighbors, clearly perceived the rising tide of opposition to all things concerning lieutenancy, and without regard to his office of deputy lieutenant turned that opposition to his own advantage.[57] In so doing he accentuated it and brought its full force to bear on the men who were primarily responsible for creating the "perfect militia", his fellow deputy lieutenants.

As we have seen, his first sally was mild enough. His refusal to entertain the sergeant sent to train his regiment in 1626 had had no disruptive effect merely because he was removed from his command. Nonetheless, he got in a parting shot at the sergeants by complaining to the deputies that the hundreds in his magisterial division were over-rated in raising the levy to pay these officers.[58] Nothing appears to have come of his complaint. Phelips refrained from giving any support to Hugh Pyne's ill-considered attack from the chair at quarter sessions on the same tax. That the two did not coordinate their efforts and that the county had not yet undergone the infuriating experience of billeting would explain why Phelips' first exhibition of animosity towards the deputy lieutenants was not supported by other complaints of over-rating.

The second attack came, however, in 1628 when the county was at the peak of estrangement from the deputies over billeting. In the Commons in April Phelips had assailed not only billeting but the authority in general by which deputy lieutenants issued their warrants, and upon his return to Somerset he gave practical expression to his verbal assault. Before the summer musters Phelips (not yet returned to his deputy lieutenancy) told the local hundred constable, one Priddle, that he was

[57] Sir Robert Phelips was a deputy lieutenant from Feb. 1624/5 until October 1625, when both Poulett's machinations and his own opposition in Parliament caused his dismissal. He was reappointed about the autumn of 1628 and served until his death in April 1638.
[58] SRO, Phelips MSS, vol. A, f. 103, Phelips to [Robert Hopton, DL, c. June 1626]. Phelips was still a justice at this time.

not to give to the deputies at the muster the powder and match brought from the hundred's magazine unless they showed him the letter of authorization from the Council. This was a cunning attack on the sufficiency of the deputies' warrants for, through an oversight, Sir John Stawell and the other deputies had omitted words to the effect that their warrants for mustering were upon order of the Council.[59] This was a factiousness on Phelips' part that Sir John and his associates might better have overlooked, especially as at law the warrants were indeed faulty. But Stawell made the error of magnifying his opponent's factiousness into a *cause célèbre*, and compounded the error by falsifying information in order to prove that Sir Robert had maliciously questioned the legality of musters. The issue, with Phelips, Priddle, and Stawell and William Walrond, DLs, as principals, came before the Council. After an exhaustive hearing the Council cleared Phelips entirely and in the process intimated that the methods used by Stawell and Walrond in pressing the prosecution were highly questionable. Their lordships strictly enjoined the three antagonists to submerge their differences and work for the King's service.[60] That service, though, had received a severe setback. Not only had the deputy lieutenants been shown to have used unlawful warrants and false information, but as well they had been successfully challenged on all counts. Sir Robert Phelips had pointed the way to effective opposition, and in succeeding years lesser men might well think they could avoid musters, fail to find arms, and stay away from Sunday drill with equal impunity.

Sir Robert Phelips, following his reinstatement as a deputy in 1628, did not again identify himself with opposition in the county until 1635, though his scathing criticism of the muster master written at about the same time as the Priddle affair had probably received wide currency in the county, encouraging his countrymen to oppose that officer and the efforts to secure his pay. Still, Phelips was not by nature a passive man. In 1633 an affront given him by one Captain John Boyse, a company commander of Poulett's regiment resident in Phelips' magisterial division, and that gentleman's refusal to take an apprentice at his hands caused Phelips to secure Boyse's dismissal from his captaincy. This was done in direct contravention of the wishes of Lord Poulett, and quite aside from his desire for revenge on Boyse, Phelips was motivated by the

---

[59] SRO, Phelips MSS, vol. A, f. 93, brief of argument by Phelips for presentation before the Privy Council [c. Sept. 1628].

[60] PRO, P.C. 2/38, p. 558, PC order, 31 Oct. 1628.

expectancy of embarrassing his enemy. This he accomplished not only by displacing Boyse but by forcing Lord Poulett to fill the vacancy with the son of a magistrate allied with Phelips himself.[61] The whole affair could have done nothing less than damage the morale and discipline of Boyse's company, perhaps of Lord Poulett's whole regiment.

When Phelips chose again to attack the other deputy lieutenants the Council had inadvertently provided him an admirable platform. The general muster order of 1635, with unexpected sharpness, charged the deputy lieutenants of the realm with "connivance and remissnes of late yeares,"[62] a well-deserved stricture. The order enjoined the strict execution of all the clauses of the July 1626 order, those concerning the preparations for the county's defence as well as the better training and arming of the trained bands. What exactly the Council intended by this unheralded show of war nerves in a period of tranquillity is somewhat obscure, though it was likely that the Council felt the mobilization would serve as visible justification for the first writ of ship money.[63] Regardless of the Council's motive, this sudden display of conciliar interest caught the Somerset deputies off balance. The deputies' almost fearful fervor, born of the awareness of their dereliction in the preceding five years, was well illustrated in their preposterous warrant to the Chewton hundred constables requiring them to appear in less than three weeks with the names of all able men in the hundred between sixteen and sixty, a full account as to the state of the beacons, and a certificate (made on an exact view) of all private arms in their hundred![64]

The deputies' nervousness offered Sir Robert Phelips a peerless opportunity to embarrass his brother deputies, Lord Poulett and Sir John

[61] SRO, Phelips MSS, vol. A, f. 144, copy of affidavit by Dr Paul Godwyn, JP, between Aug. 1632 and Jan. 1632/3; f. 145, Phelips to [PC] 14 Jan. 1632/3; PRO, P.C.2/42, p. 536, PC to Pembroke and Montgomery, 27 March 1633. The new captain was Robert Harbyn, gent., son and heir apparent of John Harbyn, JP, whose appointment as a justice Phelips had secured in 1623/4. Robert became a justice in 1639/40. He distinguished himself as a Parliamentarian officer until he went over to the King in 1643/4.

[62] PRO, P.C.2/44, p. 536, PC to Lds Lts, 27 April 1635.

[63] Gardiner (VII, 381–382) holds that Charles' emphasis on the musters was a diplomatic move directed against the partition treaty between France and the States-General, the precise terms of which he did not yet know, though he was aware of its general import and intent on avoiding its ill effects for English policy. Gardiner is probably right. However, he also states that Charles meant to deceive his subjects by inducing in them fear of a non-existent invasion threat—but gives little reason for this deception. The likeliest explanation is that the order was to justify the first writ of ship money, the monies from which were still in great part uncollected.

[64] SRO, Goodford MSS, w/55, Sir Ralph Hopton, Sir Edward Rodney, and Sir Charles Berkeley, DLs, to Chewton hundred constables, 9 Aug. 1635.

Stawell. In the summer of 1635, he launched an adroitly contrived attack well calculated to do the greatest damage to their reputations. To bring the constables under constant surveillance in the discharge of their duties, the handful of deputies required the assistance of all the justices in their various divisions. Sometime during the 1620s the justices had objected that the deputies had no authority to command their assistance, whereupon the lord lieutenant had settled the issue by directing his letters accompanying any Council order to the deputies and justices jointly. Consequently, in coat and conduct rating and the privy seal loans the justices had ungrudgingly assisted their colleagues who were also deputies.[65] Pembroke and Montgomery did not, however, follow his predecessor's practice, for during the 1630s the lord lieutenant's letters were addressed only to his deputies. In July 1635, Phelips resurrected the issue. At Phelips' instigation, John Coventrye, the son of the Lord Keeper (a recently appointed justice though not yet custos), brought the general muster order and the lord lieutenant's letter to midsummer quarter sessions, objecting vehemently at the highhandedness of the deputies in peremptorily commanding the justices to assist them. Lord Poulett and the other deputies reacted with even greater vehemence by drafting a polemic to justify their conduct, which concluded with the resounding though irrelevant assertion that if there was an earl in the county they could command him to assist them. Poulett obviously intended this argument for presentation to the Council, though there is nothing to indicate that the dispute ever got beyond the borders of the county.[66] It did not have to reach Whitehall to provoke confusion and consternation. Phelips had arranged the attack so that it fell merely on the highhanded approach of the deputies to the justices, not on the authority of the deputies to require and expect the justices' assistance. This was a reasonable objection, and it would strike a responsive chord in members of the rural bench still busy with the Book of Orders. It is impossible in the absence of documentary proof to ascertain just how strongly the members of the bench did respond to Coventrye's objection or just how widespread and

[65] After the Cadiz expedition, quarter sessions ordered the divisional justices to take the accounts of the constables for money disbursed by them on the deputies' orders, SRO, QSOB, 1620/1–1627, Mich. QS 1626, no. 2. The justices had also assisted the deputies in keeping order among the billeted troops after the Ré expedition.

[66] SRO, Phelips MSS, vol. B, ff. 252 *et seq.* This document contains the argument of Poulett and the deputies in one column, Phelips' answers to each point in the other, and notes at the end probably by Coventrye, c. July 1635. This is the sole documentary evidence of this incident.

crippling was the refusal of the justices to cooperate. However, it requires no stretch of the imagination to comprehend the disruptive effects of such a violent attack by a prestigious magistrate made before the all sorts and conditions of men who attended quarter sessions. An institution, like a man, can ill afford much adverse publicity; Coventrye had exposed the inner workings of lieutenancy to the public gaze. Precisely at the moment when the deputies—already unpopular enough—were renewing activity odious to the county, the spectacle of an institution divided and of local governors set one against the other afforded abundant encouragement to fractious and recalcitrant citizens.

It was in an atmosphere of tension, created by the county's mounting reluctance to pay ship money, that Phelips challenged for the last time the actions of the other deputy lieutenants. In the summer of 1636 he complained to the lord lieutenant's secretary that Lord Poulett had mustered his regiment in his (Phelips') division without notifying him of the muster or requesting his permission.[67] The complaint provoked Poulett to strike back at Phelips by arresting a country bumpkin named Roman Spracklinge who had joined Poulett's regiment to avoid the pressmen in 1627, carrying arms voluntarily given him by Phelips for the occasion. Once pressing was done with, Phelips had taken back the arms, and Spracklinge ceased attending musters. In the Priddle affair in 1628, one count in Stawell's information against Phelips had been his reappropriation of Spracklinge's arms, but the Council's judgment had not mentioned that point. Poulett realized that by arresting Spracklinge for not attending the muster in July 1636, he could reopen the dormant question of Phelips' actions in 1628, and in so doing place his enemy in an invidious position *vis-à-vis* the lord lieutenant. Poulett had erred, though, in assuming that Spracklinge had not attended the muster. Improperly summoned, he had appeared on the second day, but Poulett, desirous of spending no more time at musters than was necessary to make a show of dutifulness, had hurried home from the field before Spracklinge could report to him. Ignorant of this, the deputies clapped Spracklinge in gaol for his default on a *mittimus* so carelessly drafted that the date of the muster was given incorrectly. On this technicality, Phelips was able to secure his release.[68] Spracklinge then petitioned the

[67] SRO, Phelips MSS, vol. A, f. 95, Phelips to Mr. Taverner, Pembroke and Montgomery's secretary, 7 July 1636.
[68] SRO, Phelips MSS, vol. A, f. 44, warrant of arrest by 3 DLs for Spracklinge, 8 Sept. 1636; f. 45, Phelips to Ilchester gaoler, 23 Nov. 1636.

lord lieutenant (at Phelips' instigation) of the wrong done him, and Pembroke and Montgomery called on Poulett and the other deputies to answer the petition. The answer, long delayed, charged Phelips with obstruction and protested that if a trained band soldier was protected from their warrants then nobody would obey them. The lord lieutenant replied that he would suspend Phelips if Poulett proved his case,[69] and he set a date for both parties and Spracklinge to attend him at London. In May 1637 the whole business was aired before Pembroke and Montgomery and two other Councillors. Their finding—on overwhelming evidence— exonerated Spracklinge completely. The reprimand accorded Poulett at this hearing was mild compared to the harsh castigation that followed soon after. For on his return home, Lord Poulett in a fit of anger had had the hapless Spracklinge once again gaoled, in direct contempt of the lord lieutenant's judgment.[70] As a result, the "chief deputy" was in public disgrace and in very real danger of dismissal from his deputy lieutenancy by an irate Earl of Pembroke and Montgomery.

If the county needed any further proof of the oppressions of the deputy lieutenants, the Spracklinge affair seems to have provided it. Moreover, the unseemly tug-of-war between those officers charged with the supervision of the militia had undermined the authority of the deputy lieutenants in the eyes of the countrymen. What power would a warrant of John Lord Poulett have when every foot soldier felt that he could disregard it and shield himself behind the seemingly greater power of Sir Robert Phelips?

In the absence of documentary evidence of a direct link between Phelips' leadership and the county's following, it is possible to exaggerate the extent of the disruption of the militia program caused by each successful challenge of the deputies' authority by Sir Robert Phelips. Yet, the opposition to the muster master's rate proves beyond question that there was an undercurrent of active illwill present throughout the 1630s directed at the deputy lieutenants. It is not straining the evidence to argue that on those occasions between 1628 and 1637 when Phelips carried the day against all the other deputies, the latent opposition was given

[69] SRO, Phelips MSS, vol. A, f. 51, Poulett *et al.* DLs to Pembroke and Montgomery 8 March 1636/7; f. 57, Pembroke and Montgomery to Poulett, 24 March 1636/7.
[70] SRO, Phelips MSS, vol. A, f. 73, Pembroke and Montgomery to Poulett, 1 June 1637. The lord lieutenant told Poulett that, having taken the case into his own hands, "others ought not to have laide theirs uppon itt . . . which indeed I take not well. . . ." From Pembroke and Montgomery to his deputy these were strong words.

impressive expression and was encouraged and strengthened in its resolve. It is not unlikely that each successive attack by Phelips at the highest level of lieutenancy was matched at the lowest by an enervating, dragging reluctance on the part of the humblest foot soldiers. If so, that reluctance was almost as destructive of the "perfect militia" as an outright mutiny of the trained bands.

It is difficult to overstress the disruptive effects that Phelips' tactics had upon the deputy lieutenants themselves. Each attack by Phelips was upon men who had little real liking or much talent for their job. With the exception of Sir Ralph Hopton, all were civilians called upon to bring a soldier's knowledge and a soldier's proficiency to the instruction and organization of a "perfect militia." With the exception of Sir Charles Berkeley, all were justices of the peace subject throughout this decade to the unrelenting pressure of the Council and judges in furtherance of the Book of Orders. Without exception, they were the busiest of the local governors. The fact that in the relatively troublefree years of the "personal rule" so little was done by them to bring the militia to perfection bears witness not only to the magnitude of their task but also to their aversion to doing much about it. The attacks of Sir Robert Phelips on their authority made the task more difficult and rendered them even less willing to perform it. That the attacks of Phelips were successful and the deputies themselves subjected to the stinging criticism of their superiors had the important effect of engendering in them a cautiousness fast becoming inertia.

In 1640, the inertia of the deputy lieutenants was just as patent as the imperfectness of the "perfect militia."

The First Bishops' War made little call on the military might of Somerset. In November 1638 when the King and Council believed hostilities were imminent, all lords lieutenants were ordered to hold immediate musters and resume the defensive measures laid down in the July 1626 order which had been suspended after the brief flurry of activity in 1635.[71] Soldiering, hitherto a summer sport only, was even less popular when played in midwinter, though this was the most onerous duty that Somerset's trained bands were called upon to perform in this campaign. The English army (if it can be termed such) that formed around the King at York in the early spring of 1639 was composed almost wholly

[71] PRO, P.C.2/49, pp. 542–545, PC to Lds Lts, 18 Nov. 1638.

10+

of militiamen from counties north of the Trent. The lieutenants of the southern counties, including Somerset, were commanded merely to take from the trained bands a "select number" of horse and foot, supply them with coats, and exercise them weekly until they were ordered to march northwards—something of an anticlimax for the troops, who had been mobilized to be ready "at one howers warninge on payne of death."[72] These preparations came to naught, for the Pacification of Berwick ended the war almost before it had begun. In July, the men selected for special training were returned to their homes and their local companies, and the training of the militia as a whole returned to normal. It is interesting to note, though, that the King had given leave for any trained soldier desirous of staying at home to offer an "able" substitute in his place. If the King intended that his army should be an expert fighting force, it was a sad commentary on his "perfect militia" that he considered a strong-backed yokel the equal of a trained band soldier.

Although the county's militia got off lightly, the deputy lieutenants did not. Besides having to organize, prepare, and drill the men selected from the trained bands, they and their counterparts in ten other southern counties were also summoned to contribute to the expenses of the royal army. The deputies and other "principal gentlemen"—who, in Somerset, included besides the eight deputies, fourteen others, twelve of them justices—were approached through the lord lieutenant for an outright gift. The Lord Keeper was also asked to write letters "very effectually" to the gentlemen, since it was thought that his power over the justices would overcome any reluctance on their part to give. Two of the deputies contributed generously along with the custos (Coventrye, the Lord Keeper's son), three other deputies excused themselves by saying they had contributed in another way, but three deputies returned no answer at all.[73] This demand was a shameful extortion exacted from men who were in the power of the King and who were contributing without recompense their energy and time to his service. The deputies and justices would not soon forget the King's "request."

[72] PRO, S.P. 16/413, no. 111, King to Lds Lts [Feb. 1638/9] corrected draft; Asz.24/20, f. 204, order of Devon summer assizes 1639 on certificate by a Barnstaple, Devon, soldier.
[73] PRO, S.P.16/418, no. 57, PC to Earl of Hertford (Ld Lt of four Western counties) 26 April 1639; no. 45, King to Secretary of State Windebank [24 ? April 1639]; P.C.2/50, p. 299, list of gentlemen of seven Western counties to whom request for aid was made, 26 April 1639; 51, pp. 77–79, list of returns on request for aid, 26 Nov. 1639. Of the 22 canvassed, 13 Somerset gentlemen made no answer, 4 replied that they had paid another way, 2 promised to pay (total £25), and 3 paid a total of £300.

If the First Bishops' War was only a ripple to Somerset's militia, for the county as a whole it resembled a tidal wave. The rebellion of the Scots swept into the consciousness of the countryman as had few other events so far removed from his home and life. The knowledge that others of the King's subjects were in arms to preserve their rights emboldened the country to reveal openly the hostility that hitherto had expressed itself in refusal to pay the muster master rate and ship money, in reluctance to attend musters, and in isolated outbursts of puritan fervor such as the Beckington riot. The reaction to all oppressions, secular and religious, swirled to the surface. Resistance to ship money, stiffened by Hampden's example, grew rigid. The town of Yeovil as one person protested violently to quarter sessions of the oppression of a brewer licensed by a royal patentee.[74] The Beckington rioters, in contempt of a judge's order and in disregard of his leniency, refused to humble themselves before Bishop Pierce; the parishioners of St. Cuthbert's, Wells, refused a parish clerk appointed by that good prelate of Laudian proclivities; in Wells, two cordwainers, and in Stratton, a yeoman, spoke approbrious words of the archbishop himself.[75] The county was stirring, expressing its opposition to the oppressions of the "personal rule" and to Laudian churchmanship. The First Bishops' War had taken off the lid of a pot that had been boiling unseen for a very long time. The Second Bishops' War turned up the heat.

The heat was not long in coming. Charles, firmly resolved to quell his rebellious subjects and regain authority over his Northern realm, issued orders on 26 March 1640 for levying a new army. From all the shires of England and Wales, 27,600 men were to be raised by the deputies rating each hundred and making "very good choice" of trained band soldiers.[76] To ensure discipline, the haphazard system of locally appointed conductors was discarded, the officers for the field being sent to drill and then conduct the men northwards. Weekly exercising was again ordained, to be undertaken by the deputies and army officers before the men were moved to a county rendezvous on 10 May preparatory to marching northwards ten days later. In one important respect, these crisp and detailed instructions differed from those of the previous year. This

[74] SRO, Sess Rolls, 78, no. 56, Epiph. QS 1638/9.
[75] Som Asz Ords, nos. 143, 136, 160; PRO, P.C.2/50, p. 515, PC to Finch, CJCP, Justice assize Western Circuit, 14 July 1639.
[76] PRO, P.C.2/51, p. 397, PC to Lds Lts, 26 March 1640. 10,000 were to be sent by sea and 17,600 (including 2000 from Somerset) were to be marched overland to Newcastle.

time, there was to be no substitution of untrained men for trained band soldiers, no bribing of the press officers to let the trained soldier stay at home. The "perfect militia" was to be given an opportunity to prove its worth in defending King and country.

The decisiveness and aura of dispatch so evident in this order, which augured well for the King's cause, was absent in all other communiques from Whitehall during the following months. The succeeding confusion and uncertainty, stopping and starting struck at the very vitals of the war effort. In April, the deputies were urged to hurry with the levying of the men; in May, a bare week before the troops were to be taken to the county rendezvous, the move was postponed until 1 June.[77] Under the strain of extraordinary activity the post broke down, delaying important dispatches a week or ten days. In Somerset's case the delay of the letter of postponement had the unfortunate result of informing the deputies of the change in plans too late for them to prevent the useless expenditure of precious money on soldiers kept at rendezvous for a week only to be disbanded. The Council alternately cajoled and threatened the deputies with Star Chamber. With obstrusive nervousness, the lords lieutenants for the first time looked to their charges in the county. A Council order requiring their lordships to oversee personally the levying of men in the counties if any difficulties arose was interpreted by them as a mandatory injunction of personal attendance, and the King was treated to the unseemly spectacle of his nervous lieutenants stampeding towards their county charges.[78] Confusion in the highest places among the greatest men inspired no confidence in those laboring in the counties to create and preserve the King's army.

The deputies' work was feverish; it had to be in order to accomplish anything in the face of the formidable opposition that arose virtually on the day the order for levies came into the county. For the last time before the Long Parliament, the men of Somerset and the other counties expressed their loathing for the royal policy and its method of execution by refusing to subscribe the money without which the policy was doomed. Charles, his exchequer empty, had demanded once again that the counties pay coat and conduct money.[79] The Parliament that the King had hope-

[77] PRO, S.P.16/418, no. 103, PC to Lds Lts [April 1640]; P.C.2/51, p. 469, PC to Lds Lts of 31 Eng. and Welsh counties, 3 May 1640.

[78] PRO, P.C.2/51, pp. 457, 462, PC orders, 26 and 29 April 1640.

[79] PRO, P.C.2/51, p. 397, PC to his Lds Lts, 26 March 1640. The cost of keeping 2000 men at rendezvous for 10 days at 8d per man per day was £666. The coats cost £1000, though the tailor was still owed £700 of that by late summer.

fully convened in April had not granted twelve subsidies as requested. Rather, with the voice of John Pym it had assailed military impositions without ground in law, especially coat and conduct money.[80] Like Hampden's Case, this painstaking indictment by Pym hardened opposition beyond the reach of reasoning. Three successive warrants Somerset's deputies sent out for raising the money. Time and again they threatened the constables, many of whom brought in a quarter of the sum assessed, some, none at all. Commanded to give the names of those who had refused to pay, the constables replied that they "must bring in the names of every man" in some hundreds;[81] so many, in fact, that the deputies did not think fit to trouble the Council with them. Yet, councillors who had summoned three hundred and thirty from Surrey, forty-four from Gloucestershire, and countless others from Essex, Middlesex, Northamptonshire, and Herefordshire would not have paled at seeing a few from Somerset. Nor was opposition confined to refusal to pay. William Strode, the prime adversary of ship money in Somerset, politely declined the invitation of the deputies to serve as treasurer for the money collected.[82] Constables bringing money to his house found no treasurer at home, and the money came late, if at all, to the deputies' hands.

In two respects, the civilian opposition to paying coat and conduct money was fatal to the military effectiveness of the King's army. In the first place it provided a spark of contumacy that soon set the pressed men on fire. In the second place it provided the cause for ignition. There were few difficulties encountered in raising the troops initially, and so long as the soldiers were paid they were tractable.[83] But by June there was no more money. The mistake in bringing the men to rendezvous in May (occasioned by the delayed letters) had wasted over £600, and the coats had used up the rest of the money collected. The county refused to pay more. The disbandment caused by the Council's confusion and the

[80] PRO, S.P.16/450, no. 108, minute of Pym's speech, 17 April 1640. Pym was a Somerset man (from Brymore) though he was not "county" and was not a local governor. He held a lucrative office, that of receiver-general of Crown revenues in Wilts., Hants, Gloucestershire, and the Isle of Wight, in this period, PRO, E.159/470, Trin. 6 Chas. I, rot. 68, and lived with his family in Holborn, Middlesex, Bodl, Bankes MSS, bundle 62, nos. 28, 35.

[81] PRO, S.P.16/459, no. 7, Sir Thomas Wrothe, Thomas Luttrell, and John Symes, DLs, to Lds Lts of Somerset, 1 July 1640. For other counties, see P.C.2/51, pp. 558, 559, 618, PC warrants, 17 June and 4 July 1640.

[82] PRO, S.P.16/457, no. 50, Wrothe and Symes, DLs, to Lds Lts of Somerset, 17 June 1640.

[83] Pembroke and Montgomery in a letter to the Lord General, 22 May 1640, noted with satisfaction how well the pressing had progressed in Somerset, PRO, S.P.16/454, no. 64.

post's delay had sent back to their homes two thousand disgruntled soldiers. When they came again to rendezvous in June, disaffection had already begun to take its toll and far fewer than the original and required two thousand appeared at rendezvous at Bruton and Wincanton. The ones who did rendezvous there were quiet, but only so long as the money held out. Desperately, the two deputies always in attendance on them took £100 from their own pockets to pay them. It was not enough. The deputies and the army officers were "more obnoxious to their fury then any other."[84] The men deserted in droves. The constables could not or would not arrest deserters. When the men finally left Somerset on 11 June, five hundred or more soldiers had taken French leave, and Colonel Lunsford's regiment marched off to war at two-thirds strength.[85]

By the end of June desertion and insubordination had grown into mutiny. From nearly every county in the south of England came reports of mass desertion, vandalism, and murder. The Wiltshire soldiers broke open the county gaol to liberate those committed for not paying coat and conduct money. The Berkshire forces disbanded in Oxfordshire; communion rails were burned in East Anglia; a Roman Catholic subaltern was murdered by his Dorset soldiers.[86] In Somerset, at Wellington, the Devon troops turned on a hapless Romanist lieutenant named Eure, devastated his quarters, flayed him to death with ferocious brutality, and dragged his remains through the streets of the town while the constables and folk stood idly by. The commanding officer on sending to the nearest Somerset deputy for assistance received none.[87] Throughout July, the disorders and atrocities increased. The appointment of provost marshals to attend the contingents as they left their respective counties accomplished nothing.[88] Nor would the trained bands ordered out in desperation to arrest disorderly troops jeopardize the lives of their fellows by bringing them to justice. Commissions of oyer and terminer might be issued to

[84] PRO, S.P.16/457, no. 50, Wrothe and Symes, DLs, to Lds Lts of Somerset, 17 June 1640.

[85] PRO, P.C.2/51, p. 566, PC to Lds Lts of Somerset, 19 June 1640.

[86] PRO, S.P.16/460, no. 56 [Edmund Rossingham] to Viscount Conway, 21 July 1640. This professional purveyor of news complained with exasperation of further "damnable" disorders by soldiers.

[87] PRO, S.P.16/460, no. 5, Lt. Col. Gibson to [Viscount Conway] from Wellington, 14 July 1640. The Devon men walked home and boldly informed their deputies of what they had done and told them that if they were to hang one, they would have to hang all! At the winter assizes 1640/1, Wellington was fined £200 for not apprehending Eure's murders, though at the next assizes, estreat of the fine was ordered stayed, PRO, Asz.24/21, f. 35v.

[88] PRO, S.P.16/460, no. 38, minutes by Sec. Windebank of PC resolutions [9] July 1640.

the lord lieutenant, his deputies, and other justices to quell mutinous troops, but deserters and mutineers had to be caught before they could be hanged.[89] The army on which rested all the King's hopes had become in a matter of days the greatest law enforcement problem in living memory.

How far were the deputy lieutenants of Somerset responsible for this state of affairs in their county and among their troops? The Council, upon the complaint of the general of the army that the deputies of Somerset refused unless given new warrants to press more men to compensate for the desertions from their forces, ordered the lords lieutenants to call to account those deputies who had been so "scrupulous" and if necessary to appoint others, "better affected," in their place.[90] Indeed, the three deputies in question were of doubtful "affection" to the King's service. Sir Thomas Wrothe, who was also sheriff and as such was currently under strong suspicion for failing to collect ship money, made little secret of those puritan sympathies which later impelled him to take a leading part in the Parliamentary cause. John Symes was a sincere puritan who had been the warm supporter of Sir Robert Phelips both in Parliament and the county. Early in the Civil War, Thomas Luttrell proved an earnest though incompetent commander for the Parliament. Regardless, there can be no question that in the spring and summer of 1640 these three applied themselves to the task set them with a zeal undebased by either religious or political reservations. They worked alone. The seven other deputies, including Lord Poulett, Sir John Stawell and Sir Edward Rodney did not raise a hand. When the work began, all these deputies refused to assist, holding that since a new commission of lieutenancy had been issued the previous year their commissions of deputy lieutenancy had not been renewed.[91] Now it became apparent how great had been the damage wrought in the minds of those who had

[89] PRO, P.C.2/51, p. 587, PC order, 28 June 1640. A special commission for this purpose for Somerset was tested 20 July, naming the joint lords lieutenants (Pembroke and Montgomery and Hertford) and Pembroke and Montgomery's soon to be appointed successor (Philip Lord Herbert), the two judges of assize for the Western Circuit along with three serjeants-at-law who practiced there, three Somerset justices, six other Somerset justices, and two other gentlemen, PRO, C.181/5, pp. 365–366.

[90] PRO, P.C.2/51, p. 566, PC to Lds Lts of Somerset, 19 June 1640.

[91] PRO, S.P.16/455, no. 6, Wrothe, Luttrell, and Symes, DLs, to Lds Lts of Somerset, 26 May 1640. The new commission (tested 26 March 1639) had been issued to join the Earl of Hertford with Pembroke and Montgomery. Sir Ralph Hopton, DL, was in the North with Charles in command of a regiment of the horse guards; these remarks do not apply to him.

always professed and more or less practiced the King's service, by the repeated attacks of Sir Robert Phelips on their authority and the dragging, obstinate country opposition to all things military in the preceding fifteen years. The deputies had hit upon a convenient excuse to shirk their duty when they were most needed. Perhaps the excuse was more than just a quibble. If their commissions had in fact lapsed, they ran the risk of provoking the outcries of "unlawful authority" and "oppression" which had greeted them in nearly every move they had made during the past fifteen years. Sir Robert Phelips was dead, but the county did not want for others who could mount an effective attack. These deputies had abandoned the King's service at a critical moment. They were not "disaffected," neither then, nor before, nor later. They were tired and they were cautious.

It is untenable to hold that even if all ten deputies had acted with the care of Wrothe, Symes, and Luttrell, the catastrophe that was an army in open revolt could have been avoided. This service "the greatest that ever happened in our times,"[92] was by then beyond the help of fifty deputies. If the catastrophe can be laid at the feet of the deputy lieutenants at all, then the indictment must be drawn to include those years when they might have instilled in the men who deserted and mutinied in 1640 that discipline and training which had held together other armies in other times under far more adverse conditions. Despite the lack of pay, despite the total disinclination of the countryman to leave his home, despite the almost universal loathing of puritan countrymen to fight against coreligionists, despite the oppressions real and supposed of the "personal rule," men who were in truth disciplined soldiers would never have committed the outrages perpetrated by the King's troops in 1640. After all these men were not vagrants and felons—they were the soldiers of the "perfect militia."

When in 1626 the King demanded a "perfect militia" he had pitched the demand high; too high, for neither he nor his ministers took into account the fact that the institution which would have to create that militia was too weak ever to have given satisfaction. The unmartial country squires were amateurs in the one art which is always best left to the professionals. The experiment of the sergeants had been a bold

[92] PRO, S.P.16/455, no. 6, Wrothe, Luttrell, and Symes, DLs, to Lds Lts of Somerset, 26 May 1640.

attempt to provide the expert direction necessary, but it languished even before the end of the war which had afforded the militia some purposefulness. It was inevitable that with peace the sustained fervor required to train an army of part-time soldiers would vanish. It was inevitable that the years of "personal rule," unbroken by even rumors of war, would not be years in which could grow an organization nurtured only by ever-present belligerency. The old purposelessness set in and it took its old toll. Nothing was done to combat it, nothing was attempted that might have infused some spirit of urgency into the trained bands. That spirit could have come only from outside the organization, from the King and Council. Yet, beyond reiterating the demand, Whitehall did nothing during the golden years of the 1630s. In an era of peace, a demand alone was not enough to fashion an army out of actively hostile countrymen, commanded by unconcerned and squabbling squires.

Undoubtedly the King and Council were largely ignorant of this purposelessness and its detrimental effects. While demanding a "perfect militia" there was no way for them to discover that they were not getting it. Even had they known that the militia was not being perfected, there was no machinery to correct the malaise. One is struck forcibly by a comparison of the Council's real satisfaction with an unreal performance with respect to the militia during the 1630s and the Council's marked dissatisfaction with the justices' considerable efforts to enforce the Book of Orders during the same period. In one case satisfaction came from ignorance; in the other dissatisfaction came from knowledge. The judges of assize brought to the Council's notice twice yearly the shortcomings of the justices in enforcing the Book, and they transmitted the pressure of the Council onto the justices with ultimately beneficial results. In lieutenancy there was no such channel of conciliar intelligence, no such instrument for the application of conciliar pressure. Lieutenancy was the sole responsibility of the lord lieutenant, and only he could have performed for that institution the function performed by the judges in magistracy. However, he had withdrawn from any active part in the institution committed to his care, leaving the deputy lieutenants its undisputed masters. The deputies performed their duties as they willed, drafted their reports to reflect greatest credit upon themselves, and there was no one to say them nay.

The withdrawal of the lord lieutenant from active participation in lieutenancy was the basic cause of the failure to perfect the militia. Not

10*

only did it result in the severance of the one link between the government and the deputies inexpendable for the government's intelligence and the application of its pressure. The lord lieutenant's withdrawal also left the institution vulnerable to the struggle between the two factions which disordered that institution and in so doing sapped the vitality of even the most dutiful deputies. The political advantages of dominance in this important sphere of the county's government tempted the deputies to vie for power, and the lord lieutenant's absence allowed them to struggle unmolested. Their struggles were fatal to all schemes for bettering the militia. It invited one combatant to turn the hostility of those who composed the militia, indeed, of the whole populace, against his colleagues by giving aid and encouragement to the hostile. The struggle destroyed the unity among the deputies which was needed as never before to overcome the animosity of the mass of the county to anything that bore the stamp of the deputy lieutenants.

Purposelessness, personal rivalry, and opposition combined to destroy all the hopes so happily held by Charles and his ministers in 1626 that a real army could be created to support the King and give effect to the King's policy. From the failure of those hopes, partially stemmed the disastrous series of events which ultimately destroyed the King.

Chapter X ༀ *The Antagonists*

Sir Robert Phelips has loomed large in these pages. In part, this is because he alone of Somerset's local governors in this period amassed an incomparable collection of papers which his descendants preserved. It is the wealth of information contained in these papers that creates a picture of Phelips' overwhelming importance in the county's governance. But prudence demands corroboration of that picture, and fortunately such corroboration is afforded by official records from sources extraneous to Phelips. That picture is heightened, rather than diminished, by the official records. Taken singly, the official records are enough to establish Phelips as the key figure in the course of Somerset's government during this period. It is only his own papers, however, in his slanted, near-illegible hand that uncover the full extent of his acts and the motives behind them. In so doing they depict no less vividly, and only somewhat less truthfully, the acts and motives of his hated enemy and prime antagonist, John Lord Poulett.[1]

It is far easier for the historian to keep politics out of his story of county government than it was for the deputies and justices to exclude them from that institution. To the cause of history that omission would be as dangerous as politics proved to be to local government. Institutions are the shadows of men, and the shadows of these two men enveloped Somerset's government throughout these sixteen years.

[1] This chapter is based primarily upon the Phelips MSS in the Somerset Record Office, principally the volumes entitled "Musters, 1615–1667," "Duchy of Cornwall, 1613–1636," "Family letters," "Parliamentary proceedings," "Parliamentary," and various estate muniments. It was Sir Robert's systematic copying and filing of all correspondence, depositions, etc., and his careful preservation of drafts of arguments and briefs for use against his opponents that make this collection as useful to the historian as it proved to be to its creator. Beside these muniments, Phelips' parliamentary career has been followed in the printed debates of Parliaments of 1620s and various manuscript sources in the British Museum, all of which have been cited previously. Poulett's correspondence with central officials and officers of state, hitherto cited, are in the State Papers Domestic. In general, citations in this chapter are given only for quotations and where material not previously touched upon has been introduced.

Somerset's government had become the field of battle in a struggle between these two county giants that lasted for nearly a quarter of a century. The honors of war were supremacy in the county. Both contestants knew that the prize would go to him who won clear ascendancy in the county's government, and so the strategy of each was directed at obtaining that position. From such a place the victor could exercise the power and influence that marked him as the greatest man in the county. It was not a particular office that mattered, for no single office in the structure of local government was so lofty as to allow its holder unassailable power. What was sought was the recognition of the other local governors and the mass of the county's populace below them that the triumphant magnate was the magnate of magnates.

In great measure, Sir Robert Phelips had obtained that recognition tacitly, if not openly, from his fellow justices of the peace. There could be no doubt of the primacy among equals of a magistrate who ordered the clerk of the peace to obtain the release of this man and thank the chairman of quarter sessions "for his respect to me in that particular," to bind that woman in good sureties never to tipple again, to get the chairman to order this man to keep his apprentice until the next sessions, and ended with "commend me to Mr Symes [a justice] and use him in these [matters]."[2] When a justice, not of Phelips' division, was unable to attend quarter sessions, he wrote the clerk that he had excused himself to Sir Robert Phelips, adding as an afterthought that he wished also to be excused by the chairman.[3] Such recognition by Phelips' associates of the bench was very evident to the common folk. More petitions from all over the county, some of them from persons in very serious trouble, were addressed to him than to any other justice, including the chairman himself. What is even more significant is that, in nearly every case, the will of Sir Robert Phelips coincided with the finding on the cause. His authority was not limited to the confines of his division or, in its exercise to the jurisdiction of his petty sessions. Sir Robert Phelips was the greatest man on the bench at quarter sessions and his power embraced the whole county.

Phelips' dominance fell short when it came to lieutenancy. Here Lord Poulett was master, the "chief deputy"; a mastery he had assumed by

[2] SRO, Sess Rolls, 66, no. 70, Phelips to Christopher Browne, clerk of the peace, n.d., mids. QS 1631.
[3] SRO, Sess Rolls, 69 pt. ii, no. 19, Sir Henry Berkeley to Christopher Browne, 7 Jan. 1632/3. John Harington was chairman.

moving into the vacuum left by the lord lieutenant's withdrawal from an active role in county government. No one could have challenged the lord lieutenant's ascendancy in his own institution, or for that matter his supremacy in the county. His usurper though was a local governor, too much a part of county politics, too divorced from central control. So long as Poulett remained master, he invited attack. Poulett's ascendancy in lieutenancy closed to Sir Robert a sphere for the exercise of that influence essential for supremacy in the county in an era when the deputy lieutenants' control over the lives and fortunes of their countrymen reached its zenith. Inevitably Phelips challenged Poulett in his own bailiwick, thus making lieutenancy the scene of the most thunderous battles.

Every dispute that took place in this institution between Phelips on the one side and Poulett and his minion, Sir John Stawell, on the other grew out of a challenge to Poulett's dominance thrown down by Sir Robert Phelips. Sir Robert had refused to accept the four sergeants in 1626 because Poulett and the other deputies would not acknowledge him to be the senior regimental commander in point of service. Phelips' incitement of constable Priddle to refuse to give over the powder to Poulett and Stawell at the 1628 musters unless shown a proper warrant was a presumptuous claim on Phelips' part to be the prime arbiter of militia affairs even though he was not then a deputy lieutenant. In great part, Captain Boyse had been sacked and the friendly Robert Harbyn substituted in his place as a company commander in Poulett's regiment because Phelips wished to assert his authority as a deputy lieutenant and assert it at the expense of his rival. Behind the attack in 1635 that Phelips launched through the instrumentality of John Coventrye against Poulett's and Stawell's peremptory orders to the justices to aid them was the same intention of lowering Poulett in the estimation of the other local governors and the countrymen, and perhaps sullying him in the eyes of the lord lieutenant and the Council. The last great dispute (in 1636) was touched off by Sir Robert's complaint to the lord lieutenant that Poulett had not informed him of the date and place of musters and that Poulett had reviewed his regiment in Phelips' division without his knowledge or permission—a haughty claim to deference by Phelips that was sure to enrage the Lord Poulett. When that affair was settled and Poulett received from the Earl of Pembroke and Montgomery a letter so scathing as to make him fear for his place, Phelips had accomplished more than he could have hoped for short of Poulett's dismissal from his deputy lieutenancy.[4] It was not necessary for Phelips' triumph that that should have occurred. Though Phelips was not alive to see it, Poulett's withdrawal from an active part in lieutenancy in 1640 was proof of how effectively he had mauled the willpower and the authority of Lord Poulett.

These men could hardly conceive of any greater prize than supremacy in the county. It accorded the winner the deference of his inferiors, the honor of his equals, and the respect of his superiors. Inevitably, Phelips felt deeply that this should be his place as the son of a noted Elizabethan and Jacobean lawyer and statesman, as the master of the most magnificent house in Somerset. Poulett felt a like claim less by right of inheritance (though he was nothing wanting in that) than by his own attainments which had secured his elevation to the peerage, making him virtually the only peer resident in the county. Supremacy in the county allowed the magnate who attained it release from the confines of the county, release from the fetters that bound his authority and fame to his tenants, the neighboring villagers, and the inhabitants of his petty sessional division. For Sir Robert Phelips and Sir John Stawell (as earlier for John Poulett) this meant release through obtaining a county seat in Parliament and the gratifying recognition which went with it, that the honorable member spoke for the county. At Westminster, Phelips or Stawell could act upon a greater stage before a wider audience. Nor was their enthusiasm damped as the 1630s wore on and St. Stephen's lay unused. In common with most of their contemporaries, both men believed that another Parliament was just around the corner. Much of the disputation between the two and Phelips' careful solicitousness for the countryman's good throughout the 1630s convey the impression of a perpetual election campaign. Lord Poulett was no less susceptible to the appeal of a greater life beyond the county's borders. Above all, this meant to him a seat at the Board. Though his mediocre abilities and limited usefulness denied him this, he lived continually in hope that supremacy in the county would give him sufficient stature in the eyes of Charles to admit him to at least the periphery of his paradise, the Court. Even if his ambition in this was frustrated, supremacy at home was a satisfactory second best.

Quite aside from its positive virtues, supremacy in the county had one other strong attraction for both Sir Robert Phelips and John Poulett. The attainment of supremacy by one meant the exclusion of the other from

[4] For this and the preceding incidents mentioned in this paragraph, see pp. 265–270.

it. This wholly negative attraction grew out of a passionate hatred between the two which increased as the years passed and which gave added impetus to their warfare. The relations of these men had not always been disordered by such extreme loathing of one another. Until 1614 they had been good if not intimate friends. It was in that year that their friendship ended and their struggle for power began. Sir Robert, as a latecomer in a bid for one of the county seats in the Addled Parliament, met the combined forces of his friend Poulett and the ancient magnate, Sir Maurice Berkeley. Behind Phelips was his father's influence and his father's name and he expected the younger man, Poulett, to withdraw from the race in his favor. Poulett did not step back. The Poulett-Berkeley alliance, aided by the devious tactics of the sheriff at the hustings, carried both seats.[5] Phelips, the son and heir of Mr Speaker, joined the Parliament tardily, sitting for the minor Cornish borough of Saltash. He never forgot the smart of that dishonor and never forgave his onetime friend, Mr. Poulett, for his perfidy. The breach was irreparable, and when for obscure reasons Sir Robert lost the place of custos rotulorum later in the same year, the false sounding professions of regret by John Poulett indicated that there was no bond of friendship left between them.[6] From then until Sir Robert died in April 1638 hardly a year passed that one or the other, directly or indirectly, did not move to discredit his enemy. None the less, the greater engagements were destined to take place after the Earl of Marlborough and Sir Maurice Berkeley had died, leaving the long robe of county power to be scrambled for by the newly created Baron Poulett and a Sir Robert Phelips compelled by the absence of Parliament and previous loss of county office to give greater attention to county affairs. Such were the natures of the two men, the depth of their enmity, and the desirability of the robe, they would not cast lots for it.

If the end was the same—supremacy in the county—the way that each antagonist took to obtain it was different. Though both Phelips and

---

[5] Miss Edith Farnham has given a concise review of this election drawn from the Phelips MSS, which does not require revision, "The Somerset Election of 1614," *EHR* (1931) XLVI, 579–599. However, other interesting material not available to her has come to light in SRO, Sanford MSS, box 51, *inter alia*, a letter from Poulett to a supporter saying "I know we have to doe with a waveringe multitude" and admitting that Phelips "musters a great troope of justices and sirs," no. 36, John Poulett to Richard Wykes, 27 March 1614. What most infuriated Phelips was that Poulett had promised to withdraw if Phelips decided to stand.

[6] SRO, Sanford MSS, box 51, no. 35, John Poulett to Richard Wykes [1614].

Poulett followed the other's way on one or two occasions, basically they clung to their divergent strategies with the tenacity that their combat demanded. For Phelips, the way to supremacy in the county lay in the more direct approach of actively appealing to the yeomen and lesser gentlemen of the county for their support and lending aid to them in the furtherance of their interests. Poulett and Stawell believed that the means to county power was the King and his Court; a strategy forced upon them by Phelips' long-enjoyed monopoly of the county's good opinion which denied Stawell the successful use of his not inconsiderable talents of demagoguery.

Sir Robert Phelips was of a type clearly recognizable to his contemporaries. He was of the genus "popular persons . . . not the meanest, or not meane at all, but such indeed as have exacted an opinion to be thought their countries only freindes."[7] Phelips sought always the good opinion of his lesser neighbors in the county. Indeed, his rage was great when he wrote in 1628 of the rumor that he had forsaken the county's interest and turned courtier, set on foot by Lord Poulett upon his return from Parliament "upon design to withdraw the good opinion of the country from me."[8] The county's good opinion of Sir Robert was most likely to secure him a county seat, the machinations of the sheriff permitting. It was also likely to carry great weight with his fellow justices who would realize that Phelips' good opinion of them might well be the *sine qua non* for the smooth exercise of their authority within their jurisdictions. He had displayed more than once the influence that he could wield among the lower orders. He brooked no defiance from them, as Captain Boyse (that "So impudent, so proud, and so insufferable piece of humanity") well knew,[9] as the attorney Trevillian (who refused an apprentice) found out, and as Smith, the Ilchester burgess who defied Sir Robert's control of that borough, learned when forced by Council's order to publicly apologize to Sir Robert. There were other instances, too numerous to mention here, when a lesser gentleman was obliged to give Phelips public satisfaction or lost a place of some honor through questioning that magnate's authority. But it was not primarily through fear that

[7] BM, Royal MS, 17A XXXVII, "An apology of the King's agents for the enclosure of Kinges Sedgmoore in the county of Somerset." The author of this tract could not have had Sir Robert in mind, but the description was strikingly apt!

[8] SRO, Phelips MSS, vol. A, f. 93, draft brief for use against Lord Poulett and/or Sir John Stawell before the PC [Oct. 1628].

[9] SRO, Phelips MSS, vol. A, ff. 145 *et seq.*, Phelips to PC, 14 Jan. 1632/3.

Phelips gained the support of what appears to have been a remarkable cross section of the county's folk. It was through readiness to receive their petitions, take up the individual's cause and give such a voice to it that the lords of the Council as well as the justices of the county bench could not ignore it. In this era, when many individual causes and grievances coalesced into a formidable opposition, Sir Robert Phelips found the greatest opportunity to enhance his reputation among his countrymen.

Not for Lord Poulett and Sir John Stawell the pursuit of the plaudits of the "common people." The treatment they accorded their lesser neighbors was like in kind, if not in degree, to that accorded the sheriff's bailiff pressed for Ré by Stawell to gratify his own hatred for the sheriff and Phelips.[10] The browbeaten constables and the threatened trained band soldiers who came between the combatants and suffered at the hands of Poulett and Stawell bore witness to the contemptuousness with which that pair regarded the good opinion of their lesser countrymen. This indifference to their local reputation hardly injured their position, for Phelips had already captured the allegiance of the lesser folk. To Poulett and Stawell, the most fertile soils in which to sow the seeds for power were the Court and Council. The cheddar cheese for Secretary Conway, the shrewd appraisal of the widow Hele for the matrimonially inclined Secretary Dorchester, and Poulett's nauseatingly obsequious letter of grief at the Queen's miscarriage were the very careful cultivation of that soil by two master gardeners. Never, though, did they lose sight of the end, supremacy in the county. This they hoped would come from the enhancement of their prestige, particularly among the magisterial class, by the visible manifestation of his Majesty's favor and the Council's regard. At least, within the limits of Poulett's gout-induced laziness and Stawell's choleric unevenness of temper, both made a show of earning their reward. But the slackness discernible within the militia—that aspect of government which, after all, was most directly their concern and within their authority—hardly bore out Poulett's peroration in his letters to the lord lieutenant that he desired only to serve him faithfully. Poulett and Stawell, no less than Phelips, were out only to serve themselves. None the less, their profuse expressions of good affection for the King's service did cover up many of their omissions in executing it. In an era when

---

[10] *Acts PC*, 1627, p. 453, PC to JJ assize Western Circuit, 27 July 1627; PRO, S.P.16/27, no. 47, JPs of Somerset to PC, 31 July 1627.

King and Council were particularly concerned that that service should be carried to an unprecedented level of efficiency, Lord Poulett and Sir John Stawell had reason to believe that they had hit upon the way to Charles' heart.

Given another age and perhaps another king, this battle for supremacy in the county in which the two opponents fought according to two different strategies would not have been so disastrous. Either Court or country was a legitimate means to local ascendancy. However, in a decade and a half that witnessed a divergence between the King and the nation widening with phenomenal rapidity, the strategy for attaining power in the county that was based on direct appeal to the countryman was far more likely to be efficacious. As well, by emphasizing, defining, and advancing the breach it was sure to do infinite damage to the King's interest and the King's service.

It was as far from Sir Robert Phelips' intention to cripple that service as it was from Lord Poulett's and Sir John Stawell's intention to take any great pains to forward it. All three were indifferent to that service and likewise indifferent to the consequences to the service of their acts. They were opportunists. Poulett and Stawell did not scruple to jettison the King's interest when it served their ends. Affection for the service could never have included Lord Poulett's acquiescence in, if not active aid to, the organization of opposition to the disafforestation of Neroche. His lordship was aware only of the loss of his hunting; he was apathetic to his King's enrichment. Nor would the King's truly dutiful subjects connive with a disobedient judge of assize to petition for the suppression of churchales after the King had expressed his firm resolve to allow them. Poulett and Stawell with Chief Justice Richardson assumed the lead in this, not from any sympathy for puritan distaste for these rowdy gatherings nor from any concern for the preservation of order. Sir Robert Phelips had taken his revenge on the judge for having dismissed the case against Captain Boyse the previous year by informing the King and Council of the judge's insubordination in not suppressing churchales.[11] As the King's letter to Phelips and two friendly justices requiring an account of Richardson's carriage was a mark of royal favor, so it mad-

---

[11] The petition was drafted and the justices invited to sign it in the judge's chambers, by Richardson, CJKB, at the assizes where he had grudgingly revoked the former order prohibiting churchales, saying some unpleasant things about Phelips in the process, T. G. Barnes, "County Politics and a Puritan Cause Célèbre: Somerset Churchales,1633," *Trans RHS* (1959), 5th series, IX, 116.

dened Poulett and Stawell to an action that ill-became the self-styled champions of the "King's interest."

Neither did Phelips scruple to retreat from his apparent intransigence to royal policy in order to play the courtier when it suited his own interests. From the latter part of 1628 until early 1635, it was a very mild Robert Phelips who approached his magisterial duties. What ferocity he exhibited was reserved for those who like attorney Trevillian refused an apprentice, the unquiet spirits intent on preventing the enclosure of Aldermoor, and the disobedient Chief Justice Richardson—all persons, who in Phelips's vocabulary at this stage of his career, "factiously... [distract] ... the unitie and peace of this countie".[12] That the Book of Orders was applied so expeditiously throughout the county as well as in his own division owed something to Phelips. The Council thought so, and its commendatory letters must have given him solid satisfaction. This sudden change of tactics was dictated by the blow to his power that was his loss of all local office between 1626 and 1628, his imprisonment in the Tower for animosity exhibited in the third Parliament, and his consequent loss of all influence at Whitehall. Phelips could not afford to be as indifferent of his reputation at Court as Poulett and Stawell were of theirs in the county. If he was to attain ascendancy in the county, it was necessary for Phelips to retain both the favor of the King and Council and the good opinion of his countrymen. While there was not the remotest possibility of attaining supremacy without enjoying both the offices of justice of the peace and deputy lieutenant, such offices alone would not compel the allegiance of his countrymen if he was not receptive to their aspirations. In his actions, Phelips had to strike a balance, a painstaking balance evident even to his enemies, for as Poulett remarked:

> [Phelips'] ends are to gain a double reputation,... one above by pretendinge good affeccions to the service, another here by shewinge his dislikes against itt, the common people being vanely disposed to applaud any man... unwilling to lay burthens upon them....[13]

The widening breach between King and country made this balancing act infinitely difficult, but Phelips did not fall into the chasm save in those two bleak years when he had lost all favor at Whitehall. That he did not

[12] SRO, Phelips MSS, vol. A, f. 131, Phelips to King 18 Aug. 1633. Phelips was referring to Richardson's incitement of the justices to petition against churchales.

[13] SRO, Phelips MSS, vol. A, ff. 34–35, Poulett and five other DLs to the Earl of Pembroke and Montgomery, 3 Oct. 1636.

tumble between 1628 and 1635 (though he was in danger of his left foot slipping this time) was because those years were peculiarly free of royal projects likely to evoke the opposition which Phelips could not avoid leading if he was to preserve his local reputation and retain his countrymen's allegiance. During his "quiet" period, Phelips' furtherance of the King's interest was fortuitously confined to his activities in the enclosure schemes, his support of churchales, and his diligence in executing the Book of Orders. None of these projects raised a storm of opposition and in the only one that threatened to—Sedgemoor—he and his brother commissioners stepped circumspectly. Phelips felt that the calculated risk of offending a few was worth it, because when he emerged from the wilderness in 1628 he determined never to return. In the latter part of that year he was released from the Tower, readmitted to his forfeited offices, and vindicated by the King and Council for earlier having questioned the sufficiency of the deputies' warrants for musters. As well, he had the pleasure of seeing judgment in Star Chamber against Stawell for an assault on the sheriff at the 1628 county election which had returned Phelips and rejected Stawell.[14] These were all gratifying marks of royal forgiveness and they offered Phelips a chance to begin the long climb back into royal favor. The next six years were given over to building up such a reservoir of goodwill at Whitehall that when, in 1635, he once more challenged his opponents and made a bid for the county's allegiance by leading the opposition, he had a well-protected flank. But it was no affection for the King's interest that induced Sir Robert Phelips to act the part of the dutiful magistrate between 1632 and 1635 any more than it was a dislike of it that impelled him to play a far different role in the years that followed.

The exceptional parliamentary career that Phelips enjoyed was both a manifestation of his desire for a wider fame than supremacy in the county alone could afford him and a means by which he could advance his reputation in the county. At Westminster during the 1620s Phelips was in the vanguard of opposition to royal policy as he was in the county then and later. His motive was the same in both forums; in neither did it

[14] The £200 fine was respited by the Privy Council in Star Chamber, which Poulett over-optimistically took for a victory and a rout of Phelips considering that Stawell had been convicted and that the suspension of fines in Star Chamber was not unusual, PRO, S.P.16/153, no. 54, Poulett to Sec. Dorchester, 14 Dec. 1629; 232, no. 43, mitigation agenda in Star Chamber, Hil. 8 Chas. I. If Stawell hoped that in time the postponed fine would be forgotten, he was disabused in Feb. 1634/5 when it was estreated into the Exchequer for levying, PRO, E.159/474, Hil. 10 Chas. I, rot. 57.

comprise any deeply held conviction that he must defend the rights and liberties of Parliament and the people. Phelips was a politician and politics was almost an end in itself for him. As a member of every Parliament from 1603/4, save that for 1625/6 when he had been excluded by being pricked for sheriff, Phelips indulged to the full his penchant for parliamentary politics. He gloried in the role of parliamentarian, and while he played it threw all his customary energy into perfecting his performance, even to the extent of making the Rotuli Parliamentorum his vacation reading.[15] It was in the Parliament of 1620/1 that he first tasted a greater glory than that allowed most of his fellow members. During that Parliament's brief life, he stepped forward as the chief harrier of Mompesson and Bacon, and there first gathered behind him those other members who throughout the 1620s moved further and further into diametric opposition to royal policy. He appears to have gloried even more in the resultant martyrdom of spending the better part of 1621 in the Tower. James' last Parliament witnessed Phelips on the threshold of unshared leadership of the Commons. In the first of Charles, he blossomed forth as the premier spokesman of the opposition. At the Oxford session, "he virtually assumed that unacknowledged leadership which was all that the traditions of Parliament at that time permitted."[16] It is not to depreciate this handsome compliment of Gardiner nor is it to undervalue the tremendous import of Phelips' leadership in that Parliament to stress that Phelips was not an Eliot. He was a country gentleman of more than ordinary intellect with a flair for leadership and abundant egotism, but he was not then, nor was he ever to become, the courageous and selfless defender of the subject's liberty and the Parliament's privilege that was John Eliot. It was more than the accident of Phelips' exclusion from the next Parliament that left to Eliot the leadership in the last Parliament before the "personal rule." Phelips was incapable of leading so far, so rapidly as Eliot directed the House then. Throughout his parliamentary career, Phelips was always glancing over his shoulder to the countryside beyond St. Stephen's, more particularly to the countryside between the Blackdowns and the Severn Sea. He was too conscious of the effect of his words at Westminster upon his countrymen at home to advance so far that his popularity might be forfeited rather than enhanced. Receptive to the voices of his countrymen, he could not evade the limitations those

15 BM, Cotton MS, Jul. C. III, f. 294, Phelips to Sir Robert Cotton [early 1620s].
16 Gardiner, V, 432.

voices imposed. Parliament was real, parliamentary leadership earnest. Though Phelips would not have denied this, he was wholly incapable of realizing that forces were at work that made parliamentary politics something more than a zestful game and a chance to grasp at greater fame than county life allowed. There was very little of the idealist in Sir Robert Phelips, for he seldom dealt in ideals but only in the realism of politicking. That was his lifeblood; not the sentiments bound up in the words, liberty and privilege. In realizing this we avoid echoing Gardiner's veiled note of disapprobation at Phelips' apparent apostasy in 1629. Apostasy requires the abandonment of principles. Sir Robert Phelips abandoned no principles because he hardly possessed any higher than the gratification of his own yearning for excitement, power, and fame.[17]

Both the apparent imminence and the total absence of a Parliament during the 1630s increased to an incalculable degree the ferocity of the antagonists' warfare and the surge of Phelips' bid for supremacy in the county. The seeming imminence of the Parliament just-around-the-corner pitched higher the perpetual competition between Phelips and Stawell for the monopoly of the county seats. That competition gave a sharp edge to the swords with which they thrust at each other during the 1630s in swiftly multiplying flurries of blows. The absence of Parliament increased the potency of Phelips' bid for supremacy by allowing him for the first time to channel all his energies into the leadership of opposition at home without demanding that his leadership be spread over both the Commons and the county. The absence of Parliament also removed the stage which had given his yearning for excitement and fame an incomparable outlet during the previous decade. This yearning and his desire for supremacy in the county combined to place him in the vanguard of his countrymen who were at enmity with the novel and burdensome projects which dominated domestic policy during the last five years of the 1630s.

The calm was definitely ended when the first ship money sheriff made the first excessive assessment under the first writ of ship money. The

---

[17] Gardiner spoke of Phelips inclining more towards the King's interest after 1629, *Ibid.*, VII, 319. The documentary evidence necessary to place a member of Parliament against the background of his community and thus grasp the truth of his character was not available to the nineteenth century historian. The work of Sir John Neale in the Elizabethan and Prof. Wallace Notestein in the early Stuart periods goes a long way towards remedying that defect.

petition of 7 May 1635 by Phelips and the other inhabitants of Tintinhull against Henry Hodges' newly imposed assessment launched Phelips on a course of opposition halted only by his death three years later. This was Phelips, his "countries only freinde," turning the antipathy of his lesser neighbors to his own advantage by giving it a powerful and reasonable voice, a voice that by appealing for justice could not fail to be heard at Whitehall. Within a few months he had taken another irrevocable step, which shattered the uneasy truce between the antagonists that had barely existed since 1628, cracked badly by their difference over churchales and the dismissal of Captain Boyse. When John Coventrye, at the instigation of Phelips, rose at the midsummer sessions 1635 to attack the deputies' peremptory orders for assistance from the justices, the signal was given for the commencement of the final and climactic struggles between the antagonists. However, in the year that followed Phelips' disruptive activity was confined to ship money and to stirring up his neighbors to refuse assistance to the saltpeter makers.[18] Not until the summer of 1636 did Phelips touch off the conflict by informing the lord lieutenant that Poulett had mustered his regiment in his division without notifying him. The retaliatory arrest of Spracklinge by Poulett and Stawell to refire the old dispute that had lain dormant since 1628 joined the issue. The lord lieutenant's vindication of Phelips and the pawn, Spracklinge, proved the true climax of a desperate rivalry. But it was more. Since the 1628 affair, when Phelips had channelled the countrymen's grievances against coat and conduct money and billeting into alliance with him against his rivals, nothing that the deputies had done in the meantime had lessened the sense of those grievances. Rather, the countrymen's animosity towards all things connected with the militia had increased. In 1636 as in 1628 Phelips realized that the temper of the county was such that a well planned, deftly executed attack on his enemies would enhance his prestige within the county by evidencing his concern for the county's interest. The attack in 1636 had the desired result. The last writhing of his defeated opponents—Stawell's complaint that Phelips stirred up trouble against 1636 ship money—proved Phelips' success in his double object. The Council's order was the *coup de grâce*

---

[18] Phelips' incitements of his neighbors in the early summer of 1636 effectively halted the saltpeter operations in that area. As always, he justified his action on technical grounds, having told the saltpeter contractor (a rather unsavory character) that he, Phelips, "would answer . . . for his neighbours'" refusal, PRO, S.P.16/328, no. 31, Phelips to Edward Nicholas, 5 July 1636.

to Sir John Stawell (and, in effect, to Lord Poulett), and the attack on ship money by Sir Robert Phelips that had given rise to it earned for him the ultimate measure of popularity among his countrymen. Sir Robert Phelips had only a few months to enjoy it, but he wore then the long robe of supremacy.

Why did Phelips win? There is something to be learned from the answer to that question. That the will of his countrymen lay in the palm of his hand requires hardly more explanation than the repetition of Lord Poulett's statement that "the common people . . . [are] vanely disposed to applaud any man whom they find unwilling to lay burthens upon them though never soe reasonable and necessary."[19] All that need be added is that the burdens imposed in this period appeared neither reasonable nor necessary. Yet, the rout of Phelips' opponents was accomplished through King and Council, who were particularly unreceptive to power derived from mobilized opinion. With the possible exception of Coventrye's attack in 1635, all the disputes between the antagonists came to the Council's attention; most of them ended with a hearing at the Board. That Phelips was always vindicated and the ostensible supporters of the King's interest censured resulted from neither the Council's myopia nor its unjustness. Quite the contrary. The Council was more perceptive in its investigation and more just in its findings in these causes than in many other matters that came before it. It accepted the disputes for what they were: furious engagements in a long battle for ascendancy in the county. The councillors looked at Sir Robert Phelips and Lord Poulett and saw in them the motivation towards power which differed none at all from their own desires. They could perceive in the antagonists' struggles in the county the counterpart of their own struggles at Whitehall. They were not mistaken in what they saw. The moderateness of Phelips' attack, his careful avoidance of any greater issue, and his past tokens of loyalty recommended his case to the Council. There was no hint that the King's service was under attack, which indeed as such it was not. Therefore, the Council could not justly censure Phelips by the ultimate dishonor and most drastic punishment of expelling him from office. That punishment was reserved for those against whom a clear case of insubordination or disaffection could be made out, not those magnates, aggressive though they were, who limited their aggression to their recognized enemies. Though it vaguely realized the harmful effects

[19] SRO, Phelips MSS, vol. A, ff. 34–35.

of this strife on royal policy, the Council was powerless to halt it. For the Council's position was that of an arbiter, its function to make peace. All that it could do was to exhort the antagonists to lay aside their quarrels and to apportion censure among them according to the degree to which they had broken the rules of the game. It was Phelips' consummate ability to control his every act and statement, to present his case with lucidity and compelling logic that in part assured that all censure would fall upon his opponents. They took care of the other part. The lies, the trumped-up evidence, the browbeaten and perjured witnesses, the choleric and arbitrary acts which were the tactics of Lord Poulett and his minion made a sorry spectacle before the Board. That spectacle determined every finding. In the light of it, Poulett's and Stawell's professions of their love and affection for the King's service carried no more weight with their lordships than did their extreme attacks on Phelips' loyalty and integrity. Both parties had dirty hands, but the Council was not blind to whose were the dirtier.

If the King's service was not itself in question, by being caught in the crossfire of the antagonists battling for supremacy in the county it received the most grievous injury. The King's service depended upon the effectiveness with which the King's government in the counties administered it. The struggle for county power, by disrupting that administration, struck at the very vitals of the service.

Each opportunity grasped by Sir Robert Phelips to advance his reputation among his neighbors by venting their hostility to royal projects opened wider the awful gulf that stretched between the King and his people. The free gift, coat and conduct money, billeting, the militia, and ship money all suffered from the marriage of Phelips' ambition with his countrymen's grievances. Phelips was not the creator of opposition; he was its creature. Sensitively attuned to what the yeomen and lesser gentlemen thought and felt, profoundly aware of how far he could lead them before they would turn back or the Council strike him down, Phelips amplified the opposition. His position gave it an authority which it otherwise would not have had, which gained supporters for the cause and channelled the opposition to strike forcefully those local governors and their subordinates charged with perfecting the project in hand. The justice busy wheedling a benevolence from his neighbors, a sheriff working feverishly to collect ship money, a deputy attempting to keep up the strength of the trained bands felt that opposition and could not avoid slowing in his endeavors, be it only in some small measure. The constables and tithingmen recoiled beneath it and stopped altogether. Slowness and stoppage took a dreadful toll of the King's service.

Though it is difficult to calculate just how great a toll was taken thanks to Phelips' leadership of the opposition, the effect of his repeated successes against his opponents can almost be measured by counting heads. In 1640, when they were needed as they had never been needed before, six deputy lieutenants drew back, excused themselves, and avoided the service. Lord Poulett and Sir John Stawell were not only among them, but probably were responsible for confirming the others in their reluctance. Too often during the 1630s they had suffered defeat at the hands of Sir Robert Phelips for them to have retained what little genuine affection for the service they had once possessed. What other motives and other pressures were upon them tending to push them into that shiftless course, we will probably never know. But the damage wrought at Phelips' hands in the previous decade might well have been the deciding factor.

The struggle for supremacy in the county was not fought in a vacuum. It was fought within the framework of local government, between two local governors whose object was the dominance of local government. Since supremacy comprised in part the recognition of the other local governors, each antagonist appealed for the support of his brothers of the rural bench and lieutenancy. These appeals could not be ignored save by the few who, like John Harington, were capable of the greatest impartiality and devotion to duty. Such men were certainly few; to a lesser or greater extent, most of the local governors made one cause or the other their own. Friendship, ambition, family ties, animosity, ignorance, and weakness all played their part in enticing the majority of local governors into one camp or the other. Sometimes the allegiance was transitory. More often it was firm, and such was the rancor of the struggle, few men were inclined to cross over. Sir Robert Phelips could always muster in his ranks "my best friend," John Coventrye, his fervent supporter and old friend, Sir Henry Berkeley, and usually his associate of Parliament days, John Symes.[20] Robert Harbyn, who owed his justiceship to Phelips, and

[20] *Somerset Enrolled Deeds, 1536–1655*, p. 273. Phelips so alluded to Coventrye in appointing him arbiter between the trustees (including Sir Henry Berkeley) in a conveyance for the posthumous satisfaction of his debts, dated 10 April 1638, just three days before his death. He named Sir Robert Gorge, JP, Berkeley, and Symes as trustees for lands conveyed to his second son, 1630, PRO, C.142/571/157, Phelips' inquisition post mortem.

the gentle Thomas Lyte upon whom Phelips had a like claim as well as that of genuine affection were no less constant, though the latter was not a politician by nature. Thomas Brereton, whose diligence in the Neroche disafforestation earned him the not untrue though none the less slighting characterization by Poulett of a "right contrye justice, a simple man,"[21] had good cause to support Sir Robert on occasion. Equally unpleasant treatment by Poulett placed George Browne in Phelips' camp. Thomas Wyndham was sufficiently close to Phelips to have been the immediate recipient of Stawell's malice in pressing his bailiff for Ré. To judge by Sir Charles Berkeley's neutrality in the lieutenancy disputes and his readiness to follow Phelips' and his uncle's example in leading opposition to ship money, he was not unsympathetic to Phelips. The Lord Poulett's supporters while not so many in number were powerful in influence. Besides his lieutenant and alter ego, Sir John Stawell, his cousin, William Walrond, and on occasion the powerful landowner, Sir William Portman, Bart., were active in his support as deputies. Sir Edward Rodney affiliated himself wholly with this faction. Poulett could count on the regular support of most of the deputies and Phelips on only one—not surprising, considering that though Phelips aimed at Poulett and Stawell, his fire unavoidably hit the other active deputies. Indeed, it was the fact that Phelips looked for support to the justices who were not also deputies that made so disastrous the cleavage among the local governors. The attack of Phelips through Coventrye in 1635 was a clear bid for the unanimous support of the rural bench against his opponents who were deputies. While it would be dangerous to state firmly how deep the wedge was driven, that bid could not help but have had a divisive effect upon the relationship between the two groups of officers.

The struggle had a far more subtle, more basic effect as well. It permanently damaged the fabric of county government by rupturing the unity of endeavor which was essential to the smooth working of the institutions that composed county government. The relations between these men were poisoned by the polemics and excesses with which the factions waged war. The potency of the forces of polarization at work in this disrupted atmosphere is well illustrated in the cases of two magistrates who, against their wills and in contradistinction to their usual neutrality, were sucked into the conflict on occasion. Dr. Paul Godwyn, the reverend gentleman

[21] PRO, S.P.16/195, no. 12, Poulett to Sec. Dorchester, 27 June 1631.

who was an exceptionally conscientious magistrate, wrote Phelips that he would testify against Captain Boyse though he preferred not to.[22] It was not fear of Poulett that inspired reluctance in Godwyn, but a sincere desire to stay out of the conflict. More significant yet was the one occasion (in 1636) when the self-effacing and diligent Sir Ralph Hopton was forced to take a minor though distasteful part on Poulett's side in the last great dispute. Hopton was far above faction, but he could not avoid involvement when faction enveloped the whole of county government. A house divided cannot stand; an institution divided cannot function. Somerset's government was far too divided for its own health.

Sir Robert Phelips died on 13 April 1638. He had fought many battles and had won all. He had attained a measure of ascendancy in the county and fame in the nation denied to many other men. But in his climb to power he had done infinite damage to the institutions which, with his associates, it was his first duty to preserve. If his guilt was shared with his antagonists, that did not repair the damage done.

[22] SRO, Phelips MSS, vol. A, f. 144, copy of affidavit by Dr Paul Godwyn, JP [1632/3].

Chapter XI ❧ *Conclusion*

Few who write of an institution so continuous in its existence and so prosaic in its function as local government find themselves fortunate enough to possess a point of climax with which to conclude. Without straining or imposing an artificial frame on events, one writing of local government in these brief sixteen years has a ready terminus in the disorders of 1640. In local government, as in so many other areas of England's life, that year marked the end of an era, and if the beginning of the new one did not follow immediately there could be no mistaking the end of the old. The ambitious programs begun during the "personal rule" ceased abruptly, and with them ended the government's pressure that had been the dominant feature in the public life of the country gentlemen charged with county administration. Yet this year was truly a climax as well as a terminus, for in it the pressure of the government and the opposition to the program bore more heavily on the administrators than at any time previously. The crescendo of activity in local government that had begun with the King's accession ended abruptly on its highest note on the eve of the fateful Parliament which was ultimately to destroy the King.

In the case of the justices of the peace, the augmentation of labor had been gradual enough. Apparent from the summer of 1625 was the sudden though elusively subtle quickening of the justices in their normal round of magisterial duties. The forced loan of 1626–1627 with its apparatus of divisional meetings and reports brought for the first time the continuous direct stimulation of the justices by strong conciliar letters, even by the intrusion of the councillors into the counties. After the forced loan ended some of the stimulus remained and the sessions records indicate that the three years preceding the Book of Orders were marked by a greater activity on the justices' part than hitherto. It was the Book, though, that coordinated this activity. While making the routine of the justices more effective, it made their responsibilities infinitely more time-consuming and wearisome. Throughout the 1630s the program enjoined by the Book of Orders continued, and the Council through the judges' agency never lessened its demand for the more efficient administration of the whole of the statute law that fell within the justices' cognizance. All other tasks devolving upon the justices in the 1630s—under the improvement schemes, from the referrals of judges and Council, and especially from ship money—were supplementary to the work under the new, heightened routine. When the labor of the justices reached its climax in 1640 the superstructure of their work rested on the very different foundations of magistracy organized and operating in accordance with the Book of Orders.

While 1625 meant for the justices as a whole an acceleration in their normal activities not ordained from above but rather growing out of the reinvigorated atmosphere accompanying a new and younger monarch, it had meant for those of them who were also deputy lieutenants a sudden involvement in wholly unfamiliar tasks under the taskmaster of a government bent on prosecuting war. Preparedness against invasion, preparations for two overseas expeditions, the thankless tasks connected with their aftermath, and the perfecting of the militia had demanded more of the deputies' time and energy in the first five years of the new reign than had been required in the preceding quarter century; this was hardly a period of *gradual* augmentation of their duties. Nor had the opposition to the deputies' activities failed to appear with like abruptness. Both in the intensity with which the government applied and increased its constantly reiterated demand for more effectual labor on the deputies' part and in the mounting animosity that their activities evoked the deputies had a foretaste of what would befall them in 1640. That in the years following the end of the war they took so few pains to perfect the militia testified to the effectiveness of the opposition's continuing campaign as well as to their own lack of enthusiasm and their preoccupation with the struggle for county supremacy.

The sheriff waited somewhat longer for his call to greater service. Though not wholly ignored in the Book of Orders (he was the vehicle for the justices' reports to the judges) the sheriff before 1634 carried on in the same pedestrian manner the hardly onerous business long normal to his office. It was the writ of ship money that made grievous an office which hitherto had been merely irksome. Probably no other officer felt so forcibly the government's importunity, inasmuch as the sheriff stood solely responsible for procuring a vitally necessary revenue which an increasing number of his countrymen refused to provide. At the same time, he fell into the hands of commissioners appointed to compound with him and his brethren in other counties for offences which, though contrary to the law, had long been common practice.[1] This unwanted new attention and the relentless demand of the Council for ship money growing apace with the county's refusal to pay it pressed on the sheriffs between 1634 and 1640 with a weight almost unparalleled in the long history of that office. Fighting the opposition singlehandedly, desperately attempting to avoid the council's strictures, and falling hopelessly into arrears, this was the inevitable lot of the ship-money sheriff—not for just one year, but for three, four, or even five years.

For the two-score gentlemen who served in county offices during the 1630s, the "personal rule" entailed more hard work of an increasingly disagreeable nature under a stricter master than they, their fathers, or even their grandfathers had ever known.

There is ample evidence of just how burdensome county office had become, some of it contained in the county's records. It was no accident that from 1630 onwards the two annually appointed treasurers for the hospital funds were increasingly drawn from gentlemen not on the bench. Of the eight treasurers for the years 1634 through 1638 (the records are deficient after the latter date), only one was a justice. These treasurerships, never popular with the justices though hitherto grudgingly borne by them, were intolerably annoying to magistrates saddled with the increased labor, both in and out of sessions, required by the Book of Orders. They were glad to be rid of them, and so long as the laymen appointed passed proper accounts the bench was satisfied. Though the avoidance of these posts by the magistrates only slightly eased their

---

[1] PRO, C.66/2706, dorse, commission to Sir David Cunningham, Bart., *et al.* to compound with sheriffs and undersheriffs, 12 Aug. 1635. The offences, for which if the sheriffs compounded they would not be prosecuted in Star Chamber, included the undersheriff serving two successive sheriffs, which while technically a misdemeanor was a very common practice. Henry Hodges, the sheriff for 1634 and 1635 ship money, was much troubled by the commissioners though probably not without good cause. Undersheriffs had been under sporadic investigation by the commissioners for fees since 1627, though I cannot find after a careful search of the commissioners' minute books, 1627–1636 (PRO, E.165/46–49), indication that any Somerset undersheriff was proceeded against.

burden, their motive in shifting them to others was plain. In another way the county's records are even more revealing. The sessions rolls, comprising the multitudinous records of both the clerks to the justices and the clerk of the peace, cover the full range of magisterial activity and bear the imprint of the whole clerical organization at all levels of magistracy. There is a hiatus in one class of these rolls between the Michaelmas sessions 1635 and the Epiphany sessions 1638/9. When the student leaves the roll for 1635, he puts down a collection of documents drafted with some care, tidiness, and uniformity. Turning to the roll for 1638/9, he is amazed by the contrast between it and the last one he has handled. The orders and notes are scrawled, there are numerous scratchouts and a general lack of uniformity, the whole appearing to have been carelessly drafted in great haste. The contrast is striking because of the absence of documents in the intervening period; had they been preserved, the deterioration in the clerks' standards would not have been so startlingly obtrusive. The reason for this deterioration lay in the increased tempo of magistracy directed by the Book of Orders. The hand of the Council pressed on the justice's shoulder and his on the clerk's and the clerk's on the paper, leaving behind indelible proof of the weight of the Council's demand and to the justices' zeal in implementing it.[2]

At least one magistrate made no secret of how unwelcome the increased burden of his duties was to him. His complaint was penned in 1626, before the forced loan, the Book of Orders, and ship money, which provides even better insight into how wearisome the office of justice must have become in the years that followed. William Capell was a conscientious justice of long tenure, not allied with faction either local or national, and not given to extravagant comment. This letter, dated from his seat at Wrington, 28 April 1626, was addressed to his old friend and fellow justice, Robert Hopton:

> Sir, I am bold to continue my humble request unto you and ye rest of ye commissioners [for subsidies], yt I may not be raysed in ye subsidy; I shall be gladd yt it may be an occasion to putt mee out of ye comission [of the peace]. I am weary of ye burden & charge of it allredy, especially nowe there is none in ye division but myself. It is sessions with mee every day all ye day longe heere, yt I have

---

[2] SRO, Sess Rolls, 73 pt. i, no. 78. The rolls of examinations of criminals taken before justices out of sessions, drafted by the justices' clerks, are complete for this interval, and show similar decay in clerical standards.

noe time for my owne occasions hardly to putt meate into my mouth, and to adde this of ye subsidy is unmercifull. The letters would bestowe ye blessing of Ishachar upon us justices.[3]

What would Capell have said towards the end of the "personal rule"?

This question unfortunately must go unanswered, for though Capell served diligently as a justice into the 1640s no other utterance of this nature is recorded from him. Others, however, expressed then in deeds and words what he had said before. Protest at the burden of work was implicit in the refusal of Lord Poulett, Sir John Stawell, and all but three of the other available deputy lieutenants to undertake the county's commitments for the Scots war in 1640. It was explicit in the outspoken and spirited apologia the three active deputies wrote the lord lieutenant in July of that year. They had paid £100 from their own pockets in a vain attempt to pacify their mutinous troops, and had been five weeks away from their homes and families.[4] Sir Francis Rogers and John Preston, two healthy young justices, gave vent to it when they resigned from the commission of the peace in 1636 and 1640 respectively, twice causing the clerk of the Crown in Chancery to insert in his docket book the entry, omitted "att his owne request."[5]

The most striking testimony to the weight of county office during the "personal rule" was the refusal of gentlemen to undertake it. From 1635 there was a steady decline in the number of justices. Over the following five years this resulted in a net loss of ten magistrates, leaving five of the county's twelve divisions seriously undermanned and their petty sessions in danger of extinction. The decline was occasioned by the death of justice after justice, most of whom had served since James' reign and all of whom would probably have retired earlier had they not been indispensable in their divisions. Few stepped in to fill their seats on the

---

[3] SRO, Sess Rolls, 56 pt. i, no. 66. "Issachar is a strong ass couching down between two burdens: And he saw that rest was good, and the land that it was pleasant; and bowed his shoulder to bear, and became a servant unto tribute." Genesis, xlix, 14–15. Capell's complaint that he was alone in the division was quite true—and he remained alone there throughout the period, see map on p. 41, division 7.

[4] PRO, S.P.16/455, no. 6, Sir Thomas Wrothe, Thomas Luttrell, and John Symes, DLs, to Lds Lts of Somerset, 26 May 1640.

[5] PRO, Index 4212, commissions of the peace for Somerset, 1 July 1636 and 17 July 1640. These words had not before appeared in docket entries for Somerset, though justices had been expelled for political reasons and for failure to take the oaths and a number of aged ones had retired—these latter waiting until a new commission was about to be issued and a new man appointed in the division before asking to be omitted, rather than importunately requesting immediate retirement as was apparently the case with Rogers and Preston.

11+

bench; this in marked contrast to the 1620s. On Charles' accession the
first commission had, out of respect to the county's gentry, contained the
names of all former justices and a few new men as well, By the end
of 1625 the justices' numbers had been considerably reduced, a great many
aging magistrates apparently having taken the opportunity of the change
in government to retire. There was no difficulty experienced in securing
new men to fill the vacancies, and each commission added one or two
until by 1635 there were nearly as many as there had been in the King's
first commission.

After 1635 new justices were exceedingly difficult to find, either from
among the heirs of dying justices of magnate rank or from among the
newer gentlemen who had once been so eager for county office. For the
first time the almost invariable pattern of magnates' sons succeeding to
their fathers' places was broken. Prior to 1635 there was apparently not
a single case of a magnate's heir able to sit on the bench who had failed
to do so, either immediately preceding or shortly following his father's
withdrawal. In the last five years of this period four such heirs, fully
qualified in wealth, age, and political reliability, avoided an honor and
an obligation to which men of their station succeeded almost as automatically as they succeeded to their patrimonies. One other resigned
his commission within a year of his father's death. It was ironical that
the heir of the good justice, Sir Thomas Wyndham, should be included
among these. The last words of the dying magistrate to him and his
four brothers were:

> My sons! We have hitherto seen serene and quiet times; but now pre-
> pare yourselves for cloudy and troublesome. I command you to honour
> and obey your sovereign, and in all times to adhere to the Crown; and
> though the Crown should hang upon a bush, I charge you to forsake
> it not.[6]

Though three of these young men were destined to die for their sovereign,
in 1635 none of them was willing to carry on his service, which their
father had so faithfully advanced for nearly twenty years.

The reluctance of the magnates' sons was matched by that of the lesser
gentlemen who, though they had no prescriptive right to the justice's
chair, had eagerly sought it in years gone by for the recognition it

[6] Wyndham, I, 188–189. The heir, Edmund Wyndham, sat for Bridgwater in the Long
Parliament. He was a gentleman of the King's privy chamber at this time, though that was
not enough to explain his absence from the commission of the peace.

accorded of a more exalted status. There can be no doubt that the men were available in the divisions where they were so sorely needed. The commission for sewers contained a nearly inexhaustible reservoir of new men of sufficient station who would have discharged the justice's tasks quite ably. These men just did not come forward.

A place on the bench had lost most of its charm for men of any class regarded fit to fill it. Nonetheless, it had not lost any of its advantages. To the gentleman of established lineage it was still the position from which he could exert wider power than mere ownership of land accorded, still the instrument for the exercise of influence that obtained a seat in Parliament and captured the respect of his neighbors. To the gentleman barely of magisterial rank, it remained the hallmark of prestige, the next rung on the ladder of social advancement. But as never before the office of justice was equated with service. Time-serving was a thing of the past for magistrates who had, perforce, to attend to their very heavy petty sessional business or suffer expulsion from office. These considerations alone were enough to discourage many from assuming office, and even men of stronger will blanched before the load they would take up if they were joined in the commission. After all, the programs that made so vastly more time-consuming the justices' duties in the 1630s were programs implemented by officers whose only recompense was the intangible advantages office afforded. Previously, there had existed a favorable relationship between advantages and disadvantages, the former definitely outweighing the latter. It was the Book of Orders and ship money that reversed the position, making the disadvantages loom far larger than they had before—loom large enough to make many gentlemen, magnate's heir and newly-risen squire alike, feel that the office of justice of the peace was just not worth it.

This feeling was not confined to Somerset's gentry. A wholesale purge of justices of the peace in England and Wales who failed to do their duty took place in 1637. At the commencement of the winter assize circuits of 1635/6, writs of *dedimus potestatem* were directed to the judges of assize on all six English circuits and the judges of great sessions on all four Welsh circuits enjoining them to administer the oaths of supremacy, allegiance, and office to all below the rank of baron in the commissions of the peace for the various counties on their circuits.[7] A

[7] PRO, Index 4212, pp. 194 and 201, writs of *dedimus potestatem* tested 20 Feb. 1635/6 and 29 March 1636.

year was given for all justices to take the oaths, that is, to undertake the weighty responsibilities of magistracy, for once he had taken the oaths a magistrate could not avoid petty sessions work. In February 1636/7, the Lord Keeper began a systematic paring away of deadwood in the commissions of the peace. By the end of the year almost four-score justices of the peace of twenty-one counties had been expelled from the commissions of the peace.[8] Somerset, significantly, was not affected; presumably, all her justices attended the judges to be sworn. A purge of justices for this reason seems to have been unprecedented. Equally unprecedented was the unwillingness of so many justices to perform the office.

Had not war put a virtual end to county government, it is possible that the dwindling numbers of magistrates would have effectively crippled it. That, however, is conjecture. What is not is the fact that those who suffered most from the reluctance of men to become justices were the magistrates already laboring to capacity. Death might claim a member of the divisional bench, but the King's service was still there to be done, and those who remained had to do it, like the aging William Capell alone in a large division.

To the weight of magisterial work was added one further load. Not only were county offices unpaid, they were costly as well. This was an era when the government's cupidity reached unprecedented heights, compelling the Council to conjure up novel schemes to satisfy it. The magnitude of taxation, a constant theme in Parliament and the county, was proportionately greater for the local governors than for those they governed. By virtue of the fact he had assumed a county office, the government considered that the justice or deputy was of such financial status as to warrant a higher rate of taxation than those of comparable wealth who were not justices or deputies. True, the assessments to taxes levied according to law were within the power of the local governors in their role as commissioners for subsidies, and one suspects that the yeoman and minor gentlemen who served as raters often erred on the side of leniency in rating their greater neighbors. Subsidies, though, accounted for only a fraction of the money that Charles extracted from the county during these sixteen years. The local governors had little control over the assessments to the financial expedients beginning with the

[8] PRO, Index 4212, pp. 231–281. Sixteen justices only moved for reappointment, attending to be sworn.

privy seal loan in 1625 and ending with the Long Parliament's declaration of ship money's illegality. Even if the Council did not set the rate at which each was to contribute, it watched closely how much a justice or deputy was assessed to these exactions. The instructions to the commissioners for the forced loans (the justices) contained a subtle threat in the injunction that they were to subscribe first to the loan as an example to others.[9] The assessments for this imposition were established by the Council on a scale that automatically placed a local governor in a higher tax range without respect to his actual wealth. Both the earlier privy seal loan and the free gift expected more from the local governors than from others; indeed, the receipts from the latter were probably comprised largely of the justices' money, since they alone paid freely to it. Those justices who had not taken the degree of knighthood as benefited their estates were mulcted most by the compositions for that exaction.[10] The local governors fell greater prey to ship money than did their lesser neighbors, since the Council usually had the assessments to that tax at its fingertips. An assessment of a justice or a deputy too much at variance with those of his neighbors would soon be set right, that is, increased. Too, it was the deputies and the more important justices who received the Lord Keeper's "very effectual" letter in the spring of 1639 demanding a stout contribution to the King and his army encamped on the northern border.[11] That only three out of twenty local governors paid was a remarkable act of defiance which, while unlikely a decade earlier, was only to be expected then of men who had labored long in the King's service and had furnished a good deal of the financial support for it as well.

If the "personal rule" had required of the local governors merely labor of unprecedented magnitude, to be performed under correspondingly powerful pressure from the Council, it would not have borne down upon them with such terrible weight. It meant more. The growing intensity of opposition to the programs set on foot in this period struck hardest the men charged with administering them. Since one among their number in the person of Sir Robert Phelips gave aid and comfort to the

9 PRO, S.P.16/36, no. 43, directions to loan commissioners [Sept. 1626].
10 The commissioners for distraint of knighthood were instructed to allow no justice to compound for less than £25, PRO, E.178/5614-5615. The returns indicate that almost all justices were " moved " to compound for considerably more; the justices were among the highest contributors.
11 See p. 272.

hostile, the destructive effects of the counterattack were multiplied. The damage done was great, not only because opposition required an infinitely greater expenditure of effort to overcome it, but because such opposition divided the local governors from the trunk of their society. The justices, the deputies, and the sheriff were not after all alien agents of a central authority, but rather the natural leaders of a highly compact society who derived their preponderance from identification with their lesser countrymen. The programs of this era and the uncompromising pressure to execute them forced these men to choose between the desires of their neighbors and the demands of their sovereign. Whichever allegiance they chose, they stood to lose by it. Few of them could walk the tightrope upon which Sir Robert Phelips so successfully balanced; few of them were capable of his amoral, indeed, intellectually dishonest approach to this terrible and novel dilemma. Though many of them had sat in the Commons during the 1620s, with scant exception they had sat passively listening to the tumult raised by those who had joined an issue as yet but faintly perceived in the county. After each Parliament they had returned to Somerset apparently unaffected by what they had heard, to take up once more the normal round of magisterial duties. While their neutrality had died in the days of the forced loan and billeting, it was not until ship money appeared that they realized how impossible it was to reconcile two such deeply divergent loyalties. Superficially there was no conflict, for a magistrate was a magistrate, and so long as he held the King's commission he performed the King's service. Inwardly there was a conflict, for a magistrate was a county gentleman, strongly attached to his ever-present countryside, subject to the notions and prejudices that he held in common with his countrymen. It required something more than a seven-to-five judicial decision torturously arrived at to satisfy him that ship money was both legal and politic. Nonetheless, he and most of his fellows kept their doubts to themselves and carried on as they had before. But suppression gave the soul no ease, for these men realized that they were doing violence to their own principles. When 1640 afforded them the opportunity to express publicly their anxiety, their outcry gained in vehemence from the chaos in local government immediately preceding it.

The culmination of the local governors' labor, of the Council's pressure, and of the opposition's animosity came in 1640. The sheriff, in peril of arbitrary retribution, worked feverishly to collect ship money. None would pay it. The deputy lieutenants, alternately cajoled by the Council and threatened with Star Chamber, lived in fear for their lives among the hostile contingents they had raised for the royal army. Those troops deserted, mutinied, murdered, and pillaged. The justices, in the knowledge that any slackness would bring down the wrath of judge and Council, chased after deserters and mutineers and vainly attempted to preserve a peace beyond preservation. Constables would not arrest, the trained bands refused to move against their rebellious fellows, and householders sheltered those who had murdered their officers or left their colors. Local government had very nearly come to a stand-still. All order was lost. The "personal rule" was at an end.

The most momentous Parliament in England's history was convened at Westminster on 3 November 1640. From Somerset, the county and its boroughs, came sixteen gentlemen of whom nine had served as the county's governors during the "personal rule." Only one of these nine was to keep his seat after the issue had become clearly a matter of rebellion against the King. But all nine lent their support to Pym and their voices to the chorus of dissent which, in the first months of the Long Parliament, damned ship money and almost all other royal policies of the past decade. Eight cast votes condemning to death the Earl of Strafford.[12]

In the light of these gentlemen's later allegiance this unanimity, ephemeral though it was, might appear surprising. Doubtless it was born of an unreasoning fear of Strafford and of the passionate belief that the abuses of the previous decade threatening the liberty and property of the subject must be reformed. The foundation of their unanimity, though, was the common experience of many of them who had served as the handmaidens of the "personal rule" and who had witnessed

[12] The nine Somerset MPs who had been Somerset local governors were: Sir John Stawell (County MP; JP and DL throughout); William Bassett (Bath; JP from 1631, sheriff 1636–1637); Sir Ralph Hopton (Wells; JP and DL from 1629); Sir Edward Rodney (Wells; JP and DL throughout); Sir William Portman, Bart. (Taunton; JP from 1629/30, DL from 1636, sheriff 1637–1638); Sir Francis Popham (Minehead; JP throughout, DL c. 1625?–1630 at least); Robert Hunt (Ilchester; JP from 1639/40); Edward Phelips (Ilchester; JP from 1638); Thomas Smyth (Bridgwater, following expulsion of MP in Jan. 1640/1; JP from 1631). John Coventrye, JP from 1634 (custos from 1636) and a DL c. 1637–c. 1639?, sat for Evesham—a Straffordian. Of the Somerset MPs who were also local governors, only Portman voted against Strafford's attainder. Popham became a noted Parliamentarian while all the rest ultimately became strong Royalists, most of them distinguished leaders of that cause.

its destruction in the days of disorder immediately preceding the Parliament.

This common experience had been the labor to execute the Book of Orders, to collect ship money, to perfect the militia. These men had borne the brunt of the most ambitious experiments in governance that the nation had ever seen. They had been stung by conciliar disapprobation; some of them had faced an angry Board and a few had known the anguish of prosecution in the Star Chamber. In them was the frustration that men in command felt who had struggled with the growing hostility which had dogged every step taken to advance the King's service. Each had known the misery of seeing his neighbors' enmity turned against him personally. All had beheld the government's total disorganization in the months preceding, its ferocity in lashing out at those who served it in a futile attempt to avert the catastrophe that had already overtaken it. What they had seen, and more, what they had intimately experienced, raised in them contempt for the system of government and the instruments of that system. For ten years they had had a grandstand view of "personal rule." If the members of the Long Parliament were convinced "not that a few things had gone wrong, but that everything had gone wrong,"[13] certainly those among them who had been local governors knew just how wrong everything was.

Greater issues were at stake in the early weeks of the Long Parliament, and some of the members were aware of them. Yet, the bitterness with which the vast majority of the members struck down Strafford, grasped Laud, and reached out for Finch and Windebank might well have been the bitterness of men who had suffered twice over, who had suffered with the entire nation, who had suffered as their counties' governors in the era of "personal rule."

[13] Gardiner, IX, 218.

Appendix

This is a list of the resident justices of the peace (including peers and
bishops resident in the county), lords and deputy lieutenants, sheriffs, and
judges of assize for the county during this period. The dates of tenure of the
lords lieutenants, sheriffs, and judges of assize are exact. The dates of the
justices of the peace are as exact as the absence of some commissions of the
peace and the Chancery Crown clerk's errors in others will allow; however,
no attempt has been made to determine if a justice was in the commission
before 1613 (the year of the earliest commissions preserved by the clerk of
the peace) and "to end" means to the end of 1640 at least. With a very few
exceptions, the dates of the deputy lieutenants are only approximate. Indeed,
the list of deputies might not be complete, since unlike the appointments of
the other officials listed here there is no record of the deputies' appointments.

Justices of the Peace

BABER, Francis, of Chew Magna	at least 1613 to end
BABER, Dr. John, vicar of Chew Magna	1624/5–1625
BABER, John, recorder of Wells	1625–1631
BARLOW, Dr. Ralph, Dean of Wells	1622–1631
BASSETT, William, of Claverton	1631 to end
BERKELEY, Sir Henry, of Yarlington	1618 to end
BRERETON, Thomas, of Yard in Taunton	1616–1632
BROWNE, George, recorder of Taunton (omitted 1625–1629)	1618–1630
BULL, William, of Shapwick	1629 to end
BURRELL, Abraham, of Shapwick	1629 to end
BUTTON, Sir William, Bart., of Tockenham Crt., Wilts.	1618–1625
BYSSE, James, of Batcombe	at least 1613–1625
CAPELL, William, of Wrington	1616 to end
CAREW, Sir John, of Crowcombe	1628–1636

COLE, Richard, of Nailsea (omitted 1625–1630)   1623 to end
COLLES, John, of Barton Grange in Pitminster   at least 1613–1628
COURTENEY, Sir William, of Combe Sydenham   at least 1613–1625
COVENTRYE, John, of Barton Grange in Pitminster   1634 to end
CUFFE, Robert, of Creech St. Michael (omitted
    1625–1626)   at least 1613–1638
CUFFE, William, of Creech St. Michael   1639/40 to end
CURLE, Walter, Bishop of Bath and Wells   1630–1633

DAVIES, Rice, of Tickenham   1620/1 to end
DODINGTON, Sir Francis, of Barrow Gurney and
    Combe Sydenham   1630 to end

EVERY, William, of Cothay in Kittisford   1624/5 to end
EWENS, Matthew, of North Cadbury   1618–1628

FARWELL, James, of Holbrook in Wincanton
    (omitted 1625–1628)   1623–1636
FARWELL, John, of Hill Bishops nr. Taunton   1625 to end
FRAUNCIS, William, of Combe Florey   1624/5–1636

GODWYN, Dr. Paul, rector of Kingweston   1623 to end
GORGE, Sir Ferdinando, of Long Ashton   1629 to end
GORGE, Sir Robert, of Redlinch (omitted 1625–1626)   1625 to end
GORGES, Sir Robert, of Wraxhall   1631–1636
GYLL, Sir John, of ? [nr. Minehead] (omitted 1632–
    1635)   1625 to end

HALSWELL, Sir Nicholas, of Halswell in Goathurst   at least 1613–1625
HARBYN, John, of Newton Surmaville nr. Yeovil
    (omitted 1625–1626)   1623/4–1639
HARBYN, Robert, of Newton Surmaville nr. Yeovil   1639/40 to end
HARINGTON, John, of Kelston   1625 to end
HENLEY, Robert, of Henley nr. Crewkerne   1627 to end
HOPTON, Sir Ralph, of Evercreech Park and Witham
    Friary   1628/9 to end
HOPTON, Robert, of Witham Friary   at least 1613–1636
HORNER, Sir John, of Mells   1614 to end
HUNT, Robert, of Speckington   1639/40 to end

JENNINGS, Marmaduke, of Curry Rivel   1618–1625

KELLETT, Dr. Edward, rector of West Bagborough   1635 to end
KYRTON, Edward, of Castle Cary   1625–1626

LAKE, Arthur, Bishop of Bath and Wells   1614–1626

LANCASTER, Edward, of Milverton   1619–1625
LEY, Sir Henry, 2nd Earl of Marlborough, of Beck-
  ington and Wilts.   1618–1638
LEY, Sir James, 1st Earl of Marlborough, of Beck-
  ington and Wilts.   at least 1613–1628
LUTTRELL, George, of Dunster Castle   at least 1613–1629
LUTTRELL, Thomas, of Dunster Castle   1629 to end
LYTE, Thomas, of Lytes Cary (omitted 1625–1626)   1625–1639

MALLETT, Gawen, of Preston Bowyer   1620/1 to end
MALLETT, John, of Enmore (JP for short time in 1625)   1638 to end
MALLETT, Thomas, of Pointington, King's serjeant-
  at-law   1634 to end
MAY, John, of Hinton Charterhouse (omitted
  1625–1626)   at least 1613–1628
MERRIFIELD, John, of Crewkerne   1639 to end
MORE, Thomas, of Taunton   1620/1–1625

PHELIPS, Sir Robert, of Montacute (omitted 1614–
  1615/6 and 1626–8)   at least 1613–1638
PHELIPS, Edward, of Montacute   1638 to end
PHILLIPS, Sir Thomas, Bart., of Barrington Crt. at least 1613–1626
PIERCE, William, Bishop of Bath and Wells   1633 to end
POPHAM, Edward, of Huntworth in North Petherton   1614–1625
POPHAM, Sir Francis, of Wellington and Littlecote,
  Wilts.   at least 1613 to end
PORTMAN, Sir Hugh, Bart., of Orchard Portman near
  Taunton   1628–1629
PORTMAN, Sir William, Bart., of Orchard Portman
  near Taunton   1630 to end
POULETT, George, of Goathurst   1627 to end
POULETT, Henry, of ?   1638 to end
POULETT, John, 1st Baron Poulett, of Hinton St.
  George   at least 1613 to end
POWELL, Sir Edward, Bart., of ?, a Master of Requests   1630 to end
PRESTON, John, of Cricket St. Thomas   1639–1640
PYNE, Arthur, of Cathanger in Fivehead   1629 to end
PYNE, Hugh, of Curry Malet   1617–1626

RODNEY, Sir Edward, of Rodney Stoke   1616 to end
ROGERS, Edward, of Cannington   at least 1613–1627
ROGERS, Sir Francis, of Cannington   1627–1636

Rosse, James, of Shepton Beauchamp (omitted
   1625–1626)   1625 to end

Skory, Sir Edmond, of East Quantoxhead   1630–1633
Smyth, Sir Hugh, of Long Ashton   at least 1613–1628
Smyth, Thomas, of Long Ashton   1631 to end
Southworth, Thomas, recorder of Wells   at least 1613–1625
Speke, Sir George, of Whitelackington   at least 1613–1636
Speke, George, of Whitelackington and Dinnington   1634–1638
Stawell, Sir John, of Cothelstone   1620/1 to end
Still, Nathaniel, of Hutton Crt.   at least 1613–1625
Stocker, Anthony, of Chilcompton   1623 to end
Sydenham, John, of Combe in Dulverton   1626 only
Symes, John, of Poundisford Lodge in Pitminster
   (omitted 1626–7)   at least 1613 to end

Thynne, Sir Thomas, Bart., of Longleat House, Wilts.   1624/5–1625
Tynte, Edward, of Chelvey   1617/8–1630

Wake, Sir Baldwin, Bart., of Clevedon   1624/5–1627
Walker, Clement, of Charterhouse nr. Cheddar   1637/8 to end
Walrond, William, of Ile Brewers (omitted 1625–
   1626)   1623 to end
Warburton, Dr. George, Dean of Wells   1633 to end
Wood, Dr. Gerard, archdeacon of Wells   1617/8 to end
Wright, Dr. Robert, canon of Wells and later
   Bishop of Bristol   1617/8–1633
Wrothe, Sir Thomas, of Newton Forester (JP for
   short time in 1625)   1636 to end
Wyndham, Sir John, of Orchard Wyndham   at least 1613 to end
Wyndham, Sir Thomas, of Kentsford   1617/8–1635

Younge, Sir George, of Sewardswick in Compton
   Dando   1623/4–1625

    Custodes rotulorum
    Ley, Sir James, 1st Earl of Marlborough   1615–1625
    Ley, Sir Henry, 2nd Earl of Marlborough   1625–1636
    Coventrye, John   1636–1641

    "Deputy custodes rotulorum" (that is, chairmen of quarter sessions)
    Pyne, Hugh   c. 1623 ?–1626
    Harington, John   1626–c. 1651 ?

Lords Lieutenants

HERBERT, William, 3rd Earl of Pembroke	April 1621–April 1630
HERBERT, Philip, 4th Earl of Pembroke and E. of Montgomery	Aug. 1630–July 1640
SEYMOUR, William, 2nd Earl of Hertford	March 1639 to end
HERBERT, Philip Lord	July 1640 to end

Deputy Lieutenants

BERKELEY, Sir Charles, of Bruton	c. 1625–c. 1637
COVENTRYE, John, JP	c. 1637–c. 1639?
HALSWELL, Sir Nicholas, JP	c. 1625–1629
HOPTON, Sir Ralph, JP	c. 1629 to end
HOPTON, Robert, JP	c. 1625–c. 1630
LUTTRELL, Thomas, JP	c. 1639 to end
PHELIPS, Sir Robert, JP (omitted 1625–1628)	1624–1638
POPHAM, Edward, JP	1623–c. 1630
POPHAM, Sir Francis, JP	c. 1625 ?–1630 at least
PORTMAN, Sir William, Bart., JP	c. 1635 to end
POULETT, John Lord, JP	c. 1624 to end
RODNEY, Sir Edward, JP	c. 1625 to end
STAWELL, Sir John, JP	c. 1625 to end
SYMES, John, JP	c. 1637 to end
WALROND, William, JP	c. 1629? to end
WROTHE, Sir Thomas, JP	c. 1639 to end

Sheriffs

WYNDHAM, Thomas, JP	1624–1625
PHELIPS, Sir Robert, JP	1625–1626
SYMES, John, JP	1626–1627
LACH, John, of Over Langford	1627–1628
STAWELL, Sir John, JP	1628–1629
THYNNE, Sir Thomas, Bart., JP (earlier)	1629–1630
DODINGTON, Sir Francis, JP	1630–1631
LUTTRELL, Thomas, JP	1631–1632
WALROND, William, JP	1632–1633
CAREW, Sir John, JP	1633–1634
HODGES, Henry, of Haselbury	1634–1636

MALLETT, John, JP	1636 only
BASSETT, William, JP	1636–1637
PORTMAN, Sir William, Bart., JP	1637–1638
EVERY, William, JP	1638–1639
WROTHE, Sir Thomas, JP	1639–1640
HIPPESLYE, John, of Stoneaston	1640–1641

Judges of Assize, Western Circuit

BRAMSTON, Sir John, CJKB	1639/40–1640/1
CRAWLEY, Sir Francis, JCP	1639–1640
DAVENPORT, Sir Humphrey, CB	1633/4–1634
DENHAM, Sir John, B	1625/6–1637/8
FINCH, Sir John, CJCP	1634/5–1639
HEATH, Sir Robert, King's serjeant-at-law	1637/8–1638
HUTTON, Sir Richard, JCP	1618–1625
RICHARDSON, Sir Thomas, CJCP and later CJKB	1629/30–1633
TREVOR, Sir Thomas, B	1638/9 only
WALTER, Sir John, CB	1625/6–1629

Bibliography

The Public and the County Records

Manuscripts

Printed Works

Bibliography

This is not an exhaustive bibliography of the literature on the subject, but is rather the author's working bibliography of manuscript sources and printed works consulted. The manuscript sources are listed by repositories in alphabetical order, the individual manuscripts or classes of manuscripts listed sequentially by catalog references, save in the case of records in the Somerset Record Office, which are listed alphabetically by title (Clerk's of the peace records) and by collection (Deposited documents and records). Descriptive notes are provided for some of the manuscripts in this list, though the importance to this study of the Public Records and the Somerset County Records makes it advisable to treat them organically by *fonds* in an essay immediately following. The printed works, listed without differentiation between primary and secondary sources, conclude the bibliography.

THE PUBLIC AND THE COUNTY RECORDS

The Public Records and the County Records possess double significance. On the one hand, they provide the main factual basis for this study. On the other, they are almost the only vestigial remains of the institutions which created them, and as such afford evidence of the working of those institutions. This essay will emphasize both aspects of these manuscripts' value.

The Public Records

Privy Council Registers and State Papers Domestic, Charles I

The Privy Council registers, 1625–1641 (P.C.2/35–52) and the State Papers Domestic, Charles I, 1625–1640 (S.P.16) share with the county's two main classes of quarter-sessions records the distinction of being the most important sources for this study. The Privy Council registers and State Papers Domestic provide abundant information concerning virtually every county governmental matter that came to the Council's attention. The eighteen bulky volumes of Privy Council registers contain copies of the orders of the Council, letters from the Council to the local governors, a few memoranda, and minutes of appearances of persons summoned before the Board. They do not record what was discussed in the Council save for an occasional memorandum, though close study of an order or a letter will sometimes enable the student to reconstruct formative discussion. The conglomeration of miscellany which are the five hundred or so volumes of State Papers Domestic consist principally of the papers of Secretaries Conway and Dorchester and the clerk of the Council (later Secretary of State) Edward Nicholas. Preserved here are a number of notes and memoranda of Council deliberations, examinations of those suspected of political crimes and of witnesses to the same, petitions to the King and Council, proposals for reform of government institutions, and virtually any other writings bearing even remotely on matters of state which came to the hands of the Secretaries and clerks. Most significantly, they contain letters from county administrators and other officials to individual privy councillors, the Council corporate, and the clerks of the Council—thus, they comprise in part the "in" correspondence of that supreme organ. Consulted in conjunction with the "out" correspondence in the Council registers, these letters and ancillary documents afford a fairly complete picture of Council–county government relations. Among the more miscellaneous items are to be found a number of official papers created by committees of the Council or other bodies connected with conciliar activities, such as the minutes of proceedings of the councils of war (1626–1638), of the commissioners for the poor (1631 et seq.), and of the commissioners on fees (1635–1639). Two notes of warning concerning the completeness of these two classes must be sounded: a few Council letters, the originals of which are extant in private collections, were not copied into the Privy Council registers, and the State Papers Domestic by their very nature do not form a continuum of correspondence on all subjects, but contain many gaps. A useful note on the registers is E. R. Adair's "The Privy Council registers," *EHR*, XXXVIII: 410–422 (1923). The registers for March 1625 to April 1629 are excellently transcribed in *Acts of the Privy Council, Charles I* (5 vols., London, 1934–1958)—a not quite accurate title. The *Calendar of State Papers Domestic, Charles I* (22 vols. and addenda vol., London, 1858–1897) are to be eschewed as a substitute for the manuscripts; the apparent fullness of the calendars is misleading, for in reality much was omitted by their editors. The calendars should be used only as an index to the documents, and this by a page by page search, since the indexes to the calendars are too often defective.

Signet Office: Irish Letter Books

The Council correspondence, "in" and "out," is complemented by the royal letters dispatched under the signet seal, copies of which for 1627–1642 were enregistered in Signet Office, Irish letter books (S.O.1/1–3). The Public Record Office's name for this class is unfortunate. The bulk of the letters were indeed addressed to the Lord Deputy and other officials in Ireland, but such hardly exhausted the contents of these registers. Communications to foreign princes, instructions for ambassadors, and the expression of the regal will to bishops, deans and chapters, special commissioners, judges, lords lieutenants, and even private persons in matters of exceptional interest to the King customarily went out under the signet. For this study, the letters in the latter category are of prime importance. Levying of troops for the Ré expedition and other lieutenancy matters, enclosure and disafforestation projects in Somerset, ship money, oversight of county magistracy by the judges of assize, and ecclesiastical preferment were all subjects concerning which Charles' will found expression in highly informal, almost personal, signet letters.

Assizes: Western Circuit Order and Postea Books

The indispensable nexus of communication between the Council and county magistracy was the judges of assize. By a happy and unique circumstance of survival, the Western Circuit's order books, 1629–1652 (and onwards) are available (Asz.24/20–21), containing the administrative orders of the twice-yearly assizes for Somerset, Dorset, Devon, Hampshire, Wiltshire, and Cornwall, from the summer assizes 1629 to 1652, with gaps in the first volume (Asz.24/20) for 1633 and 1638 caused by the extraction of whole leaves, and some orders for 1640–1640/1 assizes missing completely. In all, one hundred and seventy-seven orders made at Somerset assizes or at other Western assizes and related to Somerset are extant for the period of this study in the first volume. These orders, most of them requiring the services of the justices of the peace, deal with the multitudinous administrative matters (bridges and roads, rating, master and servant, poor law and settlement) with which the justices usually dealt in quarter sessions, but which for a number of reasons were brought to assizes instead. Appeals from quarter-sessions orders (particularly in bastardy cases) occur occasionally, and there are a few orders made jointly by the judges and the justices. Of greatest interest are the general orders of assizes, binding on the justices in quarter sessions and out of sessions, which more than any other documents illustrate the function of the judges as the overseers of county magistracy. The Somerset portions of the first volume have been transcribed and printed in full in my *Somerset Assize Orders, 1629–1640*, with an introduction dealing with the relationship of the judges to magistracy. Unfortunately, none of the Western Circuit's records concerning criminal matters before assizes are extant. The only value to this study of the postea books, 1611–1633 (Asz.24/29–34) lies in their containing

names of attorneys who practiced in the county. Incidentally, all assize
records of all circuits for the seventeenth century have been consulted in
line with other research and points of interest to this study have been
incorporated in it.

Chancery: Crown Office Docket Books, Entry Books and Patent Rolls, etc.

Chancery, as the traditional secretariat of the central government, was the
vehicle for the appointment of the judges of assize, lords lieutenants, justices
of the peace, and sheriff as well as most special commissioners by letters
patent under the great seal. In the case of all the above patents save those
for sheriffs, the Crown Office in Chancery was responsible for drafting and
overseeing the sealing of the letters patent. Four Crown Office classes are
particularly valuable to the student in search of the names of such officials.
The Crown Office docket books, 1616–1643 (Index 4211–4212) contain a note
of every commission from that office which passed the great seal, and in the
case of the commissions of the peace the note always indicates the change
made and sometimes the reason for it. The Crown Office entry books of
commissions of the peace, etc. (C.181/3–5 for the period 1620–1645) contain
the names of all commissioners save those in county commissions of the
peace, commissions for charitable uses and for the forced loan. The Crown
Office kept a separate series of entry books for the names in the county
commissions of the peace, and a careful search of Crown Office miscellaneous
books, justices of the peace lists (C.193/12–13) turned up two, possibly eight,
such entry books among the eleven volumes in this class hitherto considered
to be all *libri pacis*. Among the Crown Office miscellaneous fiats, there is
an entry book of the names of commissioners for charitable uses, 1629–1642
(C.192/1). The names of the commissioners for the forced loan, 1626, were
not as such entered in any entry book, since they were the justices of the
peace of the various counties at the times of issue of the forced loan commissions. The importance of these Crown Office classes for the discovery of
these officials cannot be overemphasized. By this time, it had ceased to be
the practice of the Chancery to enroll fully on the dorse of the patent rolls any
commissions of this nature except commissions of lieutenancy; county commissions of the peace so enrolled are often composites of two commissions for
the year of the patent roll (C.66). Somerset is exceptionally fortunate in having
preserved about two-thirds of the letters patent commissions of the peace for
this period (see section below on the Somerset County Records); for most
other counties the docket books and entry books of the Crown Office and
libri pacis must be used to discover the names of the justices. For a complete
list of sources for the names of county justices, an assessment of their

relative values, and a detailed treatment of the machinery for appointing justices see T. G. Barnes and A. Hassell Smith, "Justices of the Peace, 1558–1688—a Revised List of Sources," *Bulletin of the Institute of Historical Research*, XXXII: 221–242 (1959). The Petty Bag sheriff rolls (C.227) consist of the lists of nominees for sheriffs. Against the name of the sheriff chosen for each county will be found the stylus mark made by the King, who "pricked" the sheriff. *Lists and Indexes*, IX, which purports to list all sheriffs from the earliest times to 1831, is not to be relied upon without corroboration.

The class Charitable uses, inquisitions and decrees (C.93) comprise the inquisitions and returns of the commissioners for charitable uses (mostly justices), who had powers of oyer and terminer in such enquiries into the disposition of charitable trusts. While different in nature, Petty Bag Office, miscellaneous rolls (C.212/20), a roll recording compositions for depopulating enclosures for a number of counties, mostly in the Midlands, served much the same function with respect to the enquiries of the special commissioners to enquire into depopulating enclosures, 1635. Somerset is not included on this roll; to judge by Exchequer, Exchequer of Receipt, issues, enrollments and registers of, warrant books (Auditor's), containing warrants for depopulations compositions 1636/7–1639/40 (E.403/3041–3042), no compositions were made with Somerset depopulators, for in this record too, Midland counties predominate. The possibility that there were such compositions, but that the record of them is no longer extant, must not be overlooked, however.

The Chancery class Inquisitions post mortem, series II (C.142), provides considerable material of importance concerning the economic position of a number of Somerset local governors and their estates or those of their immediate ancestor. Besides *Lists and Indexes*, XXXIII, to these, an *index nominum* for Somerset has been printed in *Somersetshire Archaeological and Natural History Society Proceedings* (1901), XLVII, pt. ii, pp. 1–122.

Exchequer Records

The Exchequer records have an enhanced value for an era when the government's concern with finance was even more acute than normal, and when the financial expedients employed—highly unpopular without exception—were almost all undertaken in the counties by the local governors. The class King's Remembrancer, subsidy rolls [lay] (E.179/171/361–367 and 172/371–408 for Somerset for this period), record the assessments of men of varying rank in the county to the statutory taxes and the names of the commissioners for the subsidy (mostly justices) by their divisions. More significant is Exchequer of Receipt, receipts, enrollments and registers of, register of privy seal loans, 1625–1626 (E.401/2586) which provides the assessments to and sums paid under the first of Charles' major financial exactions of an illegal or questionably legal nature. The returns of the commissioners for the composition for knighthood are Exchequer of Receipt, miscellanea, composition for knighthood, 1630–1632 (E.407/35). The accounts for ship money, including notes of the annual receipts, are among the ten account rolls of the Treasurer of the Navy for 1635–1639 in Lord Treasurer's Remembrancer, declared accounts [Pipe Office series] (E.351/2274–2283). It is worth remarking that before 1635 one roll for each year's account by the Treasurer of the Navy was sufficient, but after that year, two were required—an indication of the impact of ship money and the fleet it provided on his administration.

Aside from subsidies and financial expedients, a number of classes of Exchequer records illuminate the traditional relationship of that organ with the sheriff. Though no sheriff's accounts for the issues of manors, lands, goods, etc., are extant for Somerset in this period in King's Remembrancer, sheriff's accounts (E.199), two accounts of Somerset's sheriffs for the farm of the county (1629–1631) are extant in Lord Treasurer's Remembrancer, miscellaneous rolls, accounts of sheriffs and others (E.370/15/54 and 67). However, the whole of the financial dealings of the sheriff with the Exchequer can, in their finished form, be followed on Lord Treasurer's Remembrancer, pipe rolls (E.372). Both items of certain and casual revenue finally accounted for by the sheriff are recorded there, and whether or not they were paid can be determined from the marginal notes made by the apposers. The Lord Treasurer's Remembrancer, memoranda rolls (E.368) record (among other things) proceedings relating to and states and views of the accounts of the sheriff. Particularly valuable are the "cravings" of the sheriff for allowance of expenses incurred in providing for the judges of assize and in disposing of those convicted at assizes—the latter provides a bit of sorely needed information as to the criminal business of assizes. The "cravings" are found on the Michaelmas roll, under the heading of states and views of accounts for the county. Far more valuable than these rolls are King's Remembrancer, memoranda rolls (E.159), not so much for what they reveal of the sheriff's activities (though estreats of amerciaments on sheriffs will be found here) as for the record of cases in equity in the court of Exchequer. The disafforestation and draining enclosure schemes and suits for distraint of knighthood were Exchequer equity cases; the final settlements by which these actions were ended (the commissioners' agreements with the parties involved confirmed by the court) are recorded on these rolls. For a complete picture of Exchequer equity proceedings, King's Remembrancer, depositions taken by commission (E.134) and decrees and orders of the court of Exchequer, series III (E.125), must be consulted. In the case of both classes of memoranda rolls (E.159 and

E.368) contemporary agenda books and repertory rolls provide a fairly accurate guide to the material on these otherwise difficult-to-use records.

Two classes of King's Remembrancer records, extents and inquisitions (E.143) and bille (E.207), enable one to assess the weight on the sheriff and his officers of the levying of debts for the King and the service of Exchequer writs, respectively. The former are still in boxes, barely sorted, and are formidable to search; they indicate a certain perfunctoriousness on the part of sheriffs' officers in levying fines, amerciaments, forfeited recognizances, and other debts due to the King. The bille, among other items, contain lists of the number of returnable Exchequer writs returned by the sheriff each term, which note amerciaments on the sheriff for improper return, etc.

Estreats of fines, etc., at Somerset assizes are nonexistent and only one estreat of fines, amerciaments, etc. at Somerset quarters sessions for the period is extant in King's Remembrancer, estreats (E.137/39/7). These are the original estreats (one part of a tripartite indenture). No enrollments of Somerset estreats for the period are extant in Lord Treasurer's Remembrancer, rolls of estreats, Part I (E.362). Both classes are highly imperfect.

The bulky rolls, Lord Treasurer's Remembrancer, recusant rolls [Pipe Office series] (E.377/33–48), comprising sixteen rolls for this period, afford the names of Romanist recusants in the county and the amounts they were fined for their wilful refusal to attend church.

A considerable quantity of the records of the commissioners for the investigation of exacted fees and innovated offices (commissioners on fees) are preserved among Exchequer classes: King's Remembrancer, commission on fees (E.215), returns of schedules of fees by various officers including clerks of the peace (none for Somerset) and clerks of assize (none for the Western Circuit), King's Remembrancer, miscellaneous books II, minute books of commissioners on fees, 1627–1636 (E.165/46–51), and Augmentation Office, miscellaneous books, minute book of commissioners on fees, 1633–1634 (E.315/329). Other papers of the commissioners on fees (both Jacobean and Caroline) are in the Bodleian Library, MS Tanner 101 and 318, and the State Papers Domestic, Charles I; among the latter are two returns of fee schedules by the Western Circuit clerk of assize, 1628 and 1630 (S.P.16/528, nos. 62–63). From such returns of fee schedules much of the procedure of the courts involved can be reconstructed.

Two other useful Exchequer classes are King's Remembrancer, bills, answers, etc. (E.112/285/1383 and 1388), in which are preserved proceedings in two suits brought against sheriff Henry Hodges by subordinates, and King's Remembrancer, miscellanea of the Exchequer, *liber pacis* [28 Oct. 1626] (E.163/18/12). The latter is worth noting: this was a list of all justices in England and Wales delivered into Exchequer from the Chancery Crown

Office to enable the revenue authorities to know who the justices of the peace-cum-forced loan commissioners were at the time that that financial expedient was set on foot.

King's Bench, Common Pleas, Wards and Liveries, and Star Chamber Records

Records of four courts, two common law and two prerogative, are of exceptional value to this study. Revealed in the class King's Bench (Crown side), indictments [ancient] (K.B.9) is the extent of quarter-sessions' subordination to the central judicial authority. Besides Bills of Middlesex and coroners' inquisitions (the latter submitted at assizes), there are a number of returned writs of *certiorari* directed to quarter sessions, assizes, and leets, and the indictments or convictions called up by the writs. Common Pleas, feet of fines (C.P.25(2)/345–347 and 479–480 for Somerset, James I and Charles I, respectively) provide information of conveyances of freehold by or to local governors by collusive suit. The court of Wards, feodaries' surveys (Wards 5/36–37 for Somerset, Elizabeth I to Charles I) are surveys and certificates of values of estates of those holding of the King by knight service in chief. The survey of lands of a dead tenant in chief was cognate to the inquisition post mortem taken by the escheator, and was engrossed on parchment. The surveys must be distinguished from the paper documents found in the same class, which are certificates of values of estates (real and personal) of heirs in ward, and particularly from certificates of "improved yearly value" of the ward's property. The certificates, delivered into Wards by the feodary, show an enormous augmentation in assigned values during the period 1610–1640, in line with the court's increasing function as a revenue agency. H. E. Bell's *An Introduction to the History and Records of the Court of Wards and Liveries* (1953) is essential reading before these documents, valuable in determining the landed wealth of a number of local governors, are touched. Among the minute fraction of Star Chamber proceedings for the reign of Charles I (St.Ch.9) extant, there are none for Somerset. However, contemporary reports of and notes taken during hearings of cases in the Caroline Star Chamber preserved in other repositories (see the list of manuscripts) yield a few cases of direct relevance to this study. The Star Chamber proceedings, James I (St.Ch.8) contain a few cases concerning Somerset figures, and these have been taken into consideration in this work. Time did not permit a search to be made of civil proceedings in King's Bench (plea side), Common Pleas, Chancery, or the court of Requests for cases involving Somerset; while the relevance of such cases to the local governors might prove considerable, their relevance to local government would not be of sufficient note to warrant research so extensive as to consist of a full-scale study in itself.

The Somerset County Records

Quarter-Sessions Order Books and Sessions Rolls

Somerset is fortunate in having preserved from the reign of James I virtually every type of record connected with the institution of magistracy in the early seventeenth century. None of the series is wholly complete, but the two most important—quarter-sessions order books and sessions rolls—are nearly so for this period. From these documents can be constructed a picture of the justices' governance of the shire—the records themselves providing a concrete picture of the clerical establishment which produced or received and preserved them. These records share equal importance with the Public Records, and from the point of view of diplomatic they are almost as interesting as the more sophisticated products of the national administration.

The orders of the court of quarter sessions are preserved almost continuously from 1613 in the quarter-sessions order books, three large, thick folio volumes covering the period from midsummer sessions 1613 to Michaelmas sessions 1638, the second volume (1620/1–1627) being defective for the Easter to Michaelmas sessions, 1627, and the first volume (1613–1620) for a few of the orders of Michaelmas sessions, 1620. In the nineteenth century, these volumes were dubbed "minute books," which was a misnomer since their function was to record the orders of the court, licenses issued to badgers and maltsters, recognizances for the peace, for good behavior, etc., calendars of prisoners, grand, hundredal, and petty juries, informations and licenses to compound of common informers, abstracts of final accounts of the treasurers of the justices' standing funds. This was a relatively formal document, preeminently *the* record of the court. Though the clerical standard perceptible in the execution of the order books was not quite so high as that of the old central organs of Chancery and Exchequer, it was on a par with that of the clerks of assize and the clerks of the Privy Council as indicated by the assize order books and the Privy Council registers.

The sessions rolls for 1625–1638/9, comprising forty-three large files of about one hundred leaves each, are divided into two series: (1) examinations of suspects and witnesses to their crimes taken before justices out of sessions and sent for trial at quarter sessions and (2) drafts of quarter-sessions orders, memoranda of justices and the clerk of the peace, hundred and jury presentments, letters to the clerk and the bench from justices, other officials, attornies, informers, and private persons, certificates, bastardy orders (out of sessions), warrants, directions to constables and others, petitions, and informations—in short, every conceivable type of document, formal and informal, in any way concerning the justices' administration which came to the hands of the clerk of the peace. While supplementary to the order book, this latter series of heterogeneous documents possesses a definite integrity since they bear the imprint of the routine functioning of magistracy at every level. For the period Epiphany sessions 1635/6 to Michaelmas sessions 1638, inclusive, only the examinations series has survived.

The order books, and where defective the second series of the sessions rolls, have been edited and largely calendared in Somerset Record Society vols. XXIII and XXIV, *Quarter Sessions Records for the County of Somerset, 1607–1625* and *1625–1639*, E. H. Bates-Harbin, ed. (1907 and 1908). The editor's failure to make clear his system of editing and transcribing, the full transcribing of some items and the calendaring of others, and a number of substantial errors limit these volumes' usefulness to serving as indexes to the manuscripts.

Indictment Rolls

The twenty-eight rolls of small strips of parchment comprising the indictment rolls, 1602–1644, are far from complete. Consulted in conjunction with the examinations before justices (series 1 of the sessions rolls) and the calendars of prisoners at sessions (in the order book), it is possible to follow a number of criminal actions brought by indictment through their various stages.

Alehousekeepers' Recognizances

Alehousekeepers' recognizances—records of the bond to keep good order entered into by a publican when licensed by the justices either in or out of sessions—are sparse. Only those certified to one 1626 sessions and three sessions in 1630 remain. Yet, the recognizances for the latter three sessions indicate how many publicans were licensed just before the justices began to reduce drastically their numbers.

Wage Assessments

The wage assessments, establishing maximum wages for laborers and artisans, promulgated annually by the Easter sessions, are remarkably numerous when compared to those for many counties, seventeen remaining for 1604–1641. 1 James I, c.6 (1604) ordained that such assessments were to be engrossed on parchment and preserved among the custos's records. They afford evidence of the bench's handling of this important economic matter, especially critical in this era of recurring depression and rising prices.

Enrolled Deeds

The enrolled deeds, recording deeds of bargain and sale of land pursuant to the 1536 Statute of Enrollments, comprise twenty-eight rolls of 407 deeds, 1536–1655. They throw light on one other function of the justices and also provide information concerning the wealth of some of the local governors. They have been ably edited and calendared *in extenso* by Mrs. C. W. H. Rawlins in *Somerset Enrolled Deeds, 1536–1655*, Somerset Record Society, LI (1936).

Commissions of the Peace

The thirty-three commissions of the peace for 1625–1638/9 preserved in the Somerset Record Office represent two-thirds of the total number of commissions issued during the period, and are part of a series of 103 commissions, 1612/3–1691, in the Office. Only Lancashire has preserved a comparable series of commissions for the seventeenth century. The significance of this series has been mentioned above, under The Public Records.

Deposited Documents: Phelips MSS

While not "county records," since they are not the records of the clerk of the peace in his custody either by delegation from the custos or by direction of statute, the private muniments deposited in the Somerset Record Office have provided considerable information, in the case of one of them, a source of prime importance without which the study of the county's lieutenancy could not have been undertaken. The Phelips MSS, largely the papers of Sir Robert Phelips, furnish virtually all of the evidence extant for the functioning (and malfunctioning) of Somerset's lieutenancy in this period, notably in the volume entitled "Musters, 1615–1667." This volume contains the fullest documentary evidence for the churchales dispute of 1633, which had national implications. The volume, "Duchy of Cornwall," as well as "Musters, 1615–1667" affords ample evidence of the prolonged county-factional battle between Phelips and Lord Poulett, which did so much to disorder lieutenancy and impelled Phelips to lead the county's opposition to ship money. Two volumes, "Parliamentary" and "Parliamentary proceedings, 1628," reveal Phelips in his role of a leading parliamentarian in the 1620s. "Family letters" provide information supplementary to that contained in the other volumes of the Phelips MSS. Documents relating to Phelips' estate indicate how shaky was the financial basis for his power in the county. Once Sir Robert's nearly illegible handwriting is conquered, his papers provide a source for Somerset's government in the early Stuart period only slightly less important than the Privy Council registers, State Papers Domestic, and the quarter-sessions records.

—— Poulett MSS

Unfortunately, the Poulett MSS, consisting mostly of estate papers, contain no personal papers of comparable interest to the Phelips MSS.

——— *Sanford MSS*

For the early skirmishes of Phelips and Poulett, revolving around the 1614 election, the Sanford MSS (boxes 3 and 51) contain revealing correspondence between Poulett and one of his adherents among the lesser gentry.

——— *Hippisley MSS*

The Hippisley MSS, as yet uncataloged, provide invaluable material on lieutenancy staffing, personnel, and organization as well as a few important items concerning ship money opposition, the papers of John Preston, of Cricket St. Thomas, a trained band officer, briefly a justice, and always Sir Robert Phelips' supporter.

——— *Wyndham MSS*

The Wyndham MSS, likewise largely uncataloged, contain considerable estate materials on the important magnate family at Orchard Wyndham. This collection would reward the careful searcher on the track of the gentry's rise (or decline).

——— *Goodford MSS and Trull MSS*

The two odd items gleaned from the Goodford MSS and the Trull MSS are fascinating because of their rarity—a deputy lieutenant's warrant and a billeting rate, respectively. A score or two more of each would have been very satisfying.

MANUSCRIPTS

Ammerdown House (near Bath)

Lord Hylton's manuscripts yielded the only known copy of the Hinton rate—the key to the numerous rating disputes that disrupted the collection of ship money: "A proportion devised at Henton within the county of Somerset the 13th of July *anno regni* Elizabethe the eleaventh [1569] for the levyinge of one hundred men to be imployed in servise for Ireland." This nearly contemporary copy of the rate is written on the inside of a vellum binding of a manuscript, serial no. X. For the full transcription of the document, see *Somerset and Dorset Notes and Queries*, XXVII: 210–213 (March 1959).

Bodleian Library, Oxford

Additional MSS

  C.303 Notes of cases in Star Chamber, 1627–1630 (ff. 21–94v) and list of procurations for the diocese of Bath and Wells, early-mid seventeenth century (ff. 169–174v).

Bankes MSS (manuscripts of Attorney-General Bankes, on loan to the Bodleian)

Bundle 5 Certificate of Attorney-General Bankes and King's counsel as to legality of prosecuting sheriffs in Star Chamber and Exchequer Chamber for failure to collect ship money, 10 July 1639 (no. 40).

Summary of proceedings against sheriffs in Star Chamber for failure to collect ship money [July-Aug. 1640] (no. 41).

Bundle 6 Note of the bounds of Sir John Hippisley's lands, late parcel of Frome Selwood forest [n.d.] (no. 26).

Bundle 13 Warrant of clerk of the Council to the warden of the Fleet to deliver two Essex constables bound to answer in Star Chamber concerning ship money, 19 March 1637/8 (no. 29).

Bundle 14 Returns by aldermen, etc., in London of gentry residing there against the proclamations to return to county seats, 1632–1634.

Bundle 15 Petition of the brewers of Herts., Beds., and Hunts. to Crew, CJ, praying suppression of innholders, etc., who unlawfully brew; certificate of Crew, 12 Oct. 1626 (no. 5).

Bundle 19 Examination before the Solicitor-General of Gabriel Ludlowe (barrister prominent at Somerset QS and assizes) concerning a remonstrance against ship money in his possession, 24 Oct. 1639 (no. 7).

Bundle 24 Detailed memoranda of Robert Henley's abuses in his office of chief clerk of enrollments of pleas in King's Bench [1630s].

Bundle 42 Privy Council order to Attorney-General to examine sheriff of Hereford for prosecution in Star Chamber for failure to collect ship money and contempt of the Council, 17 May 1640 (no. 42).

Same to same to stop Star Chamber proceedings against sheriff of Staffs. concerning ship money, 11 May 1640 (no. 45).

Petition of sheriff of Oxon. concerning his failure to collect ship money— Privy Council orders Attorney-General to proceed against him in Star Chamber, 1 April 1640 (no. 47).

Bundle 43 Sign manual warrant to Attorney-General to recommence proceedings in Star Chamber against Sir Walter Norton, Bart., exsheriff of Lincs., for extortion, receiving bribes, and scandalizing the Earl of Lindsey in connection with ship money, and directions concerning the same prosecution, 20 Aug. 1638 (nos. 41–42).

Sign manual warrant to Attorney-General to prepare privy seal to empower judges of the King's Bench to deal with offenses connected with repair of highways and to devote common law fines to amending highways, recvd. 26 Jan. 1637/8 (no. 62).

Bundle 44 Names of those indicted for treason and sedition at Royalist assizes and oyer and terminer sessions in Somerset, 1642–1643/4 (no. 73).

Bundle 51 Warrant for an Exchequer commission to John Coventrye *et al.* to survey Petherton Forest for disafforestation, 30 June 1638 (no. 5).

Petition of Sir Cornelius Vermuyden and Margaret Kirby for great seal grant of King's Sedgemoor holdings of the King; warrant accordingly granted, 2 Jan. 1634/5 (no. 65).

Bundle 54 Warrant to Attorney-General to prepare a grant to Thomas Meautys, senior clerk of the Council, of the office of muster master-general of England, 14 March 1635/6 (no. 20).

Sign manual warrant to Attorney-General to prepare a grant to Thomas Warre (of Somerset) and Thomas Baven in trust for Christabel Wyndham (*née* Pyne), nurse to Prince Charles, of duties and arrears in Exchequer and the Duchy of Lancaster, 5 July 1635 (no. 35).

Bundle 62 Returns by aldermen, etc., in London of gentry residing there against proclamations to return to county seats, 1632–1634 (includes a number of Somerset gentlemen).

MSS North

b. 26 "Sedgmoor," a survey and petition, concerning draining and enclosing the moor, submitted to James I (ff. 50–51).

MSS Rawlinson

C.827 Reports of Star Chamber cases, 1636–1638.

D.720 Reports of Star Chamber cases, 1637–1639, and Lord Keeper Finch's charge to the judges of assize, 13 Feb. 1639/40 (ff. 36–53).

British Museum, London

Additional MSS

6704 Entry book of the Wigley family, of law precedents useful for a JP, early seventeenth century (ff. 100 ff.).

10114 Diary of John Harington of Kelston, Somerset, MP, 1646–1653.

11764 Reports of Star Chamber cases, Hilary 1633 (ff. 1–29v).

12496 (Sir Julius Caesar's papers) miscellaneous; includes those slain at Ré (f. 47), notes of Star Chamber hearings (ff. 125–146v), and the printed Book of Orders of 1630/1 (ff. 243 ff.).

12511 Stephen's Case in Exchequer, concerning distraint of knighthood (ff. 2–31).

14313 (Sir Julius Caesar's papers) miscellaneous; those in Somerset to receive Crown pensions and annuities, *temp.* James I (ff. 41–41v).

32093 Privy Council to JPs Somerset, 13 June 1630, with certificate of receipt by Sir Robert Phelips (f. 32).

34324 (Sir Julius Caesar's papers) miscellaneous; Lord Keeper Coventrye's charge to the judges of assize, 29 June 1626 (ff. 248–249v).

34712 Proceedings concerning the enclosure of King's Sedgemoor, *temp.* James I (ff. 192 ff.).

35251 Petition to the Commons by freeholders and tenants of manors adjoining King's Sedgemoor [temp. Charles II] (f. 21).

42077 Precedent book, probably for a JP, sixteenth century.

42078 Precedent book of William Oxenden, JP, 1555–1556.

42117 Reports of Star Chamber cases, 1632–1633 (ff. vv. 146–168).

46373 (Harington papers) Papers relating to Harington estates, 1606–1667.

46374 (Harington papers) Diary of John Harington of Kelston, MP, 1646–1653 (copy of BM Add. MS 10114 *supra*) and notes on law cases.

46500 Papers of Roger Hill of Poundisford Park, Somerset, Baron of the Exchequer in the Protectorate, 1605–1667.

47186 Eighteenth-century copy of Somerset pedigrees of 1636.

47713 Collections concerning peerages, offices, etc., c. 1605–1614. (Includes figures of trained band strength, all counties.)

48057 Reports of Star Chamber cases, 1625–1627.

48091 Parliamentary proceedings, 1625.

48092 General musters, 1573–1574.

48111 Treatise defending enclosure and draining of King's Sedgemoor, by Adam Moore, dedicated to Sir Henry Yelverton (Attorney-General) [c. 1620].

48591 Papers of Sir Bassingborne Gawdy, primarily as a commissioner of musters for Norfolk, 1599–1604.

Cotton MSS

Jul.C. III   Sir Robert Phelips to Sir Robert Cotton [early 1620s] (f. 294).

Egerton MSS

2134 Licence to John Symes to fell trees in the royal forest of Frome Selwood, 1618, and other papers.

2711 "Sir Thomas Wyatt's Poems": The Henrician poet's sonnets scribbled over by the jottings of John Harington of Kelston, who used this paper book as a commonplace book.

12+

[This unlikely looking source came to the author's notice by a brief reference in the Class Catalogue to a draft letter from Harington to Selden On inspection, this manuscript of sonnets by Wyatt proved to be also the commonplace book of Harington, chairman of Somerset quarter sessions from 1625 into the Commonwealth. Besides essays on theology, algebraic equations and geometric theorems, medicinal formulae, transcriptions of the Prayer Book in Welsh, and drafts of letters (some dealing with an apocalyptic vision of the coming civil strife), it contains notes of sermons delivered by Somerset puritan divines. Most important, the book contains notes of legal actions and other matters in which Harington acted as a commissioner (including a ship money rating dispute) and three complete charges he delivered to quarter sessions c. 1640. Harington's crabbed hand covers nearly every page. Doubtless, the volume of Wyatt's sonnets came to Harington through his grandfather, who coedited some of Wyatt's psalms in 1549. The sonnets could hardly have been pleasing to the puritan John (so unlike his father, Sir John, the luminary of Elizabeth's court) which might account for his wanton use of the book.]

2978 (Heath papers) Papers concerning Henley's King's Bench office (ff. 133–142), Parliamentarians proceeded against by the King in areas under his control, including Somerset, during the Civil War (ff. 151–152v), and other documents of interest.

3676/F Notes by William Lambarde for Bk. 2, ch. 4 of *Eirenarcha*.

Hargrave MSS

404 Reports of Star Chamber cases, 1638–1639 (ff. 72v–75v).

Harley MSS

163 Diary of the Long Parliament by Sir Simon D'Ewes.

286 Lord Keeper Coventrye to the clerk of the Crown to drop 15 JPs for parliamentary opposition, 8 July 1626 (f. 297).

1559 Notes taken in the Preston house at Cricket St. Thomas, East Coker church, Montacute House, Dunster church, and other Somerset seats and churches by an eighteenth-century antiquary.

1603 Precedent book for a justice's clerk by Nathaniel Rogers, 1606.

1622 *Liber pacis* [23–30 Jan. 1625/6].

2313 Notes on debates in the Commons in Charles I's third Parliament.

4022 Reports of Star Chamber cases, Easter–Trinity 1634.

4771 Diary of proceedings in Charles I's third Parliament.

5936 (Barford collection) Printed broadsheet of *Orders appointed by his most excellent Majestie ...*, to give maximum publicity for increased militia preparedness [c. 10 July] 1626 (no. 25)—see PRINTED WORKS *infra*.

Lansdowne MSS

53 (Burghley papers) Papers dealing mostly with the purge of JPs in 1587 (ff. 163–196), with expenses allowed judges of assize (f. 198), and similar matters.

1094 Ravenscroft's reports, 1623–1633, including Doderidge, J's, charge to the grand jury of Middlesex, Mich. 1623 (f. 8).

Royal MSS

17A XXXVII "An apology of the King's agents for the enclosure of Kinges Sedgmoore in the county of Somerset" [*temp*. James I] ff. 17–33.

Stowe MSS

152 Fairly contemporary copy of Croke, J's, opinion in Hampden's Case, Easter 1638 (ff. 56–65v) and papers relating to the Crown grant to Edmund Wyndham *et al.* of the office of pleas upon writs of error, 1632 (ff. 44 ff.).

Dunster Castle, Somerset

The Luttrell MSS provided a considerable quantity of documents relating to the holdings and activities of George and Thomas Luttrell, *temp*. James I and Charles I.

Harvard Law School Library, Cambridge, Massachusetts

L. MS 1128 "Reports of cases in the Star Chamber during ye reign of King Charles I, by an eminent practicer in that court, formerly a member of Gray's Inn," Hilary 1626 to Michaelmas 1640. The most significant single source for cases in the Caroline Star Chamber, this contained a number of cases highly relevant to this study.

Lambeth Palace, London

MS 247 Orders and instructions concerning musters, abuses perpetrated in mustering, forms, precedents, etc. (*temp*. Elizabeth), 2 parts. [Virtually a treatise on militia matters. Miss G. S. Thomson made extensive use and printed extracts of this in *Lords Lieutenants in the Sixteenth Century*.]

MS 285 A note of the musters in England, 1585 (f. 23b).

MS 932 Petition of Anthony Atkinson, customs searcher at Hull, to the Earl of Essex for authority to muster and train men, n.d. (f. 24).

MS 943 Lord Keeper Coventrye's charge to the judges of assize, 11 July 1633 (p. 221); articles, briefs, etc., concerning the altar controversy in Beckington Church, Som., late 1630s (pp. 481–518); Bishop Pierce's letter to Archbishop Laud concerning the puritan lecture at Taunton, 1637 (p. 563).

Lincoln's Inn, London

A manuscript in press C.4 entitled "Starrchamber" is the partially completed attempt of a seventeenth-century lawyer (unknown) to treat systematically the various misdemeanors triable in Star Chamber and the authorities for the same. It includes contemporary reports of a number of Star Chamber cases, 1629–1635, providing two cases (Attorney-General *vs.* Palmer, *vs.* Longe) of particular interest to this study.

Public Record Office, London (see The Public and The County Records)

Assizes

Asz.2/1   Oxford Circuit, Crown book, 1656–1678.
Asz.22/1   Western Circuit, civil minute book, 1656.
Asz.24/1   Western Circuit, bail book, 1654–1677.
Asz.24/20–21   Western Circuit, order books, 1629–1640 and 1640–1652.
Asz.24/29–34   Western Circuit, postea books, 1611–1633.
Asz.35   Essex Circuit, indictments, from 1559 (now South-Eastern circuit).
Asz.42/1   Northern Circuit, gaol book, 1658–1673 (now North-Eastern circuit).
Asz.44/1   Northern Circuit, indictments, 1607–1640.
Asz.45/1   Northern Circuit, depositions, 1613–1646.

Chancery

C.66   Patent rolls.
C.82   Warrants for the great seal, series II.
C.93   Charitable uses, inquisitions and decrees.
C.142   Inquisitions post mortem, series II.
C.181   Crown office, entry books of commissions of the peace, etc.
C.192/1   Crown office, miscellaneous fiats, entry book of charitable uses, 1629–1642.
C.193/12–13   Crown office, miscellaneous books, justices of the peace lists.
C.202   Brevia Regia (Rolls Chapel series).
C.212/20   Petty Bag office, miscellaneous rolls, compositions for depopulating enclosures, 1635 and later.
C.227   Petty Bag office, sheriff rolls.

Common Pleas

C.P.25(2)   Feet of fines.

Exchequer

E.112   King's Remembrancer, bills, answers, etc.
E.125   KR, decrees and orders of the Court of Exchequer, series III, 1 Charles I–13 Charles II.

E.134   KR, depositions taken by commission.

E.137   KR, estreats.

E.143   KR, extents and inquisitions.

E.159   KR, memoranda rolls.

E.163/18/12   KR, miscellanea of the Exchequer, *liber pacis* [28 Oct. 1626].

E.165/46–51   KR, miscellaneous books II, minute books of commissioners on fees, 1627–1636, etc.

E.178   KR, special commissions of inquiry.

E.179   KR, subsidy rolls (lay).

E.199   KR, sheriffs' accounts.

E.207   KR, bille.

E.215   KR, commission on fees.

E.315/329   Augmentation office, miscellaneous books, minute book of commissioners on fees, 1633–1634.

E.351/2274–2284   Lord Treasurer's Remembrancer, declared accounts (Pipe office series), Treasurer of the Navy accounts, 1635–1642.

E.362   LTR, rolls of estreats, Part I.

E.368   LTR, memoranda rolls.

E.370/8–59   LTR, miscellaneous rolls, accounts of sheriffs and others.

E.372   LTR, pipe rolls.

E.377   LTR, recusant rolls (Pipe office series).

E.401/2586   Exchequer of Receipt, receipts, enrolments and registers of, register of privy seal loans, 1625–1626.

E.401/2590   Exch. of Rec., privy seal loan letters.

E.403/3041–3042   Exch. of Rec., issues, enrolments and registers of, warrant books (Auditor's).

E.407/35   Exch. of Rec., miscellanea, composition for knighthood, 1630–1632.

Index 4211–4213   Chancery, Crown Office, docket books, 1616–1660.

King's Bench

K.B.9   (Crown side) indictments (ancient).

Privy Council

P.C.2   Privy Council registers.

Public Record Office, gifts and deposits

PRO.30/26/104   Miscellaneous assize documents.

Signet Office

S.O.1/1–3   Irish letter books, 1626/7–1642.

State Paper Office

S.P.14 State Papers Domestic, James I.
S.P.16 State Papers Domestic, Charles I.
S.P.38/1–25 Dockets for the great seal.
S.P.46 State Papers Domestic, supplementary.

Star Chamber

St.Ch.8 Star Chamber proceedings, James I.
St.Ch.9 Star Chamber proceedings, Charles I.
St.Ch.10 Star Chamber proceedings, miscellaneous.

Wards and Liveries

Wards 5 Feodaries' surveys.
Wards 10/24 Miscellaneous documents.

Somerset Record Office, Taunton (see The Public and The County Records)

Clerk's of the peace records

Alehousekeepers' recognizances, box 1, 1626–1630 (CQ 7/3/1).
Commissions of the peace, 3 boxes, 1612/3–1638/9 (CQ 10/1/1–3).
Enrolled deeds, 28 rolls, 1536–1655 (CQ 1–30).
Indictment rolls, 28 rolls, 1602–1644 (CQ 4/51–78).
Quarter-sessions order books, 3 vols., 1613–1638 (CQ 2/2/1/1a, 2a, 3a).
Sessions rolls, 43 files, 1625–1638/9 (CQ 3/1/53–78).
Wage assessments, 17 docs., 1604–1641 (Q/AW).

Deposited documents and records

Coker Court muniments, catalogue to, compiled in 1912 by J. H. Heayes of the British Museum. The muniments have been sold, and so cannot be consulted.
Goodford MSS, w/55 Warrant of the deputy lieutenants to the hundred constables of Chewton, 1635 (DD/X/GF).
Hippisley MSS Various (uncataloged (DD/HI).
Jones, I. Fitzroy The files of this excellent antiquary, recently deceased, have been deposited in the Somerset Record Office. They contain considerable biographical material on ecclesiastical incumbents during the seventeenth century.
Nettlecombe Court MSS Vol. 2, p. 118, commission of captaincy of a horse troop to George Trevelyan, 1638 (DD/WO).
Phelips MSS (DD/PH)

Vol. A "Musters, 1615–1667."
B "Duchy of Cornwall, 1613–1636."
C "Family letters."
D "Parliamentary proceedings."
E "Parliamentary."

} boxes 25–27

Estate documents, unbound, various, boxes 1–24.
Poulett MSS Boxes 1–30, estate and private documents, various (DD/PT).
Sanford MSS Boxes 3 and 51, private letters, etc., various (DD/SF).
Trull MSS Box 23, no. 14, rate for soldiers billetted, 1627–1628, (D/P/tru).
Wyndham MSS Various (uncataloged) (DD/WY).

Taunton Castle, Somerset (Somersetshire Archaeological and Natural History Society)

Brown MSS Copybooks of notes on Somerset wills compiled by the Rev. Frederick Brown, a late nineteenth-century antiquarian of ability. These contain invaluable biographical information, though quotations are often inaccurate and should not be used without corroboration.

PRINTED WORKS

Abstracts of Somersetshire Wills, 6 vols., Frederick Brown ed. (Taunton, 1887).
Acts of the Privy Council, Charles I, 5 vols. (London, 1934–1958).
Adair, E. R., "The Privy Council Registers," *English Historical Review*, XXXVIII: 410–422 (London, July 1923).
Addleshaw, G. W. O. and F. Etchells, *The Architectural Setting of Anglican Worship* (London, 1948).
Allan, D. G. C., "The Rising in the West, 1628–1631," *Economic History Review*, series 2, V: 76–85 (London, 1952).
Alumni Cantabrigiensis (to 1751), 4 vols., J. and J. A. Venn eds. (Cambridge, 1922).
Alumni Oxoniensis (1500–1714), 4 vols., J. Foster ed. (Oxford, 1891–1892).
Aubrey, John, *Brief Lives*, O. L. Dick ed. (London, 1950). Secondhand gossip.
Articles to be Enquired of in the Metropolitical Visitation of . . . William, Primate of All England and Metropolitan, in and for the Diocese of Bath and Wells . . . in the First Yeare of His Graces Translation (London, 1633).
Aylmer, G. E., "Attempts at Administrative Reform, 1625–1640," *English Historical Review*, LXXII: 229–259 (London, April 1957).
—— "Charles I's Commission on Fees, 1627–1640," *Bulletin of the Institute of Historical Research*, XXXI: 58–67 (London, May 1958).

—— "Office Holding as a Factor in English History, 1625–42," *History*, XLIV: 228–240 (London, 1959). This and the preceding two articles provide considerable insight into Caroline administration and the Council's intentions during the "personal rule."

Barnes, Thomas G., "A Charge to the Judges of Assize, 1627/8," *Huntington Library Quarterly*, XXIV (May 1961).

—— *The Clerk of the Peace in Caroline Somerset*, Occasional Papers of the Department of English Local History, Leicester University, no. 14 (Leicester, 1961).

—— "County Politics and a Puritan Cause Célèbre: Somerset Churchales, 1633," *Transactions of the Royal Historical Society*, 5th series, IX: 103–122 (London, 1959).

—— "Examination before a Justice in the Seventeenth Century," *Somerset and Dorset Notes and Queries*, XXVII: 39–42 (Sherborne, August 1955).

—— "The Hinton Rate, 1569," *Somerset and Dorset Notes and Queries*, XXVII: 210–213 (Sherborne, March 1959).

Barnes, Thomas G. and A. Hassell Smith, "Justices of the Peace from 1558 to 1688—a Revised List of Sources," *Bulletin of the Institute of Historical Research*, XXXII: 221–242 (London, Nov. 1959).

Bates-Harbin, S. W., *Members of Parliament for the County of Somerset* [1258–1832] (Taunton, 1939). Very useful biographical material here, scrupulously compiled.

Beard, Charles A., *The Office of the Justice of the Peace in England* (New York, 1904). A doctoral thesis drawn almost wholly from secondary sources—out of date.

Bell, H. E., *An Introduction to the History and Records of the Court of Wards and Liveries* (Cambridge, 1953). The modest title masks an admirable study of Tudor-Stuart legal and administrative procedures in an institution with important links in the counties.

Bibliotheca Lindesiana. A Bibliography of Royal Proclamations of the Tudor and Stuart Sovereigns and Others Published under Authority, 1485–1714, 2 vols., R. R. Steele ed. (Oxford, 1910). Excellent calendar, but should be used as an index to the proclamations, most of which for this period can be found in *Foedera*.

Bibliotheca Somersetensis, 3 vols., Emanuel Green ed. (Taunton, 1902). Virtually everything in print concerning the county pre-1900 finds a place in this useful bibliography, a monument to antiquarian scholarship.

The Book of Examinations and Depositions, 1622–1644, Southampton, 4 vols., R. C. Anderson ed., Southampton Record Society (Southampton, 1929–1936).

British Borough Charters, 1042–1216, A. Ballard ed. (Cambridge, 1913).

British Borough Charters, 1216–1307, A. Ballard and J. Tait eds. (Cambridge, 1923).

British Borough Charters, 1307–1660, Martin Weinbaum ed. (Cambridge, 1943). This and the preceding two volumes are essential for determining the jurisdiction of county JPs in the boroughs.

Brunton, D. and D. H. Pennington, *Members of the Long Parliament* (London, 1954).

Bulley, John A., " 'To Mendip for Coal'—a Study of the Somerset Coalfield before 1830," 2 parts, *Somersetshire Archaeological and Natural History Society Proceedings*, 1952, XCVII: 46–78; 1953, XCVIII: 17–54 (Taunton, 1953 and 1955).

Burke's Peerage, Baronetage, and Knightage, L. G. Pine ed. (London, 1949).

Byrchmore, J., *Collections for a Parochial History of Tickenham* (Taunton, 1895).

Calder, Isabel M., *Activities of the Puritan Faction in the Church of England, 1625–1633* (London, 1957).

Calendar of the Manuscripts of the Marquis of Salisbury, parts 4 and 5, Historical Manuscripts Commission (London, 1892 and 1894).

Calendar of the State Papers Domestic, Elizabeth, 1581–1590, R. Lemon ed. (London, 1865).

Camden, William, *Britannia*, 2 vols., Edmund Gibson ed. (London, 2 ed., 1722).

Cameron, A. T., *The History of the Sydenham Family* (Guildford, 1928).

Cassan, S. H., *Lives of the Bishops of Bath and Wells* (London, 1829). Totally uncritical.

Certificate of Musters in the County of Somerset, temp. Elizabeth, A.D. 1569, Emanuel Green ed., Somerset Record Society, XX (London, 1904). The introduction's usefulness is curtailed by the editor's tendency to surmise too much from too little evidence; provides some useful information concerning the organization and arming of the Elizabethan militia.

Charges to the Grand Jury at Quarter Session, 1660–1677, by Sir Peter Leicester, E. M. Halcrow ed., Chetham Society, 3rd series, V (Manchester, 1953). Admirable charges by a Cheshire magistrate-antiquary, akin to those of John Harington in Somerset, c. 1640.

Chubb, T., *A Descriptive List of the Printed Maps of Somersetshire, 1575–1914* (Taunton, 1914).

Clarendon, Edward, Earl of, *The History of the Rebellion and Civil Wars in England begun in the Year 1641*, 3 vols. (Oxford, 1712).

Clark, A., "A Lieutenancy Book for Essex, 1608 to 1631 and 1637 to 1639," *The Essex Review*, XVII: 157–169 (Chelmsford, 1908).

12*+

Cobbett's Complete Collection of State Trials, vol. III (London, 1809).

Cockle, M. J. D., *A Bibliography of English Military Books up to 1642* (London, 1900). The editor's notes contain much information on military establishments; a model bibliography.

Coke, Edward, *The Fourth Part of the Institutes of the Laws of England* (London, 1669).

——*A Little Treatise of Baile and Maineprize, written by E[dward] C[oke] Knight, and Now Published for a Generall Good* (London, 1635).

—— *La Dix[ie]me Part des Reports* (London, 1614). Ten Coke's Reports.

—— *Quinta Pars ... Relationum, de Variis Resolutionibus* (London, 1605). Five Coke's Reports. The value of these works by the age's greatest lawyer to the JPs recommend them to their historian.

Collectanea II, T. F. Palmer ed., Somerset Record Society, XLIII (Frome, 1928).

Collectanea III, T. F. Palmer ed., Somerset Record Society, LVII (Frome, 1942).

Collections for a History of Staffordshire—Staffordshire Quarter Sessions Rolls, 1581–1690, 6 vols., S. A. H. Burne and D. H. G. Salt eds., Staffordshire Record Society (Kendal, 1929–1949). Useful introductions.

Collinson, John, *The History and Antiquities of the County of Somerset*, 3 vols. (Bath, 1791), and index and supplement (Taunton, 1898). Despite much justified criticism of this work during the past century and a half, this is still the handiest single source for biographical information.

The Committee at Stafford, 1643–1645: The Order Book of the Staffordshire County Committee, D. H. Pennington and I. A. Roots eds. (Manchester, 1957).

Commons Debates, 1621, 7 vols., Wallace Notestein *et al.* eds. (New Haven, 1935).

The Commons Debates for 1629, Wallace Notestein and F. Relf eds. (Minneapolis, 1921).

Complete Baronetage, 6 vols., G. E. C[ockayne] ed. (Exeter, 1900–1909).

A Complete Collection of State-Tryals and Proceedings upon Impeachments for High Treason [etc.] from the Reign of King Henry the Fourth to the End of the Reign of Queen Anne, 4 vols. (London, 1719).

The Complete Peerage, 12 vols., G. E. C[ockayne], Vicary Gibbs *et al.* eds. (London, 1910–1953). An invaluable work, still to be completed.

A Copy of Papers Relating to Musters, Beacons, Subsidies, etc., in the County of Northampton, Joan Wake ed., Northamptonshire Record Society, III (Kettering, 1926). Formal lieutenancy papers of the variety Somerset does not possess.

Cowell, John, *The Interpreter* (London, 1701). This edition of a standard law dictionary differs little from the first edition, 1607, suppressed by James I (under pressure of opinion) for its author's sympathetic treatment of prerogative.

Cox, J. S., *Ilchester Gaol and House of Correction*, Ilchester Historical Monographs, no. 4 (Ilchester, 1949).

Croke, George, *Reports* (Charles I), part 3, Sir H. Grimston, M.R., trans. (London, 1683).

Cunningham, T., *The History of the...Taxes of England* (London, 1778). Provides a fair amount of information on subsidies.

Dalton, Michael, *The Countrey Justice* (London, 1655). 1619 (first) and 1727 editions used also. Particularly lucid justice's handbook—supplemented, though did not immediately supplant, Lambarde's *Eirenarcha*.

——— *Officium Vicecomitum: The Office and Authoritie of Sherifs* (London, 1623). The sheriff's handbook; a most useful source for the function of the office in this period.

Diary of John Rous, Incumbent of Santon Downham, Suffolk, from 1625 to 1642, M. A. E. Green ed., Camden Society, o.s., LXVI (London, 1856).

Dictionary of National Biography, 22 vols. (Oxford, 1917 et seqq.).

Dietz, F. C., *English Public Finance, 1558–1641* (New York, 1932).

——— *The Receipts and Issues of the Exchequer during the Reigns of James I and Charles I*, Smith College Studies in History XIII, no. 4 (Northampton, Mass., 1928).

Docquets of Letters Patent...Passed under the Great Seal of King Charles at Oxford, 1642–1646, W. H. Black ed. (London, 1838).

Elton, G. R., *The Tudor Revolution in Government, Administrative Changes in the Reign of Henry VIII* (Cambridge, 1953). Basic to an appreciation of the central administration of the early Stuarts.

Everitt, A. M., *The County Committee of Kent in the Civil War*, Occasional Papers of the Department of English Local History, Leicester University, no. 9 (Leicester, 1957).

Farnham, Edith, "The Somerset Election of 1614," *English Historical Review*, XLVI: 579–599 (London, Oct. 1931). One wishes the author had continued her researches into Somerset politics during the early Stuart period.

Firth, C. H., *Cromwell's Army* (London, 1921). Peerless.

Fisk, William L., "The Straffordians—a Cross Section of Conservative Political Thought," *The Historian*, XXI: 341–355 (Aug. 1959).

Foedera, Conventiones, Literae [etc.], vols. XVIII–XX, R. Sanderson ed. (London, 1726–1735). Contains invaluable sources, especially proclamations.

Foss, E., *The Judges of England*, 9 vols. (London, 1848–1864).

Fraser, I. H. C., "The Agitation in the Commons, 2 March 1629, and the Interrogation of the Leaders of the Anti-court Group," *Bulletin of the Institute of Historical Research,* XXX: 86–95 (London, May 1957).

French, Allen, *Charles I and the Puritan Upheaval* (Boston, 1956).

Gardiner, S. R., *History of England, 1603–1642,* 10 vols. (London, 1883–1884); for vols. VII–X, new ed. (1894 et seqq.).

A Genealogical Guide, 4 parts, J. B. Whitmore ed., Harleian Society, XCIX, C, CI, CII (London, 1947–1950). A ready guide to many biographical sources for many families.

Gerard, Thomas, *The Particular Description of the County of Somerset, 1633,* E. H. Bates ed., Somerset Record Society, XV (Frome, 1900). A most illuminating survey of the county and its greater families.

Gonner, E. C. K., *Common Land and Enclosure* (London, 1912).

Gordon, M. D., "The Collection of Ship-money in the Reign of Charles I," *Transactions of the Royal Historical Society,* 3rd series, IV: 141–162 (London, 1910).

Gorges, R., *The Story of a Family* (Boston, 1944). A model family history, of the Gorges of Somerset, by an American descendant.

Gough, J. W., *The Mines of Mendip* (Oxford, 1930).

Grimble, Ian, *The Harington Family* (New York, n.d.).

Hale, Matthew, *A Discourse Touching Provision for the Poor* (London, 1683). The eminent Restoration jurist indicates all the weaknesses of the Elizabethan poor law system and advocates reducing crime by solving the problem of poverty.

——— *A Short Treatise Touching Sheriffs Accompts* (London, 1683).

Hamilton, A. H. A., *Quarter Sessions from Queen Elizabeth to Queen Anne* London, 1878). The pioneer work on JPs drawn from local records, those of Devon.

Hammond, J. L. and Barbara Hammond, *The Village Labourer,* vol. I (Guild Books, London, 1948). Contains a lively account of the eighteenth-century enclosure of King's Sedgemoor.

The Harleian Miscellany, 10 vols., W. Oldys ed. (London, 1801–1813).

Hedworth Whitty, R. G., *The Court of Taunton in the Sixteenth and Seventeenth Centuries* (Taunton, 1934). Concerns the borough court.

Herne, John, *Lent 1638, the Learned Reading ... upon the Statute of 23 Henry VIII cap. 3 concerning Commissions of Sewers* (London, 1659).

Hertford County Records. Notes and Extracts from the Sessions Rolls, 1581–1698, vol. I, W. J. Hardy ed. (Hertford, 1905).

Heylyn, Peter, *Cyprianus Anglicanus* (London, 1668). Contains a very sympathetic version of Laud's part in the Somerset churchales dispute—by Laud's uncritical eulogist, his former chaplain.

Hippisley, A. E., and I. Fitzroy Jones, *Some Notes on the Hippisley Family* (Taunton, 1952).

Historical Collections, vols. I–III, J. Rushworth ed. (London, 1721–1722).

An Historical Geography of England before 1800, H. C. Darby ed. (Cambridge, 1951). Chapters 9 and 10 by E. G. R. Taylor and 11 by J. N. L. Baker are particularly valuable, dealing with the historical geography of Tudor-Stuart England.

Hoare, C. R., *Monastic Remains of the Religious Houses at Witham, Bruton, and Stavordale* (Frome, 1824).

Holdworth, W. S., *A History of English Law*, vols. IV–IX (London, 1923 et seqq.).

Holton, D. P., *Farwell Ancestral Memorial* (New York, 1879).

Hopton, Ralph, *Hopton's Narrative of the Civil War, 1642–1644*, C. E. H. Chadwyck-Healy ed., Somerset Record Society, XVIII (Frome, 1902). Gives great insight into Sir Ralph Hopton's character.

Humphreys, A. L., *The Somerset Roll of Worthies* (Taunton, 1897). Thin.

Hunt, W., *The Somerset Diocese, Bath and Wells* (London, 1885).

Hutton, Richard, *The Reports of* (London, 1682).

Instructions for Musters and Arms, and the Use Thereof (London, 1623). Twelve pages of instructions for the militia, recurrently ordered to be implemented in the years following publication—official manual.

Jones, I. Fitzroy, "Aspects of Poor Law Administration, Seventeenth to Nineteenth Centuries, from Trull Overseers' Accounts," *Somersetshire Archaeological and Natural History Society Proceedings, 1950*, XCV: 72–105 (Taunton, 1951).

Jordan, W. K., *The Development of Religious Toleration in England*, vol. II (Cambridge, Mass., 1936). The standard work on the subject, and a valuable survey of religious thought of the period.

——*The Forming of the Charitable Institutions of the West of England. A Study of the Changing Pattern of Social Aspirations in Bristol and Somerset, 1480–1660*, Transactions of the American Philosophical Society, n.s., 50 pt. 8 (Philadelphia, 1960).

—— *Philanthropy in England, 1480–1660: A Study of the Changing Pattern of English Social Aspirations* (New York, 1959). Somerset is one of the ten counties studied.

The Journal of Sir Simonds D'Ewes, Wallace Notestein ed. (New Haven, 1923).

The Journals of the House of Commons, vol. II (n.p., n.d.). For the Long Parliament, April 1640–March 1642/3.

Karraker, C. H., *The Seventeenth Century Sheriff: A Comparative Study of the Sheriff in England and the Chesapeake Colonies, 1607–1689* (Chapel Hill, 1930). A most useful survey, that gains by being comparative.

Keeler, Mary F., *The Long Parliament: A Biographical Study of its Members* (Philadelphia, 1954). An imposing piece of work; more detailed and more substantial than the similar work by Brunton and Pennington.

Kershaw, R. N., "The Elections for the Long Parliament, 1640," *English Historical Review*, XXXVIII: 496–508 (London, October 1923).

The King's Maiesties Declaration to his Subjects, concerning Lawfull Sports to bee Used (London, 1633). The Book of Sports, issued in Oct. 1633, largely because of the churchales dispute in Somerset.

Klotz, E. L. and G. Davies, "The Wealth of Royalist Peers and Baronets during the Puritan Revolution," *English Historical Review, LVIII:* 217–219 (London, April 1943).

Lambarde, William, *Eirenarcha, or of the Office of the Justices of Peace* (London, 1619); 1581 (first), 1591, 1602, and 1607 editions used also. The standard justice's handbook, treating briefly though extensively all the law, substantive and adjective, with which the JPs were concerned.

The Lancashire Lieutenancy under the Tudors and Stuarts, parts 1 and 2, J. Harland ed., Chetham Society, XLIX and L (Manchester, 1859).

Lancashire Quarter Sessions Records 1590–1606, J. Tait ed., Chetham Society, n.s., LXXVII (Manchester, 1917).

Leonard, E. M., *The Early History of English Poor Relief* (Cambridge, 1900). A pioneer work and not yet superseded, though the subject is badly in need of further investigation and reinterpretation.

Lewis, A. H., *A Study of Elizabethan Ship Money, 1588–1603* (Philadelphia, 1928).

Lipson, E., *The Economic History of England*, vols. II and III (London, 1931).

List of Sheriffs for England and Wales from the Earliest Times to A.D. 1831 Public Record Office Lists and Indexes, vol. IX (London, 1898). In need of correction.

Lloyd, D., *State-worthies* (London, 1670).

MacCaffrey, Wallace, *Exeter 1540–1640; The Growth of an English County Town* (Cambridge, Mass., 1958). Reveals borough politics and governmental mechanics, providing interesting contrasts and some similarities to county government.

Malet, A., *Notices of the Malet Family* (n.p., 1885).

March's Reports (2 ed., London, 1675). Cases in King's Bench and Common Pleas, 1639–1642.

Markham, Gervase, *The Souldiers Accidence or an Introduction into Military Discipline* (London, 1635). This and the following work appear to have received wide currency, furnishing militia officers with much practical information. This book particularly evidences familiarity with Continental military practice.

—— *The Souldiers Grammar*, 2 parts (London, 1626 and 1639).

Mathew, David, *The Social Structure of Caroline England* (Oxford 1948).

Maxwell-Lyte, H. C., *A History of Dunster*, part 1 (London, 1909).

—— *The Lytes of Lytes Cary* (Taunton, 1895).

Middlesex County Records (1549–1688), 4 vols., J. C. Jeaffreson ed., Middlesex County Record Society (London, 1886–1892).

Militarie Instructions for the Cavallrie (Cambridge, 1632). A minute treatment of Continental cavalry organization and tactics—practical.

Minutes of Proceedings in Quarter Sessions held for the Parts of Kesteven in the County of Lincoln, 1674–1695, S. A. Peyton ed., Lincoln Record Society, vols. XXV–XXVI (Lincoln, 1931).

The Montagu Musters Books, A.D. 1602–1623, Joan Wake ed., Northamptonshire Record Society, vol. VII (Peterborough, 1935). Excellent editing.

Morris, W. A., *The Medieval Sheriff to A.D. 1300* (Manchester, 1927).

Neale, J. E., *The Elizabethan House of Commons* (London, 1949).

Nef, John U., *The Rise of the British Coal Industry*, 2 vols. (London, 1932).

"Notes of Sir George Croke's Judgment in the Case of Ship Money," S. R. Gardiner ed., *Camden Miscellany VII*, Camden Society, n.s., vol. XIV (London, 1875).

Notestein, Wallace, *The English People on the Eve of Colonization, 1603–1630* (London, 1954). A simply written and compelling survey of English society then by the man more familiar with it than any person alive today.

The North Riding Record Society, Quarter Sessions Records, 9 vols., J. C. Atkinson ed. (London, 1884–1892).

Nottinghamshire County Records. Notes and Extracts from the Nottinghamshire County Records of the Seventeenth Century, H. H. Copnall ed. (Nottingham, 1915).

Orders Appointed by His Most Excellent Maiestie, and Signified by Special Letters from the ... Privie Counsell, Which All Persons within This County, of What Degree or Quality Soever, Are Straitly Commanded to Observe (London, 1626). Copy in BM, Harl. MS 5936, no. 25 (Barford collection). The broadsheet issued to supplement the instructions contained in the general muster order of 10 July 1626.

Orders and Directions Together with a Commission for the Better Administration of Justice [*etc.*] (London, 1631). Copy in BM, Add. MS 12496, ff. 243–271. The Book of Orders.

Pine-Coffin, M., *The Speke Family* (Taunton, 1914). Error-ridden.

Powell, A. H., *The Ancient Borough of Bridgwater* (Bridgwater, 1907).

Poynton, F. J., *Memoranda Historical and Genealogical Relating to the Parish of Kelston*, 4 parts (London, 1878–1885).

Proceedings before the Justices of the Peace in the Fourteenth and Fifteenth Centuries, Edward III to Richard III, Bertha H. Putnam ed., Ames Foundation (Cambridge, Mass., 1938). The introduction is very valuable.

Prynne, William, *Canterburies Doome* (London, 1646). Parliament's case against Laud, drawn by his implacable antagonist.

Putnam, Bertha H., "The Earliest Form of Lambard's *Eirenarcha* and a Kent Wage Assessment of 1563," *English Historical Review*, XLI: 260–273 (London, April 1926).

——*Early Treatises on the Practice of Justices of the Peace in the Fifteenth and Sixteenth Centuries*, Oxford Studies in Social and Legal History, vol. VII (Oxford, 1924). Contain's Marowe's Reading.

—— "Justices of the Peace from 1558 to 1688," *Bulletin of the Institute of Historical Research*, IV: 144–156 (London, 1927). This, the preceding two works, and *Proceedings before the Justices (supra)* are Prof. Putnam's most important pioneering contributions to the study of JPs.

Quarter Sessions Records of the County of Northampton. Files for 6 Charles I and Commonwealth, Joan Wake ed., Northamptonshire Record Society, vol. I (Hereford, 1924).

Quarter Sessions Records for the County of Somerset, 1607–1625, E. H. Bates ed., Somerset Record Society, vol. XXIII (Frome, 1907).

Quarter Sessions Records for the County of Somerset, Charles I, E. H. Bates-Harbin ed., Somerset Record Society, vol. XXIV (Frome, 1908).

Ramsay, G. D., "The Report of the Royal Commission on the Clothing Industry, 1640," *English Historical Review*, LVII: 482–493 (London, Oct. 1942).

Records of the Honorable Society of Lincoln's Inn, vol. I, W. P. Baildon ed. (London, 1896). Admissions.

Register of Admissions to Gray's Inn, 1521–1889, J. Foster ed. (London, 1889).

Register of Admissions to the Honorable Society of the Middle Temple, 3 vols., H. A. C. Sturgess ed. (London, 1949). Would that the admissions registers of the other three Inns of Court were as well executed as this one.

"Relation of a Short Survey of the Westerne Counties of England, 1635," L. G. Wickham Legg ed., *Camden Miscellany XVI*, Camden Society, 3rd series, vol. LII (London, 1936).

Return of the Name of Every Member [of Parliament], 1213–1874, part 1 (London, 1878).

Roberts, G., *The Social History of the People of the Southern Counties of England* (London, 1856). A useful background study.

Rowe, V. A., "The Influence of the Earls of Pembroke on Parliamentary Elections, 1625–1641," *English Historical Review*, L: 242–256 (London, April 1935).

Savage, J., *History of the Hundred of Carhampton* (London, 1830).

Sheppard, H. B., *Courts Leet and the Court Leet of the Borough of Taunton* (Taunton, 1909). As a scholarly work, it leaves much to be desired; contains factual information of value.

Shropshire County Records. Orders of the Shropshire Quarter Sessions, vol. I, R. L. Kenyon and O. Wakeman eds. (Shrewsbury, 1908).

Simpson, Alan, *Puritanism in Old and New England: A Study in the Politics of Enthusiasm* (Chicago, 1955).

Somerset and Dorset Notes and Queries, 27 vols. (1888–1959). A mine of factual information.

Somerset Assize Orders, 1629–1640, Thomas G. Barnes ed., Somerset Record Society, vol. LXV (Frome, 1959).

Somerset Enrolled Deeds, 1536–1655, S. W. Bates-Harbin ed., Somerset Record Society, vol. LI (Frome, 1936).

Somerset Incumbents, F. W. Weaver ed. (Bristol, 1889).

Somersetshire Archaeological and Natural History Society Proceedings, 103 vols. (Taunton, 1850–1959). The student's load is lightened by many erudite papers contributed by capable local scholars during the past century.

Somersetshire Parishes: A Handbook of Historical Reference to All Places in the County, 8 parts, A. L. Humphrey (London, 1905). Exceptionally useful.

State Papers Relating to Musters, Beacons, Ship Money, etc., in Norfolk from 1626, Chiefly to the Beginning of the Civil War, W. Rye ed., Norfolk and Norwich Archaeological Society (Norwich, 1907). The introduction by C. H. Firth is illuminating.

Statutes of the Realm, 9 vols. (London, 1810–1822). The Record Commission's edition, and the most authentic.

Staunforde, William, *Les Plees del Coron* (London, 1583). The standard contemporary work on the criminal law. Later editions of justice's handbooks relied heavily on it.

Stawell, G. D., *A Quantock Family* (Taunton, 1910).

Stephen, J. F., *A History of the Criminal Law of England*, 3 vols. (London, 1883). Despite its failings, this remains the most complete study of the criminal law. Dr. Leon Radzinowicz's ambitious work on the late eighteenth and nineteenth centuries' criminal law has not yet a counterpart for the earlier periods.

Students Admitted to the Inner Temple (1547–1660) (London, 1877).

Tate, W. E., *Somerset Enclosure Acts and Awards*, Somersetshire Archaeological and Natural History Society (Frome, 1948).

Tawney, R. H., *Business and Politics under James I; Lionel Cranfield as Merchant and Minister* (Cambridge, 1958). Disappointingly slim on Cranfield's administration of the Exchequer.

—— "The Rise of the Gentry, 1558–1640," *Economic History Review*, 1–38 (London, 1941).

—— "The Rise of the Gentry: A Postscript," *Economic History Review*, series 2, VII: 91–97 (London, 1954).

Thirsk, Joan, *Fenland Farming in the Sixteenth Century*, Occasional Papers of the Department of English Local History, University College Leicester, no. 3 (Leicester, 1953). Able treatment of the Lincolnshire fens, similar to Sedgemoor in Somerset.

Thomson, Gladys S., "The Bishops of Durham and the Office of Lord Lieutenant in the Seventeenth Century," *English Historical Review*, XL: 351–374 (London, July 1925).

—— *Lords Lieutenants in the Sixteenth Century* (London, 1923). A pioneer work in a still neglected field. Somewhat thin in content.

—— "The Origin and Growth of the Office of Deputy Lieutenant," *Transactions of the Royal Historical Society*, 4th series, V: 150–167 (London, 1922).

Three Centuries of Derbyshire Annals as Illustrated by the Records of the Quarter Sessions, 2 vols., J. C. Cox ed. (London, 1890).

Trevor-Roper, H. R., *Archbishop Laud, 1573–1645* (London, 1940). Strongest on Laud's policy of "Thorough," weakest on his ecclesiastical activities.

—— *The Gentry, 1540–1640*, Economic History Review Supplements, vol. I (London, 1953).

Twyford, Henry, *The Office of the Clerk of Assize ... Together with the Office of the Clerk of the Peace, Shewing the True Manner and Form of the Proceedings at the Court of General Quarter Sessions of the Peace* (London, 1682). Exceedingly valuable for the offices fifty years before.

The Twysden Lieutenancy Papers, 1583–1668, Gladys S. Thomson ed., Kent Archaeological Society, Records Branch, vol. X (1926).

Usher, R. G., *The Rise and Fall of the High Commission* (Oxford, 1913). A dated work that must be used with great care; until the court is reconsidered in a new light on the basis of newly available sources, this will continue to supply most of our information concerning Laud's ecclesiastical administration.

Victoria History of the Counties of England, Somerset, vol. II, W. Page ed. (London, 1911).

Victoria History of the Counties of England, Wiltshire, vol. V, R. B. Pugh ed. (London, 1957). Prof. Joel Hurstfield's chapter on county government, 1530–1660, is a useful survey incorporating the most recent research.

de Villiers, E., "Parliamentary Boroughs Restored by the House of Commons, 1621–1641," *English Historical Review*, LXVII: 175–202 (London, April 1952). The "restoration" of Ilchester and Milborne Port are fully treated.

The Visitation of the County of Somerset, 1531, 1573, and 1591, F. W. Weaver ed. (Exeter, 1885).

The Visitation of the County of Somerset, 1623, F. T. Colby ed., Harleian Society, vol. XI (London, 1876). Best approached with caution—corrections by an able local scholar to this indifferently edited volume will be found in *SANHS Proc.*, 1944, XC: 82–101.

Vivian-Neal, A. W., *Notes on the History of Dillington House* (Taunton, 1950).

Ward, Robert, *Animadversions of Warre*, 2 books (London, 1639). Far too theoretical to have been of much use as a text for militia officers.

Ward, W. R., *The English Land Tax in the Eighteenth Century* (Oxford, 1953). Occasional references to seventeenth century taxation are illuminating.

Warwick County Records, 8 vols., S. C. Ratcliff and H. C. Johnson eds. (Warwick, 1935–1953). The introductions to these volumes constitute a highly perceptive study of the seventeenth-century justices.

Watson, W. G. W., *A Chronological History of Somerset*, Somerset Folk Series, vol. XXI (London, 1925). Of greater value than either its title or the series would suggest, provided the information extracted is corroborated.

Webb, S. and B., *English Local Government: The Story of the King's Highway* (London, 1913).

—— *English Local Government: The Parish and the County* (London, 1906).

Wedgwood, C. V., *The King's Peace, 1637–1641* (London, 1955). An outstanding narrative with a number of brilliant insights.

Wells City Charters, D. O. Shilton and R. Holworthy eds., Somerset Record Society, vol. XLVI (Frome, 1931).

Whitelocke, James, *Liber Famelicus*, J. Bruce ed., Camden Society, o.s., vol. LXX (London, 1858). Whitelocke's patent bias against Ellesmere and others must be taken into account.

Wilkinson, John, *A Treatise...Concerning the Office and Authoritie of Coroners and Sherifes...Court Leet, Court Baron, Hundred Court [etc.]* (London, 1628). Very useful; somewhat more academic in approach than Dalton's *Officium Vicecomitum*.

Willcox, W. B., *Gloucestershire: A Study in Local Government, 1590–1640* (New Haven, 1940). A very useful study, especially of subordinate local officers.

Wilson, Jean, "Sheriffs' Rolls of the Sixteenth and Seventeenth Centuries," *English Historical Review*, XLVII: 31–45 (London, Jan. 1932).

Wiltshire County Records. Minutes of Proceedings in Sessions, 1563 and 1574 to 1592, H. C. Johnson ed., Wiltshire Archaeological and Natural History Society, Records Branch, vol. IV (Devizes, 1949). Excellent short introduction.

Worcester County Records. The Quarter Sessions Rolls, 1591–1643, 2 parts in 1 vol., J. W. Willis Bund ed. (Worcester, 1899–1900).

Wood, Anthony, *Athenae Oxoniensis*, 5 vols., Philip Bliss ed. (London, 1813).

―――― *The Life and Times of Anthony Wood, Antiquary of Oxford, 1632–1695*, 4 vols., Andrew Clark ed., Oxford Historical Society (Oxford, 1891–1900).

Wood, F. A., *Collections for a Parochial History of Chew Magna* (Bristol, 1903).

Wyndham, H. A., *A Family History*, vol. I (Oxford, 1939). A model family history of the Wyndhams, written with an eye on greater issues.

Abbreviations

Full citation for abbreviations of various classes of the Public Records and for documents in the Phelips MSS in the Somerset Record Office will be found in the Bibliography, *sub* Manuscripts, listed alphabetically by repository, class, and number.

Abp	Archbishop
Acts PC	*Acts of the Privy Council*
Add	Additional
A-G	Attorney-General
Asz	Assizes
B	Baron of the Exchequer
Bodl	Bodleian Library
BM	British Museum
Bart.	Baronet
Bp	Bishop
CB	Chief Baron of the Exchequer
CJ	Chief Justice
CP	Common Pleas
DL	Deputy Lieutenant
DNB	*Dictionary of National Biography*
Eas.	Easter or Easter Term
Eger.	Egerton
EHR	*English Historical Review*
Epiph.	Epiphany
GEC	*The Complete Peerage*, G. E. Cockayne, ed.
Harg.	Hargrave
Harl.	Harley
HLS	Harvard Law School Library
Hil.	Hilary Term
J	Judge, justice
JP	Justice of the Peace
KB	King's Bench
Ld Kpr	Lord Keeper of the Great Seal
Ld Lt	Lord Lieutenant
MP	Member of Parliament
Mich.	Michaelmas or Michaelmas Term
mids.	midsummer
PC	Privy Council
PRO	Public Record Office
QS	Quarter Sessions
QSOB	Quarter-Sessions Order Book
SANHS Proc	*Somersetshire Archaeological and Natural History Society Proceedings*
SDNQ	*Somerset and Dorset Notes and Queries*
Sess Rolls	Sessions Rolls

S-G   Solicitor-General
Som Asz Ords   *Somerset Assize Orders, 1629–1640*, Somerset Record Society, LXV
Som Rec Soc   Somerset Record Society
SRO   Somerset Record Office, Taunton
Trans RHS   *Transactions of the Royal Historical Society*
Trin.   Trinity Term
VCH Som   *Victoria History of the Counties of England, Somerset*

All dates are Old Style. The new year is taken to have begun on Lady Day, 25 March; thus, to avoid confusion, a date between 1 January and 24 March is cited by both years to which it pertains, for example, 10 February 1630/1.

INDEX

INDEX